Giants in the Sky

A HISTORY OF THE RIGID AIRSHIP

Another book by the author

THE ZEPPELIN IN COMBAT
3rd Edition 1971

Giants in the Sky

A HISTORY OF THE RIGID AIRSHIP

Douglas H. Robinson

University of Washington Press
Seattle

Copyright © 1973 by Douglas H. Robinson
Second printing, with corrections, 1975
Third printing, 1979

Printed in the United States of America

This edition is not for sale in the United Kingdom. Exclusive
rights for this territory reside with G T Foulis & Co Ltd,
Henley-on-Thames, Oxfordshire.

Library of Congress Cataloging in Publication Data

Robinson, Douglas Hill, 1918—
Giants in the sky.

Bibliography: p.
1. Air-ships—History.   I. Title.
TL657.R6   1973   387.7'3'3250904   72-11546
ISBN 0-295-95249-0

Memorial tablet in the Cathedral of the Air at the U.S. Naval Air Station, Lakehurst, from which "Shenandoah" made her final departure on 2 September 1925 (Official Photograph U.S, Navy)

Contents

Illustrations

CORRECTIONS, 1975

p. 8, fn. 4: *for* The biggest and last pressure airships ever built *read* The biggest pressure airships ever built

p. 25, 1. 38: *for* Mechanic Eisele *read* Mechanic Burr

p. 90, 11. 20–21: *for* SL 4 for the Army *read* SL 4 for the Navy

p. 137, 1. 28: *for* capacity of 2,195,800 cubic feet, and carried seven of the Maybach *read* capacity with a maximum speed of 78 mph, the first to be ready

p. 172: *delete 11. 2–7, substitute* starboard. Why this test was considered necessary I only discovered when Sir Victor Goddard, who was acquainted with most of the participants, commented on my account of the subsequent accident in the first edition of this book. Simply stated, it was an Admiralty requirement that the acceptance trials of all naval vessels should include high speed turns under full helm. Wann, Pritchard and others who knew the hazards of overstressing the lightly built hull protested in vain, Wann being told that if he refused to carry out the turning tests, he would be superseded by someone who would.[29] With each turn being sharper, and the aerodynamic loads on

p. 172, 1. 9: *delete* reckless

p. 172, fn. 29: *substitute* [29]Interview with Sir Victor Goddard, Royal Air Force Club, London, May 15, 1973. Knowing that the turning tests were to be made, Sir Victor, who was awaiting R 38's arrival at Pulham, was not surprised to hear of the disaster.

p. 173, 11. 13–14: *delete* Had Wann been in the German service, he would have faced a court martial.

P. 273, 11. 31–32: *for* At 0400 on August 25 *read* At 1600 on August 25

p. 283, 1. 17: *for* 837 feet *read* 885.8 feet

p. 289, 1. 5: *for* winter of 1937–8 *read* winter of 1936–7

p. 294, 1. 34: *for* On July 19 *read* On June 18

p. 296, 1. 2: *for* as early as February 29, 1940 *read* as early as March 1, 1940

Author's Preface

When my editor, Mr. John Hassell, first proposed that I write a history of the rigid airship, I was very much attracted by the idea, particularly as no work has ever attempted to present the entire forty-year history of these first-ever strategic bombers, long-range naval scouts, and intercontinental passenger carriers; the aims and intentions of the four nations which built them; and the courage, vision and sacrifices of the men who believed in them, constructed and flew them. On the other hand, despite my own original research in the archives of the German Naval Airship Division, I felt some doubt of my ability to deal with the programs of other countries.

This however has not proved a problem, as I have had the generous assistance of many friends who have reviewed chapters dealing with their area of special interest, and who have offered valuable advice and suggestions – Dr. Robin D. S. Higham, Mr. Charles L. Keller, Dr. Richard K. Smith, Mr. Hepburn Walker, Mr. Donald Woodward, and Mr. George E. Wright Jr. The rigid airship has been fortunate in attracting the interest of such a devoted and talented group of historians.

Others who themselves played a role during the rigid airship era have contributed to this book. Directly involved were Captain Garland Fulton USN (Ret.), former head of the Lighter Than Air Section in the U.S. Navy's Bureau of Aeronautics, to whom many of us are indebted for access to his extensive personal archives and for his advice; and Vice Admiral Charles E. Rosendahl USN (Ret.), who was navigator of the "Shenandoah" and commanding officer of the "Los Angeles" and "Akron", and who remains the most prominent advocate of the airship in America today. Sir Harold Roxbee-Cox (now Lord Kings Norton) corrected a published mis-statement on the responsibility for the R101 design. Others whom I have had the privilege of knowing and interviewing in the past have made indirect contributions – Dr. Karl Arnstein, formerly of the *Luftschiffbau Zeppelin* and Goodyear-Zeppelin Corporation; the late Dr. Walter Bleston, formerly of the *Luftschiffbau Schütte-Lanz*; the late Max Pruss, the last captain of the "Hindenburg"; Generalleutnant Friedrich Stahl, formerly of the German Army Airship Service; and the many comrades of the *Marine-Luftschiffer-Kameradschaft* who flew in the German Naval Airship Division in World War I.

xiii

While Mr. Hassell was generous in permitting me to use 100,000 words to tell my story, I did feel under some restrictions of space, and hence decided at the outset to limit myself to the 161 rigid airships *built and flown* in Germany, Great Britain, the United States, and France. Non-flying projects find space only when they relate to a program which produced flyable craft. This justifies the inclusion for instance of Britain's Airship No. 1, the "Mayfly", the metal-framed Schutte-Lanz "g" type ships, or the proposed Zeppelin LZ 132 for which Max Pruss attempted to obtain capital in 1952-60. Theoretical schemes which never achieved any degree of actuality, such as the Tsiolkovskiy airship, are necessarily ignored. Some of the opinions expressed, for which I take full responsibility, are sure to arouse controversy – such as classifying the Schwarz airship and the Metalclad ZMC-2 as rigid airships.

I am grateful to the following publishers for permission to quote from their works: Christian Wolff Verlag, Putnam & Co., Ltd., R. Oldenbourg Verlag, Societäts – Verlag, Longmans Group Ltd., Koehler Verlagsgesellschaft, Dodd, Mead & Co., Cassell & Co. Ltd., Verlag E. S. Mittler & Sohn, Yale University Press, the University Press of Kansas, H.M. Stationery Office, MacDonald & Co., and Charles Scribner's Sons.

I have chosen to express money values in the currencies of the foreign countries concerned. During much of the period covered by this work, the following rough equivalents obtained:

One mark equalled 11 3/4 pennies, or 20.4 marks to the pound.

One dollar equalled 4 shillings 2 pence, or 4.8 dollars to the pound.

Introduction
'Father, what was a rigid airship?'

"The rigid airship, my son, was one of the most extraordinary and romantic creations of man, enthralling millions during its reign from 1900 to 1940. It offered the promise of great range and load carrying capacity long before the aeroplane was really developed, serving at first as a fearful weapon of warfare, and later carrying passengers, freight and mail between the continents. Even in this age of jet transports and supersonic speeds, you will never see anything larger in the skies, nor will passengers fly in such comfort as they did in the spacious rigids. They had comfortable sleeping accomodations, smoking rooms, lounges with grand pianos, and dining rooms where passengers sat at tables draped with costly linens, eating with real silver from real plates, and drinking famous wines from bottles that stood on every table. All work stopped, traffic ceased to move, and thousands crowded into the streets to watch their majestic passage, announcing the attainment of man's dream of exploring the farthest reaches of the earth, and of connecting the nations of the world in peaceful commerce through the air."

All we have left today to remind us that man first flew with *lighter* than air craft are the blimps – three operated in the United States by the Goodyear Corporation, and one in Germany. Simple little gas filled bags of rubberized fabric, their smooth shape maintained through internal gas pressure, they have in common with the giant rigids only the principle of being sustained in the air by buoyant gas. A hundred and sixty one rigid airships were built and flown, and all but two – which were metal clad – shared fundamental features evolved by the original inventor, Count Ferdinand von Zeppelin. He it was who perceived a hundred years ago the great load carrying capacity of the really large airship, whose lift would increase with the cube of its dimensions, and which he was the first to build at Friedrichshafen in South Germany in the year 1900.

The large size he attained by constructing a light but rigid frame of aluminium or duralumin girders (some later rigid airship builders used plywood). The framework consisted of polygonal transverse rings, with radial and chord wires of hard drawn steel for bracing, tied together with longitudinal girders. The outside of the hull was smoothly faired with a fabric cover, waterproofed. Inside, between each set of transverse rings, were separate gas cells filling the entire space when 100 per cent inflated, and conferring increased safety as the ship could still stay airborne with one or even two cells deflated. To the framework were attached control surfaces at the rear, and underneath, gondolas (originally open and boat-shaped) to carry engines and the crew. These basic essentials were constant throughout the rigid airship era, though later craft were larger, better streamlined, gondolas were enclosed, and passengers eventually were carried in palatial accomodations inside the hull.

The design and construction of a rigid airship was no easy matter, and experience played as large a part as pure science and research. The designer was restricted within narrow limits by some fundamental laws of nature: the rigid airship floated in the air by displacing air itself, weighing 80.72 lb per 1000 cubic feet, with the lighter gas with which its cells were inflated. The lightest gas known was hydrogen, which is highly inflammable, weighing 5.61 lb per 1000 cubic feet in the pure state. In the United States, which has a monopoly of helium, this gas, weighing in the pure state 11.14 lb per 1000 cubic feet, was preferred because it was non-flammable. The *net* lift with these two gases was therefore 75.11 lb per 1000 cubic feet with hydrogen, and 69.58 lb per 1000 cubic feet with helium. *There was no means whatsoever of exceeding this static lifting force,* and indeed, it was in practice invariably less due to impurities in the gases used.

As already mentioned, the greater the size, the greater the gross lift. "Hindenburg," the largest airship ever built (together with her sister "Graf Zeppelin II"), had a gas volume of 7,062,150 cubic feet, and when inflated with hydrogen had a gross lift of 242.2 tons[1] under standard conditions of temperature, pressure and humidity. It was of course possible for an unskilled designer to construct a craft so strong as to be absolutely safe structurally, but at the same time so heavy that the entire gross lift would not sustain in the air the metal framework, outer cover and gas cells, not to mention the fuel, water ballast and crew needed to operate her, and the passenger and cargo capacity necessary if the airship were to be a paying proposition. Too many of the early Zeppelins, and prototype rigids constructed in other countries, were more or less useless because the

[1] This is the short ton of 2000 lb.

"Hindenburg" flying above the Zeppelin Works at Friedrichshafen. She was built in the larger of the two sheds. (Luftschiffbau Zeppelin)

dead weight of structure was excessive. On the other hand a low structural weight (vital to attain high altitudes in wartime raiding airships) meant structural weakness and possible collapse in rough air or sharp turns at low altitude. In "Hindenburg" the weight empty, including hull frame, outer cover, gas cells, power plant, crew and passenger accomodation, and tankage for fuel, oil, and ballast, totaled 130.1 tons – about 54 per cent of the gross, and a figure considered a good one for a commercial rigid which would have to be strong for passenger safety. Experience in construction, rather than theoretical design skill, served to produce an efficient craft, and the Zeppelin Company, builders of 119 of all the rigid airships ever constructed, were preeminent in this respect.

The gross lift, 242.4 tons, less the weight empty, 130.1 tons, yielded the useful lift of 112.1 tons, meaning that this was the load that "Hindenburg" could lift from the ground over and above her empty weight. It was for the airship operator to determine which of several options he would choose in loading the ship. Generally, for long flights much of the useful lift would be devoted to fuel. For a shorter journey less fuel was necessary and more freight and passengers could be carried. For a transatlantic journey "Hindenburg" loaded 64 tons of diesel oil and 3.3 tons of lubricating oil; 20.7 tons of water ballast, stores and spare parts, crew of 50 with baggage and provisions for 4½ days; and 5.5 tons for 50 passengers and baggage, 2.8 tons for their provisions and 12.7 tons of freight and mail. Needless to say, these figures far exceeded the loads carried by contemporary aeroplanes, none of which flew the Atlantic with paying passengers until two years after "Hindenburg" burned at Lakehurst.

The hull structure, 803.8 feet in length and 135.1 feet in diameter, was built up of miles of duralumin girders, different sizes serving to withstand different stresses, but generally speaking the girders were triangular in section, and built up by hand riveting stamped spacers into U-shaped channels. The main structural elements of the hull were fifteen main rings, polygons built up of girders, consisting of 18 diamond-shaped trusses arranged end to end in a circle, with reinforcements at the bottom in the region of the keel and adjacent to the gondolas in Rings 92.0 and 140.0. Nine of the rings were spaced fifteen metres (49.2 feet) apart; the four largest amidships 16.5 metres (54.1 feet) apart. Each ring was designated numerically by its distance in metres from the stern post, which was Ring 0. Wire bracing radiated from fittings in the centre of the ring to the eighteen joints of the diamond trusses, serving two purposes – transmitting the lift of the gas cells to the lower hull and keel in which the loads were concentrated; and acting as a bulkhead to prevent gas cells from surging fore and aft, or in case a cell was deflated, to prevent adjacent cells from bulging into the empty space. Eighteen heavy main longitudinal girders connected the main rings at the junctions of the diamond trusses. Eighteen lighter longitudinal girders tied together the apices of the trusses – not really strength members of the ship, they served to keep the outer cover taut. Similarly, there were two light unbraced intermediate rings between each pair of main rings, designed to reduce the bending loads on the longitudinals. All the rectangular panels formed in the hull by the intersection of rings and longitudinals were braced diagonally with hard drawn steel wire. The triangular keel in the bottom of the hull served not only as a passage way for access to all parts of the ship, but also for carrying concentrated loads, such as 660 gallon fuel oil and water ballast tanks, and spare parts, together with cargo, which might include an aeroplane or automobile. Through the centre of the hull, and supported by the radial wiring of the main rings, ran a triangular structure large enough for a man to walk upright – the axial girder, giving access to the gas cells and valves. This was accessible from the lower keel via ladders at Rings 62, 123.5 and 188. At the stern of the ship were built on the four huge fins and rudders, nearly 100 feet long and 50 feet in breadth, and eleven feet thick at the root – so roomy that the lower fin contained an auxiliary steering station in case of a breakdown of the main controls. Hull and fins were covered with large panels of cotton fabric totalling 367,000 square feet, laced to the girders and aluminium doped to reflect the sun's rays.

Inside the hull, the spaces between the main rings were filled with the gas cells, numbered from Cell 1 in the tail cone abaft the rudder post to Cell 16 in the nose. In earlier rigid airships the gas cells were made of light cotton fabric with two or three layers of gold beaters' skin glued to the inner surfaces. Superbly gas-tight, the gold beaters' skin, derived from the intestines of cattle, required special handling and some 50,000 skins were needed to line one large gas cell. In "Hindenburg," the gas cells were made of two layers of cotton with a thin layer of a synthetic gas-proof film sandwiched in between. Also, while previous gas cells were drum shaped, those in "Hindenburg" were made to hang down on either side of the axial gangway. Each gas cell had an automatic valve, spring-loaded to open at a slight pressure of 8 to 10 mm. of water, to permit the escape of gas when the internal pressure rose, as during an ascent to higher altitude. Also, ten cells had so called "manoeuvring valves" which could be opened from the control car to trim the ship or to make her heavy. In older craft the automatic valves were in the bottom of the bags, and the manoeuvring valves in the top; in "Hindenburg" both were adjacent to the central gangway, and vented into shafts leading as much as 70 feet to the top of the ship. The lift of the gas bags was transferred to the longitudinal girders and main rings by netting in the top of the ship – large-mesh netting of wire and small-mesh netting of twine – which at the same time prevented the gas cells from touching the inside of the outer cover. Though the gas cells when 100 per cent full were supposed to fill the entire interior of the hull, it was still possible for a rigger climbing on girders and wires to get at small leaks and repair them in flight.

The four engine gondolas, hung in pairs at Rings 92.0 and 140.0, were streamlined enclosures housing the four Daimler-Benz V-16 diesel engines, developing 1320 hp for takeoff and 900 hp for

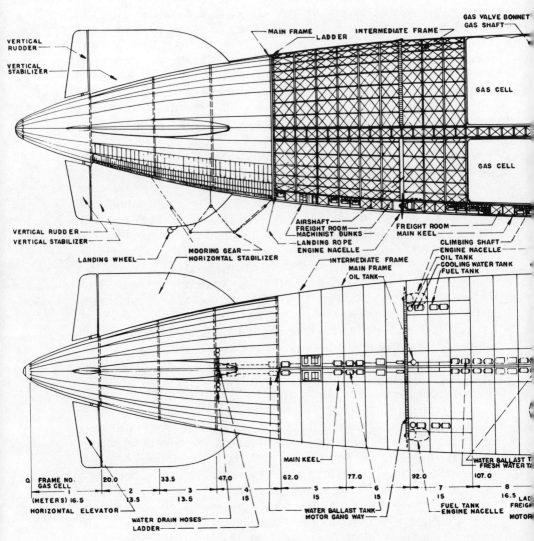

VERTICAL RUDDER

VERTICAL STABILIZER

MAIN FRAME   LADDER   INTERMEDIATE FRAME

GAS VALVE BONNET
GAS SHAFT

GAS CELL

GAS CELL

VERTICAL RUDDER
VERTICAL STABILIZER

LANDING WHEEL

MOORING GEAR
HORIZONTAL STABILIZER

AIRSHAFT
FREIGHT ROOM
MACHINIST BUNKS
LANDING ROPE
ENGINE NACELLE

INTERMEDIATE FRAME
MAIN FRAME
OIL TANK

FREIGHT ROOM
MAIN KEEL

CLIMBING SHAFT
ENGINE NACELLE
OIL TANK
COOLING WATER TANK
FUEL TANK

MAIN KEEL

WATER BALLAST T
FRESH WATER TA

FRAME NO. GAS CELL	20.0		33.5		47.0		62.0		77.0		92.0		107.0		
		2		3		4		5		6		7		8	
(METERS) 16.5		13.5		13.5		15		15		15		15		16.5	

HORIZONTAL ELEVATOR

WATER DRAIN HOSES
LADDER

WATER BALLAST TANK
MOTOR GANG WAY

FUEL TANK
ENGINE NACELLE

LAD
FREIG
MOTOR

Longitudinal partial cutaway and p

XX

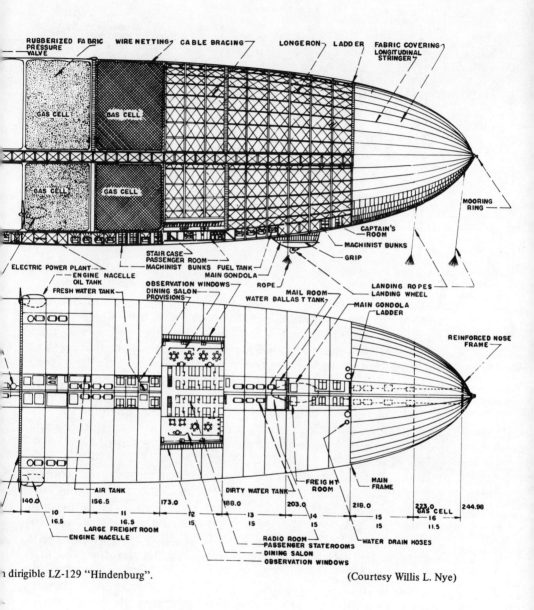

RUBBERIZED FABRIC WIRE NETTING CABLE BRACING LONGERON LADDER FABRIC COVERING
PRESSURE   LONGITUDINAL
VALVE   STRINGER

GAS CELL   GAS CELL

GAS CELL   GAS CELL

MOORING
RING

CAPTAIN'S
ROOM
MACHINIST BUNKS
GRIP

ELECTRIC POWER PLANT   STAIR CASE
ENGINE NACELLE   PASSENGER ROOM   LANDING ROPES
OIL TANK   MACHINIST BUNKS FUEL TANK   LANDING WHEEL
FRESH WATER TANK   MAIN GONDOLA
OBSERVATION WINDOWS   ROPE
DINING SALON   MAIL ROOM   MAIN GONDOLA
PROVISIONS   WATER BALLAST TANK   LADDER

REINFORCED NOSE
FRAME

AIR TANK   DIRTY WATER TANK   FREIGHT   MAIN
                                      ROOM   FRAME

140.0   156.5   173.0   188.0   203.0   218.0   223.0   244.98
                                                      GAS CELL
10   11   12   13   14   15   16
16.5   16.5   15   15   15   15   11.5
LARGE FREIGHT ROOM   RADIO ROOM
ENGINE NACELLE   PASSENGER STATEROOMS   WATER DRAIN HOSES
                      DINING SALON
                      OBSERVATION WINDOWS

dirigible LZ-129 "Hindenburg".   (Courtesy Willis L. Nye)

xxi

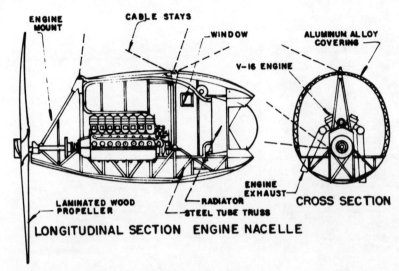

ENGINE
MOUNT   CABLE STAYS

WINDOW   ALUMINUM ALLOY
COVERING

V-16 ENGINE

LAMINATED WOOD
PROPELLER   RADIATOR   ENGINE
EXHAUST   CROSS SECTION

STEEL TUBE TRUSS

LONGITUDINAL SECTION   ENGINE NACELLE

Longitudinal section engine nacelle – "Hindenburg".

continuous cruising. An ingenious reversing gear saved weight: with the engine stopped momentarily, the cam shafts were shifted axially to bring a new set of cams into play, and the engine was then re-started with compressed air and revolved in the opposite direction. 2:1 reduction gears drove fixed pitch wooden propellers. The gondolas, about 20 feet long, had radiators in their noses behind hemispherical shutters, and were suspended from the hull on wires and held away from it by struts. Personnel in the gondolas actually controlled the throttle settings, fuel and air mixture, clutched and unclutched the propeller, etc., on orders from the control car.

The control car, forward at Ring 203.0, was a small glassed-in streamlined housing including three compartments – the control room forward, a chart room amidships, and a room for taking drift bearings on smoke bombs on the water to the rear. (The radio room was in the keel above the control car). In the nose of the control room was the wheel operating the rudders, and gyro and magnetic compasses. To the left was a wheel controlling the elevators, the huge horizontal flippers aft which raised or lowered the nose. The elevator man had in front of him an altimeter, a variometer showing the rate of ascent or descent, an inclinometer showing the nose up or down angle of the ship, and thermometers showing the gas temperature and outside air temperature. On orders from the captain or officer of the watch, the elevator man also handled the toggles of

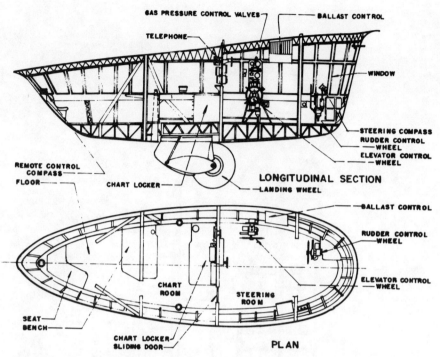

Main control gondola — "Hindenburg".

the manoeuvring valves in the middle of the gas cells, and of the ballast tanks along the keel and of the "emergency" ballast sacks at the ends of the ship — four each forward and aft containing 2200 lb. of water each, used to alter the trim of the ship. On the right side of the control room were engine telegraphs which transmitted orders to the gondolas much as in a ship between the bridge and engine room.

In earlier passenger Zeppelins the paying guests were housed in a streamlined gondola abaft the control car, but in "Hindenburg" the bottom of the bay housing Cell 12 was devoted to their accomodation. Only a small portion of the hull volume was thus subtracted; but the upper deck, measuring 49 x 92 feet, provided space for 25 two-berth sleeping cabins in the centre, and along promenade windows to port and starboard, the public rooms — a dining room, a lounge, and a writing room. On the lower deck were the galley, washrooms, a shower bath, and a smoking room, pressurized to prevent the entrance of any stray hydrogen.

Ground handling of the big rigids was always a problem,

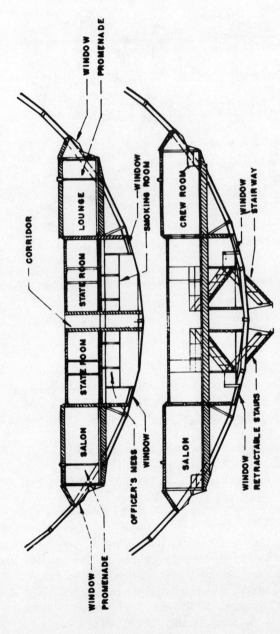

Cross section of crew and passenger accommodation — "Hindenburg".

particularly as they grew larger, and whereas the Zeppelins of World War I might be walked out of their sheds by 500 men, "Hindenburg" used mechanical devices including a tractor-drawn stub mooring mast and trolleys running on rails to which ropes were made fast. Once in the air, however, the giant rigid showed that she was simply a powered balloon, and governed by the same laws as the pioneering craft of the brothers Montgolfier and Professor Charles in 1783.

The gross lift and useful lift of "Hindenburg" previously given were under standard conditions – barometric pressure 760 mm., relative humidity 60 per cent, and air and gas temperature 0 degrees Centigrade, with hydrogen of a specific gravity of 0.1. Any change in these variables changed the lift. Generally speaking, the lift was greater with a higher density of the air, as with cold air temperatures and high barometric pressures, and lower with high temperatures and lower barometric pressures. Therefore a rigid airship could lift a greater load of fuel, passengers and cargo in winter than in summer. Humidity had a relatively slight effect, though a high air humidity

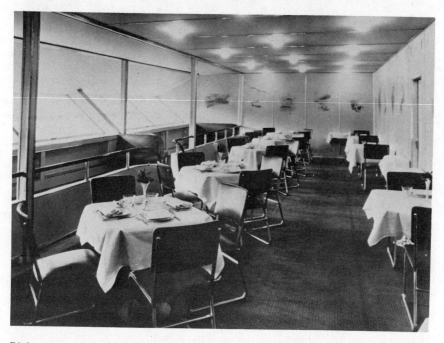

Dining room of "Hindenburg" inboard of the port side promenade deck. Murals on the wall depict the progress of an airship voyage from Germany to South America. (Luftschiffbau Zeppelin)

Lounge of "Hindenburg" inboard of the starboard side promenade deck. Note the aluminium piano in the rear corner, which weighed 397 pounds, (and the couple playing chess!). (Luftschiffbau Zeppelin)

somewhat decreased the lift. In addition, the lifting gas was constantly diffusing outward and air diffusing inward, even with "gas-tight" material such as gold beaters' skin, and this contamination obviously increased the weight of the gas and decreased the airship's lift. From time to time the gas cells had to be emptied and filled with fresh hydrogen, or in the case of American craft, the helium was sent through a purifying plant.

Temperature, barometric pressure, humidity and gas purity would be considered by the rigid airship captain in loading his craft, and on coming out of the hangar the ship was "weighed off" and in equilibrium, with the weights and lift of the gas evenly balanced. Several hundred pounds of water ballast were then dropped to give her a static lifting force at takeoff.

The static lift of the ship thereafter would be varying constantly. If the ship were 100 per cent filled with gas, she would lose lift as she ascended, while hydrogen spilled from the automatic valves. A helium filled airship would take off only partially filled, and would

A sleeping cabin in "Hindenburg", showing upper and lower berths (right), vanity table (centre) and wash stand (left). (Luftschiffbau Zeppelin)

lose no lift until reaching "pressure height," the altitude at which the cells were filled 100 per cent by the expanding helium and gas began to be vented from the automatic valves. Thus a ship would usually be heavy during the early part of her flight, and on the other hand would become statically lighter as the journey continued and she burned fuel. Dynamic lift however might compensate for a certain degree of heaviness or lightness, the hull when inclined acting as a crude airfoil. "Hindenburg" at cruising power could carry 4 tons of overload by flying 1 degree nose up, and 10 to 11 tons at 3 degrees, or a corresponding degree of lightness could be compensated for by flying nose-down. The time would come, however, when the ship would be flying at such an up or down angle that the drag would be unacceptable and the passengers uncomfortable, and the airship would then have to be brought into static equilibrium – by dropping water ballast if she were heavy, or valving gas if she were light. In addition, the static condition of the ship varied when the gas was not of the same temperature as the air – "superheating", usually from the sun's heat warming the gas, making her light as the hydrogen expanded, while "supercooling" after dark made her heavy.

Rigid airship flying was thus a complex and recondite art, in which the captain and his officers had to be thoroughly acquainted with the laws of aerostatics and aerodynamics, meteorology, some knowledge of engineering and of materials, and an awareness of the limitations and capabilities of their craft. Experience was indispensable, and German predominance in rigid airship operations in the 1920s and 1930s derived from experience gained during the pre-war and wartime years at the cost of many wrecks and mishaps. Contrariwise, the failure of programmes in Britain and America derived at least in part from relative lack of experience in the operators. Dr. Hugo Eckener, the Chairman of the Board of the Zeppelin Company and a world figure in the era before World War II, was the greatest airship pilot the world has ever seen, yet he suffered his share of mishaps in the period before 1914.

The romance of the rigid airship, the "Zeppelin fever" adroitly fostered by Dr. Eckener with the "Graf Zeppelin," and the utterly fascinating effect it had on the imagination of millions of people, is hard to comprehend today for the younger generation which has never seen one. Wrote Dr. Eckener himself,

It was not, as generally described, a "silver bird soaring in majestic flight," but rather a fabulous silvery fish, floating quietly in the ocean of air and captivating the eye just like a fantastic, exotic fish seen in an aquarium. And this fairy-like apparition, which seemed to melt into the silvery blue background of sky, when it appeared far away, lighted by the sun, seemed to be coming from another world and to be returning there like a dream — an emissary from the "Island of the Blest" in which so many humans still believe in the inmost recesses of their souls. [2]

In writing this book, I have hoped to remind the older generation of the glory and the pageantry which has departed, and to convey to a younger generation some of the fascination, the enthrallment, the awe and the majesty which these giant ships of the sky inspired in those who saw them. Further, I would like to pay tribute to the men of courage and vision who created them, believed in them, and often sacrificed their lives for them, gladly as if for a sacred cause. Hopefully, in these pages they and their creations will once more come alive.

[2] Hugo Eckener, *Im Zeppelin über Länder und Meere* (Flensburg: Verlagshaus Christian Wolff, 1949), p. 404.

I
The powered balloon

In the era of jet aircraft travel and space flight, it is easy to forget that man has been flying for nearly 200 years — not at first with wings, but with the aerostat, a displacement vessel filled with a gas lighter than air, enabling it to lift its own structural weight and a pay load of one or more persons. The brothers Montgolfier were the first, with public ascents in pre-Revolutionary France in the year 1783 with paper balloons inflated with hot air. At the end of that year the physicist, J. A. C. Charles, created the hydrogen balloon, embodying in his first craft all the essential features of the free balloon as it has existed to this day.

Great popular enthusiasm attended the early discovery of balloon flight, and daring voyages were made by the showmen-aeronauts of the day. As early as January, 1785, Dr. Jeffries and Pierre Blanchard crossed the English Channel by balloon. An early record was set by the flight of the "Great Nassau Balloon" in 1836 from London to Weilburg, a distance of 480 miles, with three persons aboard. Serious schemes were put forward to cross the Atlantic Ocean with the prevailing westerlies, while the spherical balloon, tethered on a long rope, served as an aerial observation platform in the French Revolutionary armies and on the Union side in the American Civil War. When Paris was besieged in the Franco-Prussian War in 1870-71, sixty-two balloons escaped from the encircled capital with messages, mail, and political and military personages. They landed all over Europe; some fell in the sea and were lost.

The free balloon was a means of sport and of scientific research; drifting with the wind towards no predetermined goal, it had no utility as a means of transportation. From the earliest days, inventors were busy with the problem of directing the aerostat regardless of the winds. All these early schemes failed for lack of a light-weight means of propulsion. Some projects involved harnessing eagles to a spherical balloon, or setting sails on it like those of a ship. A most ambitious and far-sighted scheme was that of the French General Jean Baptiste Marie Meusnier, who in the year 1783 proposed in a paper read to the French Acadamy of Science a large balloon,

1

streamlined to an egg shape and 260 feet long, which for the first time would contain a ballonet — an indispensable feature of all pressure airships ever since. A cloth compartment within the big gas-filled bag, the air-containing ballonet was to be kept pressurized to maintain the sleek aerodynamic shape of the outer envelope, while air could be pumped into it if the gas contracted, or be vented if the gas expanded. Three propellers were rigged in tandem close under the envelope, and the car below was to carry eighty men who would turn the propellers by means of hand cranks! The Meusnier balloon was never built, its designer was killed fighting the Prussians in 1793, and this work of inspired genius survives today only as a set of exquisitely detailed water color drawings preserved at the *Musee de l'Air* in Paris.

Others besides Meusnier dreamed of conquering the air with man- or literal horse-power; the first mechanically driven balloon or airship was not evolved until more than fifty years later. Henri Giffard, the well-to-do inventor of the steam injector, applied all his undoubted skill in the year 1852 to developing a light weight steam engine for an airship. The coke-fired boiler weighed 100 pounds empty, the engine 250 pounds, and indicated 3 hp, giving a dry weight/power ratio of 116 pounds per horsepower! Hung some 40 feet below an elongated envelope 88,000 cubic feet in capacity to minimize the risk of setting fire to the hydrogen with which it was inflated, the Giffard steam engine succeeded on September 24, 1852, in propelling the airship at 6 mph. The inventor was the sole person aboard, and this first powered airship flight extended for only 17 miles.

The steam engine was obviously too heavy for its power output to propel an airship with payload. The next significant step in powering the balloon showed little improvement in efficiency, but the craft — "La France" — designed by the French Army engineers Renard and Krebs, and built at the government balloon factory at Chalais-Meudon, was destined to influence many later inventors. The envelope, of varnished silk, was 165 feet long, 27 feet in diameter, and contained 66,000 cubic feet of hydrogen. The design was most sophisticated, the hull form being well streamlined and coming to a point at either end, and embodying a ballonet, filled by a fabric tube leading up from the gondola. The latter, a slender girder of bamboo covered with fabric and 108 feet long, contained amidships an 8½ hp electric motor weighing 210 lb and driving a two-bladed propeller 23 feet in diameter at the nose of the gondola. Most of the lift of the hydrogen was consumed by the batteries. Specially designed by Renard,[1] they still weighed 1232 pounds, and the installation including motor worked out at 210 lb/hp.

Nonetheless, the first flight of "La France" on August 9, 1884, proved that the ship was controllable. Ascending on a calm afternoon, she answered the rudder and after a flight of less than three miles, turned back to the field at Chalais-Meudon and landed safely. The flight had lasted 23 minutes and the batteries (only 704 lb of batteries were carried due to poor lift of the gas) were exhausted. In six further flights the ship returned to her starting point on four occasions; on the other two the wind was too strong and she force-landed away from her base and was deflated. The best speed of "La France" was 14½ mph. Her performance deceived several later inventors, including Count von Zeppelin, as to the amount of power that bigger airships would require. But Renard and Krebs' skilfully executed and advanced design embodied all the necessary elements of the practical small pressure airship – except a light weight power source.

The ultimate solution to this problem – the petrol-fuelled internal combustion engine – was being developed at this time by Otto and others. First to take it aloft was the German, Karl Woelfert. The primitive Daimler 2 hp engine he used was incredibly dangerous when attached to a hydrogen filled gas bag; instead of electrical ignition it relied on a platinum tube fed with petrol and kept at a high temperature by an open-flame burner! A successful short flight was made at Cannstadt with this device in August, 1888. When Woelfert attempted to fly a larger airship with a similar petrol engine at the Tempelhof Field of the Prussian Army Airship Battalion in Berlin in 1897, flaming disaster overwhelmed him. An ascent to 3000 feet caused hydrogen to be vented from the bag; this was set afire by the burner flame, and the wreckage, blazing from end to end, crashed to the ground killing Woelfert and his mechanic, Robert Knabe. Their experiments certainly did nothing to demonstrate the practicability of the petrol engine of the day as a power unit for airships.

This was successfully demonstrated at the turn of the century by a wealthy young Brazilian living in Paris, Alberto Santos-Dumont, who through pluck, determination, and self-acquired aeronautical skill, created a series of small petrol-powered pressure airships which he

[1] Captain Charles Renard, "The First Flight of 'La France'." *The Airship* (London), vol. 2, No. 8, January-March, 1936, p. 63.

demonstrated in local flights in the vicinity of the capital. Simplicity and lightness always inspired Santos' work, and his No. 1, which first flew on September 2, 1898, had a gas volume of only 6500 cubic feet, and a modified de Dion automobile engine which weighed 66 lb and delivered 3½ hp. In rapid succession he turned out modifications of his original design, larger and with better performance. His No. 6 on October 19, 1901, enthralled crowds of Parisians by flying from the Aero Club's field at St. Cloud, around the Eiffel Tower and back, a distance of 7 miles, thereby winning the Deutsch prize of 100,000 francs. This ship, rather better streamlined than some of the earlier ones, had a volume of 21,900 cubic feet and measured 118 feet long and 19.6 feet in diameter. Slung under the bag on wires was a long openwork girder keel housing a 20 hp engine amidships, the two-bladed propeller at the rear, and Santos in a wicker basket well forward. To win the Deutsch prize, No. 6 achieved a speed of 14 mph. One later ship, No. 10, with a volume of 71,000 cubic feet and a 60 hp engine, was designed to carry twelve passengers in three wicker baskets; but made only trial flights with Santos aboard. No. 9 was his smallest successful ship, only 36 feet long and containing 7770 cubic feet of hydrogen. Santos used her as a runabout, landing once in front of his home in the heart of Paris. On another occasion a famous American beauty, Mlle. Aida d'Acosta, charmed Santos into being allowed to solo No. 9 on a half mile flight.

All of which made Santos the toast of Paris, and a hero to his countrymen; but his simple little non-rigids, while demonstrating once and for all the utility of the lightweight petrol internal combustion engine for aerial use, had no useful load and did not advance the state of the art beyond "La France," Reynard and Krebs' masterpiece. True utility in terms of range and weight carrying was shortly heralded by the workmanlike products of the Lebaudy brothers.

These brothers, wealthy owners of a large French sugar refinery, directed their chief engineer, Henri Julliot, to construct an airship. Between the years 1899 and 1901 Julliot was busy with experiments and designs, and his ship, the "Lebaudy I" (nicknamed "le Jaune" because of its chrome yellow envelope made of fabric supplied by the German *Continental Caoutchouc und Guttapercha Co.* of Hannover) did not make its first flight until November 13, 1902. Julliot has never received the recognition from history that he deserves for this design, "the successful prototype of all pressure airships."[2] His inspired contribution was a flat underframe of steel tubing, oval in plan view, 70 feet long and 20 feet wide, to which the 187 foot gas bag (containing 80,000 cubic feet of hydrogen) was attached. The frame simultaneously prevented the envelope from buckling in the event of a drop in gas pressure – a problem which had plagued many of Santos Dumont's designs – while also serving for the attachment of control surfaces and the car suspended below, which contained a 40 hp Daimler engine. Because of the steel tube frame, the Lebaudy deserves to be called a semi-rigid. Able to attain 25 mph with several persons aboard, the Lebaudy I attracted the attention of the French military authorities and became the prototype of a whole series of French Army airships built before World War I.

To this period also belongs the very first rigid airship – not the creation of Count Zeppelin, but the invention of one David Schwarz, a Hungarian by birth, with no technical or engineering training, who until his forties made his living in Agram (today the Yugoslavian Zagreb) as a timber merchant. At some time in the 1880's the dream came to him of constructing a powered airship, and even more remarkably, he intended to build it of aluminium, a light metal then so novel as to be little more than a laboratory curiosity. Though no accurate information is available, it appears that Schwarz, after being rebuffed by the Austro-Hungarian War Ministry, found encouragement from the Russian military attaché in Vienna and went to St. Petersburg, where he built an experimental ship to his plans. The craft when completed would not lift from the ground, and Schwarz, fearing arrest, is said to have fled Russia under a false name and with a false passport.

In Germany Schwarz made the acquaintance of Carl Berg, a far-sighted industrialist and metal fabricator, who had brought home from the Paris Exposition of 1889 a sample of the new "silver made from clay" and since 1892 had been casting, rolling and stamping aluminium in his works at Eveking in Westphalia. The association of the two men developed into a formal partnership, which Berg not only financed completely, but also (if the only primary source available, by Berg's son, can be believed) had the engineering of Schwarz' airship worked out by his own factory personnel. Schwarz'

[2] L.T.C. Rolt, *The Aeronauts. A History of Ballooning 1783-1903.* (London: Longmans, Green & Co., 1966), p. 230.

contribution to the final product would seem to have been only that of the basic idea.

The Schwarz airship as completed was so deficient in aerodynamic efficiency that it could not possibly have realized the dreams of its creator. Cleverly fabricated of aluminium girder longitudinals and wire-braced rings, the hull was covered entirely with sheets of aluminium 2 mm. thick riveted in place. This type of construction was not gas tight, and when inflated with hydrogen the leakage was excessive. Quite innocent of streamlining, the metal-clad hull was simply a cylinder 44 feet 3 inches in diameter, with a conical nose and a slightly convex stern, measuring 156 feet long and with a volume of 114,700 cubic feet. The record speaks of 13 "compartments" between the rings, but there do not appear to have been any gas-tight bulkheads, and the entire interior seems to have constituted a single large space. Beneath the metal hull the single car was rigidly attached to girders made fast to the lower main longitudinals. The car contained a 16 hp Daimler petrol engine, which drove four propellers through an unnecessarily complicated arrangement. One pusher propeller 8½ feet in diameter was mounted between the car and the envelope, its shaft turned by belts. Two smaller propellers 6½ feet in diameter were mounted on brackets high up on the hull and driven by belts. Another 6½ foot propeller was mounted horizontally under the car to drive the ship upward or pull it downward. There were no control surfaces and aside from the possibility of operating the propellers differentially, there was no means of directing the airship. No estimate of the speed which the ship might attain appears in any of the accounts. Nor, as far as can be determined, was there a ballonet inside the big metal shell, and no provision was made for expansion or contraction of the gas as the ship ascended or descended.

Construction got underway in 1895 at the Tempelhof Field base in Berlin of the Prussian Airship Battalion, which by direction of the Minister of War gave assistance to the project. Schwarz himself is said to have directed the construction, or rather the assembly of girders and sheets fabricated at Berg's plants in Eveking and Lüdenscheid; yet he was often absent on business trips, and on January 13, 1897, he died suddenly in Vienna of a stroke. He left nobody familiar with the design and principles of the ship or who was prepared to fly it. His widow, Melanie, a most unusual figure in the pre-feminist era, was determined not to see her husband's life work abandoned, and two weeks after his death signed a contract with Berg to continue the construction, and to provide for the division of any profits. The airship was essentially complete; but there remained the problem of inflating it with hydrogen, not so simple a matter as it might seem. For merely pumping hydrogen into the air-filled hull would result in mixing it with air, degrading the purity and lift of the gas and creating a dangerously explosive mixture. Another theoretical possibility — of filling the hull with water and draining the water while piping in hydrogen — was ruled out because of the lightweight structure of the ship.[3] The problem apparently baffled Melanie Schwarz, Berg and his subordinates for months. Finally they accepted the advice and assistance of the able balloonist and technician, Premierleutnant Hans Bartsch von Sigsfeld of the Prussian Airship Battalion, who with August von Parseval had earlier invented the *Drachen* kite balloon. Von Sigsfeld's suggestion was to make a series of fabric bags shaped to fill the interior of the hull; after hanging them in place, to inflate them with hydrogen, which would force out the air inside the hull; then to release the hydrogen by cutting and removing the bags. In this manner the Schwarz airship was inflated in 2 hours 40 minutes, and found to have positive lift on the tie-down ropes. It was immediately walked out of the hangar for its first flight.

Berg and Melanie Schwarz had had difficulty finding someone to flight test the airship, and finally were forced to hire one Ernst Jägels, a non-commissioned officer of the Airship Battalion, who extracted the promise that the airship initially should be allowed to ascend tethered. On the day of inflation, however, which was November 3, 1897, everything went wrong. The weather was overcast and windy as Jägels climbed aboard. Thirteen sand bags were loaded, totalling 600 pounds of ballast, and Jägels started up the engine, first heating the platinum tube to incandescence. He started the three pusher propellers turning, and ascended to 300 feet, tethered by the 800 foot mooring line. At this point the belt drive fell off the left propeller, and the long line broke as the airship was caught by the 17 mph wind. The craft then rose free to 1300 feet, and at this point the belt drive fell off the right propeller. Jägels, becoming panicky, resolved to get down as promptly as possible and valved gas. The gondola bounced twice on the ground — not damaging the gas chamber, according to Jägels' report — but on the

[3] Thirty-two years later the similar American metal-clad ZMC-2 was inflated with helium by first filling the hollow metal shell with carbon dioxide, and then withdrawing the heavy CO_2 and admitting helium through the top of the hull.

third touch-down the hull leaned over to the left, and the metal structure collapsed. Jägels was blamed for the disastrous outcome of the trial flight; but considering the wind conditions, the numerous mechanical deficiencies of the Schwarz airship, and above all, the total lack of any means of controlling it, nobody could have done more.

The failure of the Schwarz aluminium rigid created difficulties for Count Zeppelin, whose aluminium-frame airships were seen by the public as being equally unpractical and fragile. Yet it stands as a milestone, not only being the first rigid airship, but also the first aircraft to demonstrate the supreme suitability of aluminium and its alloys for aircraft construction.

With the exception of the Lebaudy airship, none of the craft so far described had the slightest utility for commercial transportation or passenger carrying – the largest having a gas volume of slightly over 100,000 cubic feet. Only the Lebaudy carried more than its pilot, and the range and speed were insufficient for international air travel, not to mention intercontinental journeys. It was of course obvious that the airship's carrying capacity and range would increase as the cube of its dimensions, yet there were limits to the size of the fabric envelope of the pressure airship.[4] To make the powered balloon the long-range aerial vehicle of the future, some way would have to be found to build it even larger. To create such a craft was the long-standing dream of a provincial German soldier and nobleman, a native of the south German state of Württemberg – Ferdinand August Adolf, Count von Zeppelin.

[4] The biggest and last pressure airships ever built, the U.S. Navy's four ZPG-3Ws of 1959, displaced 1,516,300 cubic feet, a volume exceeded by the Zeppelins of 1916.

II
Count Zeppelin and the invention of the rigid airship

The rigid airship as it existed over forty years was the invention of a South German aristocrat, Count Ferdinand von Zeppelin, and will always be associated with his name. Of the 161 rigid airships completed and flown, 119 were produced by the company which he founded. To him, and to him alone are due the basic concepts of the large rigid craft – the enormous size, the unique metal frame which made this size attainable, and the provision of separate cells or compartments within the rigid frame to accommodate the lifting gas. Yet his contribution was far more than technical: a most remarkable strength of character, distinguished by intense and even obsessive devotion to his ideas, a fanatic determination, an unquenchable optimism and an unshakeable conviction of eventual success, left its mark on all his followers and imitators. Like the Count, they too pursued the dream of the rigid airship as if it were a holy cause with a passion and devotion remarkable even to their contemporaries. Like Count Zeppelin, they were ready at all times to give their lives for the cause, and many did.

An authentic folk hero of the Wilhelminian *Reich,* Count Zeppelin probably stood second only to Field Marshal von Hindenburg in the devotion and admiration of the German people. It was inevitable that spontaneous legends, not to mention deliberate propaganda, would distort the image of this remarkable and at the same time very human individual. He was hailed in his lifetime as an engineering genius, even as the saviour of his country. In the post-war period, when "militarism" had become a word of opprobrium, it was alleged that he had conceived and developed the rigid airship solely for peaceful commerce. The facts are remarkable enough, and his faults detract little from the credit due him both as an inventor and a person.

Though of aristocratic birth, the Count's antecedents were not remarkable. His father's ancestors had lived in the South German state of Württemberg for a hundred and fifty years, and from this

9

side the Count received the traditional "Swabian pig-headedness" which showed itself so often during the struggle to bring his invention to reality. His mother, Amalie Macaire d'Hoggeur, was French, or at least a descendant of French Huguenot refugees, and may have been responsible for the imagination, originality of thought, and international breadth of vision which distinguished the Count throughout his life from other provincial Germans. Born on July 8, 1838, at Konstanz, he was certainly the best endowed with character of the three Zeppelin children. The oldest, Eugenie, was the mother of a son, Max von Gemmingen, who was Zeppelin's successor in charge of the company after his death. A younger brother, Eberhard, though a member of the Württemberg parliament, had only a local reputation.

Educated by a tutor at home, the young Zeppelin at age 15 entered the army of his native Württemberg, at that time an independent kingdom. He took some technical courses at the War College and Polytechnic Institute, and in 1858, some studies at Tübingen, but could hardly be considered a trained engineer as a result. With Europe being at peace, Zeppelin in 1863 took the unusual step of taking a leave of absence to journey to America as an observer of the Civil War. Provided with cards describing him as "adjutant to H.M. the King of Württemberg," and with introductions to the Hanseatic Ambassador, Zeppelin was well received in Washington. From President Lincoln he obtained a recommendation to the Secretary of War that he receive a pass permitting him to move freely among the Northern armies. On May 28, 1863, he joined the Headquarters of the Army of the Potomac on the Rappahannock. At this time, the Army of Northern Virginia under Lee was advancing north through the Shenandoah Valley, and Hooker, commanding the Army of the Potomac, was following, endeavouring at the same time to cover Washington. At Ashley Gap, near Aldie, Virginia, Zeppelin was involved in a cavalry skirmish with Jeb Stuart's troopers, and came close to being captured, escaping only through the superior speed of his mount. Quite unaccountably, with the decisive and dramatic Battle of Gettysburg only a few days away, the Count quitted the northern army on June 22 and proceeded to Detroit. There followed a journey through the Great Lakes to Superior, Wisconsin, and a trek through the wilderness with two Russian gentlemen and a pair of half-breed guides. German biographers assert that Zeppelin was seeking "the source of the Mississippi," which had been discovered in Lake Itasca by Henry Schoolcraft in 1832. In fact, he seems merely to have intended a look at the American frontier. Proceeding via Crow Wing and Fort Ripley, Zeppelin and his companions returned to civilization at St. Paul on August 17. Here a significant event occurred in his life: a German-born aeronaut, John Steiner, who had served with the Union Army until December, 1862, had a balloon of 41,000 cubic foot capacity which he had inflated with coal gas on this date across the street from Count Zeppelin's hotel. Two days later, as Zeppelin wrote home in a letter, "I have just made an ascent with Professor Steiner, the celebrated aeronaut, to an altitude of 6-700 feet."[1]   Evidently this was a tethered ascent.

His month with the Army of the Potomac left the Württemberg aristocrat with a lifelong conviction of the value to their country of the American citizen army, individualists bringing to the art of war the initiative and independence of thought of the American frontier, and on his return home Zeppelin attempted to promote some of these concepts within the German military establishment. To brother officers brought up on the ferocious discipline of Frederick the Great, whose ideal was *Kadavergehorsamkeit* – the soldier obeying orders with no more question than a corpse – this was rank heresy. Zeppelin's military career suffered as a result, but characteristically, he clung determinedly to his views.

Advancement up the military ladder brought Zeppelin into close contact with his sovereign, King Karl of Württemberg, and after 1891 with his cousin and successor, King William. Zeppelin fought in the war of 1866, in which his native state sided with Austria and suffered defeat by Prussia; and in the war of 1870-71 against France. Though Württemberg thereafter was part of the new German Empire, the southern states were still allowed the fiction of independence and maintained embassies in Berlin. In 1885 Zeppelin exchanged uniform for top hat and frock coat and became Württemberg's plenipotentiary in Berlin. Two years later he was named Ambassador Extraordinary and Minister Plenipotentiary to the Prussian court. In these posts he defended the interests of his sovereign with a zeal resented by some of the Prussians among whom he was domiciled.

All the chickens came home to roost in the year 1890, when the Count, now a brigadier, gave up his ambassadorial post to return to army duty. No Württemberg brigade was available for his command, and he was given a Prussian cavalry brigade in Saarburg. Here he instituted changes based on his experiences in America, and on a

---

[1] Hans von Schiller in *Wingfoot Lighter than Air Society Bulletin,* vol. 13, No. 5, p. 9.

misadventure early in the Franco-Prussian War, where his troop was surrounded and captured in the farmhouse of Schirlenhof, only Zeppelin himself escaping. The cavalry carbine was at that time carried by the horse, not the rider, but at the Schirlenhof, as Zeppelin observed, "the horses couldn't shoot." Bugle calls were suppressed in his brigade and hand signals substituted because the bugle could warn the enemy. Naturally the innovations were not popular with know-it-all Prussians. Worse still followed when in March, 1890, he forwarded via the Württemberg War Ministry to the Prussian Foreign Secretary a memorandum on a subject which had long disturbed him: the domination of the Army of Württemberg by the Prussian War Ministry:

> The arrangement whereby the (Prussian) Commanding General is responsible for all changes in assignments of Württemberg officers has no justification either in the Imperial Constitution nor in the military convention. Most particularly, this arrangement through the manner of its operation casts H.M. the King in the role of a mere rubber stamp, while the Commanding General determines the fate of the Württemberg officers. [2]

That the authority of his sovereign over his own army was being undermined was the obvious basis of Count Zeppelin's emotional action. The Prussian reaction was predictably hostile and reached to the highest level, the Kaiser noting in the margin of the document, "am very astonished at these particularist [3] ideas being here revealed!" [4] The Imperial displeasure would not be lifted until 1908, when Zeppelin had become a national hero and the All Highest perceived the wisdom of jumping aboard the bandwagon.

Nonetheless, Zeppelin was surprised when his handling of his brigade in the autumn manoeuvres was severely criticised and he was told he could not expect to command a division. Undoubtedly his sovereign made representations on his behalf behind the scenes, but in vain. His dismissal caused dismay among many of his friends and acquaintances, but as one of them remarked, "you must have in Berlin an enemy in a place of influence." I must agree with Zeppelin's biographers who see in the criticism of him in the autumn manoeuvres a fabricated excuse to get rid of him as a troublemaker for the Prussian military establishment.

---

[2] Hugo Eckener, *Graf Zeppelin* (Stuttgart: J.G. Cott'sche Buchhandlung Nachfolger, 1938), p. 98.
[3] A dirty word in Wilhelminian politics, referring to any attempt by subordinate states to assert their independence and individuality vis-a-vis Prussia.
[4] Eckener, p. 99.

Thus, unexpectedly, Count Zeppelin at the age of 52 found himself unemployed, his military career at an end. It was not like him to retire quietly to his estates and enjoy a bucolic old age. Instead, this calamity provided the impetus for his development of the rigid airship, a project which for some years had interested him as a hobby, but which now became the all-consuming purpose of his life.

In an interview in the year 1915 the Count claimed that the balloon ascent in St. Paul 52 years previously had given him his first ideas concerning the big rigid airship; but this appears to have been a latter day deception of memory. Zeppelin's letters and diaries, carefully examined on this point in 1966 by Hans von Schiller, refer only briefly to the ascent and say nothing about the airship concept. This first appeared in an entry of March 25, 1874, and was admittedly inspired by a lecture in January of that year by Heinrich von Stephan, the founder of the World Postal Union, on "World Postal Services and Airship Travel." For Stephan to suggest that mail might be carried around the world by air showed uncommon vision at a time when the steam engine as used by Giffard was the sole power plant available. The lecture somehow fired Zeppelin's imagination (at this time he was on the sick list for several weeks due to a riding accident) and in his diary he set down some ideas:

> The craft would have to compare in dimensions with those of a large ship. The gas volume so calculated that the weight of the craft would be supported except for a slight excess. The ascent will then take place through forward motion of the machine, which will force the craft so to speak against the upward-inclined planes. Having attained the desired altitude, the planes will be angled less steeply, so that the airship will maintain a horizontal attitude. To descend the surfaces will be angled even less upward, or speed will be reduced. . .
>
> The gas compartment shall be divided into cells which may be filled and emptied individually. The machine must constantly replenish its gas. . .[5]

Other notes and sketches indicate a ship of 706,200 cubic feet capacity, with cabins for 20 passengers, together with cargo and mail holds under the hull, which would be a rigid structure made up of rings and longitudinals. (The short-range passenger Zeppelin "Bodensee" of 1919 carried 20 to 24 passengers and had this exact gas volume). There were to be 18 gas cells, and a fabric outer cover. Nothing was said about the power plant, which would have to wait on future developments. Zeppelin promptly discarded the idea of

[5] Eckener, p. 104.

lifting surfaces to sustain the airship dynamically, though the dynamic lift of the airship hull itself, driven at a nose-up angle, was often used later to carry excess loads. It never proved possible to renew the gas supply in flight. But other distinguishing features – the large dimensions, the separate gas cells and fabric outer cover – were unique in the Zeppelins, and in almost all other rigid airships, to the very end.

The qualified success of "La France" in 1884 – a military ship designed for military reconnaissance in the service of Germany's arch-enemy – caused Zeppelin to sound the alarm. In 1887 he embodied his concerns in a memorandum to the King of Württemberg:

> The defects of the captive balloon should have demonstrated to the war ministries of the Great Powers that a significant effect on military operations could be attained only with dirigible ballons, and efforts have been made towards this goal, in which Germany has been left behind, while France, which is not stingy with money when it is a matter of gaining a military advantage over her neighbors, has already obtained success in this direction. The airship "La France" of Captains Renard and Krebs, in spite of having a speed of only 5 metres per second (11 mph), has shown the undeniable possibility of controlled flight.
>
> For airship flight to be really useful for military purposes, it is necessary that the ship should be able to make progress against strong winds, and also should not have to land except at long intervals (at least 24 hours), in order to carry out long reconnaissances. It should have a large carrying capacity in order to carry personnel, cargo or explosive shells. All three requirements demand a very large gas volume, hence a large airship.
>
> Important advances in the development of the dirigible airship still have to be made in the discovery of a shape suitable for passing through the air, and in the possibility of rising without dropping ballast, and of descending without losing gas. If these problems can be solved successfully, airship travel will certainly be of inestimable further importance, not only for warfare but also for general commerce (shortest route through mountains or between places separated by sea), and for exploring the earth (North Pole and interior of Africa).[6]

More and more with the passing years it seemed as though the Count felt it was his patriotic duty to build a huge "air cruiser" to outstrip Germany's enemies in the air. "From all the statements, replies, appeals, and urgent entreaties which during the next few years he was to direct to a literally endless succession of outstanding and influential German personalities, there rings out again and again

[6] Luftschiffbau Zeppelin, *Das Werk Zeppelins, Eine Festgabe zu seinem 75. Geburtstag.* (Stuttgart: Kommissionsverlag Julius Hoffman, 1913), p. 1.

the phrase, 'help me to build the airship for Germany's defence and security!' "[7]

In the year 1891 the Count established a design department and began to investigate various materials for the structure of his airship, for outer covering and for gas cells, the properties of the motors available through the Daimler works in nearby Stuttgart, the design of propellers (of which full scale models were tested in a boat on Lake Constance), etc. The first engineer to be hired, a Herr Gross, had to be dismissed as his doubts failed to reflect the Count's optimism. He was replaced in May, 1892, by Theodor Kober, formerly with the Riedinger balloon factory in Augsburg.

Since the design evolved by Kober over the next year and a half proved to be a failure, no details of it are to be found in the writings of Zeppelin's apologists and biographers. It is possible however to present it in some detail from material in the archives of the Prussian War Ministry, from the well known patent specification of August 31, 1895, and above all, from a paper written in 1914 by Professor Müller-Breslau.

The ship itself was actually to be a multiple unit connected by elastic couplings, an "aerial express train" with a powered towing unit and trailing unpowered sections for passengers and cargo. The hull structure was in the form of a long parallel sided cylinder 36.1 feet in diameter. The forward section had a length of 385 feet, including a hemispherical nose giving a crude streamlined entry which accounted for 18 feet of the length. The gas volume of this section was 336,000 cubic feet. The useful lift was estimated at only 880 lb. The first trailing unit, designed to lift a load of 1320 lb, had a length of 52.5 feet; the second trailing unit, which terminated in a hemisphere at the stern and was designed to carry a load of 4400 lb, had a length of 131 feet.

Many reference books present photographs of a crude model of such an "aerial express train" which for years appeared in the Zeppelin Museum at Friedrichshafen; but the multiple stiff longitudinals of the model do not correctly represent the design evolved by Kober under his master's direction. This in fact was a decidedly flimsy affair incapable of resisting aerodynamic loads, and its static strength was questionable. Apparently for the sake of lightness it had only four stiff longitudinal members – these being seamless aluminium tubes less than 6 inches in diameter located at

[7] Eckener, p. 107.

the top, bottom, and both sides of the cylindrical hull. The twenty
other longitudinal members shown in the 1895 patent drawing were
simply wires, which of course had no resistance to compression or
bending loads. The longitudinals connected up a series of rings
spaced 8 m (26.2 feet) apart – incidentally, this was the spacing of
main rings in all Zeppelin airships until the year 1915. The rings were
simply hoops of the same kind of tubing 36 feet in diameter, braced
radially with 22 wires. A vertical strut spanned the diameter of each
ring, and these struts, plus the top and bottom longitudinals and
diagonal wires between the rings (apparently passing through the gas
cells), completed a truss able to resist bending and shear loads in the
vertical plane. A quantity of wire netting further strengthened the
hull and ring structure. Under the hull was a narrow walkway
suspended on wires, connecting the open boat-like gondolas rigidly
attached to the hull. There were two of these beneath the powered
section, each containing a Daimler 11 hp engine weighing 1100 lb.
Each engine drove two tiny four-bladed propellers high on the hull
on brackets near the centre of resistance. A pair of minute vertical
rudders at the nose were intended to provide directional control. To
ascend or descend in the vertical plane, the ship could be nosed up or
down by moving backward or forward a heavy weight hung beneath
the ship. Other features of the design were: taut outer cover of "silk
fabric or similar material"; individual gas cells in the spaces between
each ring, of unspecified material, each with an automatic relief valve
in the bottom and a hand-operated manoeuvring valve at the top.

Convinced that the Germany Army would immediately perceive
the strategic value of his "Deutschland" design, Count Zeppelin
turned to the military for assistance in constructing it. As early as
June 29, 1891, he was writing to Count von Schlieffen, the Chief of
the General Staff, "Your Excellency will perhaps recall a conversation
during a ride in the Tiergarten[8] concerning controllable aircraft. At
that time I did not care to pursue my ideas on the subject to the
point of experimenting, as I lacked the time to work them out and it
would have been disturbing to have been regarded as a candidate for
the madhouse. Now, when I am not permitted to do anything better
and public opinion cannot do any further injury to the profession in
which I served, but only to my person, I have again taken up
these ideas and given them substance, for the moment only in
drawings... My powered craft will be able to make fast and

[8] In the year 1890.

far-ranging journeys as they will carry fuel for 12 hours. . . Génerally these powered craft will not fly alone but usually will have transport vehicles attached for passengers and cargo. At the moment the lifting force of these is reckoned at 1100 lb."[9] Zeppelin at the same time requested that a technical officer be sent to Stuttgart to examine his plans and calculations, and Hauptmann von Tschudi, the commander of the Prussian Airship Battalion, was dispatched on this mission. Von Tschudi's report was probably verbal, for there is no record in the archives of the War Ministry, but Count Zeppelin wrote further that "he encouraged me to carry my newly-hatched project for a balloon ship to completion."[10]

The next step was to secure government support for the design which by 1893 had been completed by Kober under Count Zeppelin's direction. Zeppelin estimated the cost of building the ship – apart from procuring the necessary hydrogen – at 650,000 marks, a sum which seemingly only the Government could provide. He accordingly requested, in a letter of September 14, 1893, to Count von Schlieffen, that a commission of experts be appointed by the Government to examine his design. Should they find the airship practical, they were to direct the War Ministry to procure an example at government expense. The letter set forth at length the Count's reasons for anticipating the success of his design as a war machine: "Safe and fast-flying air trains will confer on the Army many advantages: for example, reconnaissance over hundreds of miles of enemy territory in a few hours; assured supplies for all troops from the nearest depots every day without the delays of road transport; transfer of important officers and important information from one army to the other; bombardment of enemy fortresses or troop concentrations with projectiles, etc."[11] It also promised the support of his sovereigń. King William of Württemberg did in fact intervene with the Kaiser, who caused the appointment of a commission to examine Zeppelin's claims and designs on behalf of the government. The chairman (who died shortly after its first meeting) was the renowned physicist, Hermann von Helmholtz. The other six members included a distinguished meteorologist and two professors of engineering from the Royal Technical College at Charlottenburg; and

[9] Eckener, pp. 108, 112.
[10] Eckener, p. 116.
[11] Kriegswissenschaftliche Abteilung der Luftwaffe. *Die deutschen Luftstreitkräfte von ihrer Entstehung bis zum Ende des Weltkrieges 1918. Die Militärluftfahrt bis zum Beginn des Weltkrieges 1914.* (Berlin: E. S. Mittler u. Sohn, 1941). Anlageband, Anlage Nr. 11, p. 15.

military officers representing the Prussian Airship Battalion and the War Ministry.

In later years Count Zeppelin, like other pioneers of air power, was accorded by his supporters the same Messiah treatment as was extended to General Mitchell in the United States, and Marshal of the R.A.F. Lord Trenchard in England. According to this highly partisan formula, the Count, the inspired prophet with the vision of national salvation, was reviled by the multitude, conspired against by the Pharisees and (figuratively at least) crucified for his beliefs, only to rise again and to be accepted by the people as the bearer of the True Gospel. The official records show, however, that he was treated with unusual consideration by the War Ministry, whose general principle in dealing with inventors was to demand that they construct a demonstration vehicle at their own expense before any government support would be forthcoming. Considering his past military record, the Count probably benefited little from his rank as major general; his sponsorship by the King of Württemberg was the largest factor in his special treatment.

The members of the commission, which first met on March 10, 1894, found it impossible to recommend the Count's design. Hauptmann von Michaelis in his report to the War Ministry failed to comprehend the unique properties of the large rigid airship when he criticized the large size of the craft which would make it visible at great distances, its dependency on large fixed bases, and their necessary location in the rear instead of close to the fighting lines. But other criticisms of Zeppelin's design as a fighting machine were well justified. Even the speed claimed by the Count of 20 mph was inadequate to make headway against storms and high winds. The ratio of fixed weights to gross lift was too high, and while the Count felt that a resulting ceiling of 1000 feet was adequate, Michaelis was entirely correct in asserting that the airship would promptly be shot down if it tried to reconnoitre over the enemy's country at this low altitude. Further, a higher ceiling was necessary to expand the field of vision. Lastly, Zeppelin's design could be copied by Germany's enemies, so that "both parties would extend the war into the realm of the air" — a curious objection.

More hurtful, perhaps because they came from a civilian, were the criticisms of Professor Müller-Breslau of the Technical College at Charlottenburg. With a background in bridge design, the professor was a more competent stress analyst than Theodor Kober, and his opinions commanded the respect of the other members of the commission:

> It fell to me to test the rigidity of the body of the airship. The result of my calculations were most unfavourable. The static calculations of the engineer entrusted with the working out of the details of the design were confined to the investigation of a vertical framework which passed through the airship, dividing it into two halves. . . Nothing whatever had been done in the way of providing for horizontal rigidity of the airship, or for torsional moments. . . This ship, the rigidity of which was in a high degree dependent upon the pressure of the gas, was to be anchored on the ground in the open. No hangars were provided for.
>
> It was of course possible to strengthen the framework, but owing to the very small useful lift — it was only 880 lb — it could be done only at the expense of the engines, which were already too weak.[12]

The commission accordingly reported to the War Minister on July 10, 1894, that "as a result of the calculations of Professor Müller-Breslau, we must advise the War Ministry not to involve itself with the execution of the project of Major-General Graf Zeppelin." They added, "even though the concepts at the basis of the invention are not new, in the execution many notable concepts were found and one had to credit the project with a certain originality."[13]

Count Zeppelin was quite incapable of accepting the verdict of the commission as final, and replied with a rebuttal several pages long, complaining of being denied the opportunity to defend his designs. He focused on Müller-Breslau as the chief villain, and accused the other members of the commission of being unduly influenced by him. His exaggerated claims and accusations of bias overstrained the forbearance of officers in the War Ministry, who vented their feelings with a variety of critical and sarcastic marginalia: "On this point no definite assurance was ever given to my knowledge" (the War Minister), and again, "this assumption by Count Zeppelin is in my opinion totally erroneous!" The exasperated Michaelis wrote "the opinion of Professor Müller-Breslau embodies the ultimate available judgment by this member of the commission. Somebody has to speak the last word."[14] It is all the more surprising that the War Minister, instead of brusquely dismissing the Count's arguments, should have agreed to reconstitute the Commission in order that Count Zeppelin might present his revised designs. Once again it

[12] Professor Dr. Ing. Müller-Breslau, "Zur Geschichte des Zeppelin-Luftschiffes," *Verhandlung zur Beförderung des Gewerbfleisses*, January, 1914, p. 35.
[13] *Die Militärluftfahrt,* Anlageband, Anlage Nr. 13, p. 17.
[14] *Die Militärluftfahrt*, Anlageband, Anlage Nr. 13, p. 17.

would appear that the faithful King of Württemberg had brought pressure to bear in Berlin.

The revised design abandoned the coupled sections of the "express train" and presented the forward unit only with hemispherical stern. The struts in the vertical girder had been strengthened, and the problem of lateral bending loads had been crudely solved by attaching a braced framework truss 18 feet wide to the top of the hull, extending for the whole length of the ship and attached to each ring. The Count also abandoned the idea of anchoring the ship in the open, and planned to house it in a permanent hangar.

Müller-Breslau, regarding the horizontal framework atop the hull with distaste, had to admit that "taking into consideration the assistance rendered by the gas pressure, which was never absent entirely, and in view of the slow speed of the vessel which was to be expected, the rigidity of the ship must be described as sufficient for working the ship through wind currents of moderate strength."[15]

Being more than certain that the Count's speed calculations were in error, Müller-Breslau now turned his attention to these, and found the Württemberg aristocrat even more vulnerable. In no aspect of his airship design had the Count shown himself more naively optimistic, and his calculations were based on a simple formula relating his own craft to "La France," a smaller and much better streamlined craft. Given by experiment with the French airship a speed of 12.5 mph and a thrust of 265 lb with a gasbag diameter of 27.6 feet, the Count, assuming most optimistically that his two 11 hp engines could deliver a thrust of 2080 lb., found by a simple proportional calculation that his craft could attain 20 mph. It will be remembered that the wind tunnel had not been invented; but even so, tank experiments with towed ship models had produced some information on the efficiency of streamlined bodies and on skin friction. The Count probably realized that his much larger craft would have a much higher skin friction than "La France," but was not willing to admit that any feature of the hull design contributed to the drag except for the cross sectional area. Even years later, and after having received an honorary Doctor of Engineering degree, we find Zeppelin still arguing stubbornly that

> The consideration that the speed of a ship varies only slightly from the speed of wave propagation, while the fastest airship is more than 20 times slower than the air waves caused by its progress, led me, in opposition to Helmholtz,

---

[15] Müller-Breslau

to the conviction that the laws of motion relating to ships could not be directly applied to airships, and, for example, a fining-away of the hull aft from a midships frame would not have the same effect on the speed of an airship as it would have with a surface vessel. This led me to the shape of a cylinder of small cross-section with ogival ends, to present the least possible head resistance.[16]

He continued to build long cylindrical craft with minimal cross-sectional area even after experiments in a wind tunnel by Ludwig Prandtl, the first Professor of Aeronautical Engineering at the University of Göttingen, had proved in 1910 that the Zeppelin hull shape "was not the optimum for low air resistance, (and) a more favourable bow shape could be found."

Although the new design, with the added structural weight, was to be fitted with smaller engines of 9 hp each, Count Zeppelin still expected to attain a speed of 19 mph, and even allowed himself to prophesy 28 mph! The commission however concluded that a speed of 19 mph was unattainable because firstly the air resistance had been underestimated, and secondly the efficiency of the engine and propeller combination had been overestimated. Further, it was held, an adequate power plant would be too heavy for the ship to lift. The speed with the 9 hp engines was estimated by Müller-Breslau at 11 to 13½ mph, too low for military effectiveness. The commission in fact ruled that a militarily effective craft must achieve a speed of 28 mph and a ceiling of 6500 feet. "The deficiencies mentioned in the improved design are so fundamental that we cannot recommend it to the War Ministry."

Some further correspondence followed, with the Count even claiming in a letter to the Kaiser that his ship could stay in the air as long as 7½ days, using fuel carried by coupled sections; but the Kaiser was determined that further Government attention would only be forthcoming if the Count developed a demonstration vehicle at private expense. An attempt to raise money by soliciting subscriptions from Army officers without first getting the permission of the War Ministry further heightened the bad feeling between Zeppelin and the officials in Berlin.

According to Müller-Breslau, there was a sequel to the official confrontations between him and the inventor in the meetings of the commission. Müller-Breslau set himself to redesign Zeppelin's ship to have a higher degree of resistance to stress, and for this purpose

[16] Dr. Ing. Graf Zeppelin, *Erfahrungen beim Bau von Luftschiffen* (Berlin: Verlag von Julius Springer, 1908), p. 5.

adopted the principle of the "Schwedler Cupola," a frame made up of multiple stiff longitudinals securely attached to "stiff cross walls or partitions." He enlarged the whole ship to obtain greater lift to support the stronger hull, and replaced the hemispherical ends with tapering ones. The hull was now 440 feet long and 44 feet in diameter. Müller-Breslau states that the Count was extremely grateful to him for improving the design, yet Zeppelin never gave public credit to Müller-Breslau nor did any of his biographers. The fact remains that Zeppelin's first airship, flown in the year 1900, was built of girderwork longitudinals and rings, with tapered and pointed ends, just as Müller-Breslau had proposed.

It would be tedious to follow Count Zeppelin in all his efforts to raise capital for building a full size demonstration airship. An address to the prestigious Union of German Engineers on December 21, 1896, brought from them a qualified endorsement: "After careful evaluation of all conditions we have determined to give our encouragement to the request, in spite of full awareness and knowledge of considerations appearing to weigh against it."[17] Zeppelin approached Carl Berg for assistance even before the abortive flight of the Schwarz airship, and witnessed the event on November 3, 1897, from outside the boundary of the Tempelhof Field, the Airship Battalion having ruled that he could not enter because he was a competitor. Berg offered important assistance after dissolving a contract between himself and the Schwarz heirs. On the other hand, the connection through Berg between Zeppelin and Schwarz led to accusations in later years that the Count had merely copied the Hungarian's ideas. At no time, however, was Zeppelin tempted to imitate the "metal box system" of the Schwarz airship, and correctly believed that containing the gas in unpressurized fabric cells would permit the gas volume to accomodate to changes in pressure. Nonetheless Melanie Schwarz made the accusation, and Zeppelin's advisers had to dissuade him from helping her financially by warning that any such payments could be misrepresented as "hush money." A suggestion in a public lecture by Major Gross of the Prussian Airship Battalion that Zeppelin had appropriated the Schwarz patents and bought off the widow made Gross a lifelong enemy. Count Zeppelin actually sent him a challenge to a duel, which was averted by the direct intervention of the Kaiser. There is little doubt however that Zeppelin gave up the seamless aluminium

[17] Eckener, p. 137.

tubes in favour of girders built up out of channels and profile members because these had been designed by Berg's engineers for the structural members of the Schwarz airship.

In May, 1898, Count Zeppelin established in Stuttgart the "Joint Stock Company for Promotion of Airship Travel" to raise money to build his airship. Of the total capital of 800,000 marks, Zeppelin himself subscribed 300,000, Carl Berg 100,000, and other industrialists and business men put up smaller sums. An engineer, Kübler, was hired as technical director in addition to Kober, who was responsible for the design of the new ship. At Manzell on the Count's native *Bodensee* the company began by building a huge floating shed to house the airship, the Count firstly believing that his ships could land with less damage on the water than on land, and secondly because the hangar, moored at one end, would always turn with the wind.

Work on the ship itself commenced on June 17, 1898, when the first aluminium parts arrived from the Berg factory at Lüdenscheid. The hull, designed to be cylindrical in shape with symmetrically tapered ends, was to be 420 feet long and 38½ feet in diameter. There were 24 longitudinal members in the hull, connecting 16 transverse rings which were 24 sided polygons braced with radial and chord wires. The rings were 8 metres (26.2 feet) apart except that they were spaced 4 metres apart over the two gondolas. There was no shear wiring in the hull panels as in later ships, though the aluminium bronze wire gasbag netting was attached to the longitudinals and took shear loads. The structure was made up of pure aluminium girders with a depth of slightly over 7 inches, the girders being in effect openwork I beams with no real width. They offered little resistance to compression or lateral bending loads, and photographs of LZ 1 (Luftschiff Zeppelin 1) with cover removed show many of the lower longitudinals bent and out of line. Whether the girders were designed by Kober or by Berg's engineering staff, headed by Chief Engineer Tenzer, is not known. At all events, they were fabricated at Berg's aluminium plant in Lüdenscheid. Here, in a vast barn-like three storey wooden shed, each section of the first Zeppelin was assembled and erected, then disassembled, crated and shipped by rail to Manzell. The outer cover, designed to give a smooth, taut exterior and to minimize skin friction, was of Pegamoid, a specially impregnated cotton, on top of the ship, while a lightly impregnated cotton of lesser weight covered the under side. Dope as known today in aircraft work was not used. Within the hull, 17 drum-shaped gas cells filled the spaces between the main rings; these were fabricated by the well known *Ballonfabrik August Riedinger* of Augsburg out of light-weight cotton covered with a layer of rubber. Each cell had an automatic relief valve at the bottom, and 5 of them had manoeuvring valves at the top operable from the forward car. Initially the Riedinger gas cell material leaked hydrogen so badly that Count Zeppelin corresponded with an English firm supposed to know the secret of confecting gas cells out of nearly impermeable gold beaters' skin; but eventually the Augsburg firm developed a satisfactory product.

Two open boat-shaped gondolas were firmly attached close under the hull by struts at a distance of 105 feet from bow and stern. Strongly built of aluminium sheet on an aluminium frame, they were designed to float on the water though each had a wheel protruding from its bottom. A double bottom to the gondolas was designed to be filled with water ballast, which could be released to permit the ship to ascend. Other water ballast was carried inside the ship and could be emptied from the command position in the forward gondola.

In each gondola was a Daimler 4 cylinder water cooled engine delivering 14.2 brake horsepower at 680 rpm and weighing 850 lb. All petrol for the engines was carried in the gondolas. Each engine drove through bevel gears and long shafting a pair of small propellers on brackets high on the hull just under 4 feet in diameter. One source says that the forward propellers were 4 bladed, the after ones 3 bladed. The propellers revolved at 1200 rpm, faster than the engine revolutions, according to another peculiar theory of the Count's. Later research would prove that for a slow moving aircraft at least, the large-diameter, slowly revolving geared down propeller would be more efficient. While the side propellers in later Zeppelins were made reversible, this was not true in LZ 1.

Between the gondolas stretched a flimsy walkway precariously supported on wires; along this ran tubing designed to cool the water from the engines. Control mechanisms were primitive. There were no stabilizing fins. Forward was a pair of rectangular rudders above and below the nose, and aft was another small pair snugly mounted against the sides of the ship. There were no elevating planes; instead the ship while under way was to be nosed up or down by winching a 220 lb. lead weight back and forth between the gondolas.

The total gas volume was 399,000 cubic feet, conferring a gross or total lift under standard conditions of 27,400 lb. The builders found encouragement when an actual weighing of the completed metal framework on January 27, 1900, gave a figure of 9100 lb compared to a calculated 10,570 lb. The Count had optimistically estimated that the ship could carry a useful load of 4200 lb, but the gondolas, engines, propellers, gas cells and outer cover consumed so much of the gross lift that the useful load of LZ 1 on her first flight, inflated less than 100 per cent with impure hydrogen, was only 660 lb plus 770 lb of water ballast. A speed of 20 mph was predicted, but the maximum speed actually attained at any time with this airship was not more than 17 mph.

At the end of June LZ 1 was inflated. While Count Zeppelin had not advertised his plans and expectations, the word had travelled around the *Bodensee* and large crowds lined the shore near the floating hangar, and swarmed aboard steamers and small boats on the lake. They were disappointed on July 1, for the wind was considered too strong and the ship was merely drawn out of the hangar on her floating pontoon, weighed off and the propellers run, then returned to her shed.

Conditions were better on July 2, and towards evening the huge airship was drawn out of her hangar. The manoeuvre was conducted by that experienced airshipman and aeronautical innovator, Hauptmann Hans Bartsch von Sigsfeld of the Prussian Airship Battalion, "Count Zeppelin's equal in energy and boldness, his superior in technical knowledge and skill."[18] His death in a ballooning accident in February 1902 was a tragedy for the Count as well as for German aeronautics; had he lived, Count Zeppelin's relationship with the Prussian Airship Battalion would undoubtedly have been happier.

Before LZ 1 was drawn out of the hangar on the big float, Count Zeppelin removed his hat, called for silence, and led the participants and spectators in a short prayer. Once out on the *Bodensee,* he and the rest of the flight crew climbed into the gondolas. Kübler was supposed to participate but refused because the Count had been unable to obtain insurance; Zeppelin never forgave him for this defection and he was shortly replaced as superintendent. Undeterred by insurance problems, the Count's friend, the physicist Baron von Bassus, joined him in the forward gondola; the journalist and African explorer Eugen Wolff entered the rear gondola. Mechanic Eisele manned the forward engine, Mechanic Gross that in the rear. At

[18] Hans Rosenkranz, *Ferdinand Graf von Zeppelin, die Geschichte eines abenteuerlichen Lebens* (Berlin: Ullstein, 1931), p. 123.

First flight of Count Zeppelin's first airship, LZ 1, at Manzell on 2 July, 1900. The bow is to the right of the picture. (Luftschiffbau Zeppelin)

8.03 pm came the big moment as the handling crew on the float released the gondolas to let the ship float upward. The men at the rear hung on too long, and the nose was sharply pointed upward as the ship drifted away. The movable weight soon brought it to an even keel. Then the winch mechanism for the weight jammed in the forward position, and one engine failed. Much ballast had to be released forward to prevent the nose from touching the surface of the lake. After 18 minutes in the air the Count decided to land on the lake, and was taken in tow. The light wind proved stronger than the boat, which along with the airship was dragged to shore with slight damage. With a further drop in the wind LZ 1 was returned to her hangar in the evening.

For the onlookers this first flight of a Zeppelin airship was a thrilling preview of the spectacle whereby the giant rigids excited and enthralled millions during the next forty years. A military commission appointed by order of the Kaiser, consisting of two other members of the Airship Battalion besides Bartsch von Sigsfeld, and a representative of the War Ministry, had to report that LZ 1 was "neither suitable for military nor for non-military purposes," though they added that in the LZ 1 "one possesses an experimental vehicle with which a large number of problems involving navigability of airships may be practically investigated."[19] The possibility of building and flying a large metal-framed craft with multiple separate gas cells free to expand and contract within a smooth outer cover had been demonstrated, but the useful load had been insignificant. Count Zeppelin's critics were proven right in their doubts about the speed of the craft, the correspondent of the *Frankfurter Zeitung,* one Dr. Hugo Eckener, reporting that she made no more than 8 mph. Above all, the brief trial flight had revealed a fatal flaw in the detailed design of the ship – the rigid hull was not rigid after all, as the I-beam girders in the bottom of the ship bent under compression loads imposed by the two heavy gondolas and the lead weight. One photograph shows the hull quite obviously "hogged" or bent upwards in the middle and down at both ends.[20]

An attempt was made to stiffen the hull by rebuilding the gangway as a rigid braced structure, while the movable weight

LZ 1 rebuilding in the shed at Manzell after her first flight. Note stiffening structure in the keel, also the marked deformation of the I-beam longitudinal girders, a serious design error in this first ship. (Luftschiffbau Zeppelin)

[19] *Die Militärluftfahrt*, p. 43.
[20] in Eckener opposite p. 128.

(increased to 330 lb) was brought close up under the gangway. A horizontal elevator was arranged under the nose, and the rear rudders were attached beneath the hull instead of on the sides. The next flight was delayed when on the night of September 24, 1900, rings broke from which the deflated ship was suspended in the hangar, allowing the middle section to collapse on the floor. Within 14 days the ship had been re-erected and inflated. A second flight took place on October 17, lasting 1 hour 30 minutes, and a third flight on October 24 lasted 23 minutes. On the last flight the ship demonstrated her manoeuvrability and attained her maximum speed of 17 mph. Yet von Sigsfeld, who witnessed the last of these trials, still could not recommend the expenditure of public money on the design.

Having exhausted the funds of the company, the Count saw no choice but to liquidate it. The floating hangar was set on shore and supported on piles, and LZ 1 was dismantled. The defects in her girder design would in any case have rendered her unsuitable for further experimental flights. The work force was laid off, the Count retaining only an engineer and two night watchmen.

The engineer, however, was destined to remain with the company for the balance of its existence, and to be responsible for the overall design and construction of 118 more Zeppelin airships. Ludwig Dürr was only 21 years old when he joined Zeppelin's organization in 1899, but through his theoretical knowledge as well as his practical capabilities he rapidly gained the Count's regard and stepped into the place forfeited by Kübler when the latter refused to fly in the LZ 1. Swabian provincial qualities made Dürr congenial to Count Zeppelin; but he was ill at ease in dealing with outsiders and was described by Americans 20 years later as "living almost a hermit's life. Has never traveled and has very narrow views. Believes implicitly in German theory of absolute secrecy about work; also in building just about as he pleases. . . is a very difficult man to deal with."

There followed a pause of several years in airship development in Germany, while the French Army, to Count Zeppelin's alarm, adopted and exploited the efficient Lebaudy semi-rigid design. The only potential customers for airships were the Germany Army and Navy, and now and later, the War Ministry failed to comprehend the superiority of the large Zeppelin airship for long range strategic scouting in the enemy's back areas. (The Imperial Navy, which had an urgent need for such a long-range craft at sea, showed no interest). The military in fact desired small short-range craft for tactical scouting in the zone of the armies, which at the same time should be able to land in the open and be deflated, packed and carried away by horse and wagon if necessary. The first Parseval, a small, completely non-rigid pressure airship of 81,000 cubic feet capacity completed in early 1906 at the Riedinger works in Augsburg, was intended to meet this requirement and several Army orders resulted.

Thus, Count Zeppelin once more had to raise money from private sources. An eloquent "Emergency Appeal to Save the Airship," published in the widely circulated *Die Woche,* brought in nothing. A written appeal to 60,000 leading individuals recovered only 8000 marks. Scorn and contempt were heaped on the "crazy inventor". The Union of German Engineers, previously encouraging, now took a negative attitude, one member of the committee telling Count Zeppelin to his face that "the monster will never rise again." The great mass of the German people, in contrast to their hero-worshipping attitude of a few years later, were indifferent if not mocking. Nor would it have occurred to the stiff military aristocrat to influence the populace by means of publicity releases.

That never-failing supporter, King William of Württemberg, once more came to Zeppelin's assistance, authorizing a State lottery which realized 124,000 marks. Prussia, which refused to permit the sale of the lottery tickets within its borders, made a contribution of 50,000 marks. The remainder of the 400,000 marks needed the Count raised by mortgaging his wife's estates in Livonia, part of modern Latvia. Various manufacturers assisted – Berg contributing the aluminium, Daimler the engines.

Meanwhile Dürr had been working for some years on the next design, an improvement on LZ 1. Slightly smaller, LZ 2 was to be 414 feet long and 38½ feet in diameter, with 16 gas cells containing 366,200 cubic feet of hydrogen. Instead of being 24-sided, the rings had only 16 sides.[21] The lead weight was done away with, and small elevators and rudders were fitted close under the hull. One fundamental fault was corrected when Dürr as early as November 17, 1902, proposed the use of triangular section girders which would resist bending forces in all planes. The aluminium used in LZ 2 was alloyed with zinc and copper, but the alloy was not uniform in quality and strength. Instead of the weak 15 hp motors used in the first ship, the Daimler Works had delivered two power plants rated at 85 hp each with a weight of 425 lb. Larger 3-bladed propellers with

[21] Hauptmann a.D. Hildebrandt, "Die starre System des Grafen Zeppelin" in 15. Sonderheft der "Woche," 1908, p. 14.

a diameter of 7 feet 3 inches were used, again turning faster than the engines.

Little wonder that the optimistic Count and his supporters were sure they had a winner this time; yet again there was to be a crushing disappointment. Construction of LZ 2 began in April, 1905, in the rebuilt floating hangar now mounted on piles at the water's edge. The ship was completed in seven months and on November 30, 1905, was towed out of the shed for the first flight. A knot in the tow rope caused it to jam when released, pulling the airship's bow into the water; damage was extensive to the control surfaces under the hull.

The next attempt to fly LZ 2 was on January 17, 1906. The crew comprised five mechanics, a Hauptmann von Krogh, a qualified balloon pilot, and Count Zeppelin himself. Too much ballast was released at takeoff and the ship rose to 1500 feet, valving gas, before attaining equilibrium. Here she encountered a stiff breeze from the south-west, against which she at first held her own with the power of the engines. The air speed in fact was estimated at nearly 25 mph. But LZ 2 proved to be longitudinally unstable, pitching constantly and violently first nose up, then nose down. The forward engine failed when the cooling system broke down,[22] then the after engine with a broken clutch spring. Now the huge rigid drove away to the north-east over land, a mere plaything of the wind. Near Kisslegg in the Allgaü, Count Zeppelin brought the ship down with some damage when the stern struck some trees, but during the night the ship was beaten against the ground by high winds and had to be dismantled. Only then did the crew discover that the Allgaü hamlet near which they had landed was known colloquially to the natives as "Allwind."

The misfortunes of LZ 2 proved however to be a blessing in disguise, for they brought to Count Zeppelin's side a man who immediately proved a powerful support and who in time took over the Zeppelin inheritance and so expanded it as to make his name a household word around the world – Dr. Hugo Eckener. The latter's articles for the *Frankfurter Zeitung* concerning both LZ 1 and LZ 2 had criticised both ships on technical grounds. What was Eckener's astonishment when a few weeks after the disaster in the Allgaü, Count Zeppelin called on him formally in silk hat and yellow gloves, to point out certain errors in the account of the last flight of LZ 2!

[22] The air speed of the early Zeppelins was so low that fans were mounted in front of the radiators to draw air through them. The fans were constantly breaking down or losing blades.

The meeting ended on a friendly note, Eckener was invited to dinner, and here it was the doctor himself, sympathetic to the Count's problems with governmental bureaucracy, who proposed that he write articles to educate the public concerning Count Zeppelin's airships and their value for Germany's future, militarily and commercially. The offer was accepted with thanks; but Eckener, though he was throughout his life a master of public opinion, proved himself to be more — nothing less than the greatest airship pilot of all time.

While sorrowfully directing the demolition of LZ 2 in the Allgaü, Count Zeppelin had stated publicly that he would build no more airships; but with his customary buoyant optimism, he was shortly seeking means of financing a third craft. As usual, he still hoped for military support, and in fact at this time a military commission (the member from the General Staff was Major Erich Ludendorff) was considering the question, now urgent, of what type of airship the German Army should procure in competition with the French Lebaudys already in service. Naturally, the total loss of LZ 2 made it impossible for the commission to recommend Zeppelin's airship, and in the end it advised that the German Army itself should develop semi-rigids after the Lebaudy design. Inasmuch as Major Gross of the Airship Battalion was responsible for the production of these "military" semi-rigids, the Count continued to treat him as a sworn enemy despite Gross' respect for the Zeppelin and its potentialities.[23] While the Count's supporters saw this commission as being as prejudiced as the earlier ones, its members felt the designer so deserving of encouragement that they recommended a gift from the Kaiser of 100,000 marks and permission for Zeppelin to conduct a lottery in the State of Prussia. The special intervention of the War Minister enabled the lottery to be held, with an issue of 250,000 marks, and the Airship Study Association (connected with the Parseval enterprise) made an interest-free loan of 100,000 marks.

Already in May 1906 Count Zeppelin had begun work in the shed at Manzell on LZ 3. The hull was identical with that of the LZ 2, the dimensions, the number of longitudinals and ring frames being identical with those of the ship lost at Kisslegg. The gas volume however was increased to 403,600 cubic feet. The 85 hp Daimler

---

[23] *Die Militärluftfahrt*, Anlageband, Anlage Nr. 22, p. 35, "Gutachten des Luftschifferbattalions über den voraussichtlichen militärischen Wert des Luftchiffes des Generalleutnants a.D. Grafen von Zeppelin," a report by Major Gross evaluating favorably the Zeppelin's operational potential.

engines and the 3-bladed propellers apparently were the same ones salvaged from the wreck. The same small triple box rudders were fitted close under the ship at the forward and after end of the hull, but biplane horizontal elevators were also fitted before the forward gondola and abaft the after one. The most striking innovation was two pairs of large horizontal stabilizers at the rear of the hull. These were designed to prevent the severe pitching movement which had occurred with LZ 2, and had been proposed by Dürr after some experiments in a crude home-made wind tunnel he had developed at his own expense. Yet two years would pass before the equally necessary and complementary vertical fins would be fitted to stabilize the ship about the yaw axis. The difficulties which Count Zeppelin continued to experience in directional control of his ships emphasize his refusal to engage in fundamental research on aerodynamics and structures; instead he stubbornly insisted on following his original dream, making empirical modifications as experience dictated. It may be objected that he lacked both the time and the money to engage in such research; but more particularly he appears to have been unwilling to admit that his basic engineering prejudices might have been erroneous.

With LZ 3 at last the Count scored a series of successes with none of the spectacular accidents that overtook so many of his earlier ships. LZ 3 in fact survived to a ripe old age, much modified before she was dismantled as obsolete in March 1913. On her first flight on October 9, 1906, with eleven persons aboard, she was airborne for 2 hours 17 minutes. A speed of 33½ mph was claimed, but this appears excessive and the ship was usually rated at 24½ mph. The useful load came to 6200 lb., of which up to 5500 lb. was devoted to water ballast. A second successful flight took place next day on October 10, before she was deflated and laid up in her shed for the winter.

There was considerable enthusiasm over this performance; in particular Major Gross, whom Count Zeppelin considered an enemy, was so favorably impressed that he recommended that the inventor receive half a million marks to continue his experiments with a view to obtaining a militarily effective craft. Count Zeppelin himself was inspired to make further claims so reckless and fantastic that his supporters have chosen to ignore them — all except Colsman. In a letter to the Imperial Chancellor dated December 1, 1906, the Count began by proposing that the Government buy, not only his existing ship, LZ 3, for half a million marks, but also two further craft. The proceeds would then enable him to proceed with

The studies and experiments towards a tremendous advance in airship development: with the same assurance with which I have been accustomed to predicting that I could build airships with the performance of my present one, I can assert today that I can demonstrate the possibility of constructing airships with which, for instance, 500 men with full combat equipment can be carried for the greatest distances. These airships, because they will contain no gas, will be extremely safe, and in respect to housing arrangements as well as building and operating costs will be comparatively very inexpensive. [24]

This was too much for somebody in the War Ministry, who covered the margins of the letter with sarcastic comments: "False! Inaccurate! Oh, no! If only we had millions! Don't think of it!" and with respect to the gas-less airship, "then we would do better to go right to this one!" Little wonder that this person questioned the gas-less feature; Colsman reveals briefly that the airship was to be supported by hot air, but "later experiments demonstrated that no material sufficiently light was able to withstand the high temperatures necessary for this purpose." [25]

Nonetheless, the approach to the Imperial Chancellor led to the civilian officials of the *Reich* taking an interest in Zeppelin's airships, while the military authorities continued to play their usual role. The General Staff in particular saw the French superiority as posing a severe threat to Germany, and pressed for the development of suitable German craft, without feeling able to endorse any particular system. This provoked a bitter rivalry between Zeppelin and his competitors, Major von Parseval with the non-rigid design, and Hauptmann Gross and the Prussian Airship Battalion with their semi-rigid type.

In the end, the interested authorities procured a vote by the *Reichstag* of half a million marks in favour of the Count, part of which was spent to build a new floating shed (hence known as the *Reichshalle*). On the other hand it was the Minister of the Interior, not the War Minister, who originated the requirement that the Count had to make an uninterrupted 24 hour flight to a predesignated destination and return before the Government would purchase one of his airships.

During the summer of 1907 the LZ 3 was modified. The triangular keel under the hull between the gondolas was extended forward and aft. The control surfaces, vulnerable to damage in their position under the hull, were removed, and quadruplane elevators were fitted

[24] *Die Militärluftfahrt*, Anlageband, Anlage Nr. 26, p. 47.
[25] Alfred Colsman, *Luftschiff Voraus!* Deutsche Verlags-Anstalt Stuttgart-Berlin, 1933, p. 17.

low on the sides of the ship at the forward and after limits of the parallel cylindrical body. These were found extremely effective, and even enabled the ship to take off dynamically some 1300 pounds heavy. Working up to speed, she skittered across the surface of the lake, then, setting both sets of elevators on "climb," she leaped upward, but with no inclination of the hull. Nearly 40 years later the U.S. Navy's airship arm was to introduce the "heavy" takeoff with dynamic lift as something new.

The paired rudders, mounted now between the tips of the stabilizing planes, were less efficient, and even at full speed had to be put hard over to be effective.

With the completion of the new floating shed on September 23, 1907, the modified LZ 3 was inflated in the old shed on the lake shore at Manzell. Three thousand steel cylinders, each containing 170 cubic feet of hydrogen at 150 atmospheres pressure, had been provided by the Prussian Airship Battalion, and 2413 of these were emptied during the 8-hour filling. Next day, on September 24, LZ 3 was drawn out of the shed on her float and with ten people aboard, flew for 4 hours 17 minutes around the eastern end of Lake Constance. On September 25 she made a local flight of 3 hours and 2 minutes, and on September 26 she went several times across the lake in 3 hours and 31 minutes. Four passengers were carried on this date, including Dr. Eckener and Count Zeppelin's daughter, Countess Hella, the ship landing on the lake to exchange them. On September 28, with Major Gross as a passenger, LZ 3 returned to her shed after a flight of only 41 minutes, due to a breakdown of a fan in the radiator of the after engine. On September 30, however, LZ 3 was airborne for 7 hours and 54 minutes, with a Navy representative, Fregattenkapitän Mischke, as passenger. For the first time the ship was deliberately steered over land, going north of the *Bodensee* some 20 miles to beyond Ravensburg. Flying no higher than 500 feet over the hilly terrain, the control personnel – Dürr at the elevators, Hacker at the rudder wheel – found the ship difficult to manage in up and down drafts and in air heated over open fields, and cooled by forests. The distance covered on this day was nearly 220 miles.

This ended the experimental program for the year. Due to leaking cells and shortage of gas, the ship had lost 2100 pounds of lift since her inflation. On October 8, 1907, she flew for 1 hour and 31 minutes with the German Crown Prince aboard and then was deflated. On December 14, 1907, a severe winter storm tore the

Reichshalle from its moorings and drove it ashore, severely damaging the LZ 3 hung up in the shed.

Count Zeppelin had been compelled in any case to realize that LZ 3 did not have the endurance to complete the 24 hour flight, and he would have to build a larger craft for this purpose. The authorities were sympathetic, the Chief of the General Staff, General von Moltke, pointing out that only in the Zeppelin did Germany have an aircraft potentially superior to anything possessed by the French. It was agreed that Zeppelin should receive 400,000 marks for constructing a fourth airship, and after fulfilling the 24-hour flight requirement over a distance of 435 miles, the State would purchase both airships for 2,150,000 marks.

Construction of LZ 4 began in November, 1907, in the old shore-based shed at Manzell. On June 2, 1908, after the *Reichshalle* had been salvaged and reconditioned, the completed metal skeleton of the new ship was towed out to the floating shed, and the damaged LZ 3 returned to the shore hangar. On June 17 the new craft was inflated. An enlargement of the earlier designs, LZ 4 had the same cylindrical hull form, 446 feet long, 42½ feet in diameter, and with 530,000 cubic feet of hydrogen in 17 gas cells. The useful load under standard conditions was increased to 10,150 lb, and with a more powerful Daimler engine of 105 hp in each gondola, the high speed was 30 mph. Amidships in the keel was a small cabin with windows, from which a shaft led up between two gas cells to a top platform "for taking navigational sights." The well-proven quadruplane elevators were fitted fore and aft as in LZ 3, together with similar horizontal stabilizing planes. In place of the small rudders between the planes in LZ 3, tiny rectangular rudders were fitted at both the bow and stern of the ship. These failed to control her directionally and in her short life of one and a half months, LZ 4 had her steering arrangements modified twice more: firstly by discarding the bow rudder and fitting small single rudders between the stabilizers; and then by doubling the rudders between the stabilizing fins, adding a large oval rudder at the stern 26 feet high and 16½ feet in chord and fitting huge vertical fins above and below the stern to give directional stability.

The first flight of LZ 4 on June 20 lasted only 18 minutes, and demonstrated that the small fore and aft rudders were completely ineffective, the ship making three uncontrollable circles before landing back on the lake. There was a second trial flight on June 23, and a third on June 29. On July 1 the Count boldly set out with 14 hours' fuel and twelve persons aboard including himself, on a cross country flight over Switzerland. Proceeding by way of Schaffhausen to Lucerne, he returned against a head wind via Zürich to arrive back at the hangar at Manzell after twelve hours in the air. This time far exceeded any other airship endurance record, while the distance covered was 240 miles and the maximum altitude was 2600 feet. The flight revealed a serious defect which should have received attention but did not – the ship had no fuel system to supply petrol continuously to the engines, and when the 440 lb in the main tank in each gondola had been exhausted, the engine had to be stopped while more fuel was carried by hand from the gangway in 44 pound containers.

The Count, however, was now full of confidence that in the splendid new ship he could easily reach Mainz and return to Manzell in a 24 hour period. The flight over Switzerland had produced intense interest and enthusiasm not only in the republic, but also among the German people. Zeppelin and his huge airship were news not only in his native Württemberg, but throughout the *Reich*, and his every move was now followed by hungry newspaper readers.

On July 13 LZ 4 was reinflated with fresh hydrogen in order to have maximum lift for the long flight. On the 14th she set off, but again a fan blade broke on the forward motor a few minutes after takeoff, and the ship had to turn back. Much worse happened on the following day when the ship struck the side of the shed while being towed out; several rings and longitudinals were fractured, a propeller and the port after elevator damaged, and several gas cells were leaking. Not until August 4 did the Count make another attempt.

At 6.22 am, in the cool of the morning, LZ 4 lifted off the *Bodensee* after releasing 132 lb. of ballast. Her useful lift at takeoff was 8500 lb., apportioned as follows: fuel for 31 hours for both engines, 3300 lb. Oil likewise 750 lb. Reserve radiator water 330 lb. Water ballast 1450 lb. Twelve persons with supplies and personal items 2450 lb.

Heavily loaded as LZ 4 was, Count Zeppelin was obliged to proceed at low altitude and this dictated a roundabout low level route to Mainz via the Rhine valley. Interest in the flight was intense, word had been sent ahead by telegraph, and the streets were black with crowds in all the cities along the route. First came Konstanz on the Swiss side of the *Bodensee*, then Schaffhausen. Guns fired blank charges in salute from the ancient castle. Some attempt was made at

LZ 4 as she appeared at the time of the 24-hour endurance cruise that ended at Echterdingen. Vertical fins have been added aft, also large "barn door" rudder and paired smaller rudders between fins. Note small propellers which turned at a higher speed than the engines. (Luftschiffbau Zeppelin)

dividing the crew into two watches, and several were taking breakfast when Basel appeared 300 feet below at 9.30 am. Thanks to a tail wind, LZ 4 had traveled 99 miles in three hours at an average ground speed of 33 mph. Here the ship turned north. Count Zeppelin and his men were confident that they could cover the 180 miles to Mainz in eight hours, and expected to start the return flight at 5 pm. At Strassburg, then a German city, everyone seemed to be out on the streets, and as the airship glided past the tall cathedral at a level below the top of the spire, the platform atop the tower was black with people waving hats and handkerchiefs, while cannon boomed. Soon afterwards, at 12.57 pm, the forward motor had to be stopped while the fuel tank in the gondola was filled. Heretofore the airship, though light through the sun heating the gas, had been held at low altitude by driving her nose-down with the power of the motors; but now she rose to 2700 feet blowing off quantities of hydrogen through the automatic valves. When the forward engine was restarted the ship was heavy and 132 pounds of ballast had to be released to avoid hitting a bridge. At 1.58 pm the after engine had to be stopped for the same reason, and this time LZ 4 lost more gas while ascending to 2900 feet. Beyond Worms at 3.29 pm the after engine was stopped, and this time the ship lost even more hydrogen in ascending to 3380 feet, partly because she was now flying nose up due to ballast having been dropped forward. At 4.05 the forward engine had to be stopped when a gear broke in the drive of the fan for the forward engine radiator. This could be changed; but the ship was now very heavy and because of the up angle her air speed was only 9 mph. At 5.24, eleven hours and two minutes after the takeoff from Lake Constance, and after releasing 265 lb of ballast, LZ 4 made a smooth landing on the Rhine river. The place was Oppenheim, 14 miles south of Mainz. The damage was repaired in 20 minutes, but the ship was much too heavy to go on. While 800 lb of water ballast remained on board, dropping all of this would not have lightened the ship sufficiently, while a minimum of 265 lb of ballast had to be on board for landing. In fact a further 530 lb of ballast was loaded while the ship lay alongside the river bank. As evening came on, empty fuel cans, superfluous ropes, etc., were unloaded for a total of 1550 lb, and finally, five of the crew were set ashore. At 10.20 pm, after dropping some more ballast, the ship ascended from the river and went on north. Mainz, brightly lit as a landmark, was reached half an hour later, and the airship turned south. A fan blade broke and had to be replaced, the ship this time rising to 5150 feet. At 1.27 am, shortly after passing Mannheim, the forward engine broke down completely due to melting of a crank bearing. Air speed fell to 20 mph, while a head wind from the south-west gradually freshened. The ship made little headway, and south of Stuttgart was blown backwards as the rear engine was stopped to renew the petrol supply. Count Zeppelin decided to land to have the forward engine repaired by personnel of the Daimler works at nearby Untertürkheim. At 7.51 am the ship touched down near the village of Echterdingen, south-west of Stuttgart.

Huge crowds assembled from all over the area, but were orderly and friendly. The ship was anchored as securely as possible, and soldiers came from Stuttgart to guard LZ 4 and to serve as a ground crew. Daimler engineers removed the forward engine from the ship and set up a field smithy at a distance to make repairs. The old Count napped for an hour in the midships cabin and then drove into Echterdingen. Then, towards 3 o'clock, dark thunderclouds mounted up in the western sky. A sharp gust of wind struck the big ship from the starboard side, tore the moorings out of the ground, and LZ 4 began to drift away sideways. The soldiers could not hold her, and a few were carried up on the lines before letting go. One soldier and two crew members were still aboard the derelict airship, and Mechanic Schwarz, in the after gondola, had the presence of mind to race forward through the keel to pull on the gas valves in the forward gondola. Thus the ship descended a half mile from the anchorage. The bow brushed against trees, damaging the outer cover and apparently the gas cells also, for there was a sudden burst of flame and within seconds the conflagration had raced from bow to stern, reducing the proud air giant to a mass of twisted and blackened girders. Schwarz and his two companions luckily escaped with minor injuries.

Such was the end of "the great flight" — Count Zeppelin's latest craft had not made the 24 hour cruise required by the Government for its purchase, and instead was a smouldering ruin, a symbol of the incessant and heartbreaking frustrations which had pursued this remarkable man in his single minded obsession with developing the rigid airship. Count Zeppelin was now seventy years old, and this disaster should have broken his spirit and put an end to his efforts. But it was not an end, it was a beginning: the beginning of the mass emotional phenomenon known as "the miracle of Echterdingen."

III
The Zeppelin as a nationalistic symbol

The German people had followed with mounting excitement and enthusiasm the progress of Count Zeppelin's airship on the "great flight" from Friedrichshafen to Mainz, and the reaction to the catastrophe at Echterdingen was an outpouring of grief. David Lloyd George, the future English premier, had no doubts that he was witnessing an extraordinary display of national emotion when he arrived on the scene:

> We went along to the field where the giant airship was moored, to find that by a last minute accident it had crashed and been wrecked. Of course we were deeply disappointed, but disappointment was a totally inadequate word for the agony of grief and dismay which swept over the massed Germans who witnessed the catastrophe. There was no loss of life to account for it. Hopes and ambitions far wider than those concerned with a scientific and mechanical success appeared to have shared the wreck of the dirigible. Then the crowd swung into the chanting of "Deutschland, Deutschland Über Alles" with a fanatic fervor of patriotism. What spearpoint of Imperial advance did this airship portend?[1]

From the day of Echterdingen until the day of his death nine years later, Count Zeppelin was the darling of the German people, and his giant airships, *Kolossal* symbols in the skies of Teutonic supremacy, presented an infallible antidote for the national inferiority complex. National pride demanded that Count Zeppelin continue his experiments, and with a spontaneity incomprehensible to a later and more cynical age, the rich and the poor, the simple and the sophisticated, sent their contributions to Friedrichshafen. Children donated their pennies, one little girl writing from Mainz:

> Mommy carried me from my bed out on the balcony. The sky was dark with many stars, and I saw the Zeppelin and heard its humming noise. It was so pretty. But on the next day we heard the terrible news that the beautiful airship had burned up. Then I cried a great deal and told Mommy to send to the Count everything in my bank, so that he could build a new airship.[2]

[1] David Lloyd George, *War Memoirs of David Lloyd George 1914-15.* (Boston: 1933), pp. 31-32.
[2] George Hacker, *Die Männer von Manzell* (Frankfurt am Main: Societäts-Druckerei G. m.b.H., 1936), p. 104.

On the morning after the disaster Count Zeppelin, dejected and exhausted, arrived in Friedrichshafen to be greeted by Eckener with "Congratulations, Your Excellency!" and the news that several hundred thousand marks had been sent in during the night. "Well, then, we will go on ahead!" replied the indomitable old man.[3] In fact, money equal to the cost of the lost LZ 4 arrived on the first day. A blizzard of letters, telegrams and packages descended on the Count's headquarters in Friedrichshafen, most containing money, some with advice, poems, compositions, and requests for financial assistance, not to mention gifts of hams, sausages, wool stockings – and fine wine, which was much appreciated. More and more the money mounted up, until in the end it totalled over six million marks.

Now at last, at any rate temporarily, the Zeppelin enterprise stood on a firm foundation, beholden to none of the organs of the Imperial government, but to the German people as a whole, who had but one aim in their giving – that Count Zeppelin should continue building the airships which so appealed to their sense of national achievement. On September 3, 1908, the Count founded the *Luftschiffbau Zeppelin G.m.b.H.,* with a capital of three million marks, later increased to four million. On December 30 he established the Zeppelin *Stiftung* (Foundation), endowing it with the remainder of the proceeds of the Echterdingen subscription, and to which the component parts of the Zeppelin enterprise were subordinated. Subsidiary companies erected within the parent structure of the *Luftschiffbau Zeppelin* included:

The *Maybach Motorenbau* or Maybach engine company, founded in Stuttgart in 1909 and moved to Friedrichshafen in 1910. Its purpose was to construct engines designed especially for airships by Carl Maybach, the son of Wilhelm Maybach who had collaborated with Gottlieb Daimler in the early development of the automobile engine.

The *Ballon-Hüllen-Gesellschaft* of Berlin-Tempelhof, founded in 1912 to construct gas cells of gold beaters' skin, after it had been proved that the Riedinger-built rubberized fabric cells could generate static electricity if torn.

The *Zeppelin Hallenbau* of Berlin, founded in 1913 to build large airship sheds.

---

[3] Hugo Eckener, *Im Zeppelin über Länder und Meere* (Flensburg: Verlagshaus Christian Wolff, 1949), p. 25.

The *Zahnrad-Fabrik* of Friedrichshafen, a factory erected in 1915 to manufacture gears and gear drives to the designs of a Swiss engineer, Max Maag.

The founding of the *Luftschiffbau Zeppelin* marked the end of the pioneering period, as the "men of Manzell" were well aware: collecting regular pay checks, they no longer enjoyed the relationship with the Count which had so appealed to them, that of feudal retainers serving a seigneur for fame and glory, not for gold. The business manager of the new firm was Alfred Colsman, a son in law of Carl Berg, who had first met the Count in 1899, and made a business survey of his enterprise in 1907-8. Colsman had then recommended a swampy, open area on the north side of Friedrichshafen for a permanent home for the airship enterprise. The city, determined to keep the Zeppelin works within its boundaries, purchased the area and rented it to the Zeppelin firm under a 50-year contract. In the spring of 1909 a temporary tent hangar was erected on the south-west corner of the airship field, and was first occupied by Z I (LZ 3) on May 9. Later in the year an imposing double shed was erected in the middle of the field measuring 584 feet long, 151 feet wide, and 65½ feet high. Considered at the time big enough for any airship likely to be built for years to come, it was joined during the war years by two much larger structures.

One of the aims of the Zeppelin Foundation was to build a new airship to replace the one lost at Echterdingen; but meanwhile there was still the old LZ 3 lying damaged in the shore hangar at Manzell. Furthermore, there was the prospect of selling this craft to the Government, the Interior Ministry urging its purchase while the War Ministry, which doubted that LZ 3's performance would match that of the Echterdingen ship, pressed for a performance test. Needless to say, public opinion was by now on the side of the Count, and General von Einem, the War Minister, found support only from the Finance Minister.

The extensive rebuilding of the old ship involved many changes. An extra 8 meter bay was inserted amidships, increasing the gas volume from 403,600 to 430,800 cubic feet and doubling the amount of fuel that could be carried. At the stern was a large upper vertical fin for longitudinal stability. A pair of larger Daimler engines of 105 h.p. were fitted, giving a maximum speed of 27.3 mph. On October 21, 1908, the rebuilt LZ 3 was inflated, and made three short test flights on October 23, 24 and 26. On the following day the Kaiser's brother, Admiral Prince Heinrich, and Kapitän zur See

Mischke, took part in a flight that lasted 5 hours and 55 minutes. Air enthusiasts both, they failed to budge Grand Admiral von Tirpitz from his opposition to airships.

The Imperial family was sojourning at this time in South Germany at Donaueschingen, 50 miles from Friedrichshafen, and Count Zeppelin determined to show the ship off to the Kaiser. In this scheme he was aided and abetted by the Crown Prince, who with the Crown Princess Cecelie, was always an enthusiastic supporter and friend.[4] When the LZ 3 set off on November 7 for the temporary Imperial residence, the Crown Prince was in the forward gondola. In spite of thick weather and a blustery wind, the flight succeeded, and Count Zeppelin was overjoyed to see the Kaiser standing with attendants in the courtyard of the castle. Two days later a telegram arrived in Friedrichshafen announcing "Airship Z I has been accepted by the German government."

The following day, November 10, surely was the happiest of the Count's life, as the Supreme War Lord honored him and his enterprise with a personal visit. Theatrically attired in a green calf-length flowing cape and feathered hunting hat, the Kaiser arrived by special train at Manzell together with his host, the Prince von Fürstenberg, and a swarm of princely relatives and courtiers. After an inspection of the shoreside facilities, the Imperial party was ferried out to the *Reichshalle* (Hacker had the task of running up the Imperial standard as soon as the Kaiser stepped aboard) and inspected the LZ 3, now to be known as the Army airship Z I. From the steamer they watched as the Zeppelin was drawn out of the shed and made a short flight to Friedrichshafen. The Kaiser regretted that he could not participate. With the big rigid back again in the hangar, the Kaiser congratulated the Count and presented him with the Prussian Order of the Black Eagle. Then, summoning the Count's old enemy, Major Gross, the commander of the Airship Battalion, the Kaiser, in his best parade ground voice, barked, "You have seen how it's done. Now learn it yourself."[5]

Gross was ordered to duty at the Zeppelin works, together with

---

[4] At the time of the LZ 4's Swiss flight, the Crown Prince's enthusiasm caused Zeppelin considerable embarrassment. A telegram arrived in Friedrichshafen: "Holding my fingers crossed for you. Wilhelm K." Assuming that this originated with the Kaiser, Count Zeppelin sent a message of profuse thanks (which was released to the newspapers) to the Imperial Palace in Potsdam. Subsequently he learned that the original telegram was from the Crown Prince, who in turn was warned by his irritated father, "in the future you will hold your mouth shut and not your fingers crossed". Colsman, p. 71-2.

[5] Hacker, p. 118.

Hauptmann von Jena and five enlisted men of the Airship Battalion. On March 1, 1909, eighty enlisted men arrived together with Major Sperling, Hauptmann George and Oberleutnant Masius, the first of whom was designated to command Z I.

On March 6, 1909, the airship was inflated, and beginning on March 9, the factory crew commenced training the Army personnel. On March 16 both crews handled the ship during the first deliberate landing on solid ground, put on for the benefit of General von Lynckner, the Inspector of Military Transport, and other dignitaries from Berlin. Military personnel were drawn up as a ground crew on the new Zeppelin field, but a light tail wind swung Z I around into some cherry trees, demolishing the port after elevators and damaging the port rudders. The ship made it easily back to the *Reichshalle* after temporary repairs. On April 1, the Z I, piloted by Count Zeppelin, attempted a flight to Munich to demonstrate the ship to the Prince Regent Luitpold of Bavaria. A south-west wind of 40 mph carried the Zeppelin beyond her designated landing place, but with the help of Army personnel the ship managed to land in a sheltered valley at Niederviehbach, 50 miles north-east of Munich. The experience could have been a repeat of Echterdingen; but the ship was undamaged, the wind dropped, and in the early afternoon of April 2 the Zeppelin made it back to Munich. After a ceremonial reception by the Prince Regent, the Z I took off and returned that evening to Manzell.

Henceforth the Z I was the full responsibility of the Prussian Airship Battalion and was flown by Major Sperling and his Army crew. Since her intended hangar at Frescaty, within the boundaries of the fortress of Metz, was not yet completed, she was transferred on May 9 to a temporary tent hangar on the edge of the new Zeppelin field in Friedrichshafen. On June 29, Z I departed Freidrichshafen for Metz under Sperling's command. A cloudburst forced her to land at Mittel-Biberach. Here she was moored in the open for five days of rain and wind under the care of soldiers, and went on undamaged on July 3. Truly Z I was a lucky ship to survive these experiences in open country. Furthermore, she enjoyed four more years of service in Metz, training many Army airship personnel, until she was dismantled as obsolete in March, 1913.

Meanwhile a new ship had been started in the shoreside shed at Manzell, and the transfer of Z I to the tent hangar permitted the framework of LZ 5 to be moved out to the *Reichshalle*. Two weeks later the new Zeppelin was completed, and made her first trial flight on May 26. Except for minor details she was identical with the ill-fated LZ 4. Many of the components in fact came from the Echterdingen ship, particularly the gondolas and engines. There was no cabin in the gangway amidships, and the lower vertical fin was omitted, the ship being thought to steer better without it. A second small petrol tank was carried in each gondola, so that the engine would not have to be shut down while the main tank was being refilled. For the first time the rear propellers were reversible, as it would be vital to be able to check the ship's headway in landing on fields of limited size.

Though the military authorities had already agreed in advance to purchase LZ 5, Count Zeppelin desired to demonstrate the ship's capacities through a 36 hour flight, possibly to Berlin. This was attempted with the second ascent of the ship on May 28, 1909, but aborted after encountering heavy rain which forced Count Zeppelin to release 1320 lb. of ballast – all on board. On the following evening the ship was brought out of her shed and took off at 9.31 p.m. Bitterly aware of the Count's problems with the Prussians in Berlin, Colsman shouted up as the big ship ascended, "Excellency, spit down on those fellows' heads, but don't land!".[6] Through a dark and squally night the LZ 5, flying at low altitude, followed the railway line from Friedrichshafen to Ulm, then on north leaving Augsburg to starboard. The sun rose in a clearing sky, and the new day was a holiday, Whitsunday. Holiday makers turned out to watch Count Zeppelin's triumphal progress. At Nuremberg the crew had hoped to land on a lake, the Dutzendteich, to refill the ballast sacks with buckets, but so many boats were on the surface that the plan was abandoned. Ahead lay the hills of the Franconian Switzerland, the ship pitching gently in the up and down drafts. Bayreuth was the next large city, and shortly after noon LZ 5 crossed Hof, the home town of Georg Hacker, the rudder man. So far the ship had traveled 246 miles in 14 hours 25 minutes, at an average ground speed of 17 mph. By late afternoon, at 5.15, the airship was over Leipzig. The north wind was freshening and the ground speed had been reduced to 12½ mph. While the Zeppelin might have gone on to Berlin and refueled, the aim was to make an endurance flight and return to base without landing. With two-thirds of the fuel aboard exhausted after 21 hours of flight, it was clearly necessary to turn back. After circling the field of the rival Parseval organisation at Bitterfeld, the

[6] Colsman, p. 61.

airship reversed course and steered south-south-west. Now the ground speed rose to 32 mph, and remained at 28½ mph even with one engine stopped to save fuel. Features of the ground were made out easily by moonlight. Halle passed underneath. Count Zeppelin requested a star sight, and relieved Hacker while the latter made the necessary observations. The results showed the ship to be 12½ miles north of Schweinfurt. After moonset nothing but blackness prevailed below. At 2.30 am on May 31 a cluster of lights appeared ahead, and when the Count shouted down "what place is this?" a man answered loudly "Schweinfurt station!" The Count then announced that he would return to Freidrichshafen via Würzburg, Heilbronn and Stuttgart. Although fuel for only 8 hours remained on board, the commander was choosing a course to the west of the direct line. At 8.16 am Heilbronn passed underneath; the ground speed from Schweinfurt was only 21½ mph. The wind was now more and more ahead, and at times gusty. The airship maintained a low altitude, sometimes only 30 feet above the ground, to avoid the full force of the head wind. At 9.07 am the Zeppelin was over Stuttgart.

Except for short cat naps, the flight crew had now been at their posts for 36 hours, and without the knowledge of the commander, who himself at nearly 70 years of age was the chief sufferer, an aeromedical emergency had developed: fatigue. Judgment was impaired, alertness dulled, reflexes slow. A false euphoria prevailed at the thought of home being only 80 miles away. Hacker set a course to the south, but the Count unaccountably ordered him to the east, towards Esslingen. Speed over the ground fell to 9½ mph. Shortly before reaching Göppingen the Count cried, "we will land!" Hacker relates that he had suddenly realized how tired the crew was and wanted to rest them; other sources say he wanted to take on additional fuel. With Dürr at the elevator wheel literally asleep on his feet the ship, approaching a level field, had her bow so low that Hacker could not see ahead, and she rammed her nose into a large pear tree, the only obstacle in the area. The two forward gas cells ran empty and the bow framework was badly damaged, but there was no fire. The flight had lasted for 37 hours 39 minutes, and had covered 712 miles at an average speed of 19 mph.

Luck with the weather enabled emergency repairs to be made during the next 14 hours by personnel sent up from Friedrichshafen by special train with tools, spare parts and more hydrogen. Soldiers were available as ground crew and controlled the huge crowd which gathered. The foremost four gas cells were removed, the nose framework cut off clear back to the forward gondola, the longitudinals were bent inward towards the center, and the fabric drawn tight across the foremost remaining ring. A large 8-pointed star made of hop poles reinforced the center of the new bow. To lighten the fore part of the ship, the engine and accessories in the forward gondola were removed as well as the forward propellers, the heavy drive shafts and bevel gears. Five persons formed the crew for the return to Friedrichshafen on one engine. After a further four hours on the ground due to evening cooling of the gas, the ship put down on the water by the *Reichshalle* at 6.02 am on June 2, 1909.

The LZ 5 was rebuilt, and on July 24 made the acceptance flight with the government commission on board. Z II, as she now became, was due to be delivered to the Army Airship Battalion at the new hangar in Cologne, but Count Zeppelin first was permitted to show her off at the International Aviation Exposition at Frankfurt am Main, an event which attracted huge crowds through August, September and October and aroused great enthusiasm for aviation in West Germany. The emphasis was on airships, in which the Germans were dominant, and the Parseval rivals were well represented as well as various small home-built affairs.

The flight north on July 31 was a long battle against head winds, and once the ship went through a thundersquall with hail drumming on the outer cover. Eleven hours and 50 minutes were needed for the 243-mile flight, at an average ground speed of 18½ mph. Once at Frankfurt, the ship had to be moored in the open as there was no shed large enough to house her. The intention was to go on to Cologne as soon as possible, and on August 2 the ship departed in defiance of a forecast of thunderstorms. In fact, Z II encountered severe thunderstorms beyond Coblenz. These were flown through at minimum altitude to prevent the release of hydrogen from the automatic valves, which would instantly have been ignited by the electrical discharges from the thunderclouds. Head winds forced the Zeppelin backwards, and at length she was compelled to return to Frankfurt. Another attempt on August 3 failed when shortly after takeoff the starboard after propeller broke and pieces of it were thrown through a gas cell. Still moored in the open, the airship did not get away to Cologne until August 5.

This fifth Zeppelin was destined to have a short and unhappy career in Army service, making only 16 flights. Between October 25 and November 5, 1909, under the command of Major Sperling, she participated together with Major Gross' M II, the Parseval Company's new PL 3, and the Army Parseval P I, in a series of comparative tests arranged by the War Ministry to evaluate the military capabilities and potentials of the three competing airship types – the rigid, the semi-rigid, and the non-rigid. All four ships operated from the base at Cologne. The series of flights showed that none of them could meet the requirement for a journey of 250 miles made continuously at an altitude of 3300 feet as they could not attain this altitude (not in itself sufficient for flying over the enemy in daylight) with adequate fuel on board. Z II suffered a number of mechanical breakdowns. In general, the trials supported the contention of the War Ministry that none of the airships had sufficient speed to operate in moderately strong winds: "It has been proved that the wind velocities prevailing for about 50 per cent of the year will, with the present low speed of the airships, prevent their full employment."[7] A speed of at least 36 to 38 mph would be necessary; Z II developed a mean of 28 mph in the trials. Similarly an airship suitable for war purposes must be able to maintain an altitude of at least 4000 feet; Z II during the trials did not exceed 3450 feet. The War Ministry resolved as a result of these trials not to procure any more Zeppelins until their performance was improved, and LZ 6, which the Count was building in expectation of her purchase by the Army, remained unsold.

The end of Z II came during an exercise on April 25, 1910, during which Z II, P II and M I were supposed to fly from Cologne to land before the Kaiser at the resort of Homberg some 80 miles away. The weather turned threatening while the craft were in Homburg. P II, getting away early, managed to return to the shelter of the Cologne shed despite high winds. M I was deflated at Homburg as part of the "exercise" and returned to Cologne by rail. Delayed by engine trouble, Z II was late departing from Homburg and was forced to land at Lemberg on her way home. Soldiers were called out to hold her, but a violent squall tore the ship from their hands. Unmanned, she blew up the Lahn Valley to pile up spectacularly along the railway near Weilburg. The wreckage did not burn. Count Zeppelin, as he was all too prone to do, hastened to blame the Army ground crew unfairly for the mishap, and in consequence was bitterly resented by the Airship Battalion in particular. His relationship with the military authorities sank to an all time low.

LZ 6, whose construction commenced in the shoreside Manzell shed when it was vacated by LZ 5, made her first flight on

---

[7] *Die Militärluftfahrt*, p. 98.

August 25, 1909. Hull structure and dimensions were identical with those of LZ 4 and LZ 5, but there were differences in detail. For the sake of lightness, the heavy lateral drive shafts to the propellers up on the hull were done away with, together with the bevel gears at both ends, and a steel band drive substituted. This was shortly proven to be a serious mistake. Two 115 h.p. motors were installed, but these only slightly increased the speed. Amidships in the keel was an open, railed platform accommodating a few passengers. Control surfaces were the same as in earlier craft including the "barn door" rudder right aft, but there were no vertical stabilizing fins. Lastly – a distinguishing mark in old photographs – a "rain skirt" encircled the ship's hull at the height of the midships longitudinal. This, made of stiff fabric 4 inches long, was intended to prevent rain from running down the under side of the hull and dripping on the occupants of the gondolas. The fluttering rain skirt was blamed by the crew for the disappointing speed of the LZ 6, and was not fitted in later ships.

Two days after her first flight, with no proper trials, LZ 6 was off for Berlin. Count Zeppelin saw himself as having no choice: though no goal had been announced for the Whitsunday flight of LZ 5 to Bitterfeld, thousands of Berliners, including the Kaiser and the Imperial family, had allowed themselves to believe that the capital was Count Zeppelin's destination, and had vainly waited for hours at the Tempelhof Field hoping to see the giant airship. A petulant telegram from the Kaiser must have stung the Count in a sensitive spot:

> Since 5 pm I have been waiting with Her Majesty the Kaiserin and the princes and princesses at the Tempelhof Field for Your Excellency. Together with the leading officals and personnel of the . . . Regiments, which, giving up their Whitsunday leave, had hastened here to assist Your Excellency . . . Your Excellency owes it to the Berliners to make them special amends. I request Your Excellency to advise by return mail when you will come to Berlin with the airship; since I will begin a Scandinavian vacation on August 29, the flight cannot be later.[8]

This of course constituted an Imperial command, and on August 27 the big ship was off for Berlin, loaded with 3840 lb of petrol, enough for 34.8 hours of flying; 730 lb of oil, enough for 41.2 hours; 300 lb of reserve radiator water; 1255 lb of water ballast; and 1590 lb for the eight men aboard. Dürr was in command; Count Zeppelin, after surgery for an abscess, was not fit to make the flight,

[8] Colsman, p. 65.

and with Colsman, a big man whose weight of over 200 lb made him an "unwelcome guest," was to join the ship during a refuelling stop at Bitterfeld. The first part of the journey, from Manzell to Ulm, was made at a ground speed of 29.4 mph. Less than three hours after the departure, however, a metallic crashing announced the breakage of the steel band drive to the port forward propeller. Helmsman Hacker, remembering his service aloft in sailing ships of the German Navy, climbed out on the propeller bracket high on the hull to fit a new steel band. Next, a crack in one of the cylinders forced a shut-down of the forward engine. Rain made the ship heavy, and when a wire broke to one of the ballast sacks, LZ 6 was forced to descend. An hour and a half sufficed to cut out the cracked cylinder and to repair the ballast wire lead. At Nuremberg the ship landed on the Dutzendteich before a huge crowd, and replenished with fuel and hydrogen sent up from Friedrichshafen by rail. The mechanic from the Daimler works was late arriving with the new cylinder, however, and not until 2.12 am on the 28th could the Zeppelin proceed. At 7 a m the LZ 6 was over Bayreuth. Soon afterwards the forward engine had to be stopped, and the ship, very light, ascended to 3150 feet despite hard down elevators. On descending through the cloud deck with both motors running, the crew still had Bayreuth in sight − in fact, the ship had been driven back two miles. With all four propellers turning, the ship now went on north against the head wind at a ground speed of 15½ mph. At 2.16 pm the port forward steel band broke again, while the propeller, together with shaft and thrust bearing, fell off the ship and spun down to the ground. With three propellers, the Zeppelin made it to Bitterfeld at 6.26 p.m. Informed of the crippled state of the airship, the Kaiser is supposed to have said, "If he has only one propeller left, I demand that he come tomorrow morning."[9]

Early on August 29 the big ship lifted off in heavy fog (blind flying was never a problem in airships), and with Zeppelin and Colsman aboard, arrived at the Tempelhof Field in five hours. Another hour and a half was spent in a stately tour over the capital city, to show the big ship to the enthralled multitudes, before landing on the Tegel rifle range before the Kaiser, the royal household, leading officials, and a huge crowd of spectators.

The mass excitement persisted through the afternoon and evening hours, while the Count and the flight crew were guests of the Kaiser

[9] Colsman, p. 71.

at the Imperial Palace in Potsdam. During the evening the Kaiser, Count Zeppelin and Dürr were obliged to show themselves more than once on the balcony to the throngs below.

Late in the evening LZ 6 took off for the return flight (one wonders about the condition of the crew, who could hardly have refused the liquid largesse of the Imperial cellars). They had not gone far before the forward starboard steel band drive broke, the propeller fell off, and this time a blade went through the adjacent gas cell, which promptly emptied, The ship made a hurried forced landing in a forest clearing. And here she remained for nearly three days, held by citizens and soldiers, while repairs were made. A work crew from Friedrichshafen substituted the old and proven shaft drive for the steel band drive of the forward engine, while a propeller was borrowed from the Z II at Cologne. Cell 6 was repaired and inflated, while the outer cover was patched. At 10.57 pm on September 1, LZ 6 took off to frantic cheering, and 23 hours later lay in the shed at Manzell. The near-disastrous outcome of the "command performance" flight at least proved the need for more thorough trials of new ships!

On September 4, in ideal weather, LZ 6, still with the steel band drive to the after propellers (they never gave any trouble) was in the air all day giving joy rides to members of the *Reichstag* and mayors and high officials of the local towns and government. Enormous crowds on shore and in boats on the water cheered every arrival and departure of the Zeppelin as she made six ascents from Manzell, Lindau, and the new field north of Friedrichshafen, each time carrying roughly a dozen important guests.

On September 11, 1909, LZ 6 proceeded to the International Aviation Exposition at Frankfurt. A temporary shed had been erected here for her accomodation and in a series of flights between then and September 19, the ship cruised up and down the Rhine as far as Düsseldorf. Many influential persons were carried as passengers, increasing the enthusiasm for Count Zeppelin's big rigids, and the Rhinelanders were convinced that the era of air travel had at last arrived. LZ 6 returned then to Friedrichshafen. The first experiments with radio − a set built by Telefunken − were made at this time. A third motor − the first Maybach, especially built for airships and of 140 hp − was built into the keel in place of the cabin, with two propellers on the hull. With three motors the LZ 6 made a trial flight on October 20, and reached a speed of 36 mph; but the motor was removed as it was too close to the hydrogen-inflated gas bags.

On October 27, 1909, LZ 6 transferred from the *Reichshalle* to the tent hangar on the edge of the new field. A month later the *Reichshalle* was towed away by two tugs to be broken up. Never again would the Zeppelins use the facilities at Manzell. During the winter LZ 6 was deflated and pending a reconstruction, stripped of gas cells, outer cover and gondolas, and on February 12, 1910, the bare framework was carried by massed workmen to the new double shed in the middle of the field. The ship emerged in the spring lengthened by 8 metres to accommodate an extra gas cell; with the Maybach engine in the forward gondola and the two Daimlers in the rear one; the "barn door" rudder done away with and replaced by some small rudders hung under the lower horizontal stabilizer. An upper vertical fin was at last fitted. In this guise the ship had a speed of nearly 35 mph.

The War Ministry, however, was not about to buy her, in spite of the increased speed. At the same time Count Zeppelin, the stubborn empiricist, was not interested in a programme of fundamental research designed to improve the performance of his craft. Not only were his relations with the War Ministry at an impasse: once again there arose the question of whether the Zeppelin enterprise could survive. It was Colsman who proposed a life-saving solution: why not capitalize on the mass enthusiasm for the Zeppelin by setting up an airline and flying passengers? Even though the commercial enterprise in the end made the Zeppelin a national symbol throughout the country, caught the attention of the world and favorably influenced the German Army and Navy, the old Count was hardly happy over it:

> In the use of his ships to earn money . . . he saw his ideas being profaned. Thus the enterprise remained for him, the feudal aristocrat and former military man, a tradesman's undertaking and he was accustomed to keeping its board of directors at a distance.[10]

The enthusiasm in Germany for aviation in general, and for the Zeppelin in particular, aided Colsman in raising the necessary capital of three million marks. Early in his endeavors Colsman received the backing of the shipping magnate Albert Ballin, the head of the great Hamburg-Amerika line. Ballin offered to provide 100,000 marks a year for advertising the airline, provided his offices in German cities would have the exclusive right to sell airline tickets. In fact, the

[10] Colsman, p. 112.

DELAG poster advertising "Passenger Flights with Zeppelin Airships" with "Passenger reservations through the Hamburg-Amerika Line". The map shows cities being served. The airship roughly resembles the "Schwaben" and the hangar is the one at Frankfurt am Main. (William J. Hammer Collection)

DELAG and the HAPAG remained closely associated, and the former even came to be considered a part of the shipping empire.

Swept up in the aviation fever, the big cities of the *Reich* proved willing – even eager – to put up the capital for the airline, and to build airships hangars. Frankfurt-am-Main, Baden-Baden, and Düsseldorf vied with each other to be the first cities to boast of a Zeppelin airship; in time, commercial sheds were erected likewise at Hamburg, Potsdam, Gotha, Leipzig and Dresden. On November 16, 1909, the German Aerial Transportation Company (known as DELAG from its initials in German) was founded, with headquarters at Frankfurt-am-Main.

In his capacity as business director of the DELAG, Colsman promptly placed an order with himself, as business director of the Zeppelin Company, for a commercial airship. The first Zeppelin built in the new double hangar, LZ 7, which the directors of the firm proudly but ill-advisedly resolved to christen "Deutschland," was larger than her predecessors. Four hundred and eighty-six feet overall and 46 feet in diameter, she had the usual slender cylindrical hull; a

"Deutschland," the first passenger Zeppelin of the DELAG, on a trial flight at Friedrichshafen, June, 1910. (Luftschiffbau Zeppelin)

short, blunt stern with a multiplicity of rudders aft and the usual quadruplane elevators fore and aft; and a sharply pointed nose which was particularly unfavorable for streamlining. The eighteen gas cells contained 683,000 cubic feet of hydrogen. The gross lift was 46,000 pounds, but the weight of the ship herself amounted to 35,000 pounds, leaving only 11,000 pounds of "useful lift". Some 2600 to 3300 pounds of fuel and oil were carried, the remainder of the useful lift being devoted to the crew of eight or nine (one commander, one engineer, two helmsmen, 4 or 5 machinists), to water ballast, and to the 24 passengers and their comfort. The three 125 hp Daimler engines in the two open gondolas drove the usual sheet aluminium propellers high on the hull. Trial speed was just over 37 mph, and cruising speed about 33 mph. This performance obviously would not permit all-weather intercity flights on schedule, and though the DELAG had allowed the impression to develop that it would provide such a service, it was clear that local joyrides only could be made in the vicinity of the sheds.

Since the DELAG had nothing to sell but the novelty and pleasure of an aerial journey, it was all the more necessary that the passenger quarters be safe, comfortable and attractive. The cabin amidships was solidly built, and contributed largely to the high fixed weight of the craft. As a publicity release of the DELAG described it:

> It is so constructed as an integral part of the ship that the longitudinal framing of the airship at the same time forms the framing of the cabin. It is further braced so securely in position by twelve pairs of steel cables that it will hang immovable from them even if, through some unlikely accident, a couple of struts should bend or break. All metal parts of the cabin frame are covered on the inside with mahogany while the ceiling and walls consist of mahogany plywood. Rich mother-of-pearl inlays on the ceiling beams and pillars cause the cabin to appear as an extraordinarily comfortable and elegant room. The floor, which is constructed with absolute safety of five-layered plywood, is covered with carpet. Large sliding windows permit an unhindered view in all directions. The light wicker-work furniture provides comfortable seats.[11]

On June 19, 1910, "Deutschland" was completed and between then and June 21 made four trial flights in Friedrichshafen. Lacking any real experience in the air in the short flights of LZ 6 and her predeccessors, the Zeppelin people felt constrained to hire a Captain Kahlenberg, formerly of the Prussian Airship Battalion, to command the new giant. And since the city of Düsseldorf had rushed a wooden

[11] Deutsche Luftfahrts-Aktien-Gesellschaft, *Passagier-Fahrten mit Zeppelin-Luftschiffen* (Hamburg, 1911), p. 6.

hangar to completion ahead of their rivals, it was there that "Deutschland" was transferred on June 22.

For the first cruise from the Ruhr town, on June 28, twenty-three journalists had been invited, with Alfred Colsman, the director of the DELAG, as host. Intending a flight of no more than three hours, the newspapermen were served a light breakfast of champagne and caviar soon after the take-off, which was made on time although no weather report had been received. This was the first of several errors which, piled one on top of another, turned the summer morning joyride into a nightmare journey of nine hours, from which passengers and crew were lucky to escape with their lives.

The second mistake was in proceeding with the wind towards the picturesque Wupper Valley, instead of to windward towards the less attractive Rhine plain. Thus, when the breeze unexpectedly freshened, the slow and clumsy craft found herself to leeward of her base and unable to make headway, particularly after one engine failed. Slowly the Zeppelin was forced stern-first, despite wide-open engines. Lacking radio, Kahlenberg began throwing messages overboard requesting all the Army garrisons in the vicinity to help land the ship.

Late in the afternoon the hungry and exhausted passengers of the "Deutschland" watched uncomprehendingly as the helpless vessel drove towards a towering thunderstorm looming to the north over the historic Teutoberger Forest. Reaching the storm front, the Zeppelin was tossed up like a balloon to 3500 feet. Quantities of the buoyant hydrogen blew from the overdistended gas cells during this involuntary ascent. Heavy from both gas loss and rain, there was only one way to go – down. The crew were helpless to control the airship as she plunged into the pines of the Teutoberger Forest, and in no time the proud giant, bearing the name of the Fatherland, was a twisted wreck. Miraculously, there was no fire. One crew member, leaping from the rear gondola, broke a leg. The shaken journalists were aided to climb down the thirty feet separating the passenger cabin from Mother Earth, and during the next few days the remains were cut up with saws and axes and despatched to Friedrichshafen.

One sequel to the disaster was that Colsman prevailed on Eckener to take the place of the unlucky Kahlenberg as Flight Director of the DELAG. Yet Eckener had almost as much to learn, and was to have his share of bad luck in the process.

The summer of 1910 had barely begun, and the DELAG wished to take advantage of its publicity. The lengthened LZ 6 had a cabin added amidships, and on August 21, under Eckener's command, transferred to Baden-Baden. The hangar erected by the city, at Oos on the outskirts, proved to be advantageously situated in a narrow valley where the winds were always light, and rarely blew across the shed axis during docking and undocking. Flights were made almost daily, including excursions with brief landings in Mannheim and Stuttgart. On September 14, 1910, during a similar "goal flight" to Heilbronn, motor trouble caused LZ 6 to turn back. That afternoon, in the hangar, mechanics were cleaning the gondolas with petrol. One of the engines was started; a fire broke out which turned into a fatal conflagration when another mechanic emptied a can of petrol on it by mistake. The DELAG operating personnel had received a needed lesson on the dangers of the volatile fuel, but at much cost; and this was the end of flight operations for the year. Yet the unhappy LZ 6, which had never found a buyer, was worth more to her owners dead than alive. Insurance payments of 320,000 marks from Lloyd's of London gave the Zeppelin enterprise a much needed "shot in the arm" and permitted completion of the DELAG's next ship, the LZ 8 "Deutschland II".

This craft, identical in almost every respect to her predecessor, was completed at Friedrichshafen on March 30, 1911. Meanwhile, in anticipation of a full summer of profitable passenger service, the DELAG brought out an informative brochure for prospective passengers. The first paragraph announced that the charge for excursions of 1½ to 2 hours would be 200 marks, while longer flights with landings at a distance would be priced according to the time in the air. The airship "Deutschland" was described in detail, while a chapter, "The Attraction of Airship Travel," attempted to allay the anxieties of nervous prospects:

Most people will believe that it takes great courage to entrust themselves to the gondola of an airship and to undertake a journey through the limitless realm of the air. They seem to imagine that it is a feat comparable to that of a tight-rope walker or a roofer, accustomed to working imperturbably on the highest point of a church weather vane. But whoever has sat just once in the cabin of a Zeppelin airship will abandon such fantastic ideas. He knows that the most that a Zeppelin journey requires in the way of decisiveness is that before the takeoff the novice must overcome a baseless fear, namely, the fear of dizziness threatening him in the airy heights. When he first enters the gondola he will quickly realize that all that air travel really requires of him is an open heart and open eyes. Like streaks of mist, anxiety and doubt will blow away. For the ascent of an airship takes place in such unexpected and complete tranquillity that the passenger will literally not be aware of the motion if he shuts his eyes. Or, instead of looking down at the spectators growing smaller and smaller, he lets his eyes stray towards the horizon . . . [12]

But for all this reassurance, the disaster to the first "Deutschland" was to be repeated almost as promptly with the second. Under Eckener's command, she journeyed north via Baden-Oos and Frankfurt to Düsseldorf, where she arrived on April 11. Flights were made with passengers during the next month, and on May 16 the ship was scheduled to make a further excursion. By now, the DELAG had come to regret the location of the Düsseldorf shed, sited amidst fluctuating winds which could unpredictably catch the fragile Zeppelin abeam as she was being walked out of her berth by 250 to 300 men. A high wind screen had been built 50 metres out into the field, and it was hoped that this would protect "Deutschland II" as she was being walked out. A gusty cross-wind made Eckener reluctant to fly, but the presence of a crowd of spectators, and a full load of paying passengers, swayed his judgment. Too late he recognized his mistake. As soon as the stern projected beyond the shelter of the wind-screen, the monster was driven sideways and the ground crew dragged off their feet by the force of the wind. Up over the screen went the giant hull, where it remained impaled thirty feet up in the air, the broken back suggesting a slain dragon. Amazingly, there was no fire. Fire ladders had to be erected to rescue the passengers from their precarious location. "I paid for my weak-kneed decision by damaging the ship so badly she had to be almost completely rebuilt, and thereafter was cured of such impulsive acts,"[13] wrote Eckener. Never again would he take a chance to satisfy the expectations of the public, whether his command was the "Los Angeles", "Graf Zeppelin," or "Hindenburg."

As Eckener thought over the experiences of the past year, he realized that the DELAG, blissfully ignorant of the hazards and dangers of aerial navigation, had been taking great risks with its trusting passengers, and that many changes were necessary. Firstly, from commanding officer through rudder men and mechanics, there had not been enough experience with handling the ships in the air, with the effect of temperature changes, gas purity, and rain and other loads on the lift of airships, and with the problems of rudder and elevator control at low speeds while taking off and landing. Secondly, the Daimler engines used heretofore were not reliable, and

[12] *Passagier-Fahrten mit Zeppelin-Luftschiffen*, p. 9.
[13] Eckener, *Im Zeppelin über Länder und Meere*, p. 30.

their frequent breakdowns threatened the loss of ships flying in windy weather. Thirdly, the DELAG's weather forecasting requirements could not be met by the existing meteorological service, and the airline would have to set up its own weather reporting network with observation stations at each airship base. Lastly, men alone, even 300 of them, could not control the huge ships as they were walked out of the hangars in a cross wind.

Another commercial Zeppelin, LZ 10, was already under construction at the time of the Düsseldorf disaster, and on June 26, 1911, she made her first flight. On July 15 she was accepted by the airline and christened "Schwaben" for the ancient duchy which comprised the modern Württemberg and Baden. Fated to be known as "the lucky ship of the DELAG," she was destined, under Eckener's command, to make the Zeppelin a household word throughout Germany and even in other lands; while 1553 paying passengers first ventured into the air aboard her. Shorter than the two "Deutschlands," and handier, "Schwaben" was the first Zeppelin fitted with the reliable 145 h p Maybach engine especially designed for airships, and with three of these she attained the incredible trial speed of 47 mph.

The hangar at Baden-Oos, sited in the sheltered valley, was "Schwaben's" first berth. It was Eckener's inspiration likewise to install there so-called "docking rails" extending from the shed several hundred feet out onto the field. On these rolled trolleys to which the Zeppelin was made fast fore and aft, being thereby restrained from moving sideways in cross-winds. And with all these precautions and improvements, success came at last. Through the tranquil late summer months the Zeppelin made frequent local excursions, going farther afield as the season advanced, to Frankfurt, Düsseldorf, and ultimately to Berlin. The cost of the long inter-city flights — up to 600 marks — was no deterrent. For patriotic Germans it became "the thing" to view the Fatherland from a Zeppelin. On August 3, 1911, a fifteen-week-old baby, carried in the arms of her proud parents, became the youngest person to fly. And the fresh air and the exhilaration of the flight sharpened the appetite. "Schwaben" passengers dined first class at the small tables at the open windows, as shown by menus which included Rhine, Moselle and Bordeaux wines; domestic and imported champagnes; and cold dishes such as cavir, Strassburg pâté de foie gras, Westphalian ham, and cold capon.

Following the winter lay-up in Oos, "Schwaben" was back in the air by March 30, 1912. The DELAG enterprise had expanded: still

The DELAG passenger airship "Schwaben" on a trial flight at Friedrichshafen in June, 1911. Note that all control surfaces are now at the stern of the airship. (Luftschiffbau Zeppelin)

another ship, the slightly larger "Viktoria Luise," named after the Kaiser's only daughter, had been completed and had entered service on March 4. Flying from Frankfurt, she and "Schwaben" met at Mannheim on April 4 and cruised together over Heidelberg. A setback occurred when "Schwaben" on June 28, 1912, burned on the field at Düsseldorf, the fire having been sparked by static electricity in the rubberized fabric gas cells. No passengers were aboard and no one was injured. But a sister to "Viktoria Luise," the "Hansa," was completed on July 30, 1912, to take her place. In succession, the two passenger craft used the new double hangar at Hamburg. Indeed, the first Navy airship crew began training at Hamburg on July 1, 1912, handling "Viktoria Luise" on passenger flights under the tutelage of the civilian crew headed by Captain Erich Blew. In September, as their training approached completion, the Navy men flew "Hansa" in the Fleet parade concluding the autumn manoeuvres of the High Seas Fleet. Truly, the DELAG, with its experienced civilian operating personnel, was "the university of the air," and as war approached, perhaps its most important contribution was the training of airship flight crews for the Imperial Army and Navy.

By 1913 the DELAG was a going concern. Through careful operations and observance of Dr. Eckener's safety-first precepts, hundreds of flights were made that spring, summer and fall. A third ship, "Sachsen," was completed on May 3, 1913, and was based at the new hangar in Leipzig. "Hansa" habitually operated from Hamburg, and "Viktoria Luise" from Frankfurt. In this year, also, there appeared handsomely bound guide books for sale to the DELAG passengers flying from the various bases, strikingly illustrated with many aerial photographs depicting the scenery north, south, east and west of the sheds. The captain's choice of route depended on the wind direction. Books were published for travelers flying from Hamburg, Frankfurt, Baden-Oos, Düsseldorf, Berlin and Leipzig.

Thus, in the summer before the war, all three commercial airships were in service — "Viktoria Luise" from Frankfurt, "Hansa" from Potsdam near Berlin, and "Sachsen" from Leipzig. As before, the giant craft, the symbols of Teuton supremacy, sailed serenely through the warm summer skies, loaded with proud passengers regaling themselves on the sight of the Fatherland unrolling only a few hundred feet below the cabin windows. Optimistic about the future, the DELAG ordered a new ship, LZ 26, a great advance on previous Zeppelins, with her framework of the new and lighter alloy duralumin; a better streamlined hull, with the keel partially enclosed; and clean, simple cruciform fins and control surfaces at the stern. Instead of the clumsy propellers on brackets on the hull, the forward engine at least drove a propeller directly coupled to the rear of the car. The gondolas were open as usual, but before she was accepted as the Army's Z XII on December 14, 1914, the LZ 26's cars were enclosed — the first craft to show this necessary improvement.

"Sachsen" made the last DELAG passenger flight after war was declared, on August 7, 1914. Immediately afterwards all three ships were taken up by the Army, with their crews putting on Army reserve uniform and continuing to fly them. Over a four year period the DELAG Zeppelins had made 1588 flights, and had carried 10,197 paying passengers. Many later histories assert that they flew regular passenger schedules between German cities,[14] but this was never the case.

As noted previously, the War Ministry was determined not to buy any more Zeppelins of the LZ 5 (Z II) type on the grounds that their low speed and low ceiling made them useless for any warlike purpose. The War Ministry was right, of course; but arrayed against it at this time was a great body of opinion, influenced beyond reason by the theatrical triumphs of Count Zeppelin and his glamorous symbolization of the superiority of German science and technology, and even of the German spirit and culture.

> If the military departments nonetheless refused to budge from the requirements laid down by their experts, a righteously thinking opponent of former days will today have to acknowledge their point of view all the more when it is considered that the attitude of these gentlemen was connected to a high degree with the danger of unpopularity.[15]

So wrote Colsman in 1932.

By 1911 a number of events had occurred to change the War Ministry's attitude towards Count Zeppelin's airships. Progress in the development of the aeroplane made it seem that the small, simple heavier-than-air craft might take the place of the small pressure airships in scouting in the zone of the armies. Conversely, the unique possibilities of the Zeppelin in long range strategic scouting, not to mention bombing operations, began to be perceived. The pressure airship builders tried to compete by enlarging their craft, but this

---

[14] Gordon Vaeth, *Graf Zeppelin* (New York: Harper & Bros., 1958), p. 37.
[15] Colsman, p. 45.

step, involving girderwork keels and stiffening, rendered them less demountable. In September, 1912, the War Ministry, on the advice of the General Staff, secretly decided to end the construction of pressure airships,[16] and only two of them were in service on the outbreak of war. "Schwaben" made the Zeppelin appear a practical proposition as a military weapon, particularly with her maximum speed of 47 mph. Lastly, the War Ministery found itself subjected to pressure from within the military establishment – from the Chief of the Great General Staff.

Colonel-General Hellmuth Count von Moltke had succeeded Count von Schlieffen in this post in 1905 at the Kaiser's insistence, largely because he was a nephew and namesake of the grimly efficient architect of the victories over Austria and France won by the Kaiser's grandfather, known as Wilhelm the Great. Too sensitive and imaginative to withstand the crushing responsibilities of the post – he played the cello and tried his hand at translating Maeterlinck's *Pelleas et Melisande* – Moltke the younger lost the battle of the Marne partly because he withdrew an army corps from the Western Front at a crucial moment to stem a Russian invasion of East Prussia, the dangers of which he had exaggerated in his own mind. Three years earlier he allowed himself to worry excessively about the French semirigid airships and the supposed advantage they would confer on the French armies when the war came that so many people were taking for granted. Pressure airships would not suit his purposes; he insisted on Zeppelins. Whether they were capable of military usefulness was secondary; the current Zeppelin type was the best Germany had. Subsequently, enthusiastic reports from junior general staff officers traveling aboard "Schwaben" convinced Moltke of the utility of the current Zeppelin design, though the hard-heads at the War Ministry did not budge. The General Staff's urgent demands played into the hands of the Zeppelin Company, which naturally preferred series production of an established product to the frustrations and disappointments of a research and development program. Count Zeppelin kept pointing out that he was forbidden to sell his craft abroad, and repeatedly blackmailed the service departments into ordering ships with the threat that otherwise he would have to close down and disband his company.

Initially Moltke demanded[17] only that Zeppelins be stationed in

[16] *Die Militärluftfahrt,* p. 111.
[17] In a letter of Sept. 30, 1911. *Die Militärluftfahrt,* Anlageband, Anlage 36, p. 74.

the fortresses of Metz, Cologne and Königsberg, with the "Schwaben" as a reserve. A new Army ship then under construction, Ersatz Z II (LZ 9), in fact made her first flight on October 2, 1911. Resembling "Schwaben" but with one gas cell less, the new ship made 48½ mph with her three 145 hp Maybach engines. She was however lengthened by one gas cell in the following month before being delivered to the Army base at Cologne. A similar ship, Z III (LZ 12) made her first flight on April 25, 1912. She was stationed at Metz after the old Z I was dismantled there.

No less than five Zeppelins were delivered to the German Army in 1913, while further single sheds were erected on Germany's borders. One of the new craft, Z IV (LZ 16) figured in a well advertised international incident. Having made her first flight on March 14, 1913, she was still in the hands of the Zeppelin Company when on April 3 she departed Friedrichshafen for Baden-Oos with Captain Gluud in charge. The military acceptance commission was on board and the ship was to make a high altitude flight. In solid cloud and

International incident: The Army Z 1 V making her involuntary forced landing at Lunèville in France on 3 April 1913. French-made drawings of her were transmitted to the British and United States Governments. (Luftschiffbau Zeppelin)

snow the ship was blown badly off course; when the ground appeared below the crew were lost, and were more than embarrassed to find when they landed to get their bearings that they were in Lunéville in France! The ship was held in the open by French soldiers while the German crew was obliged to disembark. On the following day the Zeppelin was permitted to proceed. In a hasty inspection the French picked up considerable information; some of it ended up in the United States Navy's archives via the naval attaché in Paris.

Three more Zeppelins were delivered to the Army in 1914 before war broke out. The entire series, from Ersatz Z II to Z IX, differed little from each other, or from the contemporary DELAG passenger ships. Gas volume rose from 628,500 cubic feet to 794,500 cubic feet. All were fitted with three Maybach engines, of 145 hp each in the early ships, 210 hp in the later ones; but maximum speed remained quite constant at 46½-52 mph. The hulls were still poorly streamlined, long and cylindrical with blunt bow and stern, small vertical and horizontal stabilizing fins aft from which depended no less than six rudders and two sets of biplane elevators, though Z IX herself, completed in July, 1914, had at last simple rudders and elevators hinged at the trailing edges of the fins. The gondolas were still open, with propellers on brackets up on the hull — two bladed ones driven by the single engine in the forward gondola, four bladed for those driven by the two engines in the after gondola. An external keel connected the gondolas, and the Army craft had a cabin amidships just as in the DELAG ships — but here it housed a wireless set and the bomb racks, if any. Each Army ship had a top platform forward with mounts for two or three machine guns.

The useful load increased from 13,200 lb. in Ersatz Z II to 20,300 lb. in Z IX. The later ships were more efficient partly because they were fully equipped with gas cells made of gold beaters' skin instead of the heavier rubberized cotton that had been used previously. Count Zeppelin had always been interested in gold beaters' skin as a gas cell material. Derived from the intestines of cattle, this membrane was superbly gas tight, but prolonged experiments had to be made before it was possible to fabricate usable cells by shingling seven layers of gold beaters' skin onto each other with a special glue. The first "Deutschland" was the first Zeppelin to fly with one gold beaters' skin cell. No mass production took place, partly because of expense, until two accidents in the year 1912 proved that the rubberized fabric cells were all too prone to generate

The Army airship service: Ersatz Z1 at Friedrichshafen in January 1913. The complicated control surfaces are typical of the period. Note the close resemblance to contemporary DELAG ships. (Luftschiffbau Zeppelin)

static electricity. In the spring, a fire occurred when the last cell of the Army Zeppelin Z III was being deflated in the hangar; there was a burst of flame and the remaining hydrogen in the cell flared up. Subsequently, tests in the dark proved that finger-length blue flames could be engendered by rubbing the rubberized surfaces together. Thus, it was suspected, had LZ 4 come to grief at Echterdingen; and this was certainly held to be the cause of the burning of "Schwaben" at Düsseldorf on June 28, 1912. These accidents led to an all-out effort by the *Luftschiffbau Zeppelin* to substitute gold beaters' skin for rubberized fabric cells; the *Ballonhüllen Gesellschaft* in Tempelhof was founded in the same year to meet this need.

The new Army ships were stationed at the various Army airship bases on the eastern and western borders of the *Reich,* and undertook mostly training flights. No outstanding exploits are recorded in the period before World War I, and they never appeared over foreign soil, though a formally arranged "showing the flag" request could hardly have been refused, and would certainly have impressed foreigners.[18] The coming of war would demonstrate how poorly prepared were the Army ships and crews to participate in military operations. It was the misfortune of the Army airship service never to enjoy the strong, centralized, dynamic leadership which the Navy later possessed in the Leader of Airships, Fregattenkapitän Peter Strasser, who not only administered his arm with outstanding imagination, forcefulness and ability, but who also made his influence felt on behalf of the Zeppelin in the highest command circles. The Army service, with its ships parcelled out in single sheds scattered around the rim of the *Reich,* was a relatively unimportant part of the Communications Troops, and never had a single head who understood and fought for it.

This did not prevent the General Staff from entertaining the most sanguine expectations of what the Zeppelins could accomplish in wartime. The airships in the west were to engage in strategic reconnaissance to determine the concentration points of the enemy armies and their lines of advance to the frontiers, together with the possibility of English troops landing on the Continent. Secondarily they were expected to bomb and destroy such military targets as airship sheds, air field facilities, radio stations, railway facilities, etc. The areas to be covered grossly overestimated the range and endurance of the primitive Zeppelins available, particularly as the missions were to be flown in daylight:

For the ship based on Düsseldorf, the area Antwerp-Grammont-Mons-Maubeuge-Namur-Liége; furthermore the coastline between Antwerp, Dunkirk, Calais and Boulogne.

For the ship based on Cologne, the area Liége-Namur-Avesnes-St. Quentin-Soissons-Rethel-Neufchateau.

For the ship based on Frankfurt, the area Verdun-Chalôns sur Marne-St. Dizier-Bar le Duc-Metz.

For the ship based on Baden-Oos, the area Nancy-Epinal-Vesoul-Belfort.

For the ship based on Trier the line of the Meuse between Dinant and Verdun and westerly thereof.

On Germany's eastern frontier, airships based at Liegnitz, Posen, Königsberg, Thorn and Allenstein had similarly extensive missions over Russian territory.

---

[18] Before 1914 the DELAG ships made only three journeys aboard, arousing extravagant enthusiasm — by "Hansa" to Copenhagen on September 19, 1912; by "Sachsen" to Vienna on June 9-10, 1913; and by "Sachsen" on November 9, 1913, to Haida in Bohemia, then a part of the Austro-Hungarian Empire.

On March 29, 1912, General von Moltke, who was most largely responsible for the build-up of the Army's Zeppelin arm, laid down that strategic scouting missions should be designated by the High Command, and that each ship should carry an officer of the General Staff. While he was designated only as an "observer", he in fact was to direct the movements of the airship and designate bombing targets, while the commanding officer played the role of a glorified chauffeur. This system of dual command and divided responsibility was hotly resented by the Army airship men.

On August 1, 1914, on the eve of war, the German Army disposed of the following airships at the respective bases:[19]

Düsseldorf	"Hansa"	Baden-Oos:	Z VII
Cologne:	Z VI	Liegnitz:	SL 2
Trier:	Z VIII	Dresden:	Z IX
Königsberg:	Z IV	Leipzig:	"Sachsen"
Posen:	Z V	Johannisthal:	P IV
Frankfurt a.M:	"Viktoria Luise"[20]		

P IV was the Parseval PL 16, the last pressure airship flown by the German Army. With a useful lift of 7500 lb and a speed of 48 mph, this small 353,000 cubic foot craft compared favorably in performance with the older Army Zeppelins.

S L 2 was the product of the Schütte-Lanz firm of Mannheim-Rheinau, which from 1909 until the end of World War I not only competed successfully with the Zeppelin Company but was also the first to introduce many improvements and refinements in rigid airship design which soon after the outbreak of war appeared in the Zeppelins also.

The guiding genius of the company was Johann Schütte, a talented professor of theoretical naval architecture at the Technical College in Danzig, who was a match for Count Zeppelin in stubbornness though lacking in popular appeal. Schütte's interest in the rigid airship was awakened by the "great flight" of LZ 4 and the disaster at Echterdingen, and soon thereafter he wrote to Count Zeppelin suggesting improvements in his design: a double outer cover, the keel gangway inside the ship, and direct drive connecting the engines and the propellers at the rear of the gondolas. The letter was

---

[19] *Die Militärluftfahrt*, p. 128.
[20] Z I, Ersatz Z II and Z III had been dismantled as obsolete. Ersatz Z I and Ersatz E.Z. I had both been lost in typical circumstances — forced to land away from their bases in storms they had been damaged beyond repair.

acknowledged but the Count declined the advice. This led Schütte to put his own ideas on paper:

1. At the present time, were there special strength calculations or other calculating methods, which were adequate to meet all the demands of this problem?
2. Were there light weight materials which on the basis of exhaustive strength investigations might prove to be especially suited for the construction of a rigid framework?
3. Could one on the basis of previous studies of the resistance of bodies in motion in water arrive at a favorable shape for a body in motion in the air?
4. With such a favorable ship's form, how were the stabilizing and steering surfaces to be arranged?
5. Was it necessary that the resultant of all thrust or driving forces should coincide as much as possible with the direction of the resultants of all resistance forces?[21]

Here at last was a skilled naval architect and engineer looking at the rigid airship, and not only with a critical eye for the eccentricities of the Zeppelin design, but also with a vision of what the efficient airship should be like. Further, Schütte was fortunate enough to secure the financial backing to develop his vision into reality. Two wealthy industrialists of Mannheim, Dr. Karl Lanz and August Röchling, undertook to back him, and on April 22, 1909, the *Luftschiffbau Schütte-Lanz* was founded with a capital of 350,000 marks. Two years later, when the first ship was completed, the partners had sunk two million marks into the project.

If the Schütte-Lanz firm never lacked for money, it paid a price in efficiency. According to a Herr Hermann Müller, the manager of the girder construction shop who fled to England in 1916,

The works organization was defective, academical ideas predominated, considerable waste of time and materials occurred. In every department extravagance prevailed. Correct ideas on recording the cost of production were absent, as a consequence the output of the works was low and discipline was far too easy going to make for efficiency.[22]

A shed was erected in the suburb of Mannheim-Rheinau and the ship, SL 1, was assembled at a leisurely pace, some of the delay being caused by the subcontractors, who included the Riedinger firm providing gas cells, gas valves and outer cover, and the Daimler motor

[21] Johann Schütte in *Der Luftschiffbau Schütte-Lanz 1909-25* (Munich & Berlin: Druck u. Verlag von R. Oldenbourg, 1926), p. 2.
[22] Great Britain, Public Record Office. 'Crown Copyright' "Examination of 'M', an ex-employee of Messrs. Schütte-Lanz Airship Constructors at Mannheim-Rheinau August 1916."

works furnishing the power plants. Much more stemmed from the experimental and pioneering nature of the enterprise. Originally to be of 495,000 cubic feet, the gas volume was enlarged to 734,500 cubic feet before construction started. Length overall was 432 feet, maximum diameter 60.4 feet.

Despite his undoubted engineering genius, Schütte made a serious mistake in his choice of structural material, which fell on plywood rather than metal, the wood selected being aspen, sliced in sheets and glued in three or more layers with one of the earliest applications of casein glue. While Schütte praised the lightness and elasticity of the plywood girders, a jealousy of Zeppelin's prestige seems to have determined him to use a different material. In practice, it turned out that the plywood girders were of uneven strength and quality, atmospheric dampness penetrated the plies despite waterproofing with lacquer and paraffin wax, and softened and loosened the glue. Humidity alone could reduce the strength of the wooden girders by fifty per cent compared to their dry state. Girder breakages were thus a constant problem in service, complained of particularly by the German Navy which had to contend with the moist atmosphere along the North Sea coast. One of Schütte's chief assistants, who obviously considered him difficult, opinionated, and egotistically prone to exaggerate the value of his own ideas, held that Schütte should have gone over to the Zeppelin type of duralumin girders with open channels and stamped profile pieces early in the war. Instead he persisted beyond all reason with the wooden girders against the advice of his subordinates, and when he saw himself forced to switch to duralumin, he was determined to be different and insisted on building his girders out of tubing. Two precious years were wasted in wartime with experiments in fabricating duralumin tube girders, and no ships with frames of this material were completed before the Armistice.[23]

The hull structure of SL 1 was unduly complicated, being made up of helically arranged longitudinals which crossed each other in a diamond-shaped pattern. Schütte saw theoretical advantages in creating merely "a sort of rigid network around the balloons," but erection was time-consuming, with false transverse rings having to be erected and then dismantled while the framework was built around them. Eventually it proved necessary to stiffen the hull internally against the gas pressure by fitting numerous vertical wires, ring

[23] Interview with Dr. Walter Bleston, Feb. 24, 1957.

Schütte-Lanz SL 1 building at Mannheim-Rheinau, 1911. This view shows helically spiralling longitudinals of the hull arranged on false frames, and on the floor to the left, preformed plywood girders. (Luftschiffbau Schütte-Lanz)

girders and radial wire bulkheads, many of the wires passing through
the gas cells with accompanying possibilities for gas leakage.
Originally the bulk of the hydrogen was to be contained in nine
spherical gas cells, the space between which was to be filled with six
doughnut-shaped cells. For the sake of weight reduction, the gas cell
number was reduced to 7 with conventional flat ends.

Nonetheless the hull was beautifully streamlined compared to
Zeppelin practice, which still presented the ugly cylindrical structure
with long parallel section amidships. In SL 1 the maximum diameter
was slightly more than a third of the distance aft from the nose, and
was 16 feet greater than the diameter of contemporary Zeppelins.
From the point of maximum diameter the lines were curved in a
graceful parabola to the rounded bow, while aft they tapered ever
more gently to a slightly rounded stern. Wind tunnel tests of the hull
were not made, but Schütte relied heavily on his experiences as
director of the model towing tank of the North German Lloyd
shipping line in the years 1899-1904.

Curiously, Schütte's correct engineering instincts failed him in
respect to the steering arrangements, and these at first were
unnecessarily complicated. Aft was a single upper vertical fin with a
large rudder mounted independently just aft of it, and two
horizontal fins with large elevators hinged to their after ends. But in
addition, Schütte felt it necessary to add biplane elevators of the
Zeppelin type under the nose, and a small box rudder just abaft the
rear engine gondola. This arrangement was soon modified, and in
May, 1912, SL 1 appeared with modified vertical and horizontal fins
aft; triple rudders hung on each side under the horizontal fins, and
small elevators under the triple rudders. The big elevators at the after
edge of the horizontal fins persisted, but the forward elevators and
small box rudders under the hull were done away with. Schütte must
have realized that this arrangement involved unnecessary drag, for
later in the year appeared the simple, correct and final
solution — elevators and rudders hinged to the trailing edge of the
four fins.

Simplicity and efficiency again were the features of the two open
gondolas, hung fore and aft in the center line under the ship. The
nose of the forward gondola was glassed in and served as a control
position. In the rear was a 240 hp eight cylinder Mercedes-Daimler
engine, bigger than the contemporary Maybachs, which drove a large
three-bladed wooden propeller at the rear of the gondola via gearing
and an extension shaft. A similar engine installation was in the

SL 1 in the spring of 1912. Note modified control surfaces. (Luftschiffbau Schütte-Lanz)

shorter rear gondola. Both propellers could be reversed. The gondolas were suspended on wires, but had no struts bracing them from the body; it was a pet idea of Schütte's that in a hard landing, the gondolas would hit the ground, the hull would be lightened by their weight and rebound, and there would be no struts to fracture or to damage the hull framework by impact loads. Only in 1915 were gondola struts introduced.[24] Ladders gave access to the interior of the ship, but there was no real interior gangway. The number of men in the crew is nowhere stated, and undoubtedly varied, probably numbering about ten persons.

SL 1 made her first flight on October 17, 1911. This could have ended disastrously, for a control cable broke and the ship made a forced landing across the Rhine, lying overnight in an open field while repairs were being made and gas added. Next day the ship took off and after three and a half hours of circling over Mannheim, she returned to the Rheinau shed. On November 1 she made a second flight over Mannheim, then was deflated for the winter and modifications made. The first flight next year, on April 18, 1912, must have been a harrowing experience for her crew. While approaching to land at noon, a vertical gust slammed the ship down on the ground, damaging all control and water ballast wires, the propellers and gondolas. The shock of the crash threw seven out of 14 crew members overboard and dumped all ballast. Lightened of all this weight, SL 1 no longer under control, ascended to 5600 feet. Her momentum carried her well over pressure height; considerable gas was lost, the ship became heavy, and since there was no more ballast, SL 1, touched down on the far side of the Rhine. Troops from Mannheim and Speyer manhandled her back to her shed the same day. Old photos show the SL 1 floating several hundred feet in the air at the end of numerous lines; when the soldiers reached the Rhine, the lines were made fast aboard a tug boat.

After approximately 40 more trial flights, SL 1 in December, 1912, was sold to the German Army for 550,000 marks. On July 5-6, 1913, she was flown from Berlin to Danzig, a feat which was turned into a celebration for Dr. Schütte, whom Danzig claimed as its own. Only a few days later, on July 16, she was lost at Schneidemühl when a thunderstorm came up whilst she was moored in the open

---

[24] The lack of struts was severely criticized by Fregattenkapitän Strasser, who observed that heavy loads on the rings as the ascending hull jerked the gondola off the ground could fracture girders. This occurred with SL 3 on March 9, 1915. *Havarien der Schütte-Lanz Luftschiffe, die nachweislich durch konstruktive Mängel verursacht wurden.*

after a forced landing. SL 1 was torn away from her anchorage and the wreck deposited in a wood some miles distant. Nobody was on board at the time.

The Schütte-Lanz works went through a crisis following the delivery of SL 1. Karl Lanz,[25] appalled at the unforseen expenditures involved in building SL 1, was ready to call it quits, but was persuaded to put up additional capital when Schütte pointed out the increasing successes of the Zeppelins. The War Ministry, in the person of General Freiherr von Lynckner, the Inspector General of Military Transport, insisted that the Schütte-Lanz enterprise must be preserved, not only as a national asset, but also as an antidote to the Zeppelin monopoly. A contract was drawn up between the firm and the War Ministry on April 24, 1913, providing for payment to Schütte of 200,000 marks compensation for his expenditures, and guaranteeing further contracts to the firm, while providing that Schütte-Lanz products should not be sold abroad.

In June and July, 1913, the War Ministry placed with the firm a contract for a second ship, which made her first flight on February 28, 1914. This SL 2, differing in many ways from her predecessor, showed Schütte's genius in every line and feature and was the first modern airship. Not only did she set the pattern for all the firm's later products, which were merely enlargements of the SL 2, but she also profoundly influenced later Zeppelin designs.

SL 2 resembled the Zeppelin hull design in having a framework consisting of transverse rings and longitudinal girders, all of plywood of course. A major reason for the change was the disappointing maximum speed of SL 1 — only 44½ mph. Schütte concluded that this was due to the high skin friction of the diamond-shaped areas of the outer cover formed by the crisscrossing girders. The hull of SL 2 was again beautifully streamlined, with no straight parallel section. Simple cruciform fins, rudders and elevators were fitted at the stern, the commander and helmsmen were accomodated in a comfortable, fully enclosed control car built onto the hull forward (with a radio cabin in the rear), and the four 185 h.p. Maybach engines were directly coupled to propellers at the rear of the open gondolas. Two of the engine cars were slung on either side of the hull amidships, the others fore and aft on the center line. The ship had a high voltage electrical system for the radio, and low voltage wiring throughout for lighting, engine telegraphs, etc. The triangular keel was inside the

[25] Who according to Müller "thought that if he could emulate Zeppelin he would obtain the social and other distinctions that he had coveted." Examination of "M".

ship, reducing frictional drag and the overall height of the hull. Eight cloth shafts led hydrogen exhausted from the 15 gas cells to the top of the hull. Length of SL 2 was 474 feet overall, diameter 59.8 feet. Gas volume was 861,900 cubic feet, and useful load 17,300 lb. Maximum trial speed was just under 55 mph. The Schütte-Lanz firm could in truth boast that theirs was the largest and fastest airship in the world. War Ministry specifications for SL 2 had been based on the performance of contemporary Zeppelins, and while useful lift of SL 2 was slightly inferior, her performance otherwise was so superior, particularly in speed, that the firm collected bonuses amounting to 280,000 marks. Between May and August, 1915, SL 2 was lengthened in Mannheim by adding a 12 metre gas cell amidships, and more powerful Maybach engines of 210 hp were installed. Her useful load thereafter was 22,880 lb, and her speed rose to 55½ mph.

After successful trials, SL 2 was accepted by the Army in May, 1914, and on May 12 arrived at Liegnitz, her base on the eastern

The lengthened SL 2 leaving the shed at Brussels-Berchem Ste. Agathe in September 1915. (Robinson)

border of Germany, where a streamlined hangar had been erected with "orange peel" doors resembling those on the Goodyear Air Dock at Akron, Ohio, U.S.A., built years later. Despite the War Ministry guarantee, no further contracts were forthcoming, and the outbreak of war a few months later found the Schütte-Lanz works completely unprepared. Not only was their only hangar partly dismantled and in the process of being lengthened; many workers had been laid off, others were called away on mobilization, and in early August there were only 5 supervisory personnel and 60 workmen on hand.

Like the German War Ministry, the Imperial German Navy was forced to take up the Zeppelin airship by the pressure of public opinion and popular enthusiasm, while having doubts about its military capabilities. The Navy Minister, Grossadmiral Alfred von Tirpitz, resisted longer than did his Army counterpart. Although subject to similar pressures, Tirpitz for long refused to spend Navy funds on the Zeppelins for two reasons. One was the basic concept of the "risk Navy," which he had been building ever since 1897 on the assumption that Great Britain – which he saw as opposing the competition of German trade and industry – would not take the risk of actually fighting Germany if the size of the German fleet made the outcome problematical. Since the German Navy was the junior service and had to fight for funds, Tirpitz spent them on offensive weapons – battleships and destroyers.

Secondly, if it came to using airships as scouting craft at sea, Tirpitz knew what he wanted and would not accept less – a large craft of long range, and above all, with a higher speed than that of the early Zeppelins.[26] And Count Zeppelin, equally stubborn and no engineer, insisted on empirical progress by small increments, and refused to build craft big enough to meet the Navy's specifications.

Following the 8-hour flight of LZ 3 in September, 1907, Fregattenkapitän Mischke claimed that "Count Zeppelin had enjoyed a decisive success, which showed that the path he was following would lead to his goal."[27] In a memorandum of April 23, 1908, Tirpitz' own Dockyard Department chief saw the airship as especially suited for strategic scouting at sea, particularly in the event of a blockade of the German coast, while "also they will eventually be

[26] In October, 1907, the naval aide-de-camp to the Crown Prince offended Zeppelin employees by remarking of the LZ 3, "we will come back as soon as the speed of the Zeppelin has increased to double that of the present one." Hacker, p. 110.
[27] *Die Militärluftfahrt*, p. 235.

able to be used with great success for independent operations against the enemy coast (attack on vital objectives thereon by dropping shells, etc.)"[28] The same memorandum called for a speed superior to a wind velocity of 33.5-47 mph.

The Echterdingen catastrophe did nothing to increase the Navy's confidence in Zeppelin's craft, and Tirpitz minuted, "the thing itself is not very safe; whether the concept is safe is very much in dispute."[29] In the following year, *Nauticus,* the ornate annual which served as a mouthpiece for the Navy minister, published an article on "The Present Status of Airship Flight with Particular Reference to Military Airship Flight." While asserting that "the question of the dirigible airship can in principle be considered solved,"[30] the article was largely concerned with the shortcomings of contemporary Zeppelins – their inadequate speed, particularly in relation to prevailing winds on the North Sea coast; unreliable engines and inadequate useful lift.

Tirpitz preferred at this time to be a spectator of the Army's experiments with Zeppelins. In 1910 he went so far as to assign a talented naval architect, Marine-Schiffbaumeister Felix Pietzker, to observe developments both in Friedrichshafen and Mannheim. Thus began the process whereby the naval architects and constructors of the Navy Ministry in Berlin forced the Zeppelin Company eventually to enlarge and improve its designs. By increasing the size of the contemporary Zeppelins and improving their streamlining, Pietzker believed that an efficient ship could be produced with a speed of 45 mph. He submitted sketches for a craft of 1,223,100 cubic feet capacity with six engines of 140 hp. But Tirpitz felt that the 3,000,000 marks needed to procure such a ship, together with base, shed and equipment, could not possibly be obtained from the *Reichstag.* And Count Zeppelin, who was not receptive to "innovations which had not been grown in his own garden,"[31] insisted he would need several years more to develop designs for larger airships. In this he was aided and abetted by Dürr, who was particularly resistant to streamlining the hulls as he found the slender cylindrical craft, with rings all identical, to be easier to build.

When in the summer of 1911, Tirpitz finally changed his mind, it

[28] *ibid.,* p. 238.
[29] *Die Militärluftfahrt,* p. 239.
[30] *Nauticus: Das Jahrbuch deutschen Seeinteressen* (Berlin: E.S. Mittler & Sohn, 1909), p. 231.
[31] Colsman, p. 157.

was in response to pressure from the Emperor and public opinion, and to increasingly disquieting reports from his attachés of airship progress in foreign navies. On April 24, 1912, a contract was placed with the Zeppelin Company for L 1 *(Luftschiff 1)*. The firm wished to build a craft of the current production model of 706,200 cubic feet; Tirpitz favored a larger 4-engine design of 882,750 cubic feet, although this still would not meet Navy requirements. The airship finally ordered was a compromise between these figures. The fourteenth in the company's series, the new Navy Zeppelin displaced 793,600 cubic feet and was practically a replica of the commercial "Hansa" and "Viktoria Luise."

Commissioned on October 17, 1912, L 1 was flown to Johannisthal near Berlin and embarked on a program of training naval personnel in airship handling. Tirpitz on January 18, 1913, was inspired by "advances in airship construction," together with "the intervention of the public in all phases of aviation,"[32] to put forward a 5-year programme of airship development:

(1) Purchase of 10 Zeppelins for two squadrons, each to consist of four operating craft with one in material reserve.

(2) Construction of a central airship base at Nordholz near Cuxhaven, to have four double revolving sheds and two fixed sheds.

(3) Subsidizing the construction of private airship hangars for use in wartime.

On January 30 the Navy Minister contracted for the first ship of the new program, which was laid down in May, 1913, under the factory designation of LZ 18. Pietzker had prepared a design for a larger craft which in case of war could reach the English coast with a load of bombs, and the Zeppelin Company agreed with some misgivings to build it. Like L 1, the new ship was 518 feet 2 inches long, while her overall height remained at 62 feet — important in that she would have to fit in the DELAG hangar at Fuhlsbüttel as well as the double building shed at Friedrichshafen. Yet by inverting the keel and placing it inside the hull, Pietzker had been able to increase the hull diameter from 48 feet 6 inches to 54 feet 6 inches, and the gas volume to 953,000 cubic feet. Because of her increased size, L 2 had four 165 hp Maybach engines in two gondolas, driving four propellers, while the commander and the controls were housed in a separate fully enclosed car attached directly to the hull some 25 feet ahead of the forward engine car.

[32] *Die Militärluftfahrt*, p. 254.

Particularly as the ship had no gas shafts[33] to carry to the top of the hull the hydrogen discharged into the gangway by the relief valves in the bottom of the gas bags, the Zeppelin designers were disturbed by having the open engine gondolas only a few feet under the internal keel. Yet Pietzker not only imposed his will with respect to these alterations, but even had wind screens fitted at the bow of each engine car, completely filling the narrow space between the gondolas and the hull. With this last triumph Pietzker sealed his own death warrant and those of 27 other men. But the terrible penalty for this mistake still lay in the future, and when the new ship was completed on September 9, 1913, Count Zeppelin so far forgot his misgivings as to congratulate Pietzker on the overall design.

After some months of local flights out of Johannisthal, L 1 was transferred to Fuhlsbüttel bei Hamburg on August 15, 1913, to participate in the autumn manoeuvres of the High Seas Fleet. On the first day of the strategic manoeuvres she reported the position of the "enemy's" main blockading force[34] as well as the activities of his cruisers and destroyers, while the surface scouting craft were still under way to the scene of the action. Admiral von Ingenohl, commanding the High Seas Fleet, wrote "these reports may be regarded as a complete success for the scouting activities of the airship, and indicate how scouting by airships without employment of surface vessels may be extended to great distances by utilizing their high speed, as is possible with favorable weather conditions."[35]

One day later, on September 9, L 1 was driven down into the sea near Heligoland when she encountered violent vertical gusts and heavy rain associated with a cold front passage. The Zeppelin broke up on the water and sank; six of the officers and men aboard were saved by rescue vessels, but 14 were drowned.

Incredible as it may seem in view of the Echterdingen catastrophe, the numerous accidents to the DELAG craft, and the dangerous combination of hydrogen and petrol in his airships, this was the first time that the loss of one of Count Zeppelin's craft had taken human life. All Germany was shaken by the disaster.

Far worse was to befall a month later with the newly completed

---

[33] These were patented by Schütte-Lanz; though the Zeppelin designers were slow to take them up even when all patents were placed in the public domain on the outbreak of war.

[34] These were relatively close to the coastline, as all German war plans assumed a close-in blockade by the Royal Navy.

[35] *Die Militärluftfahrt,* Anlageband, Anlage 99, p. 233.

L 2. On September 20, 1913, a naval crew flew her to Johannisthal and trial flights continued. An altitude trial was scheduled for October 17, and the 28 persons aboard included a party of seven (one of them Pietzker) from the Aviation Department of the Navy Ministry, and four civilians from the Zeppelin Company. Hydrogen warmed in the sun as the big ship lay on the field for two hours while a balky engine was repaired. Buoyant from the "superheat," L 2 rose quickly after takeoff to an altitude of 1000 feet, where an explosion took place that set fire to the Zeppelin from end to end. Twenty-five people were killed outright in the flaming crash; two die at the scene, and the last survivor, a lieutenant of the Queen Augusta Grenadier Guards who formed the landing crew, expired that evening in hospital.

The consequences of the L 2 catastrophe were far-reaching. Its gruesome and dramatic qualities did not fail to affect public opinion. Confidence in the Zeppelin was shaken, and for a period the DELAG flights suffered a loss in patronage. The Navy Ministry's drive to improve the Zeppelin airship for military purposes was set back for two years, as the various inquiries found that the large windscreens at the front of the engine gondolas had formed a partial vacuum in flight, and had sucked down an explosive mixture of hydrogen and air from the internal gangway close overhead. The death of Pietzker himself was a set-back; in a difficult situation he had managed to get himself accepted, even liked, by the clannish personnel of the two rival firms, the *Luftschiffbau Zeppelin* and the *Luftschiffbau Schütte-Lanz*. Count Zeppelin was more imprudent than usual in trying to throw the blame on the naval authorities. This time, to the consternation of his subordinates, he chose the public funeral service for the L 2 dead to precipitate a loud and heated quarrel with the Navy Minister. Tirpitz was enraged, and the Count desisted only when Colsman reminded him that he had congratulated Pietzker on the innovations in the ship. A wide breach opened between the Zeppelin Company and the Navy Ministry, and when it was healed, primarily through Colsman's efforts, Count Zeppelin was no longer in control of the organization. While his prestige as an authentic folk hero was unimpaired, he hung on in Friedrichshafen in the role of figurehead, embittered against the subordinates who had turned against him, and taking less and less interest in the giant craft which bore his name. With the outbreak of war, the old enthusiasm returned as he threw himself into the project of building giant 5 and

6 engined bombing planes; but in the last year of his life he was heard to say "whatever was done with the airships was all the same to him."[36]

Tirpitz, himself a stubborn man, did not scrap the airship experiment; but would seem to have retained it for reasons of prestige and national pride. The ambitious ten-ship programme was forgotten, and the small organization which survived into World War I was barely sufficient for "window-dressing" and completely inconsistent with the requirements of the High Seas Fleet. Such progress as was made was due to the initiative, drive and personal qualities of the new Chief of the Naval Airship Division, Korvettenkapitän Peter Strasser, ordered to the post two weeks after his predecessor's death in the L 1 disaster. Strasser it was who arranged the hiring from the DELAG of the "Sachsen" to continue the training of three green crews; while he also retained Dr. Eckener and Ernst Lehmann, the "Sachsen's" commander, to direct the training program. It was also at Strasser's insistence that Tirpitz, on March 21, 1914, contracted with the Zeppelin Company for a new naval airship, L 3. The Zeppelin Company, however, flatly refused to depart from their proven designs, and L 3 was practically a duplicate of L 1.

That Tirpitz accepted this inferior design is all the more remarkable in that Professor Schütte had written to him in October, 1913, offering an airship with a gas capacity of 1,112,265 cubic feet and a useful lift of 32,000 pounds. This craft would have had the internal gangway, simple tail surfaces, bomb rooms, and four engines with direct drive propellers as in SL 2, and was expected to have a speed of 47 mph. Though much larger and with better performance than contemporary Zeppelins, she would still have fitted inside the Fuhlsbüttel shed. Admiral Dick, the head of the Dockyard Department at the Navy Ministry (which included the Aviation Department) was very favorably impressed with this design, which corresponded to the Navy's requirement for an airship of 1,060,000 cubic feet. But Schütte appears to have made himself unpopular with high naval authorities. An obvious reason was that he attempted to use a friendship with Admiral Georg von Müller, the head of the Kaiser's Naval Cabinet, to influence the Kaiser in favor of the wooden-built craft. Such manipulation of the Supreme War Lord was bound to anger Tirpitz, who considered himself an expert in this

[36] Colsman, p. 181.

area; while von Müller, because of his supposed evil influence over the Kaiser (he held the job from 1906 to 1918) was regarded with resentment and suspicion by the Navy's officer corps generally.

L 3 was completed on May 11, 1914, and was transferred on May 28 to Fuhlsbuttel. She was still there, training the three Navy crews in flights along the North Sea coast, when war broke out in August. Ignored by higher authority in the Navy, the Zeppelin was totally unready to play a role as a scouting weapon for the High Seas Fleet. The Army on the other hand (or at least the Great General Staff, for the War Ministry seriously doubted the technical qualifications of the Zeppelin airship) held the most extravagant expectations of their ability to range afar over the back areas of the enemy's country, dropping bombs as well as collecting information.

The German people for years had been exposed to a barrage of propaganda about the awesome capabilities of the monster gas bags, not only from the publicity departments of the Zeppelin Company and the hand-outs of the military authorities, but more particularly, from a constant stream of chauvinistic boasts from the ultranationalistic press. The Zeppelin, they believed (the Schütte-Lanz craft had not had the benefit of such enthusiasm) was the secret weapon of Teutonic air superiority which would terrorize their enemies, beat them into submission, and win the war, which in any case was not expected to last more than a few months. The facts would be tragically different, but it would be years before the German people would turn away in disillusionment from the rigid airships.

IV

The Zeppelin as a war-winning weapon

The performance of the Army Zeppelins during the war of movement confirmed immediately the worst fears of the War Ministry concerning their vulnerability to ground fire in view of their low speed, inadequate lift and insufficient ceiling. At the same time, the overly sanguine expectations of the General Staff as to their ability to scout strategically deep in the enemy's rear areas were proved to be far beyond their capacities. The result was near-disaster, from which the Army service took months to recover.

True, against the inadequately equipped Russian armies there was a measure of success. None of the craft in the east were immediately ready on the outbreak of war, Z V and Z IV having only recently arrived in the east, while SL 2 was under overhaul in Liegnitz. Much work had to be done to prepare the ships for war service, the photographic darkroom and crew's comforts, even the wireless installation, weighing 660 lb, having to be removed to attain a ceiling of at least 6500 feet, while machine guns were mounted on the top platforms and rifles issued to the crews. No bombs had been developed, and in their places 5.9 and 8.2 in artillery shells were carried, stabilized by strips of blanket fastened to the bases. SL 2 had been assigned to the general headquarters of the Austro-Hungarian armies. Under the command of the skilled and aggressive Hauptmann von Wobeser, the big Schütte-Lanz on August 22 made a technically remarkable flight that took her nearly 300 miles east of her base to reconnoitre by daylight for advancing Russian forces. Flying west to east from Ostroviec to Krasnik and Turobin, she then proceeded south to land within the fortress of Przemysl, where von Wobeser gave his report directly to the Austrian High Command. SL 2 was held in the open by Austrian troops while numerous bullet holes were patched, and after an absence of two and half days, returned to Liegnitz, having covered a distance of 865 miles in 24 flying hours. Yet her reports did not prevent the Austrian First Army from being surprised on August 23 in an encounter battle with the Russian Fourth Army – one of a series of frontier engagements which comprised the first defeats for the Dual Monarchy.

The old Z IV, based at Königsberg, would seem to have provided some information for the outnumbered defenders of East Prussia on the westward advance of Rennenkampf's First Russian Army. Beginning on August 10, she made nightly reconnaissances all the way from Mlawa in the south to Tilsit in the north, with particular attention to the towns of Gerdauen, Gumbinnen and Insterburg on the direct Russian line of advance. A few artillery shells were aimed at Russian campfires on these flights. At the end of this period, on September 24-25, Z IV, the oldest and smallest airship in Army service, even dropped a few bombs on Warsaw.

The Z V played a part in the battle of Tannenberg, making flights on August 22 and 25 which revealed the build-up of the Second Russian Army on the southern border of East Prussia. On the other hand, an order to bomb the railway junction at Mlawa by daylight at the height of the battle on August 28 proved fatal. Badly holed by rifle and machine-gun fire, the Zeppelin became heavy, was forced to land near the target and her crew captured, many of them perishing later in Siberia.

The three Army Zeppelins in the west were even less prepared when the "threatening danger of war" telegram was dispatched on August 1. Z VI in Cologne and Z VIII in Trier were deflated and under overhaul; Hauptmann Andree, commanding the latter, was concerned at the helplesness of his ship in this condition only 7½ miles from the Luxembourg border, but was refused permission to inflate his craft. Z VI however was intended in the war plan to make an attack on the Belgian fortress of Liége, whose capture was the first item on the German timetable of conquest. On the evening of August 5 she was ready to go with seven 5.9 and one 8.2 in artillery shells. The High Command could hardly have anticipated more than a moral effect on the Belgian defenders. And even this mission, only 75 miles from the shed at Cologne, was beyond the capabilities of the airship. Due to a strong head wind, two and a half hours were required to reach the target. A low cloud deck covered the besieged city, and the commander, Hauptmann Kleinschmidt, had to descend through the clouds to 4750 feet to see where to drop the shells. At this altitude the Zeppelin was badly holed by machine guns and rifle fire. Even with the wind now helping, Z VI rapidly lost so much gas that she crash landed short of her base in a forest near Bonn.

More than two weeks passed before any use was made of Z VII and Z VIII. The loss of Z VI might be thought to have discouraged the High Command; but it appears that the Zeppelins and their commanders were more likely neglected, inasmuch as nobody at Headquarters was specifically concerned with their activities. They were remembered after troops of the French First Army, having captured Sarrebourg, were thrown out of the town by German counter-attacks and began retreating towards their own frontiers. Z VII and Z VIII were ordered to be over the retreating French troops at dawn on August 21, to ascertain their positions and to hurry their withdrawal with bombs. The fact that the Zeppelins, with their low ceiling, would be flying above the western spurs of the Vosges Mountains meant nothing to the High Command or to the General Staff officers empowered to give orders to the airships' commanders.

Z VII actually dropped most of her bombs unfused to attain a reasonable altitude above the ground. Eleven hundred pounds of bombs were dropped on French bivouacs at dawn, but the General Staff officer insisted on pressing on in broad daylight. Descending through clouds, Z VII at an altitude above the ground of only 2600 feet received such heavy infantry fire that she was forced to land at St. Quirin.

Z VIII, having farther to journey from Trier, received her baptism of fire from friendly troops, who knew nothing of the meaning of flare-gun recognition signals as these had been classified secret up until the outbreak of war. Her altitude showed 5600 feet when she encountered enemy troops, but her height above the ground was less than half of this, and she was shot up badly even though she replied with 350 lb of bombs. Z VIII crashed in the Vosges Mountains with so little gas left that she could not be set afire; her crew escaped from a French cavalry patrol and returned to the German lines after an 11-hour march.

This was the end of the reconnaisance role of the Army airships for which they had been built at such great expense, and over the opposition of the War Ministry. There remained the strategic bombing role, and ineffective night attacks, with little material result, were made on enemy fortresses, seaports and railway junctions when more ships arrived to replace losses. From these impromptu beginnings there evolved early in the war a strategic bombing policy which aimed to destroy the enemy's armament factories, cripple his transportation, and force him to divert from the active front in France men, guns and aeroplanes for home defence. Further, there were exaggerated hopes and expectations that the terror of death from the sky would undermine home front morale and force the Allied governments to sue for peace. Much has been made of the pioneering strategic bombing operations against Germany of the Independent Force, R.A.F., in 1918 under the command of Marshal of the R.A.F. Lord Trenchard; but the Germans had a strategic air force as early as 1915, composed of Zeppelins which even then could carry nearly 2000 lb of bombs to Paris or London. Not that the Zeppelins had been planned and built expressly for this role – but they were in existence, and the survival of the Fatherland demanded that they be put to this use. By contrast, there were no true bombing aeroplanes in early 1915. When the British Royal Naval Air Service in November, 1914, launched an unsuccessful air raid on the Zeppelin Works at Friedrichshafen, the aircraft used were 80 hp Avro 504's (soon to be relegated to training) carrying four 20 lb explosive bombs each.

The new Zeppelin Z IX arrived in Düsseldorf on August 10, and the ex-DELAG passenger carrier "Sachsen"[1] replaced Z VI in Cologne at the end of the month. They were under orders to bomb Antwerp, then under siege by the German armies; and the Channel ports of Dunkirk, Ostend and Calais. Between them they made three attacks on Antwerp and one on Ostend. The aggressive British Royal Naval Air Service was ordered to strike back. From Antwerp on September 22, 1914, Flight Lieutenant C. H. Collett bombed the Düsseldorf shed without results. On October 8, the day Antwerp fell, Flight Lieutenant R.L.G. Marix in a Sopwith Tabloid attacked the shed again, his bombs destroying Z IX. Her loss had a discouraging effect on the already-decimated Army airship service. At year's end it disposed in the west only of the old "Sachsen", the SL 2 transferred from Liegnitz on September 26, and the new Z X. In the east only the old Z IV remained.

While the Army was seeking a mission for the Zeppelins over land, the Navy which had previously neglected them, was abruptly discovering that they were ideally suited to meet a need unanticipated in the war plans. Quite unimaginatively, the leaders of the world's second navy had allowed themselves not only to anticipate a short war, but also had wishfully concluded that the Royal Navy would establish a close blockade of the North Sea coast, as it had off the French ports in the Napoleonic wars. Confidently the German Navy expected to decimate the close-in blockading

---

[1] Due to low performance, the DELAG ships "Viktoria Luise" and "Hansa" were relegated to training duties. The newer "Sachsen" was lengthened by one gas cell after the declaration of war, and was considered to have the performance for military operations.

cruisers and battleships with night torpedo boat attacks, following which the High Seas Fleet would fling itself on the remnants for the "decisive battle." Instead, to the consternation of the German admirals, there was established a distant blockade imposed by cruisers patrolling from the Orkneys to the Norwegian coast. The North Sea remained empty, the Grand Fleet mysteriously and menacingly inactive – until its battle cruisers, led by Admiral Beatty, descended on the High Seas Fleet's patrol craft to crush them in the Heligoland Bight battle of August 28, 1914. Now more than ever the High Seas Fleet was on the defensive. Yet its all-too-few cruisers and destroyers were intolerably overworked in maintaining the requisite patrols. The Zeppelin, all hands suddenly realized, might fulfill the role of the scouting cruiser, could cover an even wider area rapidly and do it more cheaply. The Navy, like the Army, demanded airships as fast as the building works could turn them out, while the existing Nordholz base was expanded and new bases were laid out at Hage and Tondern on the western and northern edges of the German Bight.

The Zeppelins delivered in the initial expansion program were duplicates of the L 3 and Z IX design, and ten of these were completed by February, 1915 – five going to the Army and five to the Navy. The latter service, however, regarded them as unsatisfactory stop-gaps, by reason of their small size, low speed, lift and range, and their unsuitability for foul-weather operations at sea by virtue of their open gondolas. The war emergency enabled the Navy Ministry at last to force the Zeppelin firm to produce larger craft with improved performance. The Army played little part in rigid airship development (though the Schütte-Lanz firm catered to their requirements), accepting Navy-inspired Zeppelin designs for their own use until they grew too big for the Army sheds.

On the outbreak of war a prototype Zeppelin of improved performance was already on the drawing board. In the summer of 1914 the company had commenced the construction of a passenger carrier for the DELAG, the LZ 26.[2] With 880,000 cubic feet of gas, she was roughly the same size as her predecessors, but the useful lift was 5500 lb greater. This resulted from many improvements in design. There were only 15 instead of 18 gas cells, and these were of

[2] With the outbreak of war, jigs, tools and material for LZ 26 were sent to the DELAG hangar at Frankfurt-am-Main to clear the double shed in Friedrichshafen for rapid series construction of standard craft of the L 3 type. LZ 26 was finally completed as the Army Z XII in December, 1914.

lightweight gold beaters' skin throughout. For the first time the framework, instead of being built of "hard aluminium," was of duralumin, a new and stronger aluminium alloy, containing small percentages of copper, manganese and silicon, which permitted the hull to be built lighter without sacrificing strength. For the first time since the disastrous L2 experiment, the gangway was placed partially inside the hull. The gondolas, at first open, were slung well below the body. While the two Maybach C-X 210 hp engines in the rear gondola still drove propellers on brackets high on the hull, the forward engine drove directly a propeller at the tapered rear of the gondola. The propellers were efficient wooden two-bladers, replacing the clumsy aluminium sheet ones with their paddle blades. Before her delivery to the Army, LZ 26's gondolas were completely enclosed, greatly adding to the crew's comfort and efficiency. In particular, the commander's and helmsmen's stations forward were surrounded by panes of Triplex glass giving an all-round view except astern. The hull of the new ship was better streamlined, with simple, effective fins and control surfaces. Two more near-sisters of LZ 26 (with gangways completely enclosed) were built early in 1915 – LZ 39 for the Army and L 9 for the Navy. They were the last Zeppelins constructed in the 1910 double shed in Friedrichshafen. Henceforth know as the "ring shed," this structure served for the horizontal assembly of the girderwork rings of the larger craft constructed in the adjacent hangers.

In a meeting at the Navy Ministry on August 5, 1914, Zeppelin Company representatives proposed to design an enlarged version of LZ 26, with all her improved features, a gas volume of 1,126,000 cubic feet, a fully enclosed keel, and a fourth engine driving a propeller at the rear of the gondola. With a minimum of red tape and delay, the first Zeppelin of this new type, LZ 38, was completed for the Army in Friedrichshafen on April 3, 1915, and was so successful that 21 more sister ships were built – ten for the Navy and 11 for the Army.

On the outbreak of war the Zeppelin Company became a national asset and expanded rapidly. Control passed into the hands of the Government, the Navy's construction corps playing a prominent role in supervising the work done at the factory. A great influx of engineers at last placed the Zeppelin Company's design department on a sound basis, and the "pencil-form" pre-war designs were improved beyond all recognition. Prominent in this work were Dr. Paul Jaray, an Austrian-born aerodynamicist who joined the staff in

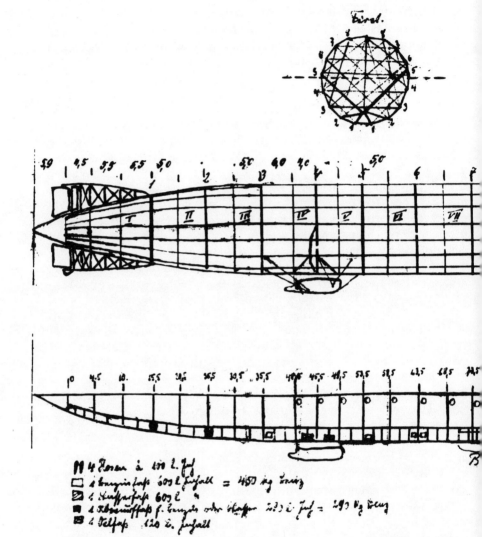

Secret and official, 1915 – The official drawing of the German Navy Zeppelin L 9, issued to members of her crew when she was building at Friedrichshafen in early 1915, and to be handled by them as a secret document. The original was crudely drawn with india ink on tracing linen. Fifty years later Herr Friedrich Kant, one of her crew members, felt able to loan the author his copy for reproduction.

L9 = L.9.

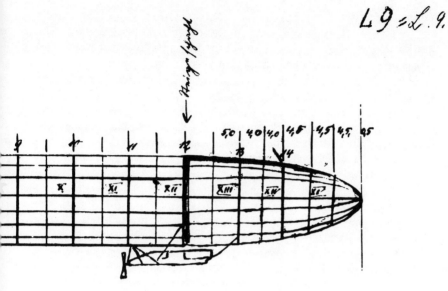

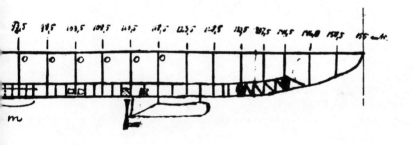

m

1914 and soon led the development section, where he made original contributions to the streamlining of Zeppelin hulls, fins and gondolas; and Dr. Karl Arnstein, who was hired in 1915 to deal with the problem of ring fractures in the current Zeppelins under loads, and who for the first time developed a detailed procedure for the stress analysis of the Zeppelin framework.

New sheds were built or requisitioned for the construction of these larger ships. At Friedrichshafen a new single building shed was begun with Navy funds measuring 629.9 x 115.4 x 91.8 feet; this is said to have been completed in two months. In nearby Löwenthal a large single shed under construction for the Army was turned over to the Zeppelin works; the ships fabricated here were assembled from parts supplied by the parent company in Friedrichshafen. The DELAG shed in Potsdam was likewise converted to airship building, and delivered its first Zeppelin, Z XI, on November 11, 1914.

Unlike the Friedrichshafen firm, the Schütte-Lanz Company already had a design for a big ship of 1,147,500 cubic feet – with slight modifications, the same as had been submitted to Tirpitz in October, 1913. Five ships were in the first wartime contract, and of these, SL 3 was built for the Navy at Mannheim-Rheinau; SL 4 for the Army in the Army shed at nearby Mannheim-Sandhofen; SL 5 for the Army in the Army shed in Darmstadt; SL 6 for the Navy in

SL 5 on trial flight at Darmstadt, May 1915. (Luftschiffbau Schütte-Lanz)

the DELAG double hanger at Leipzig; and SL 7 for the Army in the Rheinau shed. SL 3, which first flew on February 4, 1915, was then the largest airship in the world, with a length of 502 feet 4 inches and a diameter of 64 feet 10 inches. The last two ships had an added gas cell, with a length of 543 feet 5 inches and a volume of 1,240,300 cubic feet; but they all resembled SL 2 in hull shape, fins and rudders, and arrangement of the control car and the four engine gondolas.

Although they continued to find favour with the War Ministry, the Schütte-Lanz ships never became popular with the Navy. Strasser, after many girder failures in the early Schütte-Lanz ships,[3] became prejudiced against the wooden-built craft, and was known to refer contemptuously to their supporters as "glue-potters." After two and a half years of war he wrote:

> The Schütte-Lanz airships are not really combat-worthy ... I consider it would be a mistake to build more Schütte-Lanz ships, for experience has thoroughly demonstrated that wood is an unsuitable material for airship construction, because it weakens and breaks with even a moderate degree of humidity ... Building more wooden ships would only increase the number of ships useless for combat and would create personnel problems for the crews of combat-worthy aluminium ships.[4]

The routine missions of both services' airship arms were thus defined: for the Army, night bombing attacks on bases and railway junctions in the zone of the armies, and on seaports supplying them across the Channel. For the Navy, defensive reconnaissances by day by one or more Zeppelins over the North Sea, to detect the movements of enemy surface vessels and submarines. But a far more glamorous role tempted the officers of both services: strategic bombing of enemy cities in the rear areas, and particularly of the enemy capitals, with the aim of exerting pressure on the opposing political leaders and forcing them to sue for peace. The German populace supported this goal with enthusiasm, venting their hatred with particular vehemence against England. In the Autumn of 1914

---

[3] Not until George E. Wright Jr. loaned me a file titled *Havarien der Schütte-Lanz Luftschiffe, die nachweislich durch konstruktive Mängel verursacht wurden*, did I appreciate the seriousness of the Navy's problems with the Schütte-Lanz ships. The file consists of detailed reports by commanding officers and opinions and minutes by Strasser, and reveals particularly in SL 3 and SL 4 an appalling succession of girder failures, collapse of fins and rudders, and separation of ring joints, often occurring in flight, and reflecting faulty workmanship as well as the inherent weakness of the wooden girder construction.

[4] Douglas H. Robinson, *The Zeppelin In Combat* (London: G.T. Foulis & Co., Ltd., 1962), p. 36.

even the children were singing:

> Zeppelin, flieg,
> Hilf uns im Krieg,
> Fliege nach England,
> England wird abgebrannt,
> Zeppelin, flieg![5]

"Fly, Zeppelin! Fly to England! England shall be destroyed with fire!"

Thus, London, and secondarily Paris, became targets to which the Zeppelin personnel were drawn as by a magnet, with the most exaggerated expectations of what could be accomplished in forcing the hated islanders to sue for peace. As early as August 20, 1914, the Deputy Chief of the Naval Staff, Konteradmiral Paul Behncke, was agitating with Imperial Headquarters in Luxembourg for permission to launch a campaign against London as soon as the German Army should consolidate its grasp on the Belgian and French coasts. "Such attacks," he wrote, "may be expected, whether they involve London or the neighbourhood of London, to cause panic in the population which may possibly render it doubtful that the war can be continued."[6] Next to London, the naval bases at Dover and Portsmouth would be the most important targets, while the Humber and Tyne, the Firth of Forth, Plymouth and Glasgow were also mentioned. The new Chief of the Army General Staff, General Erich von Falkenhayn, who had succeeded von Moltke on November 3, 1914, waxed enthusiastic for the cause – provided the joint Army-Navy force were under Army control. Von Falkenhayn in fact produced during the autumn several plans for joint operations against England, with the Army craft occupying hangars in occupied Belgium and northern France. Thus began a rivalry between the two services to be first in attacking England – "the brutal huckster nation" – which at all times was intense, and sometimes embittered to the point where each service refused to use the other's weather stations.

Yet the generals and admirals still faced a major obstacle – the Kaiser, backed by the Imperial Chancellor, Theobald von Bethmann-Hollweg, who until his dismissal in July, 1917, looked for an accommodation with England and urged his countrymen not to "provoke" her. Months of manoeuvring went on before the

---

[5] Dr. Adolf Saager, *Zeppelin* (Stuttgart: Verlag Robert Lutz, 1915), p. 214.
[6] Robinson, p. 50.

vacillating All Highest would give his consent to starting the air war on England. In particular, the Supreme War Lord felt a tender solicitude for historical monuments in London and for the personal safety of his royal cousins, King George V and Queen Mary. Not until January 7, 1915, did the Chief of the Naval Staff obtain the Kaiser's consent to start raids on England. Even then "targets not to be attacked in London but rather docks and military establishments in the lower Thames and on the English coast."

After an abortive attempt by four Navy Zeppelins on January 13, the Navy was the first to attack England when on the night of January 19, 1915, the L 3 and L 4 reached the English coast and dropped just over a ton of bombs on Great Yarmouth, Kings Lynn and smaller places in Norfolk. Military damage was insignificant, but wild enthusiasm prevailed in Germany. The primitive Zeppelins of prewar type, with open gondolas, low speed and meagre endurance, proved barely able to reach the English coast, and appeared only once more over the island kingdom before being superseded in raiding by larger craft.

The Army, which at this time was the stronger service, was encouraged by an Imperial Order of February 12, 1915:

> 1. His Majesty the Kaiser has expressed great hopes that the air war against England will be carried out with the greatest energy.
> 2. His Majesty has designated as attack targets: war material of every kind, military establishments, barracks, and also oil and petroleum tanks and the London docks. No attack is to be made on the residential areas of London, or above all on royal palaces.[7]

The General Staff construed this directive to mean that their airships could bomb targets in London east of a line drawn through Charing Cross Station in the heart of the capital. A grandiose plan, code named FILM FETWA, was drawn up for attacking London. All possible targets in the capital east of the bombing line were listed, together with the location of known anti-aircraft guns. The force assigned included the old SL 2 in Trier, the new Zeppelins of prewar type Z X in Düsseldorf and LZ 35 in Cologne (the latter replacing the obsolete "Sachsen" which went to Allenstein in the east), and the Z XII in Frankfurt. All of these ships since the end of the year had been equipped with spherical explosive bombs of 130, 220 and 330 lb. weight, while Z XII carried the first of the famous but overrated subcloud cars *(Spähkorb)*, the joint invention of her commander, Oblt. z.S. d. R. Lehmann, and his executive officer,

[7] Robinson, p. 67.

Freiherr von Gemmingen, who was Count Zeppelin's nephew. A small streamlined nacelle hanging in clear air half a mile below the Zeppelin and connected by telephone with the control car, the *Spähkorb* enabled an observer to direct the airship hidden in the clouds above. With its steel cable and winch driven off one of the airship's engines, it weighed over half a ton. Though the sub-cloud car was fitted in many Army airships, particularly late in 1916, it served its specific purpose in only one raid, and was rejected by Strasser for the naval service on account of its weight.

After February 23, 1915, the Army airships were to be held ready for raids on London, and on receipt of the code word JAUSE ("afternoon tea") they were to proceed from their permanent stations in the Rhineland to advanced bases in occupied territory. Thus, early in March, Z X came to Brussels-Evere, SL 2 to Brussels-Berchem Ste. Agathe, LZ 35 to Gontrode, and Z XII on March 8 to Maubeuge. Their attempts to bomb London were unsuccessful. On March 17, Z X and Z XII were both prevented from reaching England by heavy fog over the Channel. Z XII however found clear air beneath a cloud deck at 4000 feet over Calais, and with the sub-cloud car hung 2600 feet below the ship, dropped 6600 lb. of bombs in two runs over the coastal town. She was damaged, however, in a forced landing in a railway cutting and was under repair for 14 days. Soon afterwards the Kaiser forbade attacks on London, as the General Staff's interpretation had gone beyond his desires and wishes. Instead, on March 20, the remaining three airships in the west attempted the first attack on Paris. While crossing the Front, SL 2 was badly damaged by gunfire over the trenches, but unloaded her bombs on Compiègne and returned to base. Z X and LZ 35 between them dropped 4000 pounds of bombs while crossing over the capital at 8000 feet and departed undamaged, leaving one dead and 8 injured. En route home Z X was so badly shot up by anti-aircraft guns at Noyon that she crash landed at St. Quentin and had to be dismantled. On April 13, LZ 35 was damaged by anti-aircraft fire in an attack on Poperinghe and wrecked in a forced landing near Ypres. Once again the Army was paying a high price for small results.

At the end of April the Kaiser was again pressed to give his consent to raids on London, and on May 5 proclaimed "London east of the longitude of the Tower permitted for air attacks; within this area military installations, barracks, oil tanks may be attacked, particularly the docks." Yet this order was held up until the end of the month.

Reinforcements for the Army Zeppelins in the war on England were coming forward. LZ 37, a small Zeppelin of prewar type, was ordered to Belgium early in April, but was badly damaged in a squall while landing *en route* at Cologne; she in fact blew away from the field with only a handful of men aboard and was brought back to the base by her quartermaster, Alfred Mühler. Thus she did not arrive at Brussels-Etterbeek until May 21. The new LZ 39, the sister of Z XII, came to Brussels-Berchem Ste. Agathe early in May. Most portentious for the future of the air war was the arrival at Brussels-Evere in mid-April of the first of the new million cubic foot Zeppelins, LZ 38.

Since these craft carried the burden of the raids against England, France and Russia until the summer of 1916 and in some cases well beyond, with 22 ships of this "p" type being built, and twelve more lengthened versions being completed as the "q" type, the design will be presented in some detail. Though there was still a parallel section 197 feet long amidships, the 536-foot hull was better streamlined

An Army "m" class ship, LZ 37 at Cologne in May 1915. First photo ever published of the craft destroyed near Ghent on 7 June 1915, by Flight Sub-Lieut. R. A. J. Warneford R.N.A.S., for which he was awarded the V.C. (Elias-Miller)

than in preceding craft. With a hull diameter of 61.35 feet, the length/diameter ratio of the hull was 8.74/1, the "fattest" of any Zeppelins yet produced. This, with a well rounded bow and finely tapered stern, made for good streamlining, and maximum trial speed varied from 57 to 60 mph. The hull was built on nineteen longitudinal girders, the top one being a double triangular girder with a "W" section. Braced rings were ten metres (33 feet) apart; lighter intermediate rings circled the hull midway between the main ones, to reduce the bending loads on the longitudinals. Right aft were large flat fins with balanced rudders pivoting at their after ends; the clean streamlined effect was marred by numerous bracing wires between the fins and the hull.

Within the hull were sixteen gas cells; these were all supposed to be of three layers of gold beaters' skin glued to cotton fabric (so-called *Stoffhaut,* designed to save the scarce intestinal membranes while making the cells stronger) but on occasion, Zeppelin commanders were required to accept the heavier rubberized fabric cells because of a shortage of the preferred type. Each gas cell had an

LZ 38, the first aircraft to bomb London, and the first of the large "p" class airships, in front of her shed at Brussels-Evere, Spring 1915. (Elias-Miller)

automatic pressure relief valve at the bottom; but no ventilation shafts existed to carry the hydrogen away. This diffused upward between the cells and the cotton outer cover, the top of which was left undoped and porous to permit the gas to escape.

Water ballast sacks and duralumin fuel tanks were arranged along the keel; the latter could be dropped through the cover if necessary as added ballast. Gravity tanks supplying the engines directly were fixed above the gondolas. Right forward and aft were "breeches," water ballast sacks shaped like half a pair of pants, which could be emptied instantly to alter the trim. Amidships, bombs were hung by their tails from the box girders running along the keel, with shutters folding inward in the bottom panel of the outer cover when the load was to be dropped. The bomb cargo comprised up to 4400 lb. of explosives and incendiaries, occasionally more.

Well forward the control car and forward engine car were faired into the same streamlined shape 46.4 feet long, though in fact they were separated by an air space of 2 to 3 inches (to prevent vibration from the engine from being transmitted to the control car) which was faired over with fabric. A double door enabled the engine car to be reached from the control car. The nose of the latter was surrounded by transparent panes, some being composed of Triplex glass and others of celluloid. Further panes in the control car roof forward permitted a view upward and ahead, while a sort of projecting shelf at the front of the car had windows permitting a view downward. Here was mounted the bomb sight, a precision instrument by Carl Zeiss of Jena, in charge of the bombing officer or executive officer, who at the same time had only sketchy training in its use. A switchboard near at hand operated the electrical bomb releases.

The floor space inside the glassed-in nose of the control car measured about 6½ by 9 feet, and here were crowded together: the rudder man right forward, steeering with a small spoked wheel and watching a magnetic compass, as the much more accurate gyro compass, developed only for shipboard use, was much too heavy for an airship. On the left side facing outboard stood the elevator man, operating the elevators with a similar wheel. His instruments included: an altimeter; inclinometer to show the up or down angle of the ship; air and gas thermometers (essential in determining the lift of the ship, particularly if the gas were superheated or supercooled relative to the air); a statascope or rate of climb indicator; and a recording barograph. The elevator man also handled (on orders from

Inside the control car of **LZ 38**. From left to right: executive officer with binoculars; elevator man with elevator control wheel, altimeter in front of him, statascope and ballast and maneouvring valve pulls overhead; rudder man in bow of car (bomb sight to his right is much simplified); commanding officer (a good likeness of Linnarz) holding speaking tube to bomb room in keel, with engine telegraphs overhead; a machinist descending ladder from the keel overhead. From a painting by Felix Schwormstadt, not published until 1917.

the officers) the toggles that released water ballast from the sacks along the keel and the "breeches" at the ends of the ship; and the handles of the manoeuvring valves fitted in the tops of some of the gas cells. All handles could be connected to a "wheel" and opened simultaneously to make the ship heavy throughout her length. The commanding officer had a chart table on the right side of this space, with engine telegraphs to relay orders to the engineers in the rear. A speaking tube led to the bomb room amidships, and another to the machine gun platform on top of the Zeppelin. The executive officer also functioned in this space, particularly in handling the bomb sight; he also spent much time in the radio room just aft, coding and decoding messages. The radio cabin, being heavily soundproofed and with a tightly fitting door with a light disconnect switch, was quite unventilated and hence the warmest place in the ship. At the rear of the control car was the "officers' lounge" with two large windows each side; in these were mounted a pair of machine guns. In the Navy Zeppelins these were the heavy water-cooled 7.62 mm. Maxim, while the Army favored the lightweight air-cooled Parabellum.

In the engine car to the rear of the control car two mechanics serviced a single six cylinder Maybach water cooled power plant. In the earlier ships of this class, this was the C-X of 210 hp; beginning with L 15 in September, 1915, the lighter 240 hp Maybach HSLu was fitted. The premature installation of the HSLu before the "bugs" had been worked out proved to be a costly mistake; for months, crankshafts fractured, connecting rods broke, and crank bearings and wrist pins overheated, melted and "froze," until air scoops were fitted to blow cool air from the slipstream through the crank case. The loss with all hands of the naval airship L 19 in a raid on England in January, 1916, was attributed to repeated failures in her unreliable HSLu's. In disgust, Strasser finally on March 4, 1916, had the five newest ships with the HSLu's laid up, the engines removed and shipped to Friedrichshafen for rebuilding, not getting them back until the end of the month. Thereafter there was no trouble.

At the rear of the gondola, driven through reduction gearing which converted the 1400 rpm of the engine to about 540 rpm, was a large wooden propeller measuring about 17 feet in diameter. A handsomely made example of cabinet work, the air screw was built up of laminations of West African and Honduras mahogany, and American walnut, and often waterproofed with a coating of walnut veneer. The rear gondola, 50 feet long, contained three similar

Inside the rear engine gondola of LZ 38, looking forward. Engine telegraph hung from overhead; radiator and drive shaft to starboard propeller seen through window; mechanics working on a Maybach C-X engine of 210 h.p. in foreground, and a gunner with Parabellum machine gun looking for attacking aircraft. From a painting by Felix Schwormstadt.

engines[8] arranged in line; the sternmost drove a propeller at the rear of the car, while the two forward ones turned propellers on brackets high on the hull. These were reversible, to check the ship's way during the landing manoeuvres. Two machine guns were mounted in side windows of this gondola. In addition, a machine gun was mounted on the rim of a small cockpit abaft the rudders to cover the vulnerable area to the rear, and on the top platform over the control car, reached by a climbing shaft from the keel, two or three more machine guns were mounted. These were manned, not by regular machine gunners, but by crew members doubling as such. The crew

[8] Franz Kollman in *Das Zeppelinluftschiff* (Berlin: Verlag von M. Krayn, 1924), Table II, has misled later historians by claiming that LZ 38 had only two engines in the after gondola. I have photographs showing the ship with 3 engines in the after gondola; the same appears in a drawing of LZ 38's rear gondola on p. 56 of Dürr, and there is a good (though unidentified) photograph of this gondola on p. 229 of Neumann's book. In LZ 38, however, the rear gondola had a flat floor, while the floor was dropped aft in the rear gondola of later ships.

of 19 included a commanding officer, an executive officer, a warrant quartermaster acting as navigator, a warrant engineer, and a sailmaker in charge of the gas cells, who were on duty throughout every flight; and two rudder men, two elevator men, two radio men, and two machinists for each engine. The latter group of enlisted men was divided into two watches, and those "off duty" rested by standing lookout at the machine guns.

Performance of the "p" class Zeppelins was markedly improved over that of the prewar types. Whereas Z X in the March 20 raid on Paris had carried only 1200 lb of bombs, 5380 lb of fuel, 6000 lb of ballast and 12 men on a flight of only 269 miles, with a maximum altitude of 7900 feet, LZ 38 in her first raid on Ipswich on April 29 carried 5400 lb of bombs, 7050 lb of fuel, 9250 lb of ballast and 14 men (some were left at home to lighten her) on a flight of 500 miles, with a maximum altitude of 11,600 feet. The cruising speed also increased from 31½ mph to 39.2 mph (usually it was nearer 45 mph). Truly the two services had good reason to be pleased with the handiness, carrying capacity, speed and ceiling of the new Zeppelins, until late in 1915 when the developing English and French anti-aircraft defences forced the Zeppelins to seek higher altitudes. The response was to add two gas cells to these craft, one 10 metres and one 5 metres in length, bringing the length overall to 585 feet 5 inches (permitting these Zeppelins to fit into the shortest of the standard hangars with less than 5 feet to spare). The gas volume rose to 1,264,100 cubic feet, and the ceiling on raids was increased by 1500 feet or so.

Despite design refinements, particularly the enclosed gondolas, duty was hard and comforts were few in LZ 38 and her sisters. Cold was the greatest hardship; the control car crew, shivering in temperatures below the freezing mark, envied the mechanics, warmed to some extent by the engines, who however suffered from the intolerable clatter and roar of the Maybachs and breathed a mixture of exhaust gases, petrol and oil fumes. During the first half of the war, service uniform and greatcoats were worn, and only later were fur lined jackets, trousers, gauntlets, boots and helmets issued. A few thermoses of tea and coffee, and a sandwich or two and some chocolate in the jacket pocket, constituted the in-flight meal. Some ships were "dry," in others, each man had a small bottle of *schnapps* in the custody of the warrant quartermaster and issued on orders of the commanding officer. Hammocks lashed to the box girders along the keel enabled some of the off-duty watch to rest during the

Close up of the first London raider on the field at Evere. Note machine gunners on the top platform. (Robinson)

crossing of the North Sea to or from England, and a few square feet of plywood adjacent to the keel constituted the crew's lounge. One ballast bag contained drinking water. Well aft and near the rudders was the "head", in later ships an imitation of a flush toilet made of light stamped aluminium.[9] In less active theatres, as in the Baltic in the summer of 1917, the officers' lounge in the control car, and the crew's space in the gangway, were fitted up with wicker chairs and tables with tablecloths, flowers and pictures, and soup or eggs could be heated on a hot plate on one of the engine exhausts.

The other Zeppelins failed to make it to England, but LZ 38, under Hauptmann Linnarz, made a series of attacks in late April and May on such coastal towns as Ipswich, Bury St. Edmunds, Southend, and Ramsgate. Defences were non-existent (though on one occasion he was pursued unsuccessfully by a naval pilot from Westgate in an

[9] My friend Peter Amesbury, who is particularly interested in the Schutte-Lanz SL II shot down at Cuffley by Lieut. William Leefe Robinson on September 3, 1916, advises that the ship's toilet seat is supposed to be in the hands of a private person in Northaw. Perhaps this individual will come forward, if he reads this note.

Avro 504). Linnarz in fact was only waiting for permission to bomb London, and when this was given, he made the first air attack on the British capital on the night of May 31-June 1, 1915. Three thousand pounds of bombs fell on residential areas in north-east London, and though only seven people were killed and £18,596 damage done, the authorities considered the consequences serious enough to clap on a strict censorship of newspaper accounts of the raid. Henceforth the regions attacked were described vaguely as "the east coast," "eastern counties," etc., the purpose being to keep the Zeppelin commanders in the dark as to where they had been over England.

Another consequence was that the British Royal Naval Air Service squadron based at Dunkirk was ordered to hunt down the raiders. On June 6, 1915, all three of the Army craft available in Belgium were sent out against various objectives. LZ 38, under orders to attack London, suffered engine trouble and returned to her shed; she was there bombed by two Henri Farmans from Dunkirk and destroyed by fire. Lieut. R.A.J. Warneford in a Morane Parasol scored a more spectacular victory when he overtook LZ 37 in flight near Ghent and set her afire with his bombs; nine of her people were killed, the first Army Zeppelin crew to be lost in the war.[10] The surviving LZ 39 and Z XII were transferred later in the month to the Russian Front, while the vulnerable advanced sheds in the Brussels area were used henceforth only briefly or in emergencies. The field was left clear for the rival Naval Airship Division.

There was a lull during the short nights of June and July, when (as the commander of the Navy's new L 10 reported after a raid on Tyneside), it never did get fully dark, but in August, Strasser was ready to start squadron raids on London. L 10, the first "p" class Zeppelin in the naval service, had commissioned in the new shed at Friedrichshafen on May 17. She was followed by L 11, the first craft built at Löwenthal, on June 8; by L 12 in Friedrichshafen on June 22; by L 13 completed in 33 days in the same shed on July 25; and by L 14 in Löwenthal on August 10.

No Schütte-Lanz craft participated in the squadron raids on London, though the Navy at this time possessed in the SL 3 and SL 4 two airships slightly larger in gross volume than the "p" class Zeppelins. Their efficiency, however, was less, while breakage of the wooden hull girders was a chronic complaint on almost every flight,

---

[10] There was one survivor, the *Steuermann,* Alfred Mühler, who as the flaming wreckage fell on a convent was thrown out of the forward gondola and into a bed. See his account in *Kyffhäuser,* Nr. 19, of 8. Mai 1938.

L 10, the first Navy "p" class airship, at Nordholz. She was the first naval Zeppelin to bomb London, and was lost with the first Navy crew in the war when struck by lightning off Neuwerk Island, 3 September 1915. (Friedrich Moch)

requiring much time for repairs. On the night of June 4, 1915, both L 10 and SL 3 were sent out to raid England. The Zeppelin carried a useful load of 29,200 lb including 6400 lb of bombs, and attained a maximum altitude of 8850 feet. The Schütte-Lanz carried a useful load of only 21,800 lb including 4400 lb of bombs, and attained a maximum altitude of only 6450 feet. Strasser relegated the despised Schütte-Lanz craft to the Baltic theatre, where the Navy had bases at Seddin near Stolp and Seerappen near Königsberg, and where the demands on them, particularly with respect to ceiling, would be less than in the North Sea.

On August 9, 1915, the L 10, L 11, L 12 and L 13, personally led by Strasser aboard L 10, set out to bomb London, while L 9 was detached during the crossing of the North Sea to attack the Humber area. Turning south-west after reaching the Norfolk coast, the bigger ships encountered thunder squalls and had to drop much of their water ballast, and even some fuel, to compensate for the weight of rain on their fabric envelopes. None of them reached London. L 11 promptly dumped all her bombs when fired on by an anti-aircraft gun at Lowestoft, and returned claiming an attack on Harwich. L 13 turned back off the coast with a dead engine. L 10 reported reaching eastern London, but she was 35 miles down the Thames from the capital and her bombs fell on the landing ground of the Royal Naval Air Station at Eastchurch on the Isle of Sheppey. L 12 was also out in her reckoning. Making her landfall at Westgate, her commander thought he was far to the north on the Norfolk coast. The lights of Margate, Ramsgate and Deal he confused with those of Yarmouth and Lowestoft, and finally he dropped his bombs on Dover mistaking it for the Harwich naval air base nearly sixty miles to the north. Anti-aircraft fire badly damaged L 12 and she failed to reach Belgium, landing on the surface of the Channel. She was towed into Ostend and caught fire while being salvaged, little being saved but the gondolas.

The faulty navigation in this raid was typical throughout the war, and the chief reason the Zeppelin raiders did not do more damage in their attacks on England was that they could not find the cities which were their targets. Wishful thinking led them to claim that their bombs had fallen on industrial centers when they might have exploded in open country. On one occasion, on a chilly May night full of snow clouds, the first Zeppelin inland started a fire with an incendiary bomb on a desolate moorland on the Yorkshire coast. At least three of the following Zeppelins aimed their bomb loads at the heath fire, believing they were over Skinningrove, Saltburn, or Stockton-on-Tees.

As anyone who has flown at night must realize, conventional navigational methods — dead reckoning at sea, and pilotage through identifying rivers, harbors or cities overland — were bound to fail. Wind direction and velocity could not be measured precisely from an airship over the sea, particularly when she was flying above clouds, hence large drift errors made dead reckoning positions worthless. Over England at night, particularly with impaired visibility, little detail could be distinguished in the blacked-out countryside, and headlands, rivers and cities all looked more or less alike. A few commanders tried taking star sights at twilight from the top platform of the airship, using an ordinary marine sextant, but celestial navigation at other times was impossible, as the modern artificial horizon sextant had yet to be invented.

Electronic aids on the ground have today solved the problems of aerial navigation at night or in thick weather, and today's jet transport flight crews do not even have to look out of the cockpit to know their position within a mile at all times. Since the Zeppelins,

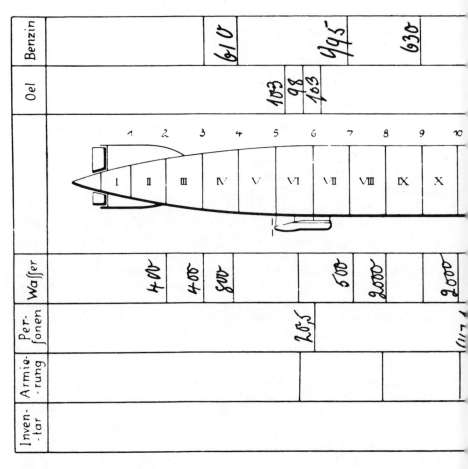

Nordholz , den 12. Juni 1915 Der Wi[

No.
d 75

Actual Ballast sheet for Airship L 11 — A book of tear-out ballast sheets was issued to each Zeppelin by the *Luftschiffbau Zeppelin*. Before each flight, a sheet had to be filled out, recording the amount of fuel, oil, water ballast, armament and bombs, personnel, supplies and equipment loaded, and their distribution through the ship; also the weather conditions at take-off. This ballast sheet was made up for L 11 for a short trial flight at Nordholz on 12 June 1915, soon after her arrival in the North Sea, and is signed by Anton Wittemann, the Zeppelin Company's representative at the naval airship bases.

us Luftſchiff „L. Z. ███ 41" „L. 11"

				kg			kg
450			3055		Benzin	3055	Paſſagiere
					Oel	347	Vorräte . . .
93			347		Beſatzung	987	Bewaffnung .
					Waſſerballaſt	8400	Munition . . .
12 13 14 15					Inventar und Reſerveteile .		Geſchoſſe . . .

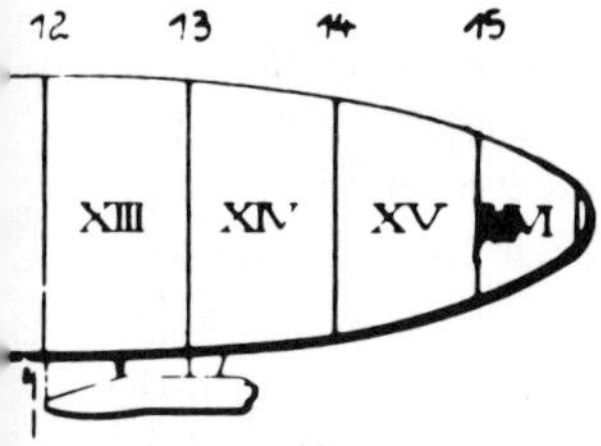

XIII	XIV	XV	XVI

Dienstladung : 13334 | Nutzladung :

Zusatzbelastung   kg
(Tau, Regen, Schnee)

Nutzlaſt bei 100 % Füllung 13334 kg

Luft :   Gas :

$b = 767.1$ mm $t = 22°,8$ C

$t = 21°,0$ C $s = 0,0454$

$rF = 86\%$

500	800	8400	987,6

Nachfüllungen   cbm

"   "
"   "
"   "
"   "

de   Der Führer

for reconnaissance purposes, already carried powerful long range wireless sending and receiving sets, the Navy early in 1915 established direction-finding stations at Nordholz and Borkum to serve its airships, later adding stations at List and Bruges. (The Army did not develop a similar service until the last month of 1915, and their ground stations were at Cologne, Metz, Strassburg, Charleville and Friedrichshafen). The airship called up the shore stations, which measured the direction of the signals and radioed the bearings to the Zeppelin, where they were plotted on a great circle chart. The Germans ignored the fact that British direction finding stations could likewise locate the airships by their wireless calls, and when the system was replaced early in 1918 by a method in which the airship was silent, it was not for the sake of security but because the special airship wavelength had become too overloaded with all the traffic required by the old procedure. The whole science of radio communication was in its infancy, and such phenomena as "night effect," which later was found to introduce gross errors in the apparent direction of the signals, was entirely unknown. Hence the bearings might give a positional error of as much as 60 miles over England. On a night in September, 1916, Kapitänleutnant Martin Dietrich, commanding L 22, was exasperated to find that three different sets of bearings gave him a wide choice of locations: the Wash, the Humber, or Flamborough Head (he was near Spurn Point at the time). In the last two years of the war, when flying at high altitude above solid cloud decks, the Zeppelins attempted to use radio bearings for blind bombing through the overcast, but without success.

Some Zeppelin commanders could draw on a sixth sense for navigation, and one of the more successful was Heinrich Mathy, "the greatest airship commander of the war" in the opinion of his enemies.[11] He was not the first naval officer over London – on the night of August 17, while Mathy's L 13 had to turn back with a broken rudder coupling, L 10 succeeded in reaching the capital. Her commander, believing he was approaching London from the north-west, reported: "bomb dropping was ordered to begin between Blackfriars and London Bridges. Collapse of buildings and big fires could be observed." Actually, through navigational error, the bomb load fell on the north-eastern suburbs of Leyton and Wanstead Flats.

Mathy's big night was on September 8. With two other Zeppelins, L 13 set out for London with nearly two tons of bombs in her

[11]H.A. Jones, *The War In The Air* (London: Oxford University Press, 1934), vol. III, p. 238.

racks – one of them being the first 660-pounder to be carried over England. Making his landfall at the Wash, Mathy proceeded south at 50 mph and from north of Cambridge had the reflected glow of the lights of the capital in sight along the horizon ahead. Coming in over the north-west suburbs at 9200 feet, Mathy, who had spent a week in London in 1909, found that "orientation over London itself was not difficult, since for example Regent's Park could be clearly recognized from the 'Inner Circle' which was lit as in peace time."

The financial houses of the City, and above all the Bank of England, were high on the German Navy's bombing list. While L 13's bombs missed the Bank, her incendiaries and explosives, raining down on the crowded textile warehouses north of St. Paul's Cathedral, started many fires. Mathy's last bombs barely missed Liverpool Street and Broad Street Stations, two of them making direct hits on motor buses and causing many casualties. The damage toll amounted to more than half a million pounds – the greatest monetary loss inflicted in any Zeppelin or aeroplane raid on England in the First World War, and over a sixth of the entire total of air raid damage in England during that conflict. Briefly, the Zeppelin must have appeared to the British Cabinet as a real threat to the war effort. Among Londoners, the shock, anger and unacknowledged fear of what the Zeppelin might accomplish never entirely disappeared. As a result of press agitation, a few days later Admiral Sir Percy Scott, a noted gunnery expert, was placed in charge of the London defences.

Five nights later, when three Zeppelins set out to raid London, L 13 held on while the other two turned back because of thunderstorms and head winds. Mathy still hoped to reach and bomb London before dawn, but near Harwich he had the bad luck to take a 6-pounder shell amidships from the gun at Felixstowe, which was firing blind into the clouds at the sound of the airship's engines. Two gas cells were holed and rapidly ran 80 to 85 per cent empty despite attempts to patch them, and the Zeppelin became very heavy. Mathy turned back at once, dumping his bombs, and headed for home by the shortest route, deliberately flying across neutral Holland to save his ship. Before reaching the Dutch coast he dumped 1750 lb of fuel. At 5.20 am L 13 was over her base at Hage. Mathy would have preferred to wait for sunrise to warm and expand the remaining hydrogen, but thunderstorms threatened to load the ship with soaking rain and he decided to land at once. Though he dropped a further 1,100 lb of oil, spare parts and radiator water, the ship fell heavily in landing. Girders were broken over the control car, gondola struts and side propeller shafts were bent, but the damage was made good in four days. Not always was the outcome so happy.

A tragedy on September 3, in which L 10 was destroyed and 19 men died — the first Navy crew to be lost in the war — taught the Naval Airship Division a hard lesson. The Zeppelin was returning to Nordholz after a reconnaissance, and had radioed her estimated time of arrival, when she encountered a local thunderstorm near Cuxhaven. Observers in the coastal batteries saw a red flame burst from the hull between the nose and the forward gondola, and then, as the flame climbed up the envelope, the bows of the airship canted downward to an angle of 80 degrees and she slowly fell, swathed in flame, to the tide flats where she continued to burn with heavy clouds of smoke. Her recording barograph was recovered from the wreckage. In his official report, Strasser wrote:

> Shortly before the crash the ship — whether on purpose or not cannot be ascertained — went over pressure height . . . The ship was thus valving gas at the time. This could have led to her being set on fire by lightning. Airships should in all circumstances try to go around thunderstorms. If this is not possible, they should go through as far as possible under pressure height as the squalls will allow. The airships of the Division now have such orders; also in thunderstorms they are ordered to reel in antennas.[12]

Only with the last raid of the year, on October 13, 1915, was London attacked by a squadron of Zeppelins simultaneously. Though L 11 jettisoned her bombs on the Norfolk villages of Horstead, Coltishall and Great Hautbois, the remaining four ships reached the vicinity of the capital. A newcomer, Kapitänleutnant Joachim Breithaupt in the new L 15, again boldly crossed the heart of London from west to east. Aiming for the War Office and the Admiralty, his bombs landed to the east and caused great damage in the theatre district north of the Strand, and farther east in the Inns of Court. L 13, after dropping part of her cargo on Shalford, which Mathy misidentified as Hampton, the site of a water works, then skirted around the south side of the capital to drop the remainder of her cargo on the Woolwich Arsenal. Fortunately the damage here was slight. L 14 crossed the lower Thames and continued south across Kent till reaching the Channel, but her commander reported that "at this time we crossed the Thames at Woolwich and attacked the dock facilities there as well as the arsenal with nine explosive bombs." These killed and wounded soldiers in an Army encampment at

[12] Robinson, p. 102.

Shorncliffe. L 14 then found her way back to London and dropped the remainder of her bomb load on Croydon. L 16 reported bombing the London districts of Stratford, East Ham and West Ham, but her bombs actually fell on Hertford, a good twenty miles to the north.

All the commanders remarked on the strength of the London defences. Mathy reporting that "compared with September 8-9, a considerable increase in the blackout and defences was noticeable." L 14's commander, attacking London for the first time, reported that "during the crossing of the city the ship was lit up bright as day by numerous searchlights (26 were counted) and was heavily fired on from all sides with explosive shells, whose bursts sometimes lay very near the ship. At the periphery of the city they were also firing incendiary rockets, some of which ascended very near to the ship." Most ominous of all was Breithaupt's observation: "Over the City four aeroplanes were observed 500 to 1000 metres (1650 to 3300 feet) below the ship; they were clearly recognizable in the searchlight illumination and by their exhaust flames." Five B.E. 2cs of the Royal Flying Corps had taken off from fields to the east of London established after Mathy's September raid, armed not with machine guns but with small incendiary bombs to be dropped on the Zeppelins from above. Only one pilot saw L 15, and she easily climbed away while he was still well below her.

Clearly, increased altitude performance would be desirable, and it was only six weeks later, on December 21, 1915, that L 20, the first of the lengthened "q" class, made her first flight in Friedrichshafen. Four more entered Navy service. The "q" class was even more popular with the Army, as these ships were the longest that could fit in most of their single sheds. Not only were seven "q"s built for the Army, but during the summer of 1916, five of their "p" class ships were lengthened to the same dimensions and gas volume at Dresden.

While the Navy was concentrating during the latter part of 1915 on North Sea patrols and raids on London, the Army was primarily concerned with the Eastern Front. During the summer of 1915, the Z XII and LZ 39, following their transfer east from Belgium, joined with the old "Sachsen" in supporting Hindenburg's great offensive against the Russian armies in Poland. Bombing attacks were made by night on the railway lines leading from Warsaw to Mlawa, Brest-Litovsk and Vilna, with great success being claimed in attacks on railway stations and junctions. Three new "p" class ships joined the eastern campaign – LZ 79 in August, LZ 85 and LZ 86 in October. The victorious advance eastward of the German armies

LZ 90, a lengthened "p" class Army ship, on the field at Wittmundhaven, unable to enter the shed because of a strong cross wind, 7 November 1916. Later in the day as the wind rose to a gale, her crew were taken off and the Zeppelin drove off unmanned into the North Sea. (Georg Blasweiler)

proved an embarrassment to the Army airship service, as their permanent hangars in Königsberg, Schneidemuhl, Liegnitz, Posen and Allenstein presently lay too far distant from the fighting zone. A new shed was completed in Warsaw in October, 1915, and still later one was constructed at Kovno in Lithuania.

The Army participated briefly in the autumn attack on England. Three big ships of the "p" class were moved forward from Rhineland bases – LZ 79 to Maubeuge, LZ 74 and LZ 77 to Namur, while the lengthened SL 2, still under Hauptmann von Wobeser, was risked closer to the enemy at Berchem Ste. Agathe, the last time that one of the Brussels sheds hangared a German airship. Ironically, only the old SL 2 accomplished anything of note. On the night of September 7, she made a daring assault on London. Her bombs fell in the dock areas of Millwall, Deptford, Greenwich and Woolwich, but von Wobeser was unlucky and his bombs mostly struck dwellings. On the same night LZ 74 dropped the first bomb on the City of London, an incendiary which landed in Fenchurch Street. Unfortunately her commander had earlier released the remainder of his payload on the glasshouses of Cheshunt! In the following month the Army High Command sent its Zeppelins to attack railway lines behind the Front in France. LZ 74 returned to her home base at Darmstadt and was lost on October 8. Descending in thick fog with engines on full power to determine her position, she rammed a hill in the Schnee Eifel and tore off both gondolas. While the injured occupants disentangled themselves from the wreckage, the hull ascended to 10,600 feet; but was brought down near Mezières when the flight engineer, who happened to be in the gangway, valved gas.

Another new front opened for the Army airship service in the Balkans, when Germany, Austria and Bulgaria mounted a campaign in the autumn of 1915 to crush Serbia and to open a ground route to Turkey. An airship base, with a single shed, was erected at Szentandras near Temesvar, Hungary, and in November LZ 81 flew from there to Sofia in Bulgaria (not yet accessible by the ground route) with high officials to negotiate with the Bulgarian government. With the landing of French and British troops at Salonika on October 5 1915, this city became the target for the Temesvar Zeppelin. LZ 85, commanded by Oberleutnant Scherzer, made two successful raids in January and March, 1916, but on May 4 was shot up by anti-aircraft guns, descended in the Vardar marshes north of the city, and the crew of 12 were captured.

With the Chief of the General Staff, General von Falkenhayn, planning the German Army's next major effort against Verdun, the Army airship service likewise turned its attention to the west. In October and November, 1915, LZ 77 in Cologne made the first Army experiment with radio direction finding. Also, whereas it had previously been believed that raids could not be made on a moonlit night as the airship would be seen too easily, some flights by LZ 77 near Cologne convinced Army observers that the Zeppelins could not be seen from the ground even on a moonlit night, hence permitting raids at any time of the month.

In an attempt to terrorize the inhabitants of the French capital, LZ 77 and LZ 79 were sent to Namur shortly before Christmas to attack "the strongly fortified armed camp of Paris." Bad weather delayed the first raid until January 29, 1916, when LZ 79 made a successful attack on Paris, but was so badly shot up by anti-aircraft guns that she crash-landed short of her base. On the following night LZ 77 claimed a raid on Paris, but was never closer to her target than the suburbs of Asnières and Versailles. This was the third – and last – Zeppelin raid on the French capital.

The Zeppelins' role in the Verdun offensive was to bomb railway junctions on the lines supplying the fortress – surely a misuse of the long-range craft which further exposed them to the concentrated defences along the Front. Because of the results of the Cologne Trials, the first raid was ordered for the evening of February 21, 1916, the day the German Army's attack opened – only three days after the February full moon. Four of the six ships available in the West were sent out that night. In the clear moonlight over the trenches, the Zeppelins stood out as they had not done in the industrial haze around Cologne. LZ 95, the first Army Zeppelin of the "q" class, was carrying 8800 lb of bombs and could not climb above 10,500 feet. Presenting a fine target for the anti-aircraft gunners, she was shot full of holes and failed to make it back to Namur, becoming a total loss. LZ 88, destined for Châlons sur Marne, turned back in the face of heavy snow squalls and landed safely at Maubeuge. SL 7, ordered to attack a station on the railway from Nancy to Verdun, returned to Mannheim claiming to have bombed La Neuville. LZ 77, after crossing the Front safely in spite of heavy anti-aircraft fire, was close to Révigny, her target, when automobile-mounted cannon firing incendiary shell set her afire. The death of her commander, Hauptmann Alfred Horn, was particularly regretted. He was one of the most experienced Army commanders, having joined the Airship Battalion in the year 1902 and had his first airship training in the Z II in 1909.

A few unsuccessful attempts were made in February and March to continue the attacks on the railway junctions near Verdun, but were defeated by snow squalls or fog. After March, 1916, no Zeppelins were permitted to cross the Front. SL 7, considered unequal to operations in the west, was transferred to Königsberg in East Prussia. Attempts to attack England singly or in pairs in April were unsuccessful. With the coming of the short summer nights, the Army ceased airship operations in the west, while LZ 87 and LZ 88 were sent east to operate with the Navy over the Baltic.

Early in the new year, on January 8, 1916, Vizeadmiral Reinhard Scheer replaced Admiral von Pohl as Commander-in-Chief of the High Seas Fleet. During the next two years there grew up between him and Strasser a respect and admiration which ensured Scheer's wholehearted support for the Naval Airship Division, and its continued existence even when the Army saw fit to abandon the Zeppelin in favour of bombing aeroplanes. Scheer was committed to a more aggressive activity against England by the High Seas Fleet, its

U-boats and airships, and on January 18 met with Strasser to discuss more widespread attacks on the whole of England.

The first result was a raid on the Midlands by nine Zeppelins on January 31-February 1. Liverpool was to be attacked "if at all possible" and two commanders claimed to have reached it, though none got farther west than Shrewsbury. They further claimed to have bombed Sheffield three times, Manchester twice, and Nottingham, Goole, Immingham and Yarmouth once each. Actually not a single bomb fell in any of these cities, but bombs fell in many places, particularly at Burton-on-Trent, which was well lighted and was attacked three times. One raider, L 19, was lost when three of her new Maybach HSLu engines failed on the way home. Dutch anti-aircraft guns damaged her when she drifted over the island of Ameland and she was carried by the wind out into the North Sea. There the floating wreck was sighted on February 2 by the Grimsby trawler "King Stephen," which refused to take the 19 Germans aboard. They were never seen again.

The outcry in the Midlands cities and towns forced a shake-up in the British defences, the most important result being that the Royal Flying Corps established a series of night flying squadrons to combat the Zeppelin menace. Originally weighted down with Le Prieur rockets and petrol bombs, their B.E. 2c aircraft by the late summer of 1916 were armed with a single Lewis machine gun firing Brock, Pomeroy and Buckingham incendiary and explosive ammunition.

During the spring Strasser continued to raid England, for nearly a week in early April sending out at least two Zeppelins every day. The first in the series was an attempt by seven ships to reach London on the night of March 31. They found the defences much augmented over the previous year. Mathy, thinking to lighten his L 13 before venturing over London, skilfully located the town of Stowmarket but could not discover the plant of the New Explosive Works. Instead his ship was badly shot up by an anti-aircraft battery. Two gas cells were holed but he made it back to Hage. Breithaupt, advancing up the Thames Estuary in L 15, was less lucky when the first salvo from guns at Dartford scored a direct hit amidships. As he turned away to the north he was pursued by a defending aeroplane which dropped explosive darts on the crippled Zeppelin from above. With four gas cells emptying fast Breithaupt threw overboard every disposable article and headed for Belgium. Suddenly the overstrained framework buckled in two places and the wrecked Zeppelin plunged into the sea near the Knock Deep Lightship. A British destroyer rescued the crew; next morning L 15 sank off Westgate while under tow. L 14 and L 16 both claimed to have attacked London, but the one dropped her bombs on Thameshaven and the other on Brentwood.

In the daily effort which followed, L 14 was first to reach Edinburgh, and achieved the most impressive result of the series of raids by burning down a whiskey warehouse in Leith to the tune of £44,000. Sunderland was badly damaged by L 11 on the night of April 1-2. Due to head winds, none of the ships out on April 4 reached England, and they landed at such distant locations as Düren and Dresden. The participants looked back wistfully in later years to "the great days of 1916, when we took off to raid three times in five days, when we came home one day at 8 in the morning and at 2 took off again for England." On April 11, 1916, the Chief of the Naval Staff reported to the Kaiser concerning the March 21-April 1 raid:

> At Grimsby, in addition to the post office and several other houses, a battleship in the roadstead was heavily damaged by a bomb, and had to be beached. At Kensington an aeroplane hangar was wrecked, near Tower Bridge a transport ship damaged, in Great Tower Street a factory wrecked, and north of the Tower a bomb fell in George Street only 100 metres away from two anti-aircraft guns. It was reported that a big fire had broken out at West India Docks, and that at Tilbury Docks a munition boat exploded (400 killed).[13]

Not a word of this was true, but the fact that it was believed, not only by the deluded populace, but also by the Supreme War Lord and his responsible advisors, underlines the role of wishful thinking in determining national policy. Count Zeppelin and his giant creations still held the adoration and devotion of the German people.

During the remainder of the spring of 1916 the Zeppelins were increasingly reserved for purely naval operations as the High Seas Fleet's activity worked up to the crescendo of the Battle of Jutland. During the bombardment of Lowestoft and Great Yarmouth by the German battle cruisers on April 25, the old L 6 and L 7 covered the High Seas Fleet's battle squadrons to the rear, while L 9 manoeuvred between the battle cruisers and the battle fleet and reported a force of British light cruisers and destroyers coming up from the south. On May 4, the L 7 was shot down into the sea in flames by two light cruisers of a British force she was reconnoitring off the Danish coast. After May 23, Scheer ordered the airships held for a fleet operation against Sunderland. With continuing bad weather, however, he had to

[13] Robinson, p. 138.

abandon the plan for an advance into the western North Sea covered by Zeppelins, and substituted an advance to the north along the Jutland coast. This resulted in the Battle of Jutland on the afternoon and evening of May 31, 1916. Five Zeppelins sent out after noon on that day saw nothing of the battle, largely due to the low cloud and mist which so handicapped the surface fleets. On the following morning, as Scheer's battered force was already retreating into the German Bight, Viktor Schütze in L 11 correctly reported dreadnoughts of the Grand Fleet off Terschelling; but Scheer paid more attention to L 24's information of a phantom fleet in Jammer Bay on the Danish coast. These, he allowed himself to believe, were part of the Grand Fleet which Jellicoe had divided after his "defeat" in the daylight action; while the vessels reported by L 11 were "reinforcements from the Channel"!

The Sunderland operation, which nearly led to a pitched battle between the fleets on August 19, 1916, showed Scheer's ideas on using the Zeppelins for strategic reconnaissance: eight were out that day, four in a line across the northern North Sea to intercept the Grand Fleet as it came south, four more along the east coast of England to report local forces issuing from the Forth, the Tyne, the Humber, the Thames, or the Channel. Four more Zeppelins were to have relieved the eight on August 20. The northern airships patrolled in vain, for the Grand Fleet, forewarned by wireless intelligence, had passed through their area a day earlier. Some of the other airships sighted Jellicoe's dreadnoughts, but Scheer refused to believe they were present. L 13, the most southerly, reported a force of light cruisers and destroyers as including battleships, leading Scheer on a wild goose chase which at least took him away from an encounter with the Grand Fleet in which he might have been worsted. World War II experience suggests that Scheer should have had a much larger force of airships to patrol the North Sea over several days. Above all, he should have been able to reconnoitre the Grand Fleet base at Scapa Flow: his three newest Zeppelins, L 30, L 31 and L 32, had the necessary range.

The day before the Jutland battle a new and impressively larger naval Zeppelin, L 30, the first of the new "r" class, arrived at Nordholz with old Count Zeppelin as a passenger. The genesis of her design went back to March, 1915, when the German Navy Ministry requested the Zeppelin and Schütte-Lanz firms to prepare designs to fit in the largest hangars then in existence in the North Sea. Dissatisfied with the resulting drawings for a 5-engined ship of

1,590,000 cubic feet, Admiral Dick of the Aviation Department of the Navy Ministry, decided on July 22, 1915, on the opposite approach — "a new project for a 6-engine ship without regard to shed measurements." Double sheds under construction at Tondern and Seddin in the Baltic were to be lengthened from 590 to 787 feet. Further, on June 17, 1915, representatives of the Navy Ministry, the Naval Staff and the High Seas Fleet Command met and decided to erect six giant double hangars for the new "big 6-engined ships" each measuring 790 feet long, 197 feet wide, and 100 feet high. One was to be added at Nordholz, one at Seerappen near Königsberg in the Baltic. The remaining four were to form an entirely new base to serve the High Seas Fleet, and would be built inland because of the danger of attack from the sea and because of the prevalence of fog along the coast. Ahlhorn in Oldenburg, nearly 60 miles from the sea, was chosen and the four Ahlhorn sheds were officially completed on September 11, 1916.

At Friedrichshafen a second large building shed measuring 787 feet long, 138 feet wide and 115 feet high was completed in the early summer of 1916. Further, both companies erected new plants especially to construct the large airships. At the insistence of the Army's Chief of Field Aviation, Oberst Thomsen, these were built in the heart of the country, lest the existing Friedrichshafen and Mannheim-Rheinau plants on Germany's borders be destroyed by air attack. In the summer of 1915 the Zeppelin Company began constructing a plant at Staaken near Berlin with two single sheds 827 feet long, 138 feet wide and 115 feet high. The Potsdam works was closed down and its staff transferred to Staaken, which completed its first Zeppelin on November 9, 1916. The Schütte-Lanz plant was at Zeesen near Berlin with a single large hangar; its first ship was likewise delivered on November 9, 1916.

Construction of L 30 started in February, 1916, in the 629-foot factory shed in Friedrichshafen. This was a tight fit for the giant new craft, with the impressive dimensions of 649.9 feet overall length,[14] 78 feet 5 inches in diameter, and 90 feet 10 inches overall height standing on the gondola bumpers. In one leap the gas volume

---

[14] Obviously L 30 and her sisters were longer than the shed, yet eight more Zeppelins of the same length were built in this hangar. The "Factory Shed I" was long enough to house these craft from bow cap to rudders, and the slender tail cone was added late in construction and protruded through the shed doors, which were left partly open. The last Zeppelin built in this shed, L 71 completed on July 29, 1918, was 693 feet long and the end of the nose stuck out at one end and the tail cone at the other.

increased by 54 per cent – from the 1,264,100 cubic feet of L 20 to 1,949,600 cubic feet. Gone was the long inefficient cylindrical section amidships, and the hull, with only a short parallel section, was much better streamlined. Paul Jaray, the Zeppelin Company aerodynamicist, wanted to design the hull with a fully streamlined shape, but certain "practical men" insisted the airship would be longitudinally unstable without any parallel portion. The smoother air flow at the tapered stern permitted smaller fins to provide adequate stability. As in previous Zeppelins, the 19 gas cells were separated by braced rings spaced 10 metres (32 feet 9 inches) apart, with intermediate unbraced rings at intervals of 5 metres. The hull was built on thirteen main longitudinals, of which the top, or "backbone" girder, was a double structure of "w" section. The 13-sided main transverse frames or rings took the loads and stresses more efficiently, and fifteen of them – Rings 30 through 170 inclusive[15] – were reinforced with kingpost bracing. To reduce tension on the cotton outer cover, twelve light auxiliary longitudinal girders were located between the main longitudinals, giving the hull from outside the appearance of a 25-sided polygon. To reduce the load on the transverse wire bracing of the main rings (as when a deflated gas bag caused adjacent cells to bulge in to the empty spaces), an axial bracing cable *(Zentralverspannung)* – a Schütte-Lanz patent – was fitted for the first time in L 30. Running from end to end of the ship, and connecting all the ring bracing at their centers, it was also a source of trouble as the cable led through each gas cell. The same was true of the shear wires which ran diagonally through ten of the largest gas cells from the top girder to the keel below. The gas-tight fittings sometimes leaked, and unless the cells were very carefully placed in position, the cables could cause them to tear.

The control car was "cleaned up" aerodynamically, and the "officers' lounge" reduced in size, but the overall length of 51 feet from the bow of the control car to the tail of the forward engine gondola indicated an unnecessarily bulky and heavy structure. Amidships were two little wing gondolas, reached by lateral gangways from the main catwalk, 19 feet long and containing one engine each, driving a geared 17½ foot propeller. The after gondola was made smaller and shorter by arranging two of the three engines side by side instead of in tandem. Here only did L 30 fail to show

---

[15] For the first time, the transverse frames or rings were numbered according to the distance in metres from the stern post, which was Ring O.

improvement over her predecessors, for two of the after engines still drove propellers on clumsy side brackets. Undoubtedly the drag of these brackets and long propeller shafts reduced the speed of these otherwise efficient ships. But they were retained because of the simple reversing gear which had been incorporated into the side propeller drive since the earliest days of the Zeppelin airship. All propellers were geared down to a 3:8 ratio. Though the need to make the propellers of the small side gondolas reversible had been recognized, the development of a new gear drive, according to Dr. Arnstein of the Zeppelin Company, required more time than the design and production of a new engine.

In two bomb rooms forward and aft of amidships L 30 could carry nearly five tons of bombs. Thirty-two droppable fuel tanks of 77 gallons capacity were hung along the triangular keel, with 8 fixed gravity tanks of 177 gallons being nested over the engine gondolas – the total of 3870 gallons being expected to last for 36 hours at cruising speed on all engines. Two hundred and ten gallons of oil could be carried in tanks near the engine cars. Along the keel were hung 14 rubberized cloth ballast sacks each containing 2200 lb of water ballast. Forward at Ring 170, and aft at Ring 30, were a total of 8 quick-release water ballast "breeches" each holding 550 lb of water. At one time, a total of 10 machine guns were carried – two in the control car, two in the after engine car, one in each of the side gondalas, one in the after gun pit behind the rudders, and no less than three on the top platform near the bows. Two lightweight boats – canvas stretched on a wooden frame – were carried as a legacy of the L 19 tragedy, one slung under the hull between the control car and the forward bomb room, the other on the top platform.

With six Maybach HSLu engines totalling 1440 hp, the maximum trial speed of L 30 was 62 mph. The ceiling in raids over England was about 13,000 feet. Out of a total lift of 141,200 lb under standard conditions, a maximum of 61,600 lb – 43.6 per cent – was available for useful load, a figure improved on in later ships of the class.

Introduced in the middle of 1916, the L 30 type of Zeppelin continued in production, with extensive modifications, to the end of the war. Furthermore, it played an indispensable role in the airship programmes of other countries. When L 33, the fourth "big 6-engine ship," made a forced landing in England in September, 1916, her design was copied in R 33 and R 34, the first successful British rigid airships. The later L 49 served as the basis for the construction of the U.S. Navy's first rigid, the ZR 1 "Shenandoah."

The Army airship service had expected to share in the production of the "big 6-engine ships," but the Navy, immediately after the Jutland battle, successfully laid claim to the entire output, citing the loss in the battle of three modern and one old light cruiser. This unexpected victory was facilitated by the fact that the Army had only four sheds large enough to house the "r" type craft — at Wildeshausen in Oldenburg, at Jüterbog near Berlin, at Kovno in Lithuania, and at Jamboli in Bulgaria.

In the summer of 1916 the Army was moving in two directions at once, expecting half the output of the new 2,000,000 cubic foot ships,[16] erecting large fixed hangars at Wittmund in East Frisia and in Düsseldorf, and furthermore building expensive revolving sheds at Schneidemühl, Düsseldorf, Mannheim-Sandhofen, Graudenz, and Dresden.[17] At the same time, the General Staff of the Army was having increasing doubts as to whether the Army airships could justify their cost in money, material and manpower. For days, even weeks at a time, raiding came to a standstill as the Army Zeppelins were confined to their sheds by cross-winds, fog, low clouds or storms:

All the more painful (for their officers) since, in contrast to the naval airship commanders, who could be kept busy with scouting flights at sea, they had no other field of activity. These were men some of whom had participated in the development of powered airship flight from the beginning, and who, through the valuable experience obtained by their practical activites since the year 1908, had stimulated and improved the construction of airships . . .
After discontinuing the attacks during the short summer nights, it was hoped that there would be real success from the planned attacks against London. Everything was thoroughly prepared, the airship radio sets were calibrated with the direction finders of the ground stations, and numerous bombing practices had been made from combat altitudes. Several commanders had equipped their ships with sub-cloud cars. Compared to the Navy, the Army was inferior in numbers, but almost equal in performance of its ships, since the Navy already disposed of 55,000 cbm. (2,000,000 cubic foot) ships which, with the technical developments existing at the time, could fly only slightly higher.[18]

[16] In the end the Army received only two of the big "r" class, the LZ 113 completing at Staaken on February 22, 1917, and the LZ 120 completing at Löwenthal on January 31, 1917.
[17] These revolving sheds were never completed. To save money and material, they were built to a novel and utterly impractical floorless design. "It would be impossible with every turn of the wind to move everything on the ground (trestles, ladders, cranes, etc.) in order to move the shed. In case of snow, the walls of the sheds would have had to be raised above the ground, otherwise they would operate as snow plows and soon be blocked by the snow." (Krell, O., *Zeitschrift für Flugtechnik u. Motorluftschiffahrt*, September 28, 1928).
[18] Hauptmann Friedrich Stahl in Neumann, Georg Paul, *Die deutsche Luftstreitkräfte im Weltkrieg* (Berlin: E.S. Mittler u. Sohn,1920), p. 344.

Army LZ 97, a "q" class ship, on a visit to Karlsruhe early in 1917. (Robinson)

For better or for worse, the Army airships in the west — LZ 90, LZ 97, LZ 98, and the new Schütte-Lanz SL 11, completed on August 2, 1916 — were thrown into the campaign.

The Navy was more confident. Strasser led off with a series of raids late in July and early in August which did little damage, but which, after a flight to England in Mathy's new L 31, caused him to write to Admiral Scheer:

> The performance of the big airships has reinforced my conviction that England can be overcome by means of airships, inasmuch as the country will be deprived of the means of existence through increasingly extensive destruction of cities, factory complexes, dockyards, harbour works with war and merchant ships lying therein, railways, etc. . . .
> I am well aware of the generally prevailing personnel problems, but believe that the personnel must be made available, if necessary through reduction in other areas, since the airships offer a certain means of victoriously ending the war.[19]

Intending to make "a big effort" against England in the raiding period from August 20 to September 6, Strasser brought to the North Sea the Schütte-Lanz SL 8 and SL 9 from the Baltic. Thirteen

[19] Robinson, p. xv.

naval airships were out on August 24, and for the first time in almost a year one of them reached London. This was Heinrich Mathy's L 31, whose heavy load of two 660 lb, forty 128 lb, and twenty incendiary bombs fell on Deptford, Plumstead, and Eltham. Damage of £130,000 was second only to that of Mathy's big raid on the City on September 8, 1915.

L 31 made a hard landing at Ahlhorn, with severe damage to hull and rear engine gondola which kept her grounded until September 21. Her commander's report encouraged Strasser to believe that the defences were not alert; L 31 had not been found by the searchlights until five minutes after dropping her bombs, and the first rounds were fired by the anti-aircraft guns as she was retreating into a cloud bank.

The next raid on September 2-3, 1916, was the biggest of the war, with twelve Navy airships proceeding from the North Sea bases, while four Army craft came up from the Rhineland sheds — the only time during the war that the airships of both services bombed the same target simultaneously. The first craft to approach London was the Army Schütte-Lanz SL 11 commanded by Hauptmann Wilhelm Schramm, who had been born in London thirty years earlier on December 11, 1885.[20] Three aeroplanes of No. 39 Home Defence Squadron were in the air. As SL 11 proceeded south over Littleheath, Northaw, Clayhill and Cockfosters, she came under fire from the guns of the northern defences, and turned back at Tottenham. As she retreated, she was overtaken by one of the Home Defence B.E. 2cs flown by Lieut. William Leefe Robinson. After firing three drums of ammunition from his Lewis gun, he succeeded in setting the Schütte-Lanz on fire, and she fell burning at Cuffley. All 16 of her crew were killed. Another pilot chasing SL 11 saw L 16 a mile away lit up by the glare of her consort's destruction, but the illumination gave out before he could come in range. The awful portent flaming in the sky, seen from as far away as Huntingdon and Harwich, understandably disheartened the other commanders making their approaches across Norfolk, Suffolk and Cambridgeshire. None pressed home the attack on London, and the great raid ended in defeat — one that had been inflicted by the night flying aeroplane armed with a machine gun firing incendiary and explosive ammunition.

[20] Peter Amesbury found Schramm's birth certificate at Somerset House, London, showing that he had been born on this date at 9 Victoria Road, Old Charlton, Kent, to Otto Karl Schramm and his wife Maria.

SL 10, of the Schütte-Lanz "e" type, on the field at Mannheim-Rheinau. On 28 July 1916, she vanished in the Black Sea with 16 men aboard during an attempt to bomb Sevastopol. (Luftschiffbau Schütte-Lanz)

Only Navy Zeppelins took part in the next raid on London on September 23-24, eight older craft being sent to bomb the Midlands cities, while four of the giant new "r" class crossed Belgium to attack London with the south wind behind them. L 33, making a direct flight up the Thames to East London, inflicted heavy damage, but herself was riddled by anti-aircraft fire and by an attacking aeroplane which perhaps because of gas loss, failed to set her on fire. Losing altitude, L 33's commander was forced to crash-land his ship near Little Wigborough behind Mersea Island. Though set on fire by her crew, it proved possible for the Admiralty's corps of draftsmen to make an accurate copy of L 33's design.

L 32, making a hesitant approach to London, veered off to the east, was picked up by searchlights after crossing the Thames near Purfleet, and was set on fire by one of the defending aeroplanes. The burning wreckage fell near Billericay; the crew of 22 were killed.

Only Mathy brought his ship home from London that night. Boldly crossing the capital from south to north, he used magnesium parachute flares to blind the defenders, and above a blanket of mist in the Lea Valley made his escape to the coast near Great Yarmouth. Though his report claimed that the bulk of his bombs fell on "Chelsea-Pimlico, in the City, and in Islington," most of the damage was in Brixton and Streatham.

Strasser's only concession to the destruction over London of two of the vaunted "big 6-engine ships" was to include in his orders "the limitation that caution is ordered in case of clear weather." On the night of September 25-26, this sent Mathy down-Channel to Portsmouth, though his bombs were not traced there. On the night of October 1-2 L 31 was shot down in flames by defending aircraft as she was poised to sweep across London with a 30 mph wind behind her. The crumpled carcass of the Zeppelin came to earth at Potters Bar. Mathy, who had jumped, was killed along with 18 other men. His death was a demoralizing blow to the Naval Airship Division, particularly for the ratings; "with him the life and soul of our airship service went out too." Though London was in the future to be ordered as a target for Zeppelin attack, it was bombed only once more by an airship, and then by accident.

Only one more raid was made before the end of 1916, and this was on the Midlands on the night of November 27-28, 1916. Nonetheless, a B.E. 2c of No. 36 Squadron shot down another "big 6-engine ship," the L 34, immediately after she dumped her bombs on the sea coast town of West Hartlepool. Another Zeppelin, L 21, after wandering as far south and west as Hanley and Stoke-on-Trent, was caught off Lowestoft by three Royal Naval Air Service aeroplanes as dawn was breaking and was shot down in flames in the sea. L 22 was also severely damaged by anti-aircraft fire and made an emergency landing at Hage, the nearest base.

The English defences, particularly the night-flying aeroplanes of the Royal Flying Corps, had established a clear-cut ascendancy over the hydrogen-filled Zeppelin raiders, operating at a ceiling of 12,000 to 13,000 feet. The reactions of the higher authorities in the German Army and Navy were diametrically opposed. Marshal von Hindenburg and his brilliant Chief of Staff, General Erich Ludendorff, summoned to the Army High Command on August 29, 1916, had been impressed by the disorganized state of German Army aviation and on October 8, 1916, had appointed an able administrator, General Ernst von Hoeppner, to command all elements of the *Luftstreitkräfte*. One of von Hoeppner's first decisions was to downgrade the role of the Army airship service, at least in the West, and to substitute large bombing aeroplanes. Following the fiery fall of the SL 11 at Cuffley, no more Army airships were sent to England. Having already been forbidden to cross the Western Front, the only possible mission for the Army airships in the West was to proceed down-Channel to attack ports and bases in northern France, such as Rouen, Étaples and Boulogne. A few successes were claimed, but the final attack of this series, by LZ 107 on February 16, 1917, was actually the last successful raid by an Army airship.

The Army airship service's last major effort was against Roumania, which declared war on August 27, 1916. Hostilities had been expected, and two Zeppelins were ready in the southeast, LZ 101 which had arrived at Jamboli in Bulgaria on August 3, and LZ 86 which reached Temesvar on August 24. LZ 101 made the first attack on Bucharest, the enemy capital, on the night of August 28, and followed with attacks on September 4 and 25. LZ 86 bombed the Ploesti oil fields on the night of September 4, and was wrecked when flown into the ground at high speed next morning while trying to land at Temesvar. With the rear gondola torn off, the badly damaged Zeppelin rebounded into the air and at an altitude of 300 feet, the control car and forward engine gondola plunged free, killing the nine occupants. She was promptly replaced by LZ 81, but in her second attack on Bucharest on the night of September 26, this Zeppelin was so badly shot up by anti-aircraft guns that she force-landed short of her base and had to be dismantled. LZ 97 replaced her, and together with LZ 101, under direct orders of the Army High Command, was sent against distant targets all the way from the Black Sea to the Aegean and the Italian Peninsula. LZ 97 attempted to raid Kishinev in south Russia, Valona in Albania, and Brindisi and Taranto in Italy, between January and April, 1917, but was invariably defeated by the weather. LZ 101 claimed a successful attack on March 20-21, 1917, on the British base on Mudros on the island of Lemnos in the Aegean; but failed in attempts to reach Mytilene on Lesbos, Odessa on the Black Sea, and Jassy, the temporary capital of Roumania. It is curious that the High Command did not assign one of the Army's two "big 6-engine ships" to this mission instead of the smaller "q" types, for the Jamboli shed at least could have accommodated LZ 113 or LZ 120. Instead the latter was tied down in Kovno attempting a raid on St. Petersburg that never succeeded, while the former went to the Navy base at Seddin on the Baltic.

In June, 1917, von Hoeppner decided to abolish the Army airship service. The big LZ 113 and LZ 120 were turned over to the Navy. The remainder – the Zeppelins Z XII, LZ 87, LZ 88, LZ 93, LZ 97, LZ 98, LZ 101, LZ 103, LZ 107, and LZ 111, together with the Schütte-Lanz SL 15, SL 16 and SL 17, were dismantled during August and September at Jüterbog, Schneidemühl, Dresden and other bases. The Army crews are said to have gone into bombing aeroplanes, particularly the 4 and 5 engined "Giants."

Strasser, whose influence with Admiral Scheer put him on the same policy-making level as von Hoeppner, chose the opposite course. Scheer in any case had an unassailable conviction of the High Seas Fleet's need for the Zeppelins as long-range scouting craft, and Strasser further persuaded him of the need to continue the raids on England:

> It was not on the direct material damage that the value of the airship attacks depended, but rather on the general result of the German onslaught upon England's insularity, otherwise undisturbed by war. The disturbance of transportation, the dread of the airships prevailing in wide strata of society, and above all the occupation of very considerable material and military personnel were considered outstanding reasons for continuing the attacks.[21]

Obviously, the performance of the airships must be improved if losses were not to continue at an unacceptable level. The Aviation Department of the Navy Ministry supported a high speed 7 or 8 engine design utilizing a new, streamlined power gondola with two engines driving a single large propeller through gearing, with speeds of 65½ and 67½ mph respectively. The ceiling, however, would remain as before at 13,000 feet with a full war load.

Strasser, however, wrote to the Navy Ministry on January 17, 1917, to recommend that the 2,000,000 cubic foot Zeppelins of the "r" class be lightened to enable them to climb to the unprecedented ceiling of 16,500 feet with full war load. This, he calculated, could be achieved by increasing the useful lift by 7,300 lb. About half of this could be saved by substituting the streamlined 2-engine gondola with the single propeller for the ungainly 3-engine after car. Much of the remainder could be saved by making the hull frame lighter. Ten days after he wrote the letter, Strasser appeared at a conference in Berlin called by Admiral Starke, the head of the Dockyard Bureau (which included the Aviation Department). Others present included Drs. Dürr and Dörr of the Zeppelin Company, and Starke's technical expert, the brilliant Marine-Schiffbaumeister Engberding. With little

[21] Walter Gladisch, *Der Krieg in der Nordsee,* vol. VI (Berlin: E.S. Mittler u. Sohn, 1937), p. 290.

argument, the conference accepted the "Front" point of view as represented by Strasser, and ordered the appointment of a commission which would embody in a ship building at Friedrichshafen the following improvements:

(1) Substitution of the 2-engine gondola with one direct drive propeller for the 3-engine rear gondola, (2) Reduction of fuel tankage to a 30 hour instead of a 36 hour supply, (3) Removal of all machine guns, of the forward and after platforms, and of the gun mounts, (4) Reduction of the bomb releases by half, leaving eight for 660 lb bombs, sixteen for 220 lb bombs, and 60 for incendiary bombs, (5) Lightened design of hull girders, (6) Design of a new, smaller control car, (7) Complete elimination of crew's quarters and comforts.

On his return to Nordholz Strasser ordered the immediate application of the conference's recommendations to the four newest airships, L 35, L 36, L 39 and L 40. One engine in the rear gondola, and all port side bomb releases were removed. The weight reduction ranged from 4,070 lb. to 4,890 lb. Brief altitude trials with simulated war loads gave ceilings between 16,100 and 17,100 feet. L 42, the first ship built to the recommendations of the January conference, was commissioned in Friedrichshafen on February 28, 1917. The hull in this ship, and in her sister L 43 − the only representatives of the "s" class − was practically identical with that of their "r" class predecessors. The stern engine in the rear car was omitted (the other two still driving propellers on outriggers), the port side bomb releases and bomb bay doors were not installed, machine-gun mounts and gun platforms were suppressed, and to hamper the English searchlights, the underside of the hull, gondolas and fins were painted black. On March 10, L 42 with Strasser aboard reached 19,700 feet in an altitude trial.

L 44, first of the two-ship "t" class, completed at Löwenthal on April 1, 1917 with a redesigned and lightened hull frame and the first streamlined twin-engined after gondola with one propeller. During the summer and autumn the new gondola was fitted to all surviving Zeppelins in place of the old after engine car with the outrigger propellers. L 46, the second "t", introduced streamlined midships power cars. A smaller, lighter control car in L 48, the first of five "u"s, made her 2,430 lb. lighter than L 46. On August 21, 1917, there was commissioned L 53, the first of the "v" type, of which ten were built. With a major change in hull structure, the "v"s had their nine largest hull frames spaced 15 instead of 10 metres apart. L 53

L 42 under major overhaul at Nordholz. Outer cover and gondolas removed, gas cells still in place but partly empty, and framework suspended from hangar roof. Fire ladder was much used for work on the outside of the Zeppelins. (Friedrich Moch)

reached 20,700 feet on her first raid. The "v" class — too lightly built to withstand full speed manoeuvres at low altitude — remained the standard type in the North Sea until nearly a year later.

With these lightened high altitude craft, Strasser achieved his major aim: the "height-climbers," as the British called them, raiding at altitudes of 16,000 to 20,000 feet, at one stroke rendered obsolete the entire British defence system. Only twice before the Armistice were any more Zeppelins shot down by aircraft in raids on England, and the anti-aircraft guns had no further successes.

But the high altitude performance of the new Zeppelins brought new and largely unforseen difficulties which sharply reduced the frequency of the raids. Navigation was more uncertain because the Zeppelins were frequently flying above solid cloud with no sight of the ground. Radio bearings became increasingly important, but with eight or ten ships in the air at one time, all calling for bearings every hour or oftener, the pandemonium in the ether sometimes beggared description. Not until early 1918 was a "passive" system introduced, whereby ther ships remained silent and took bearings on signals transmitted twice an hour from Tondern and Cleve in the Rhineland. Further, above 15,000 feet it was discovered that northerly gales could be blowing undetected by pilot balloons limited to lower levels. At high altitudes it was even harder to battle such fierce air currents, as the low oxygen content caused the engines to lose half their power. Ships capable of attaining 62 mph at sea level were reduced to 45 mph at 20,000 feet.

The flight crews suffered cruelly in every raid from oxygen deficiency, and above all, from the bitter cold. Oxygen was provided in steel flasks at all flight stations, but there was no overall doctrine concerning its use. Individual commanders, through painfully acquired experience, came to order its use for all personnel above 16,000 feet.[22] There were complaints of illness caused by impurities in the compressed oxygen, and in the early autumn of 1917 it was replaced by flasks of liquid air. Subzero temperatures going as low as $-27.5°$ F. at 20,000 feet in winter, caused frostbite, stiffened joints and dulled the senses, so that even simple activities were slowly and clumsily executed. Very little could be done about the cold except to bundle on more clothing, and many men wore layers of newspaper under their fur lined leather flight suits.

Still another, though little known reason, for a decrease in frequency of the raids was the supply of hydrogen gas. The crux of the problem was the enormous expenditure of gas by the 2,000,000 cubic foot ships in high altitude operations. In order to maintain the purity of the hydrogen and to lessen the danger of explosion, the airships had to be refilled to 100 per cent fullness after each flight, and thereafter the cells were maintained at a slight positive pressure by daily servicing, to prevent the inward diffusion of air. Yet to refill one of the standard Zeppelins to 100 per cent fullness after a high altitude flight required over a million cubic feet of hydrogen. After one raid on England in September, 1917, the six Ahlhorn ships required a total of slightly less than 6,000,000 cubic feet of hydrogen to replace what they had blown off during their ascent to high altitude.

Each of the larger bases had its own gas works, that at Ahlhorn producing in 1917 1,060,000 cubic feet of hydrogen daily. The

[22] This is within the "disturbance stage" as defined today by the United States Air Force, which directs the use of oxygen by all personnel above 12,000 feet, and above 10,000 feet on long flights.

same amount could be stored at atmospheric pressure in a conventional above-ground gas holder, while buried in the earth were numerous large steel flasks holding 4,400,000 cubic feet of hydrogen at 100 atmospheres' pressure. A further bottleneck was the capacity of the compressor which filled the high pressure store. At Ahlhorn it could handle 425,000 cubic feet of gas daily, and thus it required about ten days to refill all the high-pressure flasks. With six big ships based at Ahlhorn this was not enough, and hydrogen was imported from the Zeppelin plant at Staaken in forty railroad tank cars, whose high-pressure cylinders held a total of 2,120,000 cubic feet of gas at 100 atmospheres' pressure. Other bases were even less capable of meeting their own needs. Demand and supply were balanced most precariously, and in the summer of 1917 an explosion at the gas plant at Seddin in the Baltic forced Strasser to curtail reconnaissances in the North Sea, as part of the Nordholz and Ahlhorn output of hydrogen had to be sent east by rail.

Not until March 16, 1917, did five of the "height climbers" set out to raid England with bomb loads of 3500 to 4000 lb., lighter than in the previous year. The defences, including the night-flying aeroplanes, were unable to reach the Zeppelins, which crossed England at 17,000 to 19,000 feet. On the other hand, with a cloud deck beneath, the Zeppelin commanders had little idea of their position. Two claimed to have bombed London, but none came closer than Canterbury in Kent, and there were no casualties. The bomb damage totalled only £163. On the other hand, a north-westerly gale of 45 mph was blowing at 12,500 feet, unpredicted by the German weather service whose westernmost station, at Bruges in Belgium, had made no observations above 3300 feet. All but one of the Zeppelins were blown over France and all had difficulty in reaching safety. L 35, warned of storm conditions in north Germany, went all the way to Dresden, where she was severely damaged landing in a 40 mph wind. L40, after orienting herself near Bonn in the Rhineland, made it back to Ahlhorn with only 133 gallons of fuel remaining. L 41 likewise returned to Ahlhorn via a southerly route after nearly 27 hours in the air. L 42, with only four engines working, failed to reach England and was carried inland stern-first over Ostend by the north wind. She landed at Jüterbog near Berlin with only 1 hour of fuel on board. L 39 never made it home. Undoubtedly a victim of engine breakdowns, she was carried south-east nearly to Paris, then struggled north-east for an hour until another engine failure must have occurred, for once more she drifted south-east. At dawn she appeared over Compiègne and was set on fire by anti-aircraft shells. Seventeen men were killed.

The next raid on May 23-24 by six ships was against London, but again none reached the target. L 43 claimed to have done so, but L 42 came closest to the capital, and this was at Braintree. All the Zeppelins were carried northward across Suffolk and Norfolk by a south-west wind, and one man was killed and £599 damage done in the raid. Again the conditions at high altitude were almost too much for the Zeppelin crews. L 44, with Strasser aboard, suffered failure of all five engines over the enemy's country and fell from 18,700 to 12,800 feet. She limped home on two to three engines, and did not reach Nordholz until 6 p.m. on the 24th. L 42 flew through a squall line on her way home and was struck three times by lightning, but with little damage. Due to altitude sickness, personnel in her rear engine gondola were unable to repair a stopped engine or to drain its radiator before it froze solid.

The next raid on England on June 16-17, 1917, invited disaster, for the shortest night of the year was only five days away. For reasons unknown even to Martin Dietrich, who took part in the attack, Strasser ordered six ships to "attack in south, London." Only two of them reached England, Dietrich in L 42 bombing Ramsgate and blowing up an ammunition store. The new L 48, carrying Strasser's deputy, Korvettenkapitän Viktor Schütze, was shot down by an aeroplane after dropping her bombs ineffectively near Harwich. Because the wreck fell slowly in a near horizontal attitude, three men survived – the executive officer, Otto Mieth, who suffered two broken legs; machinists' mates Heinrich Ellerkamm who was uninjured, and Wilhelm Uecker, who died of his severe injuries on Armistice Day, 1918. Never before or after did any of Strasser's men ride down to earth with two million cubic feet of blazing hydrogen and live to tell the tale.[23]

Meanwhile a new British development forced the Zeppelins to make their daytime reconnaissance flights at high altitude – the long range twin engine flying boat, the Curtiss "Large America", which began to arrive at the RNAS stations at Great Yarmouth and Felixstowe in April and May, 1917. Sent out on the basis of radio intelligence, one of these shot down L 22 off Terschelling on May 14, 1917. Similarly another "Large America" shot down L 43

---

[23] Parachutes were issued to naval airship flight crews for a few months early in 1917, and then withdrawn because of their weight. Flight personnel had no faith in them, and no drops were ever made from a naval airship even in practice.

off Vlieland on June 14. An unsuccessful attack on L 46 on the same day revealed the secret, and the patrolling Zeppelins were now ordered to maintain an altitude of 13,000 feet. From this height it was impossible to detect or disturb submerged British submarines. The mine flights also had to be given up, as the Zeppelins could not possibly see the English "eggs" beneath the surface from two and half miles in the air. The flying boats henceforth won no further successes; but they had greatly diminished the value of the airships for their primary function of fleet reconnaissance.

Two more ineffective raids took place on the Midlands in August and September, with eight and nine ships participating. Then, on October 19, 1917, came the last big attack of the war, eleven Zeppelins being sent out to "attack middle England, industrial region of Sheffield, Manchester, Liverpool, etc." The weather over the North Sea appeared favorable, but as the Zeppelins rose to 16,000 feet on approaching England, their commanders found the wind veering towards the north, and rapidly freshening. Only one airship, L 54, reached home via the North Sea after touching the Norfolk coast, and this because her commander flew no higher than 5000 feet. The remainder, whirled south in the gale, found themselves battling desperately for survival against the wind which veered on to the north-north-east, blowing at 45 to 50 mph.

L 46's crew, from over Norfolk, could see at one glance from 19,400 feet the guns firing at Harwich, along the Thames, and even on the Western Front in Flanders, so clear was the night. Descending to 11,500 feet, the Zeppelin flew across Holland above a solid cloud deck to return to Ahlhorn. L 47, blown stern-first across the Midlands, was unable to aim her bombs accurately at Nottingham, for as pointed out by her executive officer, Walther Fischer, the bomb sight in the bow of the control car could not be aimed at the city approaching from astern! L 47 came home along the Dutch coast at an altitude of 3300 feet, and landed at Ahlhorn with only 98 gallons of fuel on board.

Other ships penetrated farther inland, and made their way home across France. Hauptmann Manger[24] in the oldest ship, the L 41, made the longest flight over England. L 41's bombs damaged the Austin Motor Works at Longbridge near Birmingham, but her commander thought he was attacking Manchester! Crossing the

[24] An Army officer commanding a Navy airship and crew, Manger came to the Naval Airship Division in March, 1915, when the Army Parseval PL 25 was assigned to the Navy complete with Army flight crew.

Western Front at La Bassée, L 41 returned across occupied Belgium to Ahlhorn.

L 53's commander believed he had bombed Birmingham and London, but was so uncertain of his position that he submitted no track chart with his raid report. L 53 was carried far to the south-east by the gale and crossed the Front near Nancy in Lorraine; she returned to Nordholz after a flight of 27 hours and 25 minutes. L 52, coming inland over the Humber, skirted the eastern edge of London and dropped bombs on Hertford and Waltham Marshes; carried by the gale into Lorraine she crossed the Front at St. Dié. Being short of fuel she landed at Ahlhorn instead of her home base at Wittmundhaven.

L 55, the newest ship in the raid and the second of the "v" type, did little damage in her progress south from the Humber. Passing west of London, she dropped bombs on Hitchin and Hatfield. Leaving Amiens to port, her commander, Kapitänleutnant Flemming, headed east and crossed the Western Front between St. Quentin and Rheims. At 8.40 am, sighting two aeroplanes to the north, he turned southeast and "climbed to 7,300 metres (24,000 feet) to make the ship heavy at the same time." Thus casually did Flemming record the greatest altitude reached by an airship in history! At 10.45 am Flemming believed he passed Maastricht on the Meuse, and shortly afterwards believed he was over Aachen, whence he steered north-north-east by compass above the overcast for Ahlhorn. In fact, L 55 had passed Mainz on the Rhine and had taken her departure from Darmstadt, 125 miles east-south-east of Aachen. The result was that when she descended late in the afternoon to look for Ahlhorn, she was in fact over the wooded hills of Thuringia. Since fuel for only two hours remained on board, a forced landing was made at Tiefenort-an-der-Werra. Badly damaged in the landing, L 55 had to be dismantled.

Others failed to make it home. L 44, likewise carried south-east to Lorraine, was overtaken by dawn on the wrong side of the trenches. French anti-aircraft guns set her afire at 19,000 feet and she fell burning at St. Clément near Nancy; all 18 of her crew were killed. Following her came L 49, so hopelessly lost that her commander, witnessing L 44's destruction, thought she had been shot down by Dutch anti-aircraft guns. Turning away from the Front, L 49 was harassed by French Nieuports which forced her to land at Bourbonne-les-Bains. The crew were captured before they could set fire to the airship, and before she was dismantled, L 49's design was copied in detail and distributed to the Allied powers.

L 50, also close by when L 44 was destroyed, turned away and flew west in broad daylight at 6500 feet as far as Tonnerre, 125 miles from the Front. Returning east, her commander saw L 49 on the ground and decided, according to his report, that he would destroy his ship by driving her vertically into the ground to crumple up her bows "like an accordion." Actually L 50 struck the ground in a more horizontal attitude, wiping off the control car and forward gondola, while several men jumped from the side gondolas. The wreck then ascended to 23,000 feet and drifted with the wind across Franche-Comté, Dauphine and Provence, to disappear over the Mediterranean off Fréjus. The derelict was never seen again, nor were four of her crewmen who were carried up with her, either injured or so disabled by altitude sickness that they could not valve gas and save themselves.

Lastly, Kapitänleutnant Kölle's L 45 made a remarkable journey "from Denmark to the Riviera by way of London and Paris in twenty hours," as one of her men put it. Coming in most northerly of the raiding Zeppelins, north of Flamborough Head, she dropped some bombs on Northampton, and then, a half hour before midnight, her astonished crew realized they were driving straight across London before the gale. A 660 pounder descended in Piccadilly Circus, and two more 660 pounders caused heavy casualties in Camberwell and Hither Green; in fact, most of the damage and casualties of the raid were caused by Kolle's bombs. Repeated engine failures, caused by altitude sickness in the crew, resulted in two of L 45's engines freezing up, and the ship drove south. At 8 a.m. Kölle realized she was crossing Lyons. An attempt was made to reach Switzerland (later Kölle regretted he had not accepted the suggestion of his warrant quartermaster that he run with the wind towards Spain), but when a third engine failed the ship again drifted south. Landing the Zeppelin in a river bed, Kölle's crew set her afire before surrendering.

Five Zeppelins out of 11 had been lost, due directly to the failure of the German weather forecasting system to predict the northerly gale at high altitude. Furthermore, Strasser, directing the raid from his headquarters at Ahlhorn, failed to issue a general recall order when he recognized the rapid southerly drift of the airships. Had he been aboard one of the airships, as was his usual custom, Strasser would surely have recognized early the development of the northerly gale in the upper air, and would have ordered the squadron back before reaching England. The loss of engine power at high altitude contributed to the helplessness with which the Zeppelins drifted before the gale, as did the effects of cold and high altitude on the crews.

The power loss at high altitude had been foreseen, and on November 3, 1917, the new L 58 arrived at Ahlhorn fitted with the first Maybach Mb IVa "altitude motors." While not supercharged, these engines, with oversize cylinders and a compression ratio of 6.08 to 1, could not be run at full throttle below 5900 feet. Below this altitude they produced a constant 245 hp, and at 19,700 feet still delivered 142 hp. With the Mb IVas, L 58 attained 67 mph at sea level, and 60 mph at 19,700 feet.

Then, on the afternoon of January 5, 1918, came a shocking disaster, when five airships − L 46, L 47, L 51, L 58 and the big SL 20 − blew up and burned at Ahlhorn in the space of a few minutes, demolishing two of the huge double hangars which housed them, and badly damaging the other two. The cause of the disaster was never definitely ascertained, though the fire began in or beneath the after gondola of L 51. There were many rumours of sabotage, but the Court of Inquiry concluded that an asbestos slab from the hangar roof had fallen through the hull of L 51, smashing a petrol tank and striking sparks which ignited the petrol pouring down on the hangar floor.

Replacements would be slow in coming, for in the summer of 1917 a dispute on the allotment of Germany's scarce supply of aluminium had gone against Scheer and Strasser. Heretofore the German Navy had been commissioning an average of two new Zeppelins per month. Now General Ludendorff, concerned with the need to expand aircraft production in anticipation of America's participation in the war, demanded that the Navy's airship program be halted completely to conserve aluminium and rubber. Scheer insisted that one Zeppelin per month would still be needed to maintain an adequate scouting force and to continue the raids on northern and central England, which he contended relieved some of the pressure on the Army in France. Should the raids be abandoned, "½ ship per month" would still have to be delivered to replace losses. The Kaiser, who had recently ruled that the Zeppelins should undertake raids only exceptionally and in unusually favorable circumstances, ruled in favour of "½ ship per month" for the Naval Airship Division.

One effect of this decree was that the Zeppelin works at Staaken discontinued airship production. The last of twelve Zeppelins built here was L 64, commissioned on March 13, 1918. The Staaken works were increasingly occupied with producing the Zeppelin-Staaken "Giant" four and five engine bombers, the only "Giant" aircraft to see combat service, which were likewise built under license by Schütte-Lanz, Albatros and Aviatik. The Schütte-Lanz Zeesen works likewise discontinued airship production with the delivery on November 26, 1917, of the SL 21, the last of three airships built there. The six Schütte-Lanz-built Staaken "Giant" bombers were constructed at Zeesen.

There were three raids on England in March and April, 1918, with five Zeppelins participating at most. Little was accomplished, but again the impotence of the defences was demonstrated, as the height-climbers of the "v" class, carrying over 6000 lb. of bombs, moved at will across the Midlands at altitudes of 21,000 feet or more. The last raid of the series on April 12, 1918, gave the country a scare: for the first time in the war, Liverpool was nearly bombed, as L 61 came within ten miles of the seaport before turning north and attacking Wigan, which her commander mistook for Sheffield. L 62 dropped 2½ tons of bombs near Coventry and Birmingham, and in the only victory of the war by an airship over a defending aeroplane, drove off an F.E. 2b of No. 38 Squadron with the pilot wounded in the head.

One new Zeppelin design entered service before war's end. As a result of the disaster in the October, 1917, raid, Strasser on December 10, 1917, urged the construction of a lengthened high speed craft with 7 engines. In April, 1918, Admiral Starke ordered the construction of four lengthened craft of 2,190,000 cubic foot capacity of 2,195,800 cubic feet, and carried seven of the Maybach about June 1. Not until July 1, however, did L 70, the first of the new "x" class, make her first flight at Friedrichshafen. Fundamentally a height climber of the "v" class with an extra 15 metre gas cell amidships, she was 693 feet 11 inches long with a gas capacity of 2,195,800 cubic feet, and crried seven of the Maybach Mb IVa "altitude motors." One was in the forward engine car and two in the rear gondola, and the remaining four in two pairs of tiny gondolas amidships, measuring not more than 12½ feet long. The fins were of thick cantilever section, eliminating much of the external wire bracing. On her trials L 70 reached 19,700 feet statically and 23,000 feet dynamically. Her maximum trial speed was 81 mph, making her the fastest airship built up to that time. It was intended that she should carry from 6,600 lb of bombs in raids on London to

10,500 lb in lower-level attacks on the industrial Midlands. In the
control car were mounted a pair of Becker 20 mm cannon — resembling the later Oerlikon — whose ball, tracer and explosive ammunition outranged the rifle caliber machine guns carried in aircraft.

Strasser waxed enthusiastic as always, hailing the new L 70 as "the
final type." Admiral Starke argued the contrary, and over Strasser's
protests, ordered a craft of still higher ceiling, the experimental
L 100 (LZ 115). This was to be a six-engined Zeppelin of 2,648,250
cubic feet, 743 feet long and 82 feet 5 inches in diameter. Her
anticipated dynamic ceiling was 27,150 feet. She was due to
complete in Friedrichshafen on November 1, 1918, but little work
was ever done on her.

Events swiftly demonstrated that Admiral Starke's doubts were all
too well justified. On July 19, 1918, the British Grand Fleet chose
the airship sheds at Tondern for the first demonstration of the
aircraft carrier against a land target. Seven Sopwith Camels, flown off
the flight deck of HMS "Furious," bombed the big "Toska" hangar
and burned L 54 and L 60. Until the Armistice the Naval Airship
Division lived in constant fear of a similar attack on one of the other
bases.

On August 5, 1918, Strasser ordered five Zeppelins out to "attack
on the south or middle (London only at order of Leader of
Airships)." He himself embarked in L 70. Unrealistic optimism was
the mood aboard the flagship, commanded by Kapitänleutnant von
Lossnitzer, a favorite of Strasser's with no combat experience in the
North Sea. A light east wind, together with Strasser's contempt for
the English defences, brought the raiding flotilla at an altitude of
only 16,500 feet to within sight of the English coast at early twilight.
Thirteen aircraft promptly ascended from the Great Yarmouth air
station, and as the squadron commander, Major Egbert Cadbury,
with the station executive officer, Captain Robert Leckie, climbed
seaward in a powerful Rolls Royce De Haviland DH 4, they were
astounded to see three Zeppelins silhouetted against the bright
evening sky to the north. At 2215, having climbed nearly to the same
altitude as the leading Zeppelin, Cadbury attacked her on an
opposite course and below. Leckie aimed his gun at the Zeppelin's
bow and the stream of incendiary and tracer was seen to enter the
giant hull three-quarters of the way aft. The Zeppelin burst into
flames, then plunged seaward, breaking in two as the wreckage
descended into the clouds far below. Cadbury turned to pursue her
two consorts, now fleeing to the east, but as they attacked one of

them, Leckie's gun jammed and could not be cleared. Otherwise the second airship would certainly have been destroyed likewise.

The doomed raider was L 70, and with her perished Fregatten-kapitän Strasser and 21 officers and men. The wreckage fell in eight fathoms of water near the Blakeney Overfalls bell buoy, and during a secret salvage operation between August 9 and September 22, much of the wreckage was recovered, together with many bodies including Strasser's and von Lossnitzer's; these were buried at sea. The wreckage itself, and a notebook found on von Lossnitzer's body, provided a wealth of information on the new design, while a dispatch case full of documents recovered in the control car undoubtedly proved of great interest to naval intelligence.

The second ship was L 65, which returned home with difficulty, having been badly holed in many of her gas cells. Since Leckie had fired only a few rounds at her, this damage must have been inflicted by a Great Yarmouth DH 9 which was lost at sea with her crew. No bombs fell on land, though the airship commanders claimed to have bombed King's Lynn, Boston, Spurn Point and Norwich, on the basis of radio bearings. Only L 56 was briefly over land near Lowestoft.

Six days later L 53, out on daylight patrol between Terschelling and the Dogger Bank South Lightship, was shot down in flames from 19,000 feet by a Sopwith Camel brought into the Bight on a lighter towed by one of the Harwich Force destroyers. For the second time it was proved that even the latest Zeppelins could be overtaken and destroyed at high altitude by high performance aeroplanes. Once again it was proposed to increase the ceiling of the Zeppelins still further. At a conference at the Navy Ministry on September 7, 1918, it was voted to lengthen and increase the gas volume of the L 71, completed on July 29, and of the L 72 under construction,[25] as well as later ships of the L 70 class. Further, the earlier L 100 design was to be discarded and replaced by a much larger L 100 approximating in size to the later "Graf Zeppelin." This ship would have been 780 feet 10 inches long, 96 feet 6 inches in diameter, displacing 3,813,480 cubic feet, with ten Maybach "altitude motors." She was expected to reach 26,200 feet statically, and 28,600 feet dynamically.

---

[25] I should like to set at rest once and for all the oft-repeated legend that L 72 was built expressly to bomb New York. When the American Colonel William N. Hensley visited Friedrichshafen in August, 1919, Captain Ernst Lehmann of the Zeppelin Company showed him the L 72 at Löwenthal and bragged that she had been built to bomb New York. The gullible Hensley accepted and reported this canard as gospel truth and it so appears in airship "histories" to this date. L 72, like the other ships of her class, was of course built solely for North Sea patrols and raids on England.

On September 18, 1918, contracts were in the hands of the Zeppelin Company for the following ships:

LZ 114   L 72 to complete Oct. 1, 1918, in Löwenthal
(LZ 115   L 100 cancelled)
LZ 116   L 73 to complete Dec. 5, 1918, in Löwenthal
LZ 117   L 74 to complete Feb. 15, 1919, in Löwenthal
LZ 118   L 75 to complete   ?   in Löwenthal
LZ 119   L 100 to complete June 1919 in Friedrichshafen

Yet with Strasser dead, the Naval Airship Division was finished as a fighting service. Scheer, his supporter, had been made Chief of the Naval Staff on August 11 and had vanished into the higher reaches of Imperial Headquarters at Spa. Hipper, succeeding him in command of the High Seas Fleet, clearly saw the airship relegated to a supplementary role while he expected large seaplanes to take over the patrol of the eastern North Sea. In fact, no scouting flights were made following the loss of L 53 until October 12, when L 63 and L 65 were out covering an operation by four battleships of the High Seas Fleet.

Korvettenkapitän Werther, succeeding Strasser as Leader of Airships, accepted the fact that they would play a minor role in 1919. On October 2 he wrote that he expected to operate with only seven "Front" ships, L 56, L 61, L 63, L 64, L 65, L 71 and L 72. L 42 and L 52 would serve as school ships. Only Nordholz and Ahlhorn, in each of which two giant double sheds had been completed in 1918, would remain in "Front" service. The new L 100 was cancelled on October 6, as was L 75 on November 2.

The Schütte-Lanz firm was still attempting to compete with their Zeppelin rivals, but with little success. They were late with the "f" type, five-engined craft of 1,989,700 cubic feet, designed to compete with the "big 6-engine ships" of the "r" class, and the first one, SL 20, did not make her first flight until September 10, 1917. She was accepted by the Navy, but her performance was inferior, with a useful load 11,250 lb less than that of L 55, her Zeppelin-built contemporary. Dr. Roeser of the Schütte-Lanz Company admitted that:

With smaller forces the wooden construction is extraordinarily favorable, but with larger forces – as in larger ships – duralumin is superior to wood . . . With the "f" type the useful load, compared with that of the Zeppelins of the same size, was 1 to 4 tons less, a sign that the most favorable size for ships with wooden hulls had already been exceeded.[26]

[26] *Der Luftschiffbau Schütte-Lanz*, 1909-1925, p. 146.

SL 21, the second "f" class ship destined for the Army, was completed on November 26, 1917, after the Army airship service was disbanded. Strasser was not interested in her, and between February 21 and 28, 1918, her stripped framework was progressively tested to destruction in the hangar at Zeesen in a series of loading experiments. The last "f" class ship, SL 22, was the last airship built by the Schütte-Lanz firm. Completed for the Navy in Rheinau on June 5, 1918, she was refused by Strasser, to the dismay of the Naval Staff and the Ministry of Finance. After visiting Nordholz and Wildeshausen against Strasser's wishes, she ended her days in Jüterbog.

It was past time for the Schütte-Lanz firm to switch from wood to metal, and following the completion of SL 22, the first of two ships of the "g" class was commenced in the Rheinau shed. These craft were to be built of duralumin tube girders, as described previously. The "g 1" (SL 23) was to have been 662 feet 9 inches long, 83 feet 4 inches in diameter, and with 2,252,800 cubic feet of hydrogen in 14 gas cells. Eight "altitude motors" were to have been carried in four twin-engine gondolas. Though larger than SL 22, the duralumin hull frame of SL 23 was calculated to be 15,300 lb lighter. However it was the "g 2" (SL 24) which was laid down first. Lengthened by two 15 metre gas cells, this craft was to have had a capacity of 2,754,200 cubic feet. Though SL 24 is said by some authorities to have been completed at the Armistice, and then destroyed to prevent capture by the French, I am satisfied after correspondence with surviving officials of the firm that the framework was only partly erected.

The Schütte-Lanz firm was not invited to the September 7 conference at the Navy Ministry, but prepared a design for the "h" type to compete with the Zeppelin firm's big L 100. She was to have been 782 feet 6 inches long, 99 feet 9 inches in diameter, and would have had a gas capacity of 3,964,250 cubic feet with ten engines. She remained only a paper design.

With the building sheds in Rheinau and Zeesen demolished in 1921 by order of the Inter-Allied Commission of Control, the Schütte-Lanz firm made no further effort to build rigid airships in Germany. They kept their design staff together for some years and made determined efforts to raise capital in America for construction of large transatlantic airships, even offering a design by Dr. Schütte in a 1928 United States Navy airship competition, but nothing came of these efforts. In 1922 the Mannheim firm, hoping to capitalize on their experience with new techniques in fabricating plywood, was reorganized as the *Schütte-Lanz Holzwerke G.m.b.H.* The firm exists today in Rheinau as a large producer of plywood, but is still known colloquially to Mannheimers as "the airship works."

With the signing of the Armistice, the Navy's sixteen surviving airships were hung up in their sheds and deflated. At Versailles, the Allied powers debated how to divide them up among themselves. Two days after the scuttling of the High Seas Fleet at Scapa Flow on June 21, 1919, groups of conspirators consisting of former flight crew members destroyed all the Zeppelins at Nordholz, and two of those at Wittmundhaven. The Allies demanded the remainder, and in the summer and fall of 1920 the LZ 113 and L 72 went to France, L 71 and L 64 to England, and L 61 and LZ 120 to Italy. Belgium received L 30, but had her dismantled at Seerappen. Japan was awarded L 37, but her new owners broke her up at Seddin and merely saved important parts. SL 22 was dismantled at Jüterbog and specimens of her structure were distributed among all the victorious powers. All the Army and Navy sheds, and even the building sheds, were ordered demolished by the Interallied Commission of Control; the work was done by German contractors during 1921. Some of the sheds were delivered in pieces to the Allies, but only the Jüterbog hangar was re-erected, at Kasumigaura in Japan where it housed the "Graf Zeppelin" in 1929 on her world flight. For various reasons the three Zeppelin building sheds in Friedrichshafen were spared, together with one building shed at Staaken, and the small hangar at Seddin-bei-Stolp.

Of all the surrendered Zeppelins, only one, the L 72, in the hands of the French Navy's Lieutenant de Vaisseau Jean du Plessis de Grenedan, accomplished anything of note, of which more later. Post-war apathy and economic stringency resulted in the remainder becoming "hangar queens." In addition, after two years of neglect, the ships were in bad condition, particularly their gas cells. Lastly, they were unsuited for any peace-time commercial employment, having been designed expressly for bombing from great altitudes, and so lightly built that only highly trained crews could fly them safely.

The hydrogen-inflated rigid airship ended World War I completely discredited as a combat weapon, even in Germany, where 106 were completed during the conflict. Only the United States would procure them in the future for military purposes, and the United States had a monopoly of the non-inflammable lifting gas, helium. In the early days of the war the Zeppelin possessed a real potential as a weapon of aerial superiority. With low-powered and unreliable engines, the aeroplane could not then lift from the ground enough fuel to fly for extended periods, while the rigid airship, supported in the air by buoyant gas and using its engines only for forward motion, could carry quantities of fuel and had an endurance of several days. Yet the Zeppelin had failed to realize its potential as a war-winning weapon, and this was clear even to its most ardent supporters – the German people – by the end of 1916. The hated enemies' cities were not lying in ruins, their populations were not cowering in abject terror, their leaders were not begging for peace; in fact, minimal damage had been done in the bombing raids, at enormous cost in resources and personnel. The Army was well justified in dismantling its airships in mid-1917. The Navy might have been well advised to do the same, but continued to procure Zeppelins because of Strasser's fanatic belief in them, and Scheer's exaggerated opinion of their value as scouts.

A very large amount of technical and operating knowledge had been obtained, however, and the design staffs of the Zeppelin and Schütte-Lanz concerns, together with the naval architects and engineers of the Navy Ministry connected with airship activities, constituted a large reservoir of talent. Furthermore, the wartime services had trained at least a thousand men as Army and Navy flight crews. One conspicuous feat – a 95 hour flight covering 4200 miles from Jamboli in Bulgaria to Khartoum and back – had demonstrated the possibility of the large rigid airship in intercontinental commerce.[27] With the still primitive state of the aeroplane, the rigid airship was seen as the only vehicle capable of crossing the oceans and linking the continents by air.

[27] The flight of L 59 to Africa in November 1917 with 15 tons of supplies for German troops under General von Lettow-Vorbeck will be dealt with in Chapter VII.

V
The imitators: British military rigids

Great Britain was second only to Germany in the number of rigid airships built, a total of 15 being completed during the 1908-21 period considered in this chapter. The official British attitude towards the rigid airship reveals a painful, even insoluble ambivalence: on the one hand during the war years the official and popular press propaganda (encouraged by the success of defending R.F.C. aircraft against the London raiders in the autumn of 1916) alleged that the German Zeppelins were overrated, clumsy, ridiculous, and a great waste of German resources; while on the other hand, and secretly, the British Navy in particular, through its Intelligence Department, revealed an insatiable curiosity and envy concerning the German weapon of air superiority. The pitiful crushed wreckage of the Zeppelins brought down over England was searched and researched with a thoroughness which one is tempted to label Teutonic. Zeppelin crewmen taken prisoner were questioned again and again to extract the last morsel of operational and technical information. In one case, involving an elaborate masquerade, a German-speaking British officer disguised as a sick German officer for ten days shared the hospital room of an injured Zeppelin officer survivor in a vain attempt to obtain information.[1] British agents also engaged in extensive espionage inside Germany to obtain Zeppelin secrets. Major Trench, the head of Admiral Hall's German section in the Division of Naval Intelligence, boasted to a captured Zeppelin commander that during the war he had spent a day in Friedrichshafen,[2] while there is much evidence that selected German Navy ratings in key positions were bribed to supply information.[3] And as will be related in due course, two of the British

[1] Public Records Office, Air 1/540. The German officer was Leut.z.S. Otto Mieth, the executive officer of L 48, shot down at Theberton, Suffolk, on June 17, 1917.

[2] Robinson, p. 186.

[3] v. the highly detailed maps of the German naval airship bases at Nordholz, Wittmundhaven, Ahlhorn and Tondern in Air Ministry (Confidential), *Enemy Aircraft North Sea and Baltic, 1918* (this was in the days before long range aerial photo reconnaissance!). In *U-Boat Intelligence* (London: Putnam, 1969), p. 175, Robert M. Grant relates how three ratings at V U-Boat Flotilla Headquarters in Bremerhaven fled to Holland and delivered to Allied Intelligence the War Diaries of submarines in the flotilla.

wartime rigids were built to plans smuggled out of Germany by a former Schütte-Lanz employee.

The object of all this effort — and only the Royal Navy was involved — was to create in imitation of the Germans a fleet of large shore based rigid airships to scout in the North Sea for the Grand Fleet. (Had the programme been successful, other rigids would undoubtedly have patrolled the Atlantic approaches to England to escort convoys and attack German U-boats). Particularly after Jutland and the Sunderland Operation of 1916, during which it had been helpless to shake off shadowing Zeppelins, the Grand Fleet and its leaders developed an exaggerated estimate of the value to their enemies of the large gasbags in the sky, and an obsession concerning their own need to match them. Had earlier programmes been energetically and persistently pursued, the Royal Navy might have possessed such long range aerial scouts by 1916. Instead, the grandiose programme undertaken in November, 1916, was too late to produce results before the Armistice. In fact, in late 1916 the first British rigid to fly had barely been completed, and she was more or less a copy of the unlucky German Army Zeppelin Z IV which had made the forced landing at Lunéville in France in April, 1913. The Germans, at this time, were producing the 2,000,000 cubic foot "super-Zeppelins" at the rate of two per month.

That the German military rigid programme was a success (at least technically and numerically) and the British one a failure reflects profound differences in the attitude of the two countries towards the big airship. At no time was there in England any public enthusiasm or interest in the big rigids; on the contrary, British success in building over 200 small pressure airships during the war militated against the acceptance of the rigid. The latter, it is true, had its advocates in the Royal Navy in such men as Murray Sueter, Reginald Bacon, and E.A.D. Masterman — Sueter as Inspecting Captain of Airships in 1911-14 and head of the Admiralty Air Department in 1912-15,[4] occupied a position somewhat analagous to that of Fregattenkapitän Peter Strasser as Leader of Airships in the German Navy. In Sir John Fisher, First Sea Lord 1903-10, Sueter had a chief as ardent as Scheer in his advocacy of the rigid airship, and even

---

[4] Sueter, an outspoken personality, had apparently made himself unpopular with some of his superiors and was thereafter sent to the Mediterranean. Stephen Roskill in *Naval Policy Between the Wars,* vol. I (London: Collins, 1968), p. 361n, reveals how Sueter in December, 1917, destroyed his career by writing to King George V proposing himself for a decoration for his role in inventing the tank.

more powerful. Fisher again showed his interest in the airship when once more in power between October 1914 and May 1915. Other senior officers and Cabinet members had a negative attitude towards the airship. In particular it is surprising to find that Winston Churchill, otherwise airminded, as First Lord of the Admiralty twice intervened, in the autumn of 1911 and again in the spring of 1915, to discontinue programmes involving the development of prototype rigids. The time lost by his decisions, and worse still, the dispersion of trained personnel and plant facilities, were the major reasons that the British wartime rigid airship program never bore fruit.

The beginning was made by a brilliant protégé of Fisher's, Captain Reginald Bacon, who had played a major role in the early development of British submarines, and who on July 21, 1908, proposed to his chief the appointment of a Naval Air Assistant to the Admiralty Staff, and the placing of an order with the Vickers armament firm (who had developed the Royal Navy's early submarines) for construction of a large rigid airship. The latter was intended to serve as an experimental prototype, with a view to developing long range aerial scouts to serve the Fleet at sea. The interest of Fisher in such a craft at this time is all the more remarkable in that Count Zeppelin had not yet made the "great flight" which ended in disaster at Echterdingen, and his endeavors were receiving no encouragement from Admiral von Tirpitz.

With the approval of the Treasury and the Committee of Imperial Defence, on May 7, 1909, the Admiralty signed a contract with Vickers for the airship. Already a design had been prepared by Bacon, Sueter, Commander Oliver Schwann, and a Vickers design team headed by Mr. Charles Roberton, Chief Engineer. It is to be noted that all these persons, particularly Bacon and Sueter, had been involved in the earlier Vickers submarine programmes and saw the airship, floating by displacement of a medium in which it was completely submerged, as being analagous to the submarine.

Specifications required that the ship, designated H.M. Airship No. 1 (popularly known as "Mayfly") should be able to fly for 24 hours at 40 knots, attain a ceiling of 1500 feet, be capable of mooring to a mast on the water (or possibly on land also), and carry radio equipment and quarters for a crew of 20.[5] The design was ambitious, even in some respects ingenious and original, owing little to Zeppelin practice, and it is unfortunate that a lack of concern for weight

[5] Air Department, Admiralty, *Handbook on Rigid Airship No. 1* (Confidential). Parts I and II and Appendix, 1913, p. 1.

problems caused her in the end to be unsuccessful. The hull, 512 feet long and 48 feet in diameter, was built on twelve longitudinal girders with 40 transverse rings – twelve-sided polygons – spaced at 12½ foot intervals. The main radially braced rings were however spaced as closely as 12½ and 25 feet apart over the gondolas and midships cabin, and 37½ feet apart elsewhere, so that of the 17 gas bags, nine were 37½ feet long, five 25 feet long, and three 12½ feet long. Valves were of the Parseval type, in the top of the ship and both automatic and manually actuated. Total gas volume was 663,518 cubic feet. "Mayfly" was thus larger in volume than contemporary Zeppelins and her size was not surpassed until L 1 – the German Navy's first airship – was completed in the autumn of 1912.

A daring step forward was made when Vickers determined, with Admiralty approval, to fabricate the hull framework of duralumin, rather than the "hard aluminium" used in the Zeppelins until Z XII was completed in December, 1914. The decision was well justified as the new alloy had a much higher resistance to stress, enabling the hull framework to be built over a ton lighter for the same strength.

Other decisions were not so fortunate. Like the Zeppelins, the hull shape featured a long parallel section with rounded nose and tapering stern, but these were characteristics of a shape recommended by an early American aerodynamicist, Professor Albert Francis Zahm, who claimed (erroneously) that his hull form produced only 40 per cent of the drag of the contemporary Zeppelin. Beneath the hull, and connecting the two gondolas, was a triangular keel, broadening amidships to form a cabin housing the radio equipment. The hull framework was admittedly heavy to provide the strength needed for mooring the ship at sea. As in the first Zeppelin, the girders were I beams formed of two U-shaped channels strutted 1 foot apart and diagonally braced with wire. Those in the main rings in the upper part of the ship failed under gas pressure loads during inflation and had to be replaced with triangular section girders.[6] The bracing wires were likewise made of duralumin; these snapped continuously under tension and had to be replaced by steel.

The gas bags were manufactured by Short Brothers from rubberized fabric provided by the *Continental Caoutchouc u. Guttapercha Co.* of Hannover, Germany; the British Army airship service, with experience with small pressure airships, advised against gold beaters' skin as it tended to become brittle. The outer cover was

[6] Captain F.L.M. Boothby, "Early Days of the R.N. Airship Section." *The Airship.* v. 5, no. 19, Sept.-Dec. 1938, p. 35.

made of silk, waterproofed with a compound trade-named "Ioco." Thirteen years before the Zeppelin LZ 126 appeared with an aluminium-doped outer cover, "Mayfly" was so treated on her upper half to minimize heat absorption; the under half of the hull was "a beautiful primrose color." Horizontal and vertical stabilizing fins were fitted aft, with quadruple box rudders and triplane box elevators fitted to their trailing edges; in addition, large triplane elevators were fitted well forward, and small triple rudders immediately abaft the rear gondola. All these surfaces were built to Messrs. Short's Reversible Aerocurve patent, and flexed rather than being hinged.

The open gondolas, designed to float on the water, were made of two-ply mahogany sewn with copper wire by the Consuta process, developed by Saunders & Co., of Cowes. Each gondola contained a 180 hp Wolseley 8 cylinder engine weighing 1800 lb. The forward engine drove two propellers 11 feet 10 inches in diameter on outriggers, the after one drove a single 15 foot propeller at the rear of the car.

Water recovery equipment was fitted to the engines to condense moisture from the exhausts and to prevent the ship from becoming lighter as fuel was consumed – again years in advance of similar developments by the Americans. It was claimed that 70 per cent of the weight of fuel consumed could thus be recovered. The equipment weighed half a ton, however, while petrol, water and compressed air tanks, piping and equipment were also unduly complicated and therefore added to the empty weight. This was further increased by the requirement that "Mayfly" carry such nautical gear as a capstan weighing 225 lb, an anchor weighing 74 lb, and hawsers weighing 650 lb.

Whether inspired by the Zeppelin example at Manzell, or by the desire to make of "Mayfly" a truly seagoing unit, the builders decided that she should take off and land from the water. The building shed was therefore erected on piles in the Cavendish Dock at Barrow, being completed in June, 1910. The ship herself was then commenced, but the novelty of the enterprise caused many delays. By January, 1911, the hull framing was completed, the keel added, and gondolas, fins and rudders in place. Inflation commenced on April 30, 1911, and was completed on May 21. It then became clear that "Mayfly" was overweight and could not meet the stipulations of the contract. Gross lift with gas cells 95 per cent full under standard conditions was 19.665 tons, the empty weight of the ship 19.589

tons![7] Nonetheless, it was decided to proceed with a programme of mooring trials.

The naval crew had been present since September 29, 1910, when they had arrived in Barrow aboard the obsolete light cruiser "Hermione". Sueter became her captain and another of the early British airship pioneers, Commander E.A.D. Masterman, was detailed to supervise inflation of the big rigid. "Mayfly's" captain designate was Lieutenant Neville Usborne – killed in February, 1916, in a daring experiment designed to carry a night fighting aeroplane aloft under a blimp envelope for anti-Zeppelin work. His second in command was Lieutenant Talbot. Both these officers had had submarine experience.

On May 22, 1911, "Mayfly" was brought with some difficulty out of the shed, which was really too small for safely docking and undocking her, and moored by the nose to a mast atop a pontoon in the center of the dock. For three days she remained at the mast with a crew of 9 officers aboard, and on May 23 withstood a wind of 45 mph. She was too heavy to rise from the water, however, though at times the rear gondola ascended as gusts lifted the stern. Boothby, who was a member of her crew, claims that the airship even then could have been made to fly with fuel for full speed for 12 hours and a reduced crew, and as he says, "had the public seen her in the air subsequent history might have been different."[8] The Admiralty, however, insisted she meet the terms of the contract, so on May 25, three hundred sailors returned her to the shed for modifications.

The shed was too short to increase the capacity of the airship by cutting her in two and adding further gas cells. One of the drastic lightening measures was to remove the keel between the cars; this was supposed not to impair the strength of the ship, but in fact weakened the hull disastrously.

> Without the keel the ship was not a pleasant sight. She hogged amidships and sagged over the cars. The removal of the keel was a great mistake, but it must be remembered that there was no other way to get the required lift. The opinion was then held, and held for a long time afterwards, that an airship which would stand up to her handling stresses on the ground would stand up to anything she might get in the air, and this was probably true while speeds were low, but failed disastrously when they were above 60 knots.[9]

Other weights were less regretted: the water recovery apparatus, the forward "aeroplanes" (elevators), the two forward propellers

---

[7] British airship constructors used the long ton of 2240 lb.
[8] Boothby
[9] *ibid.*

"Mayfly" in Cavendish Dock, Barrow, May 1911, for trials at the mooring mast. Original configuration with keel between gondolas, large triplane elevators, forward twin propellers on outriggers driven by the engine in the forward gondola, and triple rudders abaft the rear gondola. Note the high drag of the multiple control surfaces fitted to the fins aft. (Vickers Ltd.)

replaced by a single direct drive 10-footer; the metal tanks and piping of the water trimming service replaced by fabric ones; some hawsers discarded; even the crew's tool boxes replaced by cloth bags and holes drilled in the engine handling levers. The capstan and anchor remained, but the clutch of the former was discarded. The net result was to give "Mayfly" a disposable lift of 3.21 tons.[10] On September 22, 1911, she was inflated, and two days later was drawn out of her shed, the crew of 11 on board expecting to fly her immediately. While being manoeuvred on the water by means of winches, the ship suddenly broke in two ahead of the after gondola, whose occupants had to dive overboard and swim for it. Further damage was caused

[10] George Whale, *British Airships, Past, Present and Future* (London: John Lane, the Bodley Head, 1919), p. 144.

by a jackstay along the top of the ship ripping out successive frames. Various accounts blame the breaking of the hull on a sudden squall or an overstraining of the hull by the mechanical handling gear, but it was certainly fatally weakened by removal of the keel. With much trouble "Mayfly" was returned to her shed a total wreck, and later dismantled.

Bacon, Sueter, et. al., had learned a great deal and had a solid foundation of experience on which to build in a regular programme of rigid airship development; but it was not to be. The Court of Inquiry found that "Mayfly" was structurally weak, and was further memorable for the revealing remark of the president, Rear Admiral Sir Doveton Sturdee, who on viewing the wreck exclaimed "the work of an idiot!" Sturdee's views were echoed more or less widely at the Admiralty, Jellicoe, the Controller, being an exception. Fisher had been replaced as First Sea Lord by Arthur Wilson, no innovator, and Churchill, the new First Lord, refused to endorse further experiments with airships. The personnel were dispersed, and Sueter put on half pay.

The Germans of course were not standing still, and presently their successes with Zeppelins – exaggerated in the eye of the distant beholder – forced a reappraisal of the airship question at the Admiralty. Late 1911 and early 1912, it will be remembered, was the time when the successes of the DELAG Zeppelin "Schwaben" were causing great excitement in Germany and envy and admiration abroad. Jellicoe's interest in the rigid airship led him during a visit to Germany to take an excursion flight on November 15, 1911, in "Schwaben," then based at Potsdam, together with the Naval Attaché in Berlin, Captain Watson. At about this time, according to Alfred Colsman, the business manager of the Zeppelin firm, Watson attempted to get in touch with him to sound him out on procuring a Zeppelin for the Royal Navy.[11] The meeting never took place, and in any case the Zeppelin Company would have been forbidden by the German Government to build a rigid to foreign account; but Colsman used the fact of Watson's interest to persuade Admiral von Tirpitz to place an order for the first German naval airship, L 1.

Jellicoe was impressed by the capabilities of "Schwaben"; six months later Sueter and Colonel Mervyn O'Gorman, the superintendent of the Royal Aircraft Factory at Farnborough, went to the continent disguised as Americans to obtain more information on airship developments in France, Germany and Austria. The high

[11] Colsman, p. 156.

point of their trip was a 5½ hour flight in "Viktoria Luise" on July
9, 1912, from Hamburg to Lübeck and return via the Kiel Canal,
with the first German naval airship crew under Kapitänleutnant
Hanne aboard for a training flight. On their return they reported to
the Committee of Imperial Defence that

> In favorable weather the German airships can already be employed for
> reconnaissance over vast areas of the North Sea, and one airship, owing to the
> extensive view from high altitudes under favorable weather conditions, is able
> to accomplish the work of a large number of scouting cruisers. It is difficult
> to exaggerate the value of this advantage to Germany. By a systematic and
> regular patrol of the approaches to the coast, it will be possible in fair
> weather for German airships to discover the approach of an enemy and to
> give timely warning of the attack.[12]

Recognizing the corresponding need to expand Britain's aviation
strength, the Committee urged *inter alia* that the Admiralty negotiate
with a British firm for a rigid airship to serve as a naval scouting
prototype and to train personnel. Interest in procuring a British rigid
was heightened by the widespread belief that the Germany Navy's
L 1, on a trial flight with Count Zeppelin in command, had flown
over Sheerness on the night of October 14, 1912. This was not true,
but the German craft was quite capable of such a flight, and the
naval and military authorities knew it. Early in 1913 the Committee
of Imperial Defence approved an order for a new rigid.

Again Vickers, the pioneer firm, got the contract for what was to
be known as H.M. Airship No. 9.[13] They re-assembled their design
team and opened an airship department in April, 1913, the chief
designer being H.B. Pratt and one of his subordinates being the later
celebrated Barnes Wallis. The order for No. 9 was placed on June 10,
1913, and the final contract signed in March, 1914. The leisurely
pace was justified to a degree by the fact that the unlucky Cavendish
Dock shed was also too small, and a larger one, measuring
540 x 150 x 98 feet clear inner dimensions, was to be erected on
land on Walney Island near Barrow. No. 9 was designed to the
requirement that she should achieve 45 mph at full power, have a
minimum disposable lift of 5 tons, and a ceiling of 2000 feet. The
"Mayfly" design having proven unairworthy, No. 9 was to copy
Zeppelin practice, and the French plans of the German Army

[12] Raleigh, Sir Walter, *The War In The Air,* vol. I. (London: OUP, 1922), p. 181.
[13] British naval airships were numbered indiscriminately regardless of type. Airships No.2-8
were pressure craft. The prefix R (Rigid) was not applied until so ordered by the Admiralty
on December 18, 1917.

Zeppelin Z IV, obtained after her forced landing at Lunéville on April 3, 1913, were secretly made available soon afterwards to the Vickers design team.[14]

Again the requirement that she be strongly built to resist mishandling by crews in training resulted in a heavy ship. The hull shape resembled that of contemporary Zeppelins; with blunt bow, short tapered stern and long parallel portion. Five hundred twenty six feet long and 53 feet in diameter, it was built on 17 longitudinal girders with 18 transverse main frames. These were spaced 30 feet apart, and two light intermediate rings between each main frame were formed of "Mallock tubes." The girders were again of duralumin, triangular in section and followed Zeppelin practice. Seventeen gas cells of rubberized fabric lined with gold beaters' skin contained 890,000 cubic feet of hydrogen. Beneath the hull a keel ran almost the entire length, with a wireless cabin amidships. Vertical and horizontal fins at the stern carried triple rudders and biplane elevators as in the German prototype. There were two enclosed gondolas, each containing two 180 h.p. Wolseley Maybach engines driving swiveling propellers which could be rotated to provide ahead or astern thrust, or to force the ship upwards or pull her down. In each gondola was mounted a 1-pdr. gun, and two machine guns were to be carried on a platform atop the hull, accessible by a climbing shaft.

Changes in design, and worse yet, changes in policy, delayed the first flight of No. 9 until 2½ years after the signing of the contract! Material was assembled in the summer of 1914, but work proceeded very slowly after the outbreak of war. Nobody at the Admiralty was now interested in her completion, even though a war was on, and on March 12, 1915, Churchill ordered the construction of No. 9 to be cancelled. The excuse was that the war would be over before she was completed; but the real reason was his undoubted prejudice against the rigid airship and his bias in favor of the aeroplane.

Arthur Balfour succeeded Churchill as First Lord on May 25, and partly as a result of the early Zeppelin attacks on the country, the Admiralty on June 19 decided to resume construction of No. 9. Several months passed before the design staff was reassembled (Pratt and Wallis having enlisted in the Army) and material reassembled. Actual erection of the hull began in the autumn of 1915, and by the end of June, 1916, this was completed. Because of the addition of

[14]Robin Higham, *The British Rigid Airship 1908-31.* (London: G.T. Foulis & Co., Ltd., 1961), p. 125.

armament at the request of the Admiralty, the contract useful lift requirement was reduced to 3.1 tons. When the ship made her first flight, however, on November 27, 1916, it was found that her useful lift was only 2.1 tons and the Admiralty refused to accept her. The maximum speed also was no more than 42½ mph.

Modifications by Vickers included a new set of lighter gas bags, while the two engines in the rear gondola were replaced by an actual German Maybach HSLu of 240 hp, obtained from the wreck of the German naval Zeppelin L 33 brought down in England in September, 1916. This was connected to a single direct drive propeller. With a useful lift of 3.8 tons the ship was accepted on April 4, 1917, and sent to the Rigid Airship Trial Flight at Howden in Yorkshire, where she was used for training and experimental work. From May 26 to October 29, 1917, No. 9 spent 33 hours testing mooring systems, latterly at the airship station at Pulham in Norfolk. Here it is said that after sustaining damage, she was slung up in her shed and finally dismantled in June, 1918. In all, she flew only 198 hours 16 minutes, which is said to have included a few offshore patrols. Four years behind her Zeppelin prototype, No. 9, with her low useful lift and inadequate performance, was useless for war purposes. The early "height climber" Zeppelins being completed at the time she was accepted, with gas volumes of 2,000,000 cubic feet, flew at combat altitudes of 16,000 feet and had a useful lift of 37 tons.

The same June 19, 1915 Admiralty conference which had resurrected No. 9 voted to procure four more rigid airships, involving additional firms in their production, while operating bases were planned to match. Eventually these were constructed at Howden in Yorkshire, at Pulham in Norfolk, and at East Fortune on the Firth of Forth, while building sheds with 2 berths in each were contracted for at Inchinnan on the Clyde (Beardmore), Selby (or Barlow) in Yorkshire (Armstrong Whitworth), Cardington in Bedfordshire (Short Brothers) and Flookburgh in Lancashire (Vickers: They were refused the steel for this shed, meaning that Vickers had no place to build large rigids). The first three rigids ordered on October 16, 1915, constituted the No. 23 class, slightly enlarged versions of No. 9 and no improvement over her. Vickers again created the design, with a length of 535 feet, a diameter of 53 feet, and a gas volume of 940,000 cubic feet in eighteen bags. The hull had the same external keel and long parallel section as in No. 9, while the stern was fuller and less well streamlined. The control surfaces showed improvement, in that simple elevators and rudders were hinged to the trailing edges of the fins as in the German Army Z IX, completed just before the outbreak of war. There were three gondolas, the forward and after ones each containing one 250 hp Rolls Royce engine driving two swiveling propellers. Amidships was a small gondola containing two 250 hp Rolls Royce engines with a dry weight of 907 lb, driving fixed propellers. Speed was to be 52 mph maximum and the useful lift 8 tons. No. 23 was built by Vickers at Walney Island, No. 24 by Beardmore, and No. 25 by Armstrong-Whitworth; a fourth ship of the class, R 26, was ordered from Vickers in January, 1916.

Though expected to be completed in the autumn of 1916, it was not until September and October, 1917, that the first three ships were placed in service; R 26 followed on March 20, 1918. Again the airships were overweight and useless for war service. The machinery installation was 4000 pounds overweight, and other modifications added to the fixed weights, so that No. 23 came out with only 5.7 tons of useful lift under standard conditions. Subsequently the heavy rear engine car was replaced by one of the small midships gondolas of the wrecked German L 33, dynamos, bomb racks, radio generator, buffer wheels and cabin furniture were removed, bringing the useful lift to something over 6 tons. No. 24 came out with 5.1 tons of useful lift; after similar alterations the figure was increased to 6.18 tons. The useful lift of No. 25 as completed was 5.8 tons. R 26, built with the modifications listed above, had a useful lift of 6.28 tons. These ships were generally used for training and some coastal patrols. R 26, based at Pulham, was present for the surrender of the German U-boats at Harwich on November 20, 1918. No. 25 was a failure in that her construction permitted marked fore and aft surging of the gas bags, rendering her statically unstable. No. 23 in the summer of 1918 carried a Camel fighter aloft from the airship station at Pulham and released it to glide down unmanned; in a later experiment on November 6, 1918, the aircraft was flown by Lieut. R.E. Keyes of No. 212 Squadron at Great Yarmouth. All but No. 25 were used for mooring experiments in the period before and after the Armistice, and were scrapped during 1919.

With a modification of the No. 23 design, known as the 23X class, British rigid airship constructors at last achieved a useful craft with a disposable lift of more than 8 tons. The improvement was largely due to a daring move never imitated by the Zeppelin concern – the elimination of the keel, which contributed little to the strength of the hull and which saved over 3 tons of weight. Ballast bags and fuel tanks were attached to the radial wiring of the main frames, and an internal corridor, kept open by light U-shaped formers, permitted communication between the gondolas. The design was approved in June, 1916, for completion in mid-1917; four ships (R 27-30) were to have been built, but R 28 and R 30 were cancelled in 1917 due to a decision to discontinue the outmoded British designs and to concentrate on copying the latest German "super-Zeppelin," an example of which, L 33, had been captured reasonably intact on September, 1916. As far as the needs of the Grand Fleet were concerned, this decision was unfortunate, for none of the L 33 copies were completed until March, 1919. Long before then, suggests Dr. Higham, it would have been possible to mass produce considerable numbers of the useful 23X class (Vickers claimed to be able to turn them out in eight weeks) in time to serve the Fleet in the North Sea, and to escort ocean convoys at the height of the unrestricted U-boat war.[15]

R 27, built by Beardmore at Inchinnan, was commissioned on June 29, 1918, and based at Howden. Here, after 89 hours and 40 minutes of flying, she was destroyed in a spectacular accident on August 16. Some spilled petrol was accidentally set afire by an American Navy crew fitting the old envelope of the non-rigid SSZ 23 to a new car; the small blimp went up in flames together with SSZ 38, SS 54, and R 27.[16]

R 29, built by Armstrong-Whitworth at Selby, was commissioned on June 20, 1918, and based at East Fortune on the Firth of Forth. Her useful lift was 8.66 tons, the highest of any British rigid yet built. During 1918 she flew 337 hours 25 minutes, and 100 hours and 33 minutes more in 1919. Her longest flight was 32 hours, 20 minutes on July 3-4, 1918. She was employed on antisubmarine patrol and received partial credit for the destruction of UB 115 near the coast north of Sunderland on September 29, 1918. Two old destroyers and a pack of trawlers finished off the U-boat with depth charges, but it was the rigid, escorting a Scandinavian convoy, which sighted oil on the surface and dropped a 230 lb bomb to indicate the submarine's location.[17]

Two other rigids ordered at this time, R 31 and R 32, not only

[15] Higham, p. 157.
[16] Indicative of the lack of interest of historians in the British rigid airship programme is the fact that Dr. Higham first learned of the Howden disaster from an interview by Charles L. Keller with an American survivor, Frank Peckham, at Lakehurst in 1959. Whale, whose book published in 1919 is the only other volume on the wartime British rigids, says nothing of this event; he was of course gagged by the Official Secrets Act.
[17] Robert M. Grant, *U-Boats Destroyed* (London: Putnam, 1964), p. 129.

marked a step forward in the British rigid airships programme, but also resulted from a spectacular success in the cloak and dagger war of espionage. The ships had wooden girder hulls and were inspired by the Schütte-Lanz type; that they were ordered in May, 1916, from Short Brothers at Cardington resulted from the arrival in England a few months earlier of a Swiss, Hermann Müller, who claimed to be a former employee of the Schütte-Lanz firm in Mannheim, and who in fact had been the manager of the girder construction shop. He was put in touch with the airship design department of the Admiralty and the design of R 31 and R 32 was prepared with his assistance. Subsequently, in 1918, Müller appeared in the United States, but the naval authorities there were not impressed with his knowledge. In fact, while undoubtedly competent at constructing wooden girders, Müller had no engineering knowledge, proposing to the Admiralty designers that the radio cabin be placed on top of the ship! Nonetheless, the British design was highly sophisticated, and the resemblance to the contemporary Schütte-Lanz "d" type (the first of

Schütte-Lanz SL 7 on her first flight at Mannheim-Rheinau, 3 September 1915. Plans of this "d" type Schütte-Lanz ship were brought to England by Hermann Müller, and used as the basis for the wooden-girder R 31 design. (Georg Blasweiler)

which, SL 7, had made her first flight at Mannheim on September 3, 1915) is so complete that I have been obliged to conclude that Müller brought with him to England *actual general arrangement drawings* of this Schütte-Lanz ship, and probably detailed drawings as well. The similarities are too numerous to be coincidental:

The diameter of the British ships was 64 ft. 10 in., the SL 7 diameter was identical. The hulls of all three craft were built on 20 longitudinals arranged in Schütte-Lanz fashion with two top longitudinals instead of the single top backbone girder as in Zeppelin practice. True, there was a difference in length, the R 31 and R 32 being 614 ft. 8 in. long, the German ship 534 ft. 5 in long, and the British craft had 1,500,000 cubic feet of hydrogen in 21 gas cells, to 1,240,300 cubic feet for the SL 7 in eighteen gas cells. R 31 and R 32 had an axial cable connecting the centers of the braced rings, just as in SL 7. Though the hulls of R 31 and R 32 were longer, they had the same streamlined shape as in SL 7, the fin profiles were closely similar, and above all the main rings in all three ships were 9 meters apart, while there were three sets of rings 5 meters apart to which the engine cars were attached. With a smaller volume, the German craft had a useful lift of 15½ tons compared to 16½ tons in the larger British ships.

Where SL 7 had carried four 210 hp Maybachs in the conventional arrangement — two in the midline forward and aft, and two on each side amidships — R 31 had six 250 hp Rolls Royces in individual gondolas driving pusher propellers directly. Two gondolas were well up on the hull to port and starboard amidships, while the other four were in two pairs slung close together under the hull fore and aft. R 31 with this installation made 70 mph on her trials, while R 32, which had only one engine car fitted aft, still made 65 mph with 1250 hp.

Another advance was in the control car which, with the radio cabin, was built close up against the hull in a streamlined shape. This was hailed as something new in the later Zeppelins "Bodensee," LZ 126 and "Graf Zeppelin."

Again, neither R 31 nor R 32 were to serve the Fleet. R 31 made her first flight in August, 1918. On her second trial flight on October 16 the port side bracing of the upper fin carried away and she returned to Cardington with the fin and rudder laid flat on the hull to starboard. On November 6, 1918, she was commissioned and set off for East Fortune. En route the wooden girders began to break (Strasser could have told the Admiralty about this Schütte-Lanz

R 31 on an early trial flight. Compared to SL 7, the hull has been lengthened to carry two additional power plants, the control car has been built onto the hull for the first time, and engine gondolas have been modified. (Garland Fulton collection)

failing!) and an emergency landing was made at Howden. The ship
was placed in the shed in which R 27 had burned three months
before, damaged roof and all, and when she was examined some
months later it was found that rain and moisture had hopelessly
rotted and softened the glued plywood girders. R 31 was dismantled
beginning in February, 1919, having flown a total of only 8 hours
and 55 minutes!

R 32 did not commission until September 3, 1919. She ran some
full scale tests for the National Physical Laboratory and was then
employed in 1920-21 training the American crew of R 38, a large
rigid under construction which was to be sold to the United States
Navy. In April, 1921, she was tested to destruction by
overpressurizing one of the gas cells, and the wreck was then
dismantled. She had flown 212 hours 45 minutes not counting flight
time in American charge.

One wonders what happened to the mysterious Herr Müller. An
Intelligence interrogator opined that he was "solely inspired by
money motives."[18] Presumably he returned to his native Zürich and
lived in obscurity; certainly he never published anything about
himself.

By the middle of 1916, no rigid airship of British design had yet
flown, despite the fact that the war had been going on for nearly two
years, and despite the performance of the Zeppelins as scouting craft
for the inferior German fleet. True, a large pressure airship
programme was bearing fruit, with Sea Scout and Coastal airships
already available for antisubmarine patrol, and a large pressure
airship, the North Sea, of 360,000 cubic feet, for scouting with the
Grand Fleet. (Thirteen were built, and with most of them based at
East Fortune after July, 1917, they did a certain amount of work
with Beatty's ships).

Then, over a three month period, three events focused attention
anew on the value of the big long range rigid for naval purposes: (1)
the Battle of Jutland on May 31—June 1, 1916; (2) the Sunderland
Operation of August 19, 1916; and (3) the capture of the latest of
the German Navy's "super-Zeppelins," L 33, on September 24,
1916.[19]

As the reader is aware, the Zeppelins played no significant role at
Jutland, in fact, Scheer's operational plan for the sortie of the High

[18]Great Britain, Public Record Office, "Examination of 'M', an ex-employee of Messrs.
Schütte-Lanz Airship Constructors at Mannheim-Rheinau August 1916."
[19] see p. 124

Seas Fleet that day was designed for the contingency that they would not be available. Nonetheless, all hands in the Grand Fleet's battleships and battle cruisers who saw Schütze's L 11 disdainfully observing them on the morning after the battle had an uneasy though exaggerated impression of the capabilities of the German Zeppelin fleet. The legend grew up subsequently that it was the Zeppelins, not the *Gefechtskehrtwendung* or battle turn, which had enabled Scheer's inferior force to escape the might of the Grand Fleet. This false impression was reinforced in the Sunderland Operation of August 19, during which the Grand Fleet failed to come to grips with the High Seas Fleet in the western North Sea, while the British units felt themselves to be under constant surveillance by Zeppelins. Actually only eight were out, and only four of them sighted British units, but even Jellicoe gained an exaggerated impression of their ubiquity:

> From 8.28 onwards Zeppelins were frequently in sight from both the Battle Fleet and the Battle Cruiser Fleet, and were fired at, but they kept at too long a range for the fire to be effective. The *Galatea* sighted the first at 8.28 a.m., and the second was seen by the Battle Fleet at 9.55 a.m.; at 10 a.m. Commodore Tyrwhitt, who was at sea with the Harwich Force, reported himself in position Lat. 52.50 N., long. 3.38 E., and also being followed by a Zeppelin. He stated later that his force was shadowed by airships during the whole period of daylight on the 19th. Reports were also received from the patrol trawler *Ramexo* that she had two Zeppelins in sight in Lat. 57 N., Long. 1 E. It was evident that a very large force of airships was out. A total of at least 10 was identified by our directional wireless stations and they appeared to stretch right across the North Sea.[20]

Little wonder then that British proponents of the rigid airship, writing on September 20, 1917, were believed when they asserted that the German Zeppelins were watching the Grand Fleet on both days of the Jutland battle, and in the Sunderland Operation, were actually directing the U-boats which sank two light cruisers:

> From the results already given of instances it will be seen how justified is the confidence felt by the German Navy in its airships when used in their proper sphere as eyes of the Fleet. It is no small achievement for their Zeppelins to have saved the High Seas Fleet at the Battle of Jutland: to have saved their cruiser squadron on the Yarmouth raid (April 25, 1916), and to have been instrumental in sinking the "Nottingham" and "Falmouth" (on August 19, 1916). Had the positions been reversed in the Jutland battle, and had we had

[20] Admiral Viscount Jellicoe of Scapa, *The Grand Fleet, 1914-16* (London: Cassell & Co., Ltd., 1919), p. 439.

rigids to enable us to locate and annihilate the German High Seas Fleet, can anyone deny the far-reaching effect it would have had in ending the war? [21]

None of these claims were true, but given the Grand Fleet's inferiority complex about the German Zeppelins, they were believed, and even advanced as true by American rigid airship advocates as late as 1926.

And then, at the height of the excitement, a usable copy of the latest German "super-Zeppelin" fell into British hands. All previous plans were scrapped, and two of the four R 23X class rigids were cancelled, as the Admiralty yielded to the natural temptation to copy "the latest thing" produced by their rivals across the North Sea. A team of Admiralty draftsmen under Commander C.I.R. Campbell of the Royal Corps of Naval Constructors camped out in tents at Little Wigborough for several weeks until they had made complete sets of drawings of L 33's hull, girder work, wiring, gondolas, etc. [22] In November, 1916, the Cabinet authorized production of two copies, R 33 and R 34. In January, 1917, three more were ordered, R 35, R 36 and R 37. Two uses for the new ships were contemplated − scouting for the Grand Fleet in the North Sea, and convoy escort over the Atlantic. To attack higher flying Zeppelins in the North Sea, R 33 and R 34 were to be armed with two 2 pdr guns on the top platform; two 2 pdrs were to be mounted in the hull framework amidships, and a 1 pdr in a gondola ahead of the lower fin. The convoy escort ships were to carry a 12 pdr for attacking submarines. In addition they would carry four 550 lb bombs and twenty 100 lb bombs. Furthermore, there was the hope and expectation, after America entered the war in April, 1917, that she would be able to provide non-flammable helium to inflate the North Sea craft at least. To maintain secrecy, the helium was referred to as C-gas, Currenium, or deceptively, argon.

Not until December 9, 1917, did Beardmore lay down R 34 at Inchinnan, while presumably R 33 was commenced by Armstrong's at Barlow at about the same time (no building berths were available until No. 24 and No. 25 had been completed and delivered to East Fortune and Howden in October). In the end, the two ships were not

[21] *The Uses of Airships for the Navy (British)*, Sept. 20, 1917. Copy provided by Captain Garland Fulton, USN. The writer has never been identified, but I agree with Dr. Higham that it was probably Wing Commander E.A.D. Masterman.

[22] These were published in CB 1265 and CB 1265A, *German Rigid Airships* (Confidential), Admiralty War Staff, Intelligence Division, London, February, 1917, along with quantities of detailed photographs of the wreck.

Chinese copies of L 33. In particular, they had the streamlined twin engine after gondola with single propeller fitted in the later "height-climbers," as exemplified by L 49 captured in France after the "Silent Raid" of October 19-20, 1917. The engines were 250 hp vee-12 Sunbeam Maoris, specially designed for airships, but less reliable than the German Maybachs. The three later ships were modified further in view of information derived from German "height climbers," notably from L 48 brought down in Suffolk in June, 1917. R 35 was to have had an extra gas cell and a ceiling of 16,500 feet; R 36 and R 37 were to have an extra cell and lightened structure to reach 17,000 feet. Of the three, only R 36 was completed, and in much modified form.

No ships of this advanced programme were of course finished at the time of the Armistice, and suddenly after this event there was no urgent need for their completion. Economy became the watchword, and the Admiralty saw an opportunity not only to save money, but also to smother the infant Royal Air Force by dumping the expensive rigid airship programme on the unwanted rival service. In practice, the ships continued under naval command, the Admiralty was responsible for design and construction, personnel were transferred to the R.A.F., but never felt themselves a part of the organization. In addition, there was the pious hope that commercial interests, with a minimum of government encouragement, might buy the ex-military ships and use them to set up air lines to India, Australia and South Africa. Nothing came of these schemes, and the military airships in any case were unsuited for the purpose, being too lightly built among other things.

With R 34, however, a determined attempt was made by a small band of enthusiasts within the Air Ministry to demonstrate the superior capabilities of the large rigids in long range commercial operations. The guiding genius was the Air Ministry's Director of Airships, Air Commodore Edward Maitland Maitland, a much beloved leader possessed of great personal charm, an Army airship officer from pre-war days, and a dedicated believer in the future of the rigid airship.

R 33 was the first to fly on March 6, 1919, R 34 followed on March 14, but the latter ship, though she had a shorter life, was more often in the limelight. On March 24 she left the building works at Inchinnan for the operating base at East Fortune. A jammed elevator caused a sudden rise the next morning at a 40 degree up angle from 3000 to 7800 feet; several petrol tanks tore loose in the keel, one bursting on the after gondola, whose engines were stopped in time to prevent a fire. Shortly before the signing of the Versailles Treaty, R 34 made a 56 hour flight along the North German coast into the Baltic, designed to overawe the Germans.

An excuse for Maitland to set up a transatlantic flight had been offered in March, 1919, when the president of the Aero Club of America invited the British Government to send an airship to a meeting of the association in May. The project rapidly became an official one of the American services together with the British Air Ministry; the Admiralty was persuaded to station the battle cruisers "Renown" and "Tiger" along the proposed route. R 34 would not make the first transatlantic aerial crossing – the U.S. Navy's NC-4 seaplane had arrived in England on May 31, 1919, and Alcock and Brown made their non-stop flight from Newfoundland to Ireland on June 14-15. But R 34 would make the first round trip, above all carrying a number of persons in comfort – a fact destined to influence commercial aviation planners for the next twenty years.

At 2.42 am on July 2, R 34 lifted off from the air station at East Fortune, her goal Roosevelt Field, Long Island, New York. On board were thirty persons, including Maitland; Major G.H. Scott, the captain; two watch standing officers; an engineer officer; a navigator; a meteorological officer; a radio officer; Lieut. Comdr. Zachary Lansdowne representing the United States Navy; two coxswains; five riggers; two radio men; eleven engineers; and a stowaway, a member of the ship's crew who was to have been left behind, but who hid in the hull between the gas bags. R 34 was also carrying 15.8 tons of petrol; 9 tons of oil; four tons for crew, baggage and bedding; 0.2 tons of spares and 0.42 tons of drinking water, leaving only 3 tons for water ballast.[23] The ship had to climb dynamically to clear the hills of Scotland at the outset, losing two tons of lift and requiring that she be flown 10 to 12 degrees up by the bow. This of course diminished her air speed. On the first night out, supercooling of the gas plus loss of hydrogen due to superheating caused the ship to be 4 to 5 tons heavy, and she had to be flown again at a 10 degree up angle. Indeed, the low speed caused by the need to carry excess loads dynamically was a major reason for the slowness of the westbound flight, which took 108 hours 12 minutes at an average ground speed of 33 mph. Further, much of the journey was made on only three engines to conserve petrol. Initially Scott was lucky with

[23] Edward M. Maitland, *The Log of H.M.A. R 34* (London: Hodder & Stoughton, 1920), p. 24

the weather, being able to find tail winds around the north sides of two low pressure areas – the first example in a transoceanic crossing of what today is called "pressure pattern flying," namely using the winds circulating around high and low pressure areas to increase the ground speed of the aircraft. On the other hand, following her landfall at Trinity Bay, Newfoundland, at 1.30 p.m. on July 4, R 34 encountered strong headwinds and several isolated thunderstorms. Her ground speed was so reduced that it appeared doubtful she could reach New York before exhausting her fuel supply; Scott considered landing at Chatham, Massachusetts, and then Montauk Point, Long Island. By working all night draining the storage tanks along the keel and transferring the petrol by hand into the gravity tanks over the engine cars, the crew were able to get R 34 into Roosevelt Field with a mere 140 gallons of fuel left, enough for two hours at full speed.

Nowhere in America was there at that time any proper hangar for a large rigid airship, and during her three days there R 34 was precariously moored in the open by the three wire method. By day she was held on the ground by a large handling party of soldiers; at night she was allowed to rise on the wires to 150 feet with nobody on board. Heavy rain from a thunderstorm brought her to the ground on the first night. Next day the casting in the hull to which the mooring point was attached pulled out, but jammed in the shackle, otherwise the ship might have blown away. The return flight, commencing on July 10, required only 75 hours 3 minutes with following winds, even though one of the after engines was irreparably damaged by being allowed to race unclutched. This decided Scott against showing the ship over London; there was further disappointment when the Air Ministry ordered R 34 to land at Pulham because of unfavorable winds, while the crew's families were waiting at East Fortune.

The flight, though it occupies a place in the standard aviation histories, was little remarked at the time and there were no public receptions or decorations for the crew. That there were no further transoceanic experiments was not so much due to the marginal showing on the westward journey (though Newman Alcock feels that the 183-hour time for the double crossing, with fuel consumption of 8260 gallons, could have been reduced to 133 hours and 5850 gallons if the ship had not been flown at such large up angles to secure dynamic lift, and if the propellers had been more efficient).[24]

[24] *Wingfoot Lighter Than Air Society Bulletin,* vol. 8, No. 3, January, 1961.

It was simply lack of interest in the government, lack of funds, and lack of any support for the ambitions of Maitland, Scott, Masterman, *et. al.* In fact, little was accomplished with the other airships either, and on May 31, 1921, the British Government ordered the airship service closed down as an economy move. All airships on hand were to be sold to private companies or turned over to the Disposal Board to be scrapped by August 1.[25]

R 34 did not fly again until February, 1920, and did only 7 hours 55 minutes in that month, and 13 hours 55 minutes the next. She did not then fly until January, 1921, and on the 27th of that month, on a training flight out of Howden, struck a hill at night damaging the control car and the forward and after propellers. She was brought to Howden on two engines but could not be housed in a gusty wind; made fast to a three-wire mooring in the open her fore part was beaten to pieces and she had to be dismantled.

R 33 did nothing spectacular, and nobody wrote a book about her; but she was the longest lived of any British rigid, albeit much of her existence was spent laid up. On July 1, 1919, she made a 31 hour flight over the Midlands, North Wales, the Isle of Man and the Irish coast with a band on board on behalf of the "Victory Loan." On September 10 she flew to Holland and back with beds and a chef aboard in an attempt by the Air Ministry to demonstrate the suitability of airships for carrying passengers. Between February 2 and June 7, 1921, she made 50 flights from the mooring mast at Pulham, to which she was attached for 111 out of 126 days. During a flight from the Pulham mast in April one of the after gas cells deflated completely when a rigger fell through it; by dropping ballast aft and sending men into the nose R 33 was re-trimmed and landed at the mast, where a new bag was fitted. The ship's ability to stand the strain of the deflated bag caused much satisfaction to her British operators. In June R 33 was used by the police to control race traffic at Epsom Downs, and in July she appeared at the Hendon air show. She was laid up next month, but will reappear in Chapter VII.

Though R 36 was conceived and designed as a "height climber," she was completed as a passenger ship. She was begun at Inchinnan before the Armistice, at which time work was suspended. In 1919 she was ordered to be completed as a civil airship and received the civil registration G-FAAF. Originally designed to have four 350 hp

[25] Trenchard, the Chief of the Air Staff of the R.A.F., did not want to keep the airships, not because of prejudice but due to the heavy drain they would make on the slim appropriations for his service. "He had to jettison liabilities to preserve the R.A.F. itself" (Higham, p. 210).

Sunbeam Cossack engines, she ended with two Cossacks in two gondolas amidships and a third one in a center line gondola aft. In addition, two small wing gondolas from the German L 71, containing two Maybach Mb IVa "altitude motors," were attached to the hull forward.[26] Right under the hull amidships was a 131-foot long and 8½ foot wide cabin with the control car in its forward end. This, with wicker chairs, 2-berth cabins, toilets and a galley was supposed to accommodate 50 passengers, while the crew totalled 28. The disposable lift was only 16 tons after the addition of the passenger accommodations, and though the Air Ministry's Department of Civil Aviation touted R 36 as being able to carry 30 passengers and a ton of mail from England to Egypt in 72 hours, she never flew outside England. Indeed, she could not have carried the 13.65 tons of fuel and oil which the same official department estimated she would require for the run to Egypt.

R 36 made only a few flights between her first one on April 1, 1921, and her last on June 21. She flew to Pulham on April 3 and moored to the mast there. On April 5, near Bristol, the upper and starboard fins collapsed and she dived from 6000 to 3000 feet. She was halted by stopping all engines and sending men aft, and her captain, Major Scott, then succeeded in getting her back to Pulham. On June 14 she was used by the police to control the Ascot race traffic, with journalists aboard. On June 21 she was badly damaged while mooring at Pulham in a wind; due to a failure of the winch at the base of the mast, the 675-foot rigid overran the mast and was brought up all standing on the wire with such violence that the bow longitudinals were bent downward aft to Frame 2, deflating the foremost two gas bags. The damage made it impossible to moor her to the mast, but with all berths in the Pulham sheds filled, the only way to house her was to evict L 64, which was dragged out of her hangar in bits and pieces during the night. R 36 was further damaged when a gust blew her against the shed door smashing many longitudinals "with a noise like breaking large sheets of glass." Supposedly she was repaired in 1925, but never flew again.

There remains the story of the supreme British rigid airship effort of the war – a conscious attempt on the part of Admiralty constructors to surpass their rivals across the North Sea in every

[26] After being surrendered at Pulham on July 21 and July 1, 1920, respectively, L 64 and L 71 were deflated and never flew again. For the demise of L 64 on June 21, 1921, see below. Nobody knows when L 71 was dismantled – probably in 1923, according to Ralph Booth *(Wingfoot Lighter Than Air Society Bulletin),*vol. 10, No. 7, May 1963.

respect – size, carrying capacity, ceiling, range, and speed. In charge
was Constructor-Commander C.I.R. Campbell, who had modified the
23 class to create the successful 23X class, and who was confident of
his ability to produce an all-British giant superior to the Zeppelins. In
June, 1918, the Naval Staff formulated a requirement for a rigid able
to patrol in the North Sea for 6 days as far as 300 miles from her
base. R 38, the first of the class, was ordered in September, 1918,
from Short Brothers at Cardington; subsequently, in February, 1919,
the Government nationalized the Short establishment and
rechristened it the Royal Airship Works. The design, known as the
"Admiralty 'A' type," was for a highly streamlined craft with only a
short parallel portion amidships, 699 feet long, 85.5 feet in diameter,
and with 2,724,000 cubic feet of hydrogen in 14 gas cells. The hull
was built on 13 main longitudinals with 12 intermediate
longitudinals, and for the first time in a British rigid the main rings
were spaced 15 meters apart as in the latest German "height
climbers." Main rings, anticipating the German LZ 126 of 1924, had
diamond-shaped trusses instead of the king-post bracing then
customary in the Zeppelins, and there were two light intermediate
rings between each main one. The corridor or keel was a trapezoidal
structure, instead of having the customary triangular section, and was
criticised as being potentially unstable under loads. Fins were of
cantilever construction, this innovation having been discovered
through a secret salvage operation which during August and
September, 1918, recovered much of the wreckage of L 70 off the
Norfolk coast. The rudders had large balance areas ahead of the hinge
line. Altogether the hull structure was built as light as possible to
attain a combat ceiling of 22,000 feet with fuel for 65 hours at full
speed. On the other hand, it was revealed much later that Campbell,
in designing a hull with an obviously low factor of safety, had
calculated only the static loads and had hoped that a factor of safety
of 4 would take care of the aerodynamic loads. Actually, Campbell
was ignorant of the fact that in turns, much higher bending loads
were imposed on the hull than wind tunnel tests so far had indicated;
though the turning experiments in R 32 might have been helpful if
they had been completed. The actual factors of safety of R 38 under
worst conditions of loading are given by Lewitt as: Intermediate
transverse frame 2.22 (failed locally); main transverse frame 1.4
(failed in deflated gas bag test); and longitudinal girder 1.07 (failed in
flight).[27]

[27] E.H. Lewitt, *The Rigid Airship* (London: Sir Isaac Pitman & Sons Ltd., 1925), pp. 196, 198, 209.

Yet R 38 was heavily engined, and intended to develop a maximum speed of 70.6 mph. There were six Sunbeam Cossack engines of 350 hp each, carried in two gondolas close under the hull forward at Ring 5; two more laterally to port and starboard at Ring 7; and an after pair close under the hull again at Ring 9.[28] The control car forward was a small affair, with radio cabin in the rear, built right onto the hull as in the earlier R 31 and R 32. R 38 was to carry four 520 lb bombs, eight 230 lb bombs, a 1 pdr gun on the top platform forward, and twelve machine guns, paired on the top platform forward, on a top after platform ahead of the fins at Ring 12, in a cockpit at the extreme tail and under the hull aft, and singly in the midships gondolas and control car.

Work on R 38 apparently started about February 1919; her sister R 39 was commenced at this time, and R 40 and R 41 were also ordered. In October, 1919, the first two main frames of R 38 were erected and the remaining frames were erected up to November, 1920.

In the meantime, with the Government desiring to economize, the Treasury requested cancellation of some of the airships under construction, this leading to the cessation of work on R 35, R 37, R 39, R 40 and R 41. R 38 was at first included, but the Admiralty held out for her continuation because of her advanced design. A definite reprieve for the new giant came through the interest of the United States Navy in obtaining the largest and most advanced rigid airship in the world, while at the same time the British were glad to unload her for the sum of £300,000. On October 9, 1919, the Cabinet approved R 38's sale to the United States Government. At the time the Americans of course had no realization of her defects, though some were to become exceedingly concerned about her shortcomings before the ultimate disaster.

Having no rigid airships of their own, the Americans expected, indeed were obliged, to obtain training of their personnel in Britain. Eight American officers and 18 ratings (many with previous pressure airships experience in England during the war) were sent across the Atlantic under Commander Louis H. Maxfield, and in April, 1920, began training as the so-called "Howden Detachment." Several months were spent reconditioning R. 32, then flying in her commenced on August 11. As R 32 was scheduled to be deleted, she was always in American charge through March, 1921. The Americans then trained further in the metal-hulled R 80 (see below), which

[28]Cossacks were substituted aft for lighter 275 h.p. Maoris. Charles Keller advises that the hull structure was correspondingly stiffened.

however was always under British control. Between March 26 and June 1, 1921, R 80 flew 8 hours and 45 minutes with American trainees.

Already, as R 38 approached completion, there were certain individuals in both the British and American services who had doubts about her structural integrity. Questions had arisen in Washington as early as May, 1920, when the American representative in Cardington, Commander H.C. Dyer, complained that he had not yet obtained factors of safety calculations, figures on the factor of safety of the main ring with a gas bag deflated, or strength in a turn with elevators or rudders hard over. Part of the Americans' problem was that the harassed Campbell, who apparently was most largely responsible for the new ship's design features, was no longer in charge of her construction but had been saddled with the additional responsibilities of managing the Royal Airship Works and even with making trips (by sea of course) to the United States to consult with the American designers of the ZR 1 U.S.S. "Shenandoah."

In March, 1921, Flight Lieutenant J.E.M. Pritchard, a veteran of R 34's transatlantic crossing and the officer in charge of trials, proposed that R 38 do 100 hours of test flying in British charge, including rough weather flying, followed by 50 hours in American charge before the U.S. Navy crew took her across the Atlantic. Pritchard seems to have appreciated as did no one else the structural fragility of the lightly-built "height climber." At a later date Pritchard urged that R 38 be tested in the same manner as the German "height climbers" at a minimum altitude of 7000 feet where the aerodynamic loads would be less due to diminished air density. Maitland, the Director of Airships, though less a technician than Pritchard, wanted at least 90 hours of trials according to some of his suriviving notes. On the other hand, less knowledgeable persons in authority pressed to curtail the test programme. The Director of Research of the Royal Air Force, ignoring the unprecedented dimensions and new features of the R 38, insisted that her trials could be completed in 50 hours, and economy caused others to join in the chorus. Maxfield, the prospective American commander, did not want more than 50 hours on the ship before he took her over; a brave man, he was no technician either. The American crew generally were eager to set off for their home land in the largest and finest airship ever built, though a few had misgivings.

These were reinforced by several misadventures on the trial flights. During the first one, of about 7 hours' duration on the night of June

23-24, it was discovered that the control wires were slack and the control surfaces overbalanced. The balance area of the top rudder only was reduced. During the second flight on the night of June 28-29, it was found that as speed built up to 45 knots, the other surfaces also overbalanced; all balance areas were reduced by ten per cent. In addition the cantilever fins showed weaknesses and were braced externally with wires.

The third flight on July 17-18, intended also as a transfer flight to Howden, revealed the handwriting on the wall, but those in authority ignored it. At 50 knots, R 38 began to hunt vertically over a range of 500 feet; one account says the balance areas of the elevators took charge and she went into a dive. Pritchard intervened personally to take the elevator wheel and reduce speed; simultaneously word came from the keel that transverse girders amidships near Frame 7 had failed. This damage was certainly caused by excessive aerodynamic bending loads at high speed acting on the light structure, and should have raised the gravest doubts about R 38's airworthiness at her designed full speed; but Campbell incredibly attributed the girder failures to the slip stream of the midships propellers. Here indeed he seems to have revealed a remarkable ignorance of aerodynamic forces.

Instead, after repairs and some reinforcement, plans were made to fly R 38 to Pulham, moor her to the mast there, and load her for the transatlantic flight to Lakehurst, where the United States Navy had at last completed a huge double hangar for her reception. On the morning of August 23, 1921, R 38 departed Howden with a mixed crew of 28 Britishers including Maitland; seventeen American naval officers and ratings; Commander Campbell, the designer and head of the Royal Airship Works; and four men from the National Physical Laboratory with photographic and other equipment to record the ship's reactions to sharp turns.

Fog at Pulham caused Flight Lieutenant Wann, the commanding officer of R 38, to decide to spend the night in the air and return to Howden. Next day, for the first and last time, the engines were brought up to full power and a maximum speed of 62 knots (71.3 mph) was recorded. Shortly afterwards, the ship being then about 2500 feet over the city of Hull and the air speed being 54.5 knots (62.8 mph), the officers in the control car began the turning tests.

With no reduction in speed, the rudders were put over to port, then to starboard, and back again, the angle evidently increasing until they were being moved from hard over to port to hard over to starboard. Why this test was considered necessary has never been revealed, nor is it clear who ordered it; Flight Lieutenant Wann, the sole survivor from the control car, was too seriously injured to testify at the Court of Inquiry, but Air Commodore Maitland was in the control car and if he did not order the tests, he certainly agreed to them.[29] With each turn being sharper, and the aerodynamic loads on the rudders increasing, the strain on the hull built up, and in retrospect, it was inevitable that this reckless misuse of the controls at high speed and low altitude should cause a major structural failure. Longitudinals in the top of the bay between Frames 9 and 10 fractured, the ship broke in two just abaft the rear engine cars, and the two parts fell into the River Humber, the city of Hull narrowly escaping a major disaster. Two violent explosions shattered glass over a wide area (these undoubtedly involved several of the gas cells which were known to be of low purity and contaminated with air)[30] and the forward two thirds of the rigid hull fell in flames, only Flight Lieutenant Wann surviving from this section. The after third sank more slowly and landed on a sand bar; three men were rescued from the rear gunner's cockpit, while a fourth survived in the keel. The British dead included Maitland, Pritchard, Campbell, and Pannell, the head of the National Physical Laboratory team; only one American, a rating, survived. So decimated was the Howden Detachment of the United States Navy that British officers and men assumed the honor guard alongside the coffins of their sixteen American shipmates for the impressive funeral services at Westminster Abbey.[31]

The various investigations of the accident concentrated on the faulty design of R 38, Campbell's failure to calculate the structure for aerodynamic loads, and the fact that some of the National Physical Laboratory papers on aerodynamic stresses in turns were apparently not known to him. There was no second guessing about what should have been done following the girder failures on the third flight. The Aeronautical Research Committee Sub-Committee which investigated the disaster was of the opinion that:

[29] John McCarthy, a former member of the Howden Detachment who had flown with Maitland in the R 32, asserted emphatically that he could not have ordered the final manoeuvres of R 38. "The General never intervened in the operation of the ship." Interview, Lakehurst, N.J., June 25, 1971.

[30] Four cells were below 90 per cent purity; Cell 5 was down to 76.4 per cent purity. Charles Keller, letter May 16, 1971.

[31] Richard E. Byrd, *Skyward* (New York: G.P. Putnam's Sons, 1928), p. 133.

The accident must be ascribed either to inadequate strength of the ship or to stresses produced by the use of the controls. Since the Committee are of the opinion that the use of the controls was legitimate, they are forced to the conclusion that the structure possessed inadequate strength.[32]

So R 38 stands condemned to this day – a bad airship badly designed by Constructor Commander C.I.R. Campbell, who died in her. But in the light of my knowledge of German practice, I must disagree with the findings of the sub-committee. Because the ship's strength was marginal (after all, she was built as light as possible for high altitude operations), the use of the controls was *not* legitimate, and therefore the immediate cause of the disaster was the misuse of the controls to produce violent changes of direction at high speed and at low altitude in dense air. Had Wann been in the German service, he would have faced a court martial. Listen to the late Admiral Walther Dose, who commanded two of the German Navy's "height climber" Zeppelins, the L 51 in 1917 with 10 metre frame spacing and the L 65 in 1918 with 15 metre spacing:

The hull of L 65 was much more fragile and delicate than in the L 51. If I had run the starboard engine full speed ahead, and the port engine full speed astern, I would have broken the main ring.[33]

This is not to say that R 38, even if handled with caution at low altitudes, would have survived for long. With her low factors of safety, and in the hands of an untrained American crew, she would sooner or later have been overstressed and broken up in rough weather flying.

The deaths of so many brave men from both sides of the Atlantic brought an outcry against the rigid airship, and together with the economy drive which closed down the British airship service after August 1, 1921, the R 38 disaster seemed to put paid to a costly experiment which had failed to produce any results. It was of course a fact that only two militarily useful British rigids had entered service before the Armistice, and aside from R 34's transatlantic flight, nothing of real value had been accomplished afterwards. But two technical achievements which advanced the state of the art deserve to be recorded: the first all-streamlined British airship, and the development of the mooring mast.

Vickers, the pioneering British firm and the only private corporation in England which had assembled a competent design

[32] Higham, p. 224.
[33] Interview, Hamburg, Germany, July 31, 1957.

staff, was treated with remarkable ingratitude by the Admiralty, for which it had designed and built Airship No. 1 (the "Mayfly"), No. 9, and the No. 23 class, of which it had built No. 23 and the R 26. While Armstrong, Shorts and Beardmore received allotments of scarce steel to build construction sheds for the large ships authorized in late 1916 and early 1917, Vickers, as we have seen, was refused the steel for the large shed they had proposed to build at Flookburgh in Lancashire, and thus they were effectively frozen out of the 1916-17 airship programme. All they had left to them was the Walney Island shed in which they had constructed No. 9, No. 23 and R 26, and which was much too small for ships of the R 33 class.

Faced with the dilemma, Vickers proposed to the Admiralty that they be allowed to proceed with a design of their own, small enough to fit in the Walney Island shed, and in November, 1917, permission was received after waiting only 7 days! The result was a free hand for Barnes Wallis, the engineering genius who in 1916 had become Vickers' Chief Airship Designer, and who had numerous original ideas on the subject of airship design. Convinced that the pencil-form Zahm shape of previous British designs was in error, Wallis as early as 1916 conceived the perfect streamlined shape of the rigid airship destined to become R 80.[34] Measuring 535 feet long and 70 feet in diameter with a gas volume of 1,200,000 cubic feet, this craft had 16 main frames spaced 10 metres apart, resembling the main frames of contemporary Zeppelins except that their king posts were braced with wires instead of girders. Light intermediate frames alternated between the main ones. There were 11 main longitudinals and 10 intermediate ones, giving the outside of the hull a 21-sided appearance, though just ahead of the fins the intermediate longitudinals were eliminated. Mooring gear was added to the nose after R 80's completion, and to balance her statically, she had to carry a ton of permanent ballast aft. The gondolas were most carefully streamlined, the forward gondola, about 50 feet long, being cleanly faired with a transparent nose section forward, and two 230 hp Wolseley Maybach engines to the rear driving a single large propeller. Amidships between Frames 16 and 18 were a pair of single engined gondolas to port and starboard, again highly streamlined. These had buffer and flotation bags, for the ship had no rear gondola. Best of all, out of a gross lift of 38.5 tons, R 80 had a

[34] Even Dr. Higham, whose *The British Rigid Airship 1908-1931* is truly exhaustive, has been unable to discover why so many numbers were skipped between R 41 and R 80. Higham, p.xv.

disposable lift of 17.8 tons. Here at last we see a home grown ship equal to the Germans' best, created by a designer sure of himself, and producing a rigid airship which reflected credit both on himself and his country.

Unfortunately, R 80 ran head on into the run down of airships after the war. Commenced in late 1917, she still was not completed at the Armistice, and did not make her first trial flight until July 19, 1920. She was damaged by excess gas pressure on this first flight, and not commissioned in the Royal Air Force until January, 1921. On February 24 she was flown to Howden, with the intention of scrapping her. Instead, in view of the loss of R 34 she was made available to the Americans for training. On September 20, 1921, she made her last flight, to Pulham, where she was laid up after only 73 hours' flying time. In 1925 she was scrapped. The Americans were quite interested in her and she formed the basis for a series of Vickers designs for commercial airship in the postwar period, R 80 herself appearing with a passenger cabin in a book on commercial airships by a member of the Vickers design team.[35] Unfortunately no money was forthcoming to build them for civil air services.

In spite of the R 38 disaster, airships would be resurrected in Great Britain, and in this latter-day effort, Barnes Wallis would play a prominent role.

A significant British innovation was the development of the mooring mast. This far sighted step is all the more remarkable in that the Germans, until forced by the Americans in connection with the LZ 126 contract in 1922-24, never experimented with any kind of system for mooring in the open nor fitted their ships for such a purpose. (Though it must be admitted that the fragile height climbers of 1917-18 would have had to be much strengthened, thereby increasing their weight, to withstand the stresses of mooring to a mast). Operationally, the Germans were much handicapped by their reliance on sheds and large handling parties, and there were occasions during the war when the Zeppelins could not leave their sheds for raids or scouting flights because of cross winds, while they could easily have slipped from a mast.

The very first British rigid, No. 1, the "Mayfly," was designed to float on the water moored to a mast, and it will be recalled that she did so for three days from May 22 through 25, 1911. The mast was a heavy steel girder 38 feet high fixed in a pontoon which in turn

[35] H.B. Pratt, *Commercial Airships* (London: Thomas Nelson & Sons, Ltd., 1920). R 80 appears as Figure 4 on p. 63.

R 80 training American personnel of the "Howden Detachment". Note the fully streamlined hull, and careful attention to stream-lining of the large forward gondola with two engines in the rear, and the midships cars containing one engine each (J. H. Collier)

swivelled around a concrete bollard sunk in the basin at Barrow, which here was only 8 feet deep. A meshwork wind screen was rigged on a 38 foot spar inclined 23 degrees to windward, and crossing 34 foot topsail and lower yards, but this was later abandoned. The idea of using the pontoon was that if the mast were overloaded by a gust of wind acting on the airship, there would be some "give" as the pontoon heeled over. On being drawn out of her shed, Airship No. 1 was made fast by shackling the ship's 4 inch mooring wire, 43 feet 6 inches in length, to a 111 foot length of 4 inch wire reeled on a winch on the pontoon and carried over the top of the mast. No. 1 was then reeled as close in to the top of the mast as possible, but not locked to the mast with any special fitting. The mooring trial was considered a success when the airship rode out winds blowing a steady 36½ mph gusting to 42-45 mph.

The British Army made further experiments with mooring their non-rigid airships to a mast at Farnborough as early as February, 1912, but of course no experiments could be made with rigids until such craft were available after early 1917. The first mooring experiments were made in 1917 with No. 9 at Pulham with what was termed the "three-wire system."[36] This, thought at one time to hold much promise, involved three wires made fast to a mooring point under the ship's nose, and rigged to terminate in three ground anchors at the apices of a triangle, which measured 550 feet a side. Thus, a large area of ground was required. In the winter of 1918-19, R 26, then scheduled for deletion, was strengthened with added wiring over Frames 2 and 3 forward, and spent 10 days aloft on the three-wire system in February, 1919. The ship of course had to be "light," and was found to ride best at an angle of 4 to 5 degrees down by the stern, with the same number of degrees of rudder to keep her slightly off the wind to prevent yawing. A quick means of adding ballast had to be provided as with superheating the stern might rise dangerously, yet this was difficult to provide, nor was it easy to change crews. In the end, a heavy fall of snow brought R 26 to the ground and terminated the experiment. The three-wire mooring method was used during R 34's layover in the United States in July, 1919, and again gave trouble. After R 34 damaged herself on January 28, 1921, she was put on the three-wire mooring on her

[36] At some time No. 9, and later R 26, were towed by Army tanks fitted with short masts. On one occasion No. 9, in a high wind, lifted the tank off the ground! It remained for the Americans ten years later to develop a mechanical means of moving the rigids in and out of their sheds.

return to Howden (which had no mooring mast), but the ship's mooring point tore out.

Late in 1917 it was suggested that trials be made with a rigid airship made fast to a wire braced pole mast 120 feet tall with a revolving top, and in March, 1918, Vickers was ordered to construct such a mast.[37] Originally the mast was to be erected at Barrow, but in May, 1918, it was decided to erect it at Pulham and R 24 was flown there from Howden on May 31. There was an unbelievable delay in this important experiment, both with respect to airship and mast, for which Higham gives various excuses.[38] Suffice it to say that not until June, 1919, was R 24 reinflated. after addition of bow stiffening, a bow coupling and winch in the bow, removal of the midships gondola and addition of further ballast tanks. The Barrow mast was erected in one piece at Pulham in March, 1919, but not until May 30 was the mast ready, with gas and water ballast mains to the masthead, telephone and electrical leads. R 24 was walked out to the mast on July 11, 1919, and moored there until July 31 when she was returned to her shed for an inspection and overhaul. She was again moored to the mast September 1–October 15, and again from November 7 until some date in December. Compared to later mast mooring operations, these early experiments were primitive, the ship being on the ground when the ship's wire was shackled to the mast wire and the nose hauled *up* to the masthead. Yaw guys to check swinging as the nose approached the mast were still in the future.

No further mast trials were made until 1921. During the interval a new mast head had been designed by Major Scott in September 1920 to permit the ship to be hauled down from a position in the air above the mast, and in January, 1921, the "Bedford/Pulham" fitting was mounted on the mast. R 33, under Flight Lieutenant Thomas, was sent down from Howden to Pulham to test the mast on February 2, 1921, and spent much of the next half year on the mast in tests, as previously related. On the first mooring the ship as before was landed on the ground, walked over to the mast and the ship's cable shackled to the mast wire, after which 2200 lb, of ballast was released to allow the ship to rise. R 33 was then allowed to ascend on 1400 feet of wire, and then slowly reeled in to the mast head, with the wing engines being used to keep her head to the wind. The ship's mooring cone fitted precisely into the mast socket and was then locked in

[37]Captain T.B. Williams, "Airship Mooring in England." *The Airship*, vol. 5, No. 18, April-June 1938, p. 16.
[38]Higham, p. 352.

place. The winch used at the foot of the mast to haul in the wire was "an ordinary farm steam engine with the necessary modifications," later criticised by the U.S. Naval Attache as "of the home-made, kitchen variety" when it played a major role in severely damaging R 36 at the same mast on June 17, 1921.

On February 4, R 33 was made light and let up about 300 feet, then winched down and secured. On February 7, 1921, she for the first time slipped from the mast 500 lb. light and made a flight of 2 hours and 22 minutes. On her return, instead of landing on the ground near the mast, R 33 let out all her 600 feet of mooring wire in a bight and at 200 feet dropped the end, which was shackled to the end of the mast wire which had been laid out 800 feet to leeward of the mast. Five hundred pounds of ballast was then released and R 33 rose to 1200 feet, from which altitude she was reeled down to the mast. When about 100 feet from the mast head she swung somewhat rapidly, and just before the mooring cone entered the coupling, she over-rode the mast head and the outer cover was

The experimental mooring mast at Pulham: R 33, shown here in RAF colours, spent many months in 1921 in mooring trials at this mast, working out the "high" mast techniques for both the British and American services. (Charles Keller)

punctured. Only 22½ minutes passed from dropping the mooring wire to securing at the mast head. In a second flight on February 18, the time to secure the ship was reduced to 10 minutes. This routine continued to be the normal one for mooring and unmooring at the high mast, though at a later date, wire yaw guys were led to port and starboard from the airship's nose, to prevent her from swinging as she approached the mast.

The many days spent at the mast demonstrated that constant changes in lift were a problem, and a watch had to be kept aboard at all times to handle the elevators, to valve gas if superheat made the ship light, or to release ballast if she became heavy; while hydrogen and water had to be available at the mast head at all times. The elevators were used to keep the angle of inclination of the ship between 3 degrees up and 9 degrees down. The rudders were kept amidships at all times. Strong winds up to 55 mph in gusts were no problem; light rain made the ship heavy to a certain point, after which the excess dripped off; dry snow did not accumulate, but wet snow was a problem to the end of the airship era. Captain Thomas even devised snow clearing gear consisting of an endless wire atop the ship between Frames 7 and 34, which dragged lengths of 2½ in. hemp rope forward and aft along the airship's outer cover. On June 3, 1921, a heavy rain squall forced the tail of the ship to the ground despite release of ballast aft; fortunately the lower fin landed in a pond and was submerged without damage. It was thought that the dynamic force of the falling rain drops on the large area of the cover, rather than the weight of the water, was what brought R 33 to the ground on this occasion. To prevent the stern from rising when superheated, pairs of artillery wheels weighing about 7 cwt. each were attached at Frames 21 and 34 by bridles which lifted them off the ground when the stern rose 3 to 4 degrees. The changes in static lift at the mast, and the need to keep a full watch aboard at all times, later caused the Americans (who copied the English "high" mast) to develop the stub mast which held the airship low to the ground, while the rear car or lower fin rested on the ground atop a mooring car which rode around the "mooring out circle" as the ship weather-vaned into the wind.

The Pulham experiments with R 33 ended in August, 1921, with the closing down of airship activity in Britain. The Pulham mast remained unique in England, until a much larger tower was built at Cardington in connection with a later programme.

The British rigid airship programme is more remarkable politically than technically or operationally. Money was spent lavishly to build copies of German Zeppelins which were three to four years out of date when completed; a minimal amount of flying was done, necessarily most of it for training, and the only outstanding achievement was the double crossing of the Atlantic by R 34 in July, 1919. Nor was this an outgrowth of policy, but represented the initiative of the Director of Airships, Air Commodore Maitland, and the enthusiasts around him. The most ambitious technical advance, the design and construction of R 38, resulted in catastrophe; R 80, however, proved that Britain had at least one designer with skill and ability.

The purpose behind the British rigid airship programme was to give the Royal Navy a means of long range aerial reconnaissance at sea equal or superior to the Zeppelins of the Imperial German Navy. The purpose was not achieved. Vacillations in policy and a lack of sense of purpose among those in power represented "muddling through" at its worst. The fifteen rigid airships built in Great Britain between 1908 and 1921 deserve to be mentioned in this history; but they did little to advance the state of the art, no originality was shown in their employment, and their neglect by the historian would seem deserved in view of their generally sterile operational record.

VI

The innovators: American military rigids

Long after the Germans and British had abandoned the rigid airship as a military weapon, the American Navy, up to the eve of World War II, persisted in attempts to develop the rigid as a naval scout. The reasons for this continued effort were various, but may be summed up in naval requirements for a possible Pacific war, and in the American monopoly of helium, a non-flammable lifting gas only slightly heavier than hydrogen.

In a few years, from the Spanish-American War of 1898 to the end of World War I, the United States Navy had grown from sixth to second largest in the world. In addition, it had assumed responsibility for a Pacific empire captured from Spain, and had begun to feel concern about the expansionist ambitions of Japan as revealed by the Twenty-One Demands on China in 1915, aggressive intervention in Siberia in 1918, and resentment of the United States after the passage of the Japanese Exclusion Law of 1924. The Washington Treaty of 1922, setting a 5 : 5 : 3 strength ratio among the British, American and Japanese Navies, in some ways aggravated the problem. The American war plan was based on a local defence of the Philippines while the United States Fleet, consisting of battleships, cruisers, and train, fought its way across the wide Pacific in the face of a powerful and aggressive Japanese fleet, operating from a large number of bases in the Marshalls and Carolines generously offered to the island empire by the architects of the Versailles Treaty. Such an advance – or any warlike operation in the incomprehensible vastness of the world's largest ocean – would require far-flung reconnaissance to divine the enemy's movements and intentions, and the rigid airship was seen as peculiarly suited for this role by reason of its great range and endurance.

At the same time, the United States Navy had become increasingly air-minded from the year 1911, when the first naval officers had taken flight training with Glenn Curtiss; and had made a major effort to establish a naval air service in Europe in 1917-18. Technical advances, and an awareness of the increasing capabilities of the air weapon, caused the Navy with the approval of Congress to establish a

182

Bureau of Aeronautics on July 12, 1921, to control and direct the development of aviation in the Navy. The choice of Rear Admiral William A. Moffett for Chief of the Bureau was extraordinarily fortunate. Far more than the flamboyant exhibitionist, General William L. Mitchell, Moffett laid the foundations for the sea-air victory over Japan in 1941-45. His mission was simply "to take aviation to sea with the Fleet," and in the process he fostered and developed the aircraft carrier, the attack group of carrier aircraft, the light-weight, high powered air cooled radial engine, and the long range flying boat. Moffett also took a great interest in the rigid airship throughout his three terms as Chief of the Bureau (1921-33), and a considerable measure of support came from his successor, Rear Admiral Ernest J. King (1933-36). The rigid airship cause was further supported by the large Goodyear industrial combine, the president of which, Paul W. Litchfield, established an alliance with the *Luftschiffbau Zeppelin* which resulted in the creation of the Goodyear-Zeppelin Corporation.

Official interest in European rigid airships commenced in 1913, when Admiral David W. Taylor, the able and far-sighted Chief Constructor of the Navy, sent one of his most brilliant subordinates, Naval Constructor (Lieutenant Commander) Jerome C. Hunsaker, to Europe to study recent developments in naval aircraft. Hunsaker had already distinguished himself by founding in that year at Massachusetts Institute of Technology one of the earliest courses in aeronautical engineering taught in the United States, and through the years he continued to be a prominent figure in the rigid airship program. On the trip to Europe, he was allowed to inspect the outside of the DELAG passenger ship "Viktoria Luise" and made a flight in her over Berlin.[1] On his return he observed that "the principal function of the dirigible in naval warfare is to supplement the work of scout cruisers, and its offensive powers would rarely be called upon."[2] Such was the rationale behind the U.S. Navy's interest in the rigid airship throughout the period of its employment. Through the naval attaché in Berlin, samples of gas cell material picked up at the site of the L 2 disaster were forwarded to Admiral Taylor's Bureau of Construction and Repair and identified as gold beaters' skin, leading to interest in fabricating this material in

[1] Hunsaker, J. C. *The History of Naval Aviation.* Vol. VI, "The Development of Rigid Airships," p. 1. Typescript, 1923, copied and mimeographed by Charles L. Keller, 1960.
[2] Hunsaker, J. C. "The Present Status of Airships in Europe." *Journal of the Franklin Institute,* vol. 177, No. 6, p. 597-639.

America; while samples of girders from the wrecks of L 3 in Denmark, L 20 in Norway, and LZ 77 in France, were made available by the naval attachés in these countries and determined by analysis to be duralumin as described in Wilm's original patent of 1909. This aided the Bureau in persuading the Aluminium Company of America and other firms to commence production of duralumin beginning in 1916.

War in Europe, and the spectacular Zeppelin raids on London, focussed increasing attention on the rigid airship and its possible usefulness for the U.S. Navy. As early as June 24, 1916, the General Board of the Navy, an advisory committee of senior admirals headed by George Dewey, the victor of the Battle of Manila Bay, issued a study of "the possible naval uses of aircraft" which recommended among other matters the procurement of one rigid airship, one semirigid and three small non-rigid airships.[3] A further step was the joint proposal by Admiral Taylor and General G.O. Squier, the Chief Signal Officer of the Army, that the War and Navy Departments cooperate in designing and building rigid airships. The matter was referred by the Secretaries of War and Navy to the General Board, which on October 19, 1916, replied that Zeppelins were "a matter of great importance to the Navy and demand immediate attention."[4] This led to the establishment on January 15, 1917, of a Joint Airship Board of Army and Navy officers charged with designing an airship of the Zeppelin type under the direction of the Chief Constructor of the Navy.

Mr. Starr Truscott, a civil engineer, was named Chief Engineer to the Board, and was largely responsible for the evolution during 1918 of a design for a rigid airship 615 feet long. Unfortunately Hermann Müller, the British Admiralty's Schütte-Lanz "expert," had now appeared in Washington sponsored by the Naval Attaché in London, and he was responsible for the hull framework being designed with wooden girders. Müller's incompetence as an engineer was recognized and he was released after a few months; but the design had some startling features for which Truscott was responsible – thick cantilever section fins which only then were appearing on the latest Zeppelins, and four engines enclosed in the keel driving propellers on brackets. Such an internal power plant installation would only have been possible if the ship were inflated with helium. Subsequently the

[3] Archibald J. Turner and Clifford L. Lord, *History of United States Naval Aviation* (New Haven: Yale University Press, 1949), p. 63.
[4] Hunsaker, *The History of Naval Aviation*, Vol. VI, p. 5.

faults and weaknesses of the wooden girders were apparent and the Board decided not to build this design. In fact, no American rigid was laid down or procured during the war years.

A great effort was made during 1917-18 to make helium available for military airship use, the British being particularly concerned to obtain the gas for the rigids being built for military operations in the North Sea. First discovered in the solar spectrum in 1868, and isolated in the laboratory in 1895, the rare, inert gas continued to be a laboratory curiosity even after Dr. H.P. Cady of the University of Kansas identified helium in natural gas from a well in Dexter, Kansas, in 1905. It soon became clear that helium was present in natural gases occurring in Kansas. It is now known that helium is found in significant amounts only in the United States, and "about 90 per cent of the helium is concentrated in a small area within 250 miles of Amarillo, Texas."[5]

In the year 1917, the scientists and chemists were investigating the properties of the new gas, costing $2500 per cubic foot when produced in minute amounts in the laboratory, with no idea that it might have a practical application. It was Sir William Ramsay, acting on behalf of the British Admiralty, who first drew the attention of officials of the U.S. Bureau of Mines to the possibility of procuring helium for airship use from sources in the United States. With America in the war, the Airship Board on July 26, 1917, took up a proposal by the Bureau of Mines to set up an experimental helium plant, and £100,000 of military funds were approved for the project. Subsequently, and largely at British insistence, the program was enormously expanded. Under U.S. Navy direction, two separate experimental plants were erected in Fort Worth, Texas, to extract helium from the natural gases of the Petrolia field, Plant 1 (designed by Linde Air Products) being completed on March 6, 1918, and Plant 2 (by the Air Reduction Company) on May 5, 1918. In both facilities, the extraction process involved liquefaction of the major constitutents, methane and nitrogen, while the helium, still gaseous, could be recovered in a 70 per cent pure state. Subsequent purification improved the figure to 90 per cent. By Armistice Day the two Fort Worth plants had produced 150,000 cubic feet of helium. Some of this was in gas cylinders on the dock at New Orleans on this date, ready for shipment to Europe. A contract for a large production plant was signed with Linde on October 22, 1918, but

[5] Clifford W. Seibel, *Helium, Child of the Sun* (Lawrence: The University Press of Kansas, 1969), p. 20.

this was not completed until April, 1921. Steady improvements in extraction methods were carried out by Navy personnel under Lieut. Comdr. Zeno W. Wicks, the officer-in-charge, but on July 1, 1925, the Bureau of Mines succeeded in gaining control of the helium producing organization through an Act of Congress. Through January 10, 1929, this production plant at Fort Worth delivered a total of 46.1 million cubic feet of helium, supplying the needs of the early post-war U.S. Navy rigid airship program.[6]

In December, 1917, the Airship Board sent a technical committee abroad to investigate airship development in England and France. The committee report led the Board on July 19, 1918, to recommend to the Secretaries of War and Navy that four rigid airships be purchased at once — two in England for use abroad, and two to be built in the United States. It was recommended that the Navy be solely responsible for design and construction of the American ships, providing information to the Army. Following the Armistice the 4-ship program was abandoned, but in 1919 Congress appropriated funds for two airships, one to be purchased abroad, the other to be built at home; and for establishment of an airship base. This led to the purchase of the British R 38, numbered ZR 2 in the American series,[7] the design and construction in the United States of the ZR 1 U.S.S. "Shenandoah," and the acquisition of the Army's Camp Kendrick in New Jersey and its conversion into the U.S. Naval Air Station, Lakehurst, with a giant double hangar 804 feet long, 264 feet wide, and 193 feet high, "clear inner dimensions."

Despite the established policy that the Navy alone would be responsible for design and construction of rigid airships in the United States, the Army made a bold attempt to procure a large airship from the Zeppelin Company. The subterfuges employed, the indifference to established legal procedures and the disregard of operational realities (neither the Army nor the Navy at the time possessed a large airship hangar in the United States) bear the stamp of Brigadier General William Mitchell, then Chief Training and Operations Officer of the Army Air Service. His instrument was a certain Colonel William N. Hensley, who was sped on his way by being assigned as observer aboard the R 34 on her eastbound flight from Long Island to Pulham, England, in July, 1919. Hensley's orders were to "acquire as much information as practicable concerning airships and airship

[6] Seibel, p. 41-49.
[7] The Z designation applied to all Navy lighter than air craft from 1919 to 1961; the R indicated rigid.

stations in England."[8] He was also encouraged to visit Germany, France and Italy in search of further information. On August 20, 1919, Hensley received orders from the War Department to proceed to The Hague "for the purpose of carrying out confidential instructions with reference to the original Zeppelin Airship Corporation."[9] These resulted from an attempt by the Zeppelin Company to sell the last wartime airship, L 72, which they considered their personal property — an approach disapproved by the Joint Army-Navy Board on Aeronautics, on the grounds that L 72 would be disposed of by the Allied powers under the Peace Treaty. Together with the military attaché at The Hague, Colonel Edward Davis, Hensley proceeded to Berlin on September 5 to discuss sale of the L 72 with Zeppelin Company representatives. Going on to Friedrichshafen, Hensley inspected the Zeppelin works and flew in the passenger airship "Bodensee," while his deluded partner advised Washington "we now have tentative plans to fly airship L 72 from Berlin across Asia to Philippine Islands, thence across Pacific via Honolulu to the United States and afterwards back to Berlin if desired."[10] Yet on September 5 the Inter-Allied Aeronautical Commission of Control had awarded the L 72 to France.

For Hensley this was a small matter, as he had been made acquainted in Friedrichshafen with the "America airship," the reworked design for the big L 100 of 3,800,000 cubic feet, ordered for the German Navy in September, 1918, and cancelled a month later.[11] To secure one of these monsters, bigger even than the R 38 then building in England, would be a real triumph for Hensley personally, and for the Army Air Service — all the more attractive when the price of eight million inflated marks came to only $360,000. The money was made available, and at the end of October the War Department agreed to a higher price — twelve million marks, equal to $500,000. Hensley, expecting to be commanding officer, wired home for 13 officers and 37 men to form a crew. On November 26, 1919, Hensley and Alfred Colsman of the Zeppelin Company signed a contract for construction of the ship, known as the LZ 125, and to be 774 feet long, 97 feet 11 inches in diameter, and with 3,532,000 cubic feet of gas in 16 cells and twelve 240 hp

[8] Charles L. Keller, "The Hensley Affair." *Journal of the American Aviation Historical Society*, vol. 10, No. 4, Winter, 1965, p. 282.
[9] *ibid.*
[10] Keller. There were of course no facilities for housing or servicing rigid airships in Asia, the Philippines, or Hawaii.
[11] See p. 139.

Maybachs in ten power cars. Though forbidden to do so by Article 201 of the Versailles Treaty, the Zeppelin Company began work on the new craft.

Abruptly Hensley's dream was shattered when he was advised on December 1, 1919, that the Secretary of War, Newton D. Baker, had ordered the project abandoned and no more expenditures were to be made. Hensley got nowhere with protests that the contract already had been signed, nor did the Zeppelin Company with threats to bring a claim for damages. What seems to have happened is that Baker had been kept more or less in the dark concerning the activities of his ambitious subordinates. As he later explained to the properly indignant Secretary of the Navy,

> Under an erroneous assumption that the dirigible referred to at that time was one to be procured under conditions similar to those which would have brought about the purchase of the L 72, I permitted negotiations to be entered into ... When I became fully acquainted with the facts in the matter and realized that we were entering into negotiations with nationals of a country with which we were still at war ... I therefore promptly gave instructions to cancel the contract and to drop the matter entirely.[12]

Though the United States Army continued to fly pressure airships until 1937, it never succeeded in procuring a rigid.

Of the two ships of the Navy's 1919 programme the first to fly was the ZR 2, as the British R 38 was to have been known in the American service. The history of this unfortunate craft has already been told, including the story of her last flight and crash on August 24, 1921, in which her prospective commanding officer, Commander Louis H. Maxfield, and 15 other American officers and men were killed.[13] Maxfield's death was particularly painful, for "it was largely due to his enthusiasm and energy that the Department (and the General Board) agreed to approve a rigid airship program and the Lakehurst station."[14] It is to be noted that the timing of the ZR 2's delivery flight across the Atlantic was influenced by the completion date of the Lakehurst hangar, which was approximately August 1,

---

[12] Keller. The United States Senate's refusal to ratify the Versailles Treaty led to a state of war with Germany continuing until October 18, 1921, when the Senate ratified a special peace treaty with Germany.

[13] Though R 38 had not been transferred to the U.S. Navy at the time of the crash, she was wearing the American star-in-a-circle insigne and American vertical red, white and blue stripes on her rudders. Neither Charles Keller nor Robin Higham know of an American name selected for her, and Keller doubts that one had yet been chosen.

[14] Hunsaker, Vol. VI. p. 15.

1921.[15] The tragedy left in the American naval authorities and airship operators a lasting distrust of British designs and methods: painfully aware of their own lack of knowledge and experience, they had trustfully accepted the role of pupils to the British, only to find their confidence had been betrayed at the cost of many irreplaceable lives. "The United States was perhaps at fault in not detailing a competent naval constructor and an engineer to act as inspectors with the usual full authority," wrote Hunsaker with the benefit of hindsight.[16] Determined not to be cheated again, the United States Navy resolved that the replacement ship to be procured abroad should be safe and efficient without question, and therefore would be built in Friedrichshafen by the Zeppelin Company. This led shortly to a contract with the Friedrichshafen firm for the ZR 3 "Los Angeles."

For the ZR 1 design the U.S. Navy Department and the designers of the Bureau of Construction and Repair decided to use German models. During the 1917-18 visit to Europe of the Technical Committee of the Joint Army and Navy Airship Board, Truscott had received a promise of the drawings of the German Zeppelin L 49, which had force-landed in France after the "Silent Raid" of October 19-20, 1917, and from which complete plans were made by Naval Constructor Sabatier. These were given to Hunsaker in late 1918 when he was in Europe to inspect German naval Zeppelins as a member of the Inter-Allied Aeronautical Commission. The first American design, Fleet Airship No. 1 as it was then known, was a copy of the L 49 with American engines. The British designer of R 38, Naval Constructor C.I.R. Campbell, made two visits to Washington in December, 1919, and September, 1920, and made many suggestions, which included lengthening the ship, increasing the number of the engines, and replacing the flat fins of the L 49 with thick cantilever ones. The latter suggestion was at first not accepted, but four variants of the FA 1 design were prepared, two of them with two added gas cells and six engines. Lack of knowledge of bending stresses in turns led to the addition of only one gas cell. Cantilever fins were added to the design after the Americans obtained data on the fins in L 72, and after wind tunnel tests. It must not be assumed that the Americans slavishly copied the

[15] The Naval Air Station, Lakehurst, was commissioned on June 28, 1921. Charles Keller believes the ZR-2 would have landed at Lakehurst, and then have based at Cape May where a wartime shed was being enlarged to 705 ft. long x 106 ft. wide x 109½ ft. high.
[16] Hunsaker, Vol. VI, p. 15.

Zeppelin design, for independent stress analyses were made by Mr. Charles P. Burgess of the Bureau of Construction and Repair, with the famous warship designer, Professor William Hovgaard, as consultant. After the R 38 crashed due to structural failure, the Bureau undertook to obtain an independent check of their calculations through a committee named by the National Advisory Committee for Aeronautics. The committee's report was highly favorable; but it must be noted that Burgess and his fellow designers had worked in more material to strengthen the light "height climber" hull, particularly in the lower intermediate longitudinals.

The final ZR 1 design, as approved by the Secretary of the Navy on October 31, 1921, was for a rigid airship 680.25 feet long, 78.7 feet in diameter, and with a gas volume 95 per cent full of 2,115,174 cubic feet in twenty gas cells. The hull form and structure closely followed Zeppelin practice with kingpost braced main frames 10 metres apart, intermediate unbraced rings 5 metres from the main frames, and thirteen main longitudinal and twelve intermediate longitudinal girders. The bow structure was strengthened for mast mooring and fitted with a mooring cone; the cantilever fins resembled those in L 72, the rudders and elevators being flat surfaces and fitted with external balancing areas ahead of the hinge line. Six Packard 6 cylinder in-line liquid cooled engines of 300 hp at 1400 rpm were carried in an arrangement resembling that of L 72. Five of them were installed in small power cars with radiators in the nose of the gondolas, the air flow being controlled by adjustable hemispherical shutters. One gondola was fitted aft at Ring 60 and two more to port and starboard at Ring 90; these had 18 foot geared down propellers, reversible in the pair at Ring 90. Another pair at Ring 120 had direct drive 10 foot propellers. The sixth engine was fitted abaft the control car, which was slung below the hull on struts and wires as in Zeppelin practice.

All parts of the airship were fabricated at the Naval Aircraft Factory at Philadelphia and trucked to Lakehurst for assembly in the big hangar. The work at Lakehurst was directed by Commander R.D. Weyerbacher, assisted by Anton Heinen, a former Zeppelin Company flight test crew captain brought to the United States by Weyerbacher in 1922; and a Mr. Farlam, a British Admiralty overseer familiar with airship work. (Hunsaker reports that the two former enemies acted as inspectors and got on very well!) The first ring, 105, was completed and hoisted into place on April 24, 1922, and by January 1, 1923, the structure was complete except for the bow and tail sections. The

"Shenandoah" as completed, with 6 engines, above the Hudson River. (U.S. Navy)

tail was completed by April, the outer cover laced on, and inflation commenced (with helium, of course) on August 13. ZR 1 floated free in her shed on August 20, and her first flight was made on September 4, 1923. It was the first ascent ever made by a helium-inflated rigid airship.[17] The command arrangement on this first flight was a curious one: the ship's designated commander was Captain F.R. McCrary, but as ZR 1 in effect was making her builder's trials, Weyerbacher was nominally in charge. Since both U.S. naval officers lacked practical experience, all directions and commands were in fact given by the German operating expert, Heinen.

There followed flights in which ZR 1 showed herself over New York, and Washington, generating great enthusiasm as traffic stopped in the streets and people rushed out of houses and buildings to see the great silver ship in the sky. On October 1-3 forty-four hours were put on the ship as she flew from Lakehurst to St. Louis for the

[17] Though on December 5, 1921, the U.S. Navy's non-rigid C 7, under the command of Zachary Lansdowne, had made the first flight of a helium inflated airship from the Naval Air Station Hampton Roads to Anacostia (near Washington) and return.

National Air Races, returning with Admiral Moffett aboard for his first airship flight. On October 10 the airship was commissioned and christened by the wife of the Secretary of the Navy with the name "Shenandoah," an Indian term meaning "daughter of the stars." On November 11, 1923, the new ship made a 14 hour flight to Boston. Among the enthralled spectators was a small boy of 5 who was (and still is) convinced that no more beautiful or romantic vehicle had ever appeared in the skies as this graceful silver monster bearing the red, white and blue star-in-a-circle and vertical rudder stripes, and the legend "U.S. Navy" amidships. Majestically she passed from the northeast to show her broadside, turned to starboard and glided down the sky to the southwest, effortlessly, almost soundlessly. I have never forgotten to this day the high excitement of those moments, nor have I ceased to regret that my dream of flying in a rigid airship has never been fulfilled.

"Shenandoah" promptly became a guinea pig for working out many practical details of rigid airship operations as the U.S. Navy thought they should be conducted. Sharing the British determination that their ships should not be caught in their sheds by cross winds, the Americans were resolved to keep their airships moored to the mast as much as possible. The 160-foot Lakehurst "high" mast was not a copy of the British experimental mast at Pulham, being a stout triangular steel tower with elevator, gas, fuel and water mains to the masthead, winches at the base of the tower for the main mooring wire and the yaw lines, and around the tower on a circle of 500 feet radius were 48 snatch block anchorages to take the port and starboard yaw lines regardless of the direction from which the ship approached. A similar mast was built by Henry Ford at his own expense in Detroit, and on the after deck of the Navy tanker "Patoka" another triangular mast was erected with a height of 141 feet. "Semiportable" field masts were erected at Fort Worth, San Diego, Camp Lewis in the State of Washington, Guantanamo Bay in Cuba, and Ewa, Hawaii, being 160 foot steel poles braced with three sets of guys. "Shenandoah" made her first mooring to the Lakehurst mast on November 16, 1923, and during her 2-year career made 26 mast moorings, plus 7 to the tender "Patoka." As in the R 33 experiments, difficulty was experienced with rapid changes in lift, and a watch had to be kept on board at all times to "fly" her at the mast.

With "Shenandoah" being the first rigid airship to fly with helium, the problems peculiar to the use of this gas instead of hydrogen were

The 160 foot "high" mooring mast at Lakehurst, with "Shenandoah" riding to it, prior to the "break-away" flight of 16 January 1924. (R. S. Clements)

worked out with her. While to the layman the non-flammable lifting medium might seem an unmitigated blessing, to experienced American airship men it often appeared as a curse. Indeed, there were arguments that in wartime particularly, hydrogen should be employed because of the higher performance, greater weight carrying capacity and ceiling which could be attained with the lighter gas. [18] Such proposals however received no countenance from the Bureau of Aeronautics, which after an intensive campaign to convince Congress and the country of the advantages of the expensive but "safe" helium, was committed to evolving techniques for its use.

The commanders of the "Shenandoah" and later American rigids were faced with essentially two problems in respect to helium: one being the actual decreased performance relative to hydrogen, and the other being the need to conserve the gas, which in fiscal 1922-23 cost $120.22 per thousand cubic feet vs. $2 to $3 per thousand cubic feet for hydrogen.

As for the loss of performance, a comparison of the 2,115,000 cubic foot "Shenandoah" with the German L 70 of 2,195,800 cubic feet is instructive. Under standard conditions with hydrogen of a specific gravity relative to air of 0.1 (the efficient gas plants at the German Navy's North Sea bases were able to turn out hydrogen with a gravity of 0.09) the gross lift of the German Zeppelin was 159,400 lb. In the slightly smaller "Shenandoah" inflated with helium the gross lift was only 131,100 lb. Part of the problem here was that the helium as produced by the Fort Worth plant was little more than 90 per cent pure. [19] While the light weight German "height climber" had a weight empty of 62,300 lb, that of "Shenandoah" was 77,500 lb as of October 10, 1923, increased by May 22, 1924, to 83,600 lb. With higher structural weight and lower gross lift in the helium ship, the big difference appears in the useful lift – 97,100 lb. in the German hydrogen ship, only 53,600 lb in "Shenandoah" on October 10, 1923, decreasing to 47,500 lb on May 22, 1924. [20]

Not only was helium expensive in the year "Shenandoah" was first inflated, but the plant in Fort Worth had difficulty in keeping up with the demand – in fact a real shortage in 1924 prevented the

[18] Department of the Navy, Bureau of Aeronautics, *Rigid Airship Manual* (Washington: Government Printing Office, 1927), p. IX-8.
[19] Writing of the Amarillo helium plant opened in 1929, Seibel comments: "The added purity (98 per cent) over the standard of the plant at Fort Worth would have given an airship like the old 'Shenandoah' an additional payload of about 10 per cent." Seibel, p. 81.
[20] Figures for "Shenandoah" from Charles L. Keller, *U.S.S. "Shenandoah."* (1965: World War I Aero Historians Inc., West Roxbury, Mass.), p. 22.

operation of more than one airship at a time. All sorts of expedients were devised to minimize the valving of gas. In the hangar "Shenandoah" was kept only 85 per cent full of gas. This was contrary to German practice, which required that cells be gassed daily to 100 per cent fullness with as much overpressure as the automatic valves would tolerate to prevent the inward diffusion of air, which would produce a dangerously explosive mixture of oxyhydrogen. On the other hand, no danger resulted from air diffusing into helium, and the helium itself could easily be purified in a liquefaction plant right at Lakehurst. With 85 per cent inflation the pressure height — that at which the gas expanded to fill the cells 100 per cent full — was 4500 feet, and "Shenandoah" therefore flew ordinarily below this altitude to prevent loss of helium through the automatic valves. Furthermore, all sorts of expedients were used to increase or decrease the lift of the ship through superheating or supercooling, all without changing the amount of gas on board. Takeoff with "hangar superheat" involved bringing the airship out of the warm hangar and into the cold night air, which would confer a temporary superheat of as much as 15 degrees with corresponding increase of lift. By the time the gas temperature had cooled to that of the surrounding air, the ship was aloft and able to carry the added load dynamically with the power of her engines.

A favorite device for getting away with a relatively large amount of fuel was to bring the airship out to the mast the evening before a flight, or early in the morning. As the sun rose into the sky, the helium warmed and expanded, and fuel was piped aboard as the superheat and lift increased. Again because of the superheat problem, landings were not made in the middle of the day, but in the evening or at night when the gas was supercooled and the ship relatively heavy. Valving helium to bring the "Shenandoah" down for a landing was religiously avoided, regardless of the operating schedule.

Yet valving helium could not have been avoided unless the lightness of the ship after burning petrol could somehow be compensated for. The theoretical answer was to recover from the engine exhausts the water formed by combustion of the petrol. In theory, 145 lb of water could be recovered in the exhaust from burning 100 lb of petrol; in fact, the water recovery equipment installed on engines 1, 4 and 5 of the "Shenandoah" recovered 110 to 122 lb of water for every 100 lb of petrol burned. This was piped to ballast bags in the keel, thus maintaining the static condition of the ship; but the equipment was not popular with the ship's commanding officers. Each water recovery unit consisted of a nest of piping measuring 5 feet across, hung in the air stream above the gondolas where it created added drag; while the weight of each unit appears to have been approximately 450 lb.

In a radio broadcast in the summer of 1923 Admiral Moffett had suggested that "Shenandoah" should fly to the North Pole. Preparations were made with the aid of the noted Arctic explorer, Vilhajalmur Stefansson. In December President Coolidge approved the flight. Mast moorings were stepped up during December, 1923, and January, 1924, to train the crew as "Shenandoah" would have to exist at a mast ashore or aboard "Patoka" in the Arctic. On the evening of January 16, 1924, a serious accident occurred which could have had fatal results for the ship, particularly if she had been inflated with hydrogen: while riding to the mast in a gale, the cover of the upper fin tore to pieces, and in a gust of 74 mph the "Shenandoah" ripped free of the tower, leaving the mooring fitting on the mast. Structural damage caused the two forward gas cells to deflate. Personnel on board, directed by Heinen, dropped ballast, started the engines and got the damaged ship under control, bringing her back to Lakehurst next morning after the storm had abated.

The resulting repairs kept "Shenandoah" grounded until May 22, 1924. The fins, which had shown signs of weakness on the St. Louis flight, were reinforced. The badly damaged upper fin and the nose were rebuilt. The No. 6 engine abaft the control car was removed and its place taken by a motor-generator set for the radio and a cook stove with two petrol burners. Despite removal of the heavy Packard, the total weight of "Shenandoah" increased, largely due to the addition of water recovery apparatus.

In addition, the ship had a new commanding officer. Continuing tensions among the commanding triumvirate of McCrary, Weyerbacher and Heinen, coming to a head on the "breakaway flight," when one of "Shenandoah's" officers had refused to accept Heinen's orders, led to McCrary being replaced on February 12, 1924, by Lieut. Comdr. Zachary Lansdowne, who continued in command until the final tragedy a year and a half later. An officer of the highest professional qualifications, and an unforgettable figure in the history of the rigid airship, Lansdowne's constant preoccupation was to make the rigid airship a useful scouting tool for the Fleet.

A short flight of 1 hour and 13 minutes on May 22, 1924, served to test the repairs and to train the crew. Following some flights to New York, Philadelphia, Buffalo and Scranton, "Shenandoah"

"Shenandoah" moored to the "Patoka" off Newport, 8 August 1924. Obviously it was possible for the airship to swing over the tanker if wind and tide did not coincide, and the latter's superstructure and masts were cut down accordingly. (U.S. Navy)

proceeded to Newport, R.I., to moor for the first time to the "Patoka," newly commissioned with a mast at her stern. "Patoka" was intended to be the mobile base for "Shenandoah" on the polar flight, and much depended on the success or failure of her equipment.[21] The mooring operation on August 8 took an hour, but differed little from mast moorings at Lakehurst, and there were no unusual problems. Instead of the mooring wire being dropped on the field to be coupled to the mast wire, the two were picked up in the water by a boat and coupled manually (this proved so time consuming that later a grapnel on the airship's wire coupled automatically to the mast wire). The yaw guys, led from 80 foot booms at the base of the mast, were similarly connected and the "Shenandoah" drawn to the mast while the "Patoka" steamed slowly ahead. After nearly 20 hours on the mast, "Shenandoah" cast off and returned to Lakehurst.

[21] The "Patoka's" sister tanker "Ramapo" was to be fitted with a mast also, but cancellation of the Arctic flight caused this project to be dropped.

Now came a daring *tour de force* intended to prove the design and construction of "Shenandoah," the feasibility of her numerous innovations including helium inflation and water recovery, and the question of whether she could operate over a period of time from mooring masts without having access to a hangar. In preparation for the Arctic flight, the big rigid was to cross the country to the West Coast, proceed north to the State of Washington, and return to Lakehurst. That success was achieved with a prototype airship and a rudimentary ground organization stands to the credit of Zachary Lansdowne, her skilled and determined commander, and to the crew which he had trained and inspired by his outstanding personal qualities.

Flying the flag of Admiral Moffett, "Shenandoah" departed the Lakehurst mast on October 7, 1924, and after an uneventful flight of 37 hours made a night mooring to the mast at Fort Worth. The next stage, across the Continental Divide to San Diego, was known to be the most difficult of the journey, for the airship would have to ascend to a higher altitude than she had yet reached even to make her way through the passes at the southern end of the Rocky Mountain chain. To ascend to high altitude and clear the peaks was out of the question, not only because of the large loss of helium that would ensue through the automatic valves, but also because so little lifting gas would remain that the airship could not carry enough fuel to reach her destination.

Thus, although "Shenandoah" was flying low above the ground, she was gradually forced up higher by the rising terrain of West Texas as she proceeded west-south-west from Fort Worth. At Van Horn she was already flying at 6,600 feet, with helium blowing off from the automatic valves. By moonlight the airship crossed El Paso, proceeding via Deming and Lordsburg to pass through Dos Cabezos Pass between Bowie and Cochise. Here the gusty head wind at one point swung the long hull towards a mountain side despite having hard over rudder in the opposite direction, and control car personnel held their breath. Dawn showed Tucson ahead. Proceeding down the Gila River, "Shenandoah" traversed Mohawk Pass and reached Yuma. Heading up the Imperial Valley to avoid head winds on the more direct route, "Shenandoah" was enveloped in a snow squall which drove her to within 300 feet of the ground — as demonstrated by the lead "fish" at the end of the radio antenna being carried away! At 11.30 p.m. on October 10 the ship touched down on the landing ground of the Naval Air Station, North Island, San Diego,

"Shenandoah" on the transcontinental flight, moored to the 160 foot semi-portable mast at San Diego, 10-16 October 1924. (U.S. Navy)

preparatory to being walked to the mast, 37 hours and 44 minutes after departing Fort Worth. Here occurred the only accident of the cruise, as the inexperienced ground crew stood back and allowed the rear gondola to strike the ground hard. Girders were damaged in the hull above, but repairs were made at the mast during the next 5 days.

There followed a scenic flight of 58 hours up the Pacific coast on October 16-18, prolonged by fog obscuring the mast in the early morning when "Shenandoah" arrived at Camp Lewis, Washington, near Tacoma. By the time the fog had burned off the ship's helium was so superheated by the sun that she could have landed only by valving large amounts of the expensive gas. So Lansdowne cruised all day nose down to counteract the ship's lightness dynamically, landing at 6.30 p.m. after the gas had cooled. Here Admiral Moffett disembarked.

The flight back down the coast to San Diego on October 19-21 consumed only 47 hours despite stiff head winds off San Francisco. The return eastward across the Continental Divide was a more strenuous test of the ship than the westbound flight, as she was obliged immediately to ascent to 6000 feet before having a chance to burn off fuel. Only by driving her at a 12 degree up angle with full speed on the engines was it possible to hold her at this altitude with 18,000 lb of fuel on board, and with supercooling of the gas after sunset over western Arizona, it was necessary first to drop a ton of ballast, and then in succession four 724 lb. tanks of petrol. This ended Lansdowne's hopes of making the flight to Lakehurst non-stop with the prevailing westerlies, and "Shenandoah" landed at Fort Worth to fuel and take on helium. The return to Lakehurst across the central plains was easy, and just before midnight on October 25, the airship landed outside the big hangar. Total time in the air was 235 hours 1 minute.

The West Coast flight caused great excitement and interest among the American public – it must be remembered that in the year 1924 there was no transcontinental air passenger service, and only mail was being flown from New York to San Francisco by the Post Office Department in rebuilt World War I de Havilands. Thus it was easy to see the "Shenandoah's" transcontinental flight as the precursor of commercial passenger service. Abroad, the cruise convinced British and German airship men that the Americans meant business, were learning their trade thoroughly, and that their innovations including the use of helium were practical.

Among those who congratulated Lansdowne and his officers was Dr. Hugo Eckener, the chairman of the Zeppelin Company, who had arrived at Lakehurst on October 15 in command of the new ZR 3, the Zeppelin-built LZ 126. With the meagre output of the Fort Worth helium plant the United States did not possess enough helium to fly two large airships, so it was decreed that "Shenandoah" should be laid up and her helium transferred to the new ship. Not until June 26, 1925, did Lansdowne get his craft back in the air, and then only by getting his helium back from the ex-German sister ship. Meanwhile some further modifications were made in "Shenandoah," the most drastic involving a reduction in the number of gas valves, both automatic and manoeuvring.

"Shenandoah" as completed followed German practice, with eighteen automatic valves at the bottom of her twenty gas cells (the two smallest cells at the ends of the ship had no valves, but communicated with their neighbors instead), and sixteen manoeuvring valves in the top of the gas cells, these being operated by wires from the control car. In addition, she had a non-German

Two rigids at Lakehurst but only one flying! "Shenandoah" at left is deflated, with framework suspended from the overhead and supported from below. "Los Angeles" at right has received her helium and is tied down in the shed. Taken in 1925 before 26 June. (R. S. Clements)

innovation, a fabric inflation manifold 2 feet in diameter connecting all the gas cells. This was intended to permit filling them through the nose of the ship while at the mast, but increasingly was used by Lansdowne to equalize the pressure differences between the cells in flight. Lansdowne had developed something of an obsession with conserving helium, not only by reason of its cost (down to $55 per thousand cubic feet by 1924), but more particularly because of the meagre amounts being delivered by the Fort Worth plant due to the exhaustion of the Petrolia field.[22] No valve was ever completely gas-tight, and helium could leak from the manoeuvring valves in the top of the ship, while air leaked into the cells through the automatics in the bottom. Even before the West Coast flight, Lansdowne had removed eight of the manoeuvring valves. Further, gas-tight "jam

[22] The much larger Cliffside field, with a higher percentage of helium in the natural gas, had been discovered near Amarillo, Texas, in 1920. In April, 1929, a modern and efficient production plant at Amarillo began shipping helium from the Cliffside field, and thereafter there was an adequate supply for the American rigid airship program.

pot" covers were devised to cover the automatic valves. At first these were in place only in the hangar, later Lansdowne kept them on when flying, to be removed by the riggers on watch in the keel if the "Shenandoah" approached pressure height.

During the long lay-up Lansdowne further insisted on having ten of the automatic valves removed, together with the chimneys between the gas cells into which they vented. The Bureau of Aeronautics accepted this modification with great reluctance, as 12 of the cells now did not have automatic relief valves and could only relieve themselves of overpressure by venting through the manifold into the eight cells that still had valves. The rate of gas loss was thus much reduced, and the Bureau pointed out that "Shenandoah" could not now ascend at a rate greater than 400 feet per minute without experiencing dangerous overpressure in the gas cells. Lansdowne's reply was that in the event of a faster rise, the eight manoeuvring valves could also be held open by hand. Following the ship's loss in September, 1925, there was much debate as to whether gas cell overpressure actually caused a breakup of the ship's rigid structure, and a body of opinion in Germany held that it was the reduction in the number of automatic valves which in fact caused "Shenandoah's" destruction.

During the summer of 1925 President Coolidge, to the great disappointment of Admiral Moffett, the Bureau of Aeronautics, and the "Shenandoah" crew, decided against the polar flight. At the same time, with the failure of the ZR 3 to complete a scheduled flight to Minneapolis on June 7-8, Lansdowne was ordered to inflate "Shenandoah" and make the flight himself. America's first rigid airship was well known on the eastern seaboard, and had appeared on the West Coast; now there was a demand from congressmen, mayors and civic leaders that she show herself over the towns and cities of the Midwest. Lansdowne protested on the grounds of hot weather decreasing the useful lift, and the prevalence of thunderstorms on the route. The flight was postponed until mid-September.

Meanwhile there was a series of publicity flights, and a first attempt at cooperating with the Fleet: on July 3-5, "Shenandoah" flew to Bar Harbor, Maine, and moored to the "Patoka" mast for the Governors' Conference. In July and August the big rigid participated in Atlantic Fleet gunnery problems, mooring to the "Patoka" at Newport, Rhode Island, and once at Cape Charles. She towed target sleeves, and took part in scouting exercises with Admiral Charles F. Hughes, Director of Fleet Training, on board. Bad weather caused her to lose contact after finding the "enemy," and helium problems forced her to leave the exercises ahead of time. Lansdowne recommended subsequently that experiments be made in carrying an aeroplane which could be launched and retrieved by the airship to assist in the scouting mission. This represented an advance over Zeppelin scouting tactics, and was taken up by the U.S. Navy within the next few years.

There remained the Midwest flight, now scheduled for the first week in September so that "Shenandoah" could appear at a long list of state fairs. The route and times had been publicised in advance, and Lansdowne was expected to adhere to the schedule. At 2.52 pm on September 2 the big ship departed the mast at Lakehurst with 43 persons, 16,620 lb of fuel, 9075 lb of water ballast, 861 lb of oil, and 948 lb of reserve radiator water on board. The itinerary included a landing at the Army's lighter than air base at Scott Field near St. Louis; to Minneapolis, and to the Ford mooring mast at Detroit. "In laying down the route on charts in preparation," wrote Rosendahl, "Lieutenant Commander Hancock and I for some strange reason decided not to lay down the return path until we should start back. We came back by totally unexpected routes."[23]

Early the following morning, in the vicinity of Ava, Ohio, "Shenandoah" encountered weather conditions of unusual severity, and despite every effort by her crew, broke up in the air and was destroyed with the loss of 14 lives. The "Shenandoah" disaster is often ascribed to a line squall, but I accept the subsequent analysis of the ship's aerologist, Lieutenant J.B. Anderson, that a massive flow of cold air from the north-west, overrunning warm air flowing from the south-west, abruptly created severe atmospheric instability over a wide area of Ohio, with the simultaneous appearance in many places of thunderstorms, some of considerable violence.[24] First intimation of trouble for "Shenandoah's" officers was the appearance of thunderstorms in the distance, particularly to the north and east. A stiffening head wind held the ground speed to practically zero, and little progress could be made despite numerous course changes. At 4.20 am, being then at an altitude of 1600 feet, the ship began to rise in ascending air and continued upward at an average rate of 225 feet per minute, despite being 1200 lb heavy and being driven down with the engines at an angle of 18 degrees. Briefly she levelled off just

[23] Charles E. Rosendahl, *Up Ship!* (New York: Dodd, Mead & Co., 1931), p. 65.
[24] "Technical Aspects of the Loss of the U.S.S. 'Shenandoah.' " *Journal of the American Society of Naval Engineers*, vol. XXXVIII, No. 3, p. 515.

above 3000 feet, rolling and pitching, then rose faster than ever to an altitude of just over 6000 feet. The last part of the ascent was at the rate of nearly 1000 feet per minute. Realizing that the eight automatic valves alone could not handle the expansion of gas, control car personnel opened all the manoeuvring valves at 4100 feet and held them open for 5 minutes. A rush of cold air entered the ship at the top of the rise, and at last she began to fall, being now some 7370 lb heavy. Some 4300 lb of ballast was dropped, and crew members in the keel were ordered to stand by to slip fuel tanks, but "Shenandoah" was still 3000 lb heavy when at 3000 feet her descent was abruptly checked by another rising current of air. The atmosphere was violently turbulent, with the long 682-foot hull spinning counterclockwise. A blast of air forced the nose up to an angle of 25 to 30 degrees, and "with a terrific crashing of metal and a combination of noises hard to describe," the hull broke in two at Frame 125, just forward of engine cars 4 and 5.

Mute evidence on the ground graphically depicted the sequence of events as the "Shenandoah" disintegrated and crashed to earth. Four men had the ill fortune to be standing in the keel at Frame 125, the very spot where the break occurred, and only one of them survived. Aviation Pilot Cullinan was thrown immediately through the opening, and his body, marking the spot where this occurred, was found half a mile to the north-east of the main wreckage. For a minute and a half, drifting with a 20 mph north-east wind, the two halves of the broken hull were held together by the massive rudder and elevator cables leading from the control car aft into the tail. These, heavily strained, pulled the control car aft, breaking its suspension struts and wires, and when the cables finally parted, the big gondola fell like a rock, tossing out Lansdowne, Hancock, Lawrence, Houghton, and the rudder and elevator men. For 15 to 20 seconds the separate radio car must have been carried along on the bow before falling with two ratings inside. With the final separation of the hull a further break occurred at Frame 110, precipitating to the ground the two forward engine cars with their three occupants, and Aviation Machinist's Mate O'Sullivan, one of the unlucky quartet caught at Frame 125. The after half of the ship, with considerable helium left in its gas cells, drifted down more slowly and landed a third of a mile from the control car and engine cars 4 and 5. Fourteen men survived uninjured in this section, while four more lived when the "crew space" at Frame 105 was brushed off as the tail section dragged through trees.

Lightened of the weight of the control car, the bow section of "Shenandoah" ascended possibly as high as 10,000 feet, carrying seven people of whom the senior was Lieut. Comdr. Charles E. Rosendahl, the "Shenandoah's" navigator. Briefly also it carried an eighth, for the ship's engineering officer, Lt. (j.g.) E.W. Sheppard, who was standing at the break at Frame 125, managed to grasp some wreckage as he fell. Aviation Machinist's Mate Shevlowitz, just forward in the remains of the keel, tried to reach Sheppard and heard him say, "never mind me — look out for yourself!"[25] just before the structure he was clinging to tore free. The engineer officer's body, still clutching in one hand a piece of girder and in the other a wire, was found in the woods a quarter mile south-west of the wrecked tail.

Watches of the dead in the control car stopped at 4.45 and 4.47. Not until 6.45 a.m. did Rosendahl, by valving gas and dropping some ballast, bring the free-ballooning bow to earth near Sharon, some 12 miles south of the main wreckage.

The Court of Inquiry found that "the final destruction of the ship was due primarily to large, unbalanced, external, aerodynamic forces arising from high velocity air currents."[26] There was a great deal of effort devoted to the contention, most articulately advanced by Captain Heinen, that the gas valve capacity remaining had been inadequate to prevent excessive pressure at the peak altitude, with resulting fatal damage to the rigid structure of the hull. The Court, in continuing its opinion, added "whether the ship, if entirely intact and undamaged, would have broken under the forces existing, or whether prior minor damage due to gas pressure was a determining factor in the final break-up are matters which this Court is unable definitely to determine." It added, "the change resulting in a reduction of the number of gas valves was inadvisable," a censure of Lansdowne hotly resented by the surviving crew members, who prepared a lengthy "Brief Submitted by Interested Parties" in rebuttal. All testimony of survivors in the keel indicated that the gas cells were closely watched during the second ascent for signs of excessive pressure, and none were found. On the other hand, the sound of snapping wires high in the hull was heard just before reaching the peak, and possibly of girders breaking also, even though it was felt the hull structure was not being stressed aerodynamically.

[25] Rosendahl, p. 79.
[26] "Technical Aspects of the Loss of the U.S.S. 'Shenandoah'," p. 691.

Certainly violent stresses were inflicted on the hull when the descent
was abruptly checked at 3000 feet; gas cells amidships immediately
began to deflate, and this would seem to have resulted from failure
of upper longitudinal girders in compression. With cells 9, 10, 11, 12
and 13 deflating, the ship was very heavy amidships with a severe
sagging moment, and the violent gust under the nose during the final
rise sufficed to cause a catastrophic failure of all girders in the bay
between Frames 120 and 130, beginning on the upper port side.

The death of Lansdowne was particularly regrettable for the
future of the rigid airship in the United States, and events would
undoubtedly have taken a different course had he survived.
Dedicated to the airship cause, and keenly aware of the airship's
potential role in strategic scouting at sea, he would have been an
increasingly effective partner to Moffett through the years as he grew
in experience, influence and rank.

On the other hand, the senior survivor, Lieut. Comdr. Charles E.
Rosendahl, became a public figure through his prominent role before
the Court of Inquiry, and has continued to this day in the public eye
as the leading American advocate of the rigid airship.

The disaster forced a re-evaluation on the part of American airship
designers of the structural requirements of rigid hulls in respect to
aerodynamic loads of unusual severity ("no European designer could
possibly imagine the violence of weather conditions in the American
Midwest," Dr. Karl Arnstein told me in 1955). As a result of
"Shenandoah's" loss, future American airships were built stronger,
notably with a lower fineness ratio. Since all but three of the deaths
in her resulted from the carrying away of gondolas slung below the
hull on struts and wires, future designs incorporated the control car
built directly onto the hull, and engines enclosed within the
structure.

Lastly, despite its disadvantages, helium was responsible for saving
twenty-nine lives. Had "Shenandoah" been inflated with hydrogen,
she would surely have burned in the air after the breakup.

The American ZR 3, destined to be named "Los Angeles," was
built expressly for the United States Navy by the Zeppelin Company
in Friedrichshafen. As noted previously, the loss of ZR 2 (R 38) in
August, 1921, provided the incentive for the Americans to seek to
have the Zeppelin Company build them a new ship; but the origin of
the ZR 3 contract went back to June, 1919. On the 23rd of that
month, two days after the scuttling of the High Seas Fleet at Scapa
Flow, seven of the fourteen surviving German Navy Zeppelins were

wrecked by their crews at the North Sea bases. Two of the craft destroyed, L 65 and L 14, were to have been allotted to the United States.[27] In the summer of 1921 the Allied representatives got around to deciding Germany's punishment for the "Scapa Flow" at Nordholz and Wittmundhaven: two small post-war commercial Zeppelins were to be confiscated (Italy received one, France the other), and the countries scheduled to receive the other five ships destroyed were to be compensated in cash *or in kind.* This unusal provision not only secured for the United States Navy the latest example of Zeppelin construction, but also saved the works on the *Bodensee* from destruction.

For a variety of reasons, relations between the Zeppelin Company personnel and American airship men were always more cordial and intimate than with those of France and Britain,[28] and as early as the year 1920, Zeppelin representatives had approached the American military commission in Berlin to inquire if they might build an airship for the United States Navy. The Germans' situation was truly desperate: the Hensley contract had been repudiated, their two small commercial ships had been seized, and their building works were marked for destruction. The American Navy Department showed interest, which hardened into resolve after the ZR 2 crash. The Germans were forbidden, however, to build airships larger than 1,000,000 cubic feet, and an exception had to be negotiated with the Council of Ambassadors in Paris. From motives of jealousy, both the French and British were obstructive, but after the ZR 2 crash Secretary of State Hughes demanded and obtained the diplomatic support of the British. The American desire to obtain a 3,800,000 cubic foot ship of the LZ 125 type was vetoed, and at French insistence the volume was limited to 2,500,000 cubic feet, the smallest size that could fly the Atlantic. On December 16, 1921, the Council approved the American request to have a ship of this size built by the Zeppelin Company, but at the last minute the British inserted the stipulation that the Zeppelin was to be devoted to "civil purposes."

There was some haggling with the Zeppelin Company over the contract, the Germans complaining that the 3.2 million gold marks'

[27] Garland Fulton papers. Another document states that the United States was to have received L 42, L 52 and LZ 120.

[28] After the Zeppelin L 72 was flown to Maubeuge by a German crew on July 13, 1920, her new French owners found a large variety of insults painted on channels and girders. Capitaine de Frégate de Brossard, *Lâchez Tout!* (Paris: Editions France Empire, 1956), p. 156.

payment stipulated by the Allies would not cover the cost of the ship. The Americans agreed to pay a further $100,000. Furthermore, Dr. Eckener, representing the Zeppelin Company, found it necessary to pledge the assets of the firm as security in case the ZR 3 was lost on her delivery flight. This was easy for him to do, for he knew that if the ship were lost the Zeppelin Company would be destroyed likewise. The intervention of the Foreign Minister, Walther Rathenau, was necessary to overcome objections raised by the *Reichs* Minister of Finance. On June 24, 1922, the contract was signed at the Foreign Ministry by Dr. Eckener for the Zeppelin Company, and by Commander Weyerbacher and Commander Fulton for the United States Navy. Rathenau himself was not present, having been assasinated by extremists while on his way to preside at the ceremony.

During the two years that the LZ 126 was under construction in Friedrichshafen, Garland Fulton as Inspector of Naval Aircraft played a vital but unobtrusive role. Not only did he ably represent the U.S. Navy in the construction of the airship, but through patience, tact, and genuine friendliness he gained the confidence of Dr. Eckener, the Chairman of the company, and Dr. Arnstein, the chief designer, and through them was given access to much of the design information of the Zeppelin Company. Such were his abilities that through the remainder of the rigid airship era Fulton occupied a key position in the Bureau of Aeronautics as head of the Lighter-Than-Air Design Section. Here, until his retirement from the Navy in 1940, he not only supervised development and construction programs, but also was constantly consulted on matters of airship policy as well as technology by Admiral Moffett, and to a lesser extent by his successor, Admiral King.

Believing that LZ 126 would be the last Zeppelin ever built, the men at Friedrichshafen spared no effort to make her as sound and perfect as she could be, with a view to leaving a lasting impression on the aeronautical world. The ship was an advance on the wartime high altitude craft in many respects, and owed something to the two small commercial airships of 1919. With a nominal gas volume of 2,471,000 cubic feet she was slightly larger than the L 57, L 59, L 71 and L 72, and the largest Zeppelin built up to that time.[29] The weight empty was 77,836 lb, the gross lift 179,266 lb, and the useful

[29] The nominal gas volume figure corresponded to the 70,000 cubic metres authorized by the Council of Ambassadors. Actually the gas capacity with 100 per cent inflation was 2,762,100 cubic feet.

lift 101,430 lb.[30] The fully streamlined hull was 658.3 feet long including the mooring fittings incorporated in the nose at American insistence; the maximum diameter was 90.7 feet. Main rings had diamond trusses and were spaced 15 metres apart, with two intermediate rings at 5 metre intervals. The keel was unusually sturdy, constituting an upright V with stout lateral bracing at each main ring. There were 14 gas cells, but only thirteen of them were numbered. The long tapering tail cone abaft the rudder post was large enough to contain an unnumbered "stern cell" of 15,892 cubic foot capacity. The fins were of thick full cantilever construction with two cruciform structures at Frame 0 (the rudder post) and 10. Further, the fins at their trailing edges, instead of being flat as in the last wartime ships, had a certain thickness, as did the control surfaces, and were therefore stronger. The five engine gondolas were arranged conventionally – one on the center line aft at Frame 50, and the others in pairs at Frames 80 and 110. The engines were Maybach VL-1s, a new vee-12 power plant especially developed for the ship, with a dry weight of 2,437 lb, and with a full power output of 400 hp at 1400 rpm. A shifting camshaft enabled the engines to be stopped and restarted in reverse without the weight of heavy gears. The Maybach factory encountered unusual difficulty with crankshaft breakages during the developmental period, and indeed, the completion of the ship was much delayed by teething troubles with the new power plants.

In accordance with the requirement that LZ 126 be used for "civil purposes," she was designed to carry 20 passengers, and was the first airship ever to provide sleeping accomodations for passengers on voyages of several days' duration. Following the example of the post-war commercial ships, the passenger accomodations were combined with the control car in a single streamlined structure nearly 75 feet long built directly onto the keel forward. In the fore part of the long gondola was the control room, laid out as in earlier ships but with some advanced instruments including for the first time a gyro compass with repeaters (called by the Germans the "mother compass" and "daughter compasses"). Abaft the control room on the port side was the wireless cabin. For the first time electricity was obtained with an outboard generator outside the radio room, driven by a 6-bladed wooden propeller spinning in the slipstream. The

[30] In American service with 95 per cent inflation with helium the figures were: volume 2,624,000 cubic feet, gross lift 153,000 lb., weight empty 90,400 lb., and useful lift 63,100 lb. Richard K. Smith, *An Inventory of U.S. Navy Airships*, p. 13.

generator simultaneously provided alternating current for the radio and direct current for the ship's lighting. Compared to the previous electrical system involving generators driven by the main engines, the windmill generators provided power where it was needed, eliminating long and heavy electrical cables through the ship, and delivering current whenever the ship was under way, whereas a breakdown of the generator-equipped engine formerly meant a total loss of electrical power. In the body of the forward gondola were five staterooms, three to starboard and two to port, with settees which could be made up at night into berths for 20 passengers. Aft to starboard was a kitchen with two electric hot plates, hot water heater, and baking and roasting ovens with current supplied by a separate windmill generator. Aft to port were wash rooms and toilets.

Another innovation in LZ 126 was that for the first time in Zeppelin practice, powdered aluminium was mixed with the dope on the outer cover, giving a silvery appearance. The purpose was probably to minimize the loss of precious helium through solar heating. Previous Zeppelins, being clear doped, presented the natural buff color of the cotton material, or printed-on patterns of fine blue dots or lines.

Under the command of Dr. Eckener, LZ 126 made her first brief flight on August 27, 1924. The ship handled well in passing through a fairly turbulent squall line, and developed 79½ mph with full power, and 70 mph at cruising speed with 300 h.p. from each engine.

The four subsequent factory flights during September, 1924, were ostensibly to prove the ship and engines in long cruises before the ocean crossing to America, but were also deliberately planned by Eckener to cover the length and breadth of the *Reich*, and to remind his fellow countrymen of German predominance in the lighter than air field. For the first time in five years a German rigid airship was to be seen in the skies over the Fatherland, and the popular enthusiasm was all that Eckener could have wished. Great crowds thronged the streets of the major cities to see what was supposed to be the last Zeppelin, and with tears in their eyes sang "Deutschland über Alles." More and more the departure of LZ 126 for America promised to be an overwhelming emotional experience, with a minority of die-hard nationalists vowing that no foreigner would ever possess this supreme example of German genius. Eckener's life was even threatened.

Privately, he viewed the ocean crossing with some apprehension. Not only had it never been flown before by a Zeppelin airship, but with the limited gas volume of LZ 126, the range and fuel endurance were somewhat marginal. With a useful lift of 43 tons, some 33 tons of fuel could be carried, which would confer a range of 5400 nautical miles in 70 hours at full power. Since Eckener had to expect an average head wind of 13 to 15½ mph on the westward crossing, it was decided to cruise at reduced power which would enable the ship to go 5350 miles in 96 hours against such a head wind.[31] This would suffice to reach Lakehurst from Friedrichshafen via the Azores. In fact the flight was made over a distance of exactly 5000 miles in 81 hours' flying time, at an average speed of 61½ mph.

One reason for making the flight in less than the anticipated time was that Dr. Eckener utilized "pressure pattern flying" to accelerate his progress, i.e., ascertaining from the weather map the centers of high and low pressure over the ocean, he took advantage of the clockwise circulation around the highs, and the counterclockwise circulation around the lows, to minimize head winds and provide tail winds if possible. Furthermore, Eckener had devised a system of dead reckoning navigation so accurate that even in later years, celestial navigation, radio direction finding, and ground pilotage played secondary roles. The system involved frequent checks of the drift by dropping an acetylene filled smoke bomb which served as a fixed point, giving off smoke by day and flame by night. Steering first with the wind, and then changing course by 45 degrees, the navigator took bearings, plotted them graphically together with the air speed, and the resulting vectors gave both the desired heading and the speed over the ground.

After a false start on October 11, on which occasion the fully loaded ship did not lift due to warming of the air, LZ 126 got away on the following day with 33 tons of fuel, 2.2 tons of oil, and only 7300 lb of water ballast. The crew numbered 27, the passengers included three United States Navy officers and one Army officer.

Eckener had decided to cross by the southern route, via Cape Finisterre to the Azores, as the northern part of the Atlantic was dominated by low pressure areas offering nothing but head winds. The flight across France was uneventful, LZ 126 leaving the country at the mouth of the Gironde. Towards midnight the airship was passing north of Cape Finisterre, and by noon of the 13th was in sight of San Miguel in the Azores. Now, however, there was a check to the ship's progress, for a sight of the ocean below indicated that a

[31] Hugo Eckener, "Der Amerikaflug des ZR III" in Hans Hildebrandt (ed.), *Zeppelin Denkmal für das deutsche Volk* (Stuttgart: Germania-Verlag G.m.b.H., 1925), p. 366.

LZ 126 landing at Lakehurst on the morning of 15 October 1924. (Luftschiffbau Zeppelin)

strong south-west wind had sprung up — blowing at 31 mph and reducing the ship's speed to the same figure. Under these circumstances it would have taken 70 hours to reach New York, and fuel for only 50 remained on board. In this crisis Eckener looked at the big picture: weather reports from two United States cruisers, "Milwaukee" and "Detroit," indicated that a low pressure center lay south of Newfoundland. Boldly Eckener set a north-west course to go around the north side of the low, and was rewarded by finding a strong north-east wind on the afternoon of the 14th. Making 78 mph over the surface, LZ 126 now steered direct for Boston. In the early dark hours of the 15th Boston was in sight, and after sunrise the ship passed over New York. At 9.37 a.m. LZ 126 settled on the field at Lakehurst and was walked into the hangar, becoming the ZR 3 of the United States Navy. Not only was the transatlantic flight of the LZ 126 a personal triumph for Dr. Eckener and his men; it aroused great enthusiasm in America, and served to wipe out some of the bitterness of the war.

The hydrogen in ZR 3's cells was promptly valved off into the atmosphere, and the helium of the decommissioned "Shenandoah" was used to reinflate her. Red, white and blue stripes were painted on the rudders and elevators, the star-in-a-circle insigne in the usual places – under the nose, on top of the hull amidships, and on both quarters – and "U.S. Navy" in black amidships. Water recovery apparatus was installed on all five engines. On November 25, 1924, ZR 3 flew to Anacostia Naval Air Station where the wife of President Coolidge christened her "Los Angeles," and she was commissioned into the Navy.

Thus began a remarkable career that spanned nearly 8 years, during which "Los Angeles" made 328 flights totally 4092 hours 41 minutes in the air. Though she never accomplished anything spectacular, neither did "Los Angeles" ever kill a man; while her value to the U.S. Navy was incalculable, both in training large numbers of men in rigid airship handling (she had seven commanding officers) and in being the subject for numerous technical experiments in connection with the design of the next generation of American rigids.

During the first half of 1925 "Los Angeles" made a number of long distance cruises, proceeding twice to Bermuda and twice to Puerto Rico, mooring three times to the "Patoka." Then, on June 7, while attempting to fly to Minneapolis, two engines broke down, and the ship turned back over Cleveland. A thorough check of the ship showed other problems: the original German gas cells were hopelessly porous, and the ill-judged use of calcium chloride as an antifreeze in ballast bags had caused corrosion of girders at many points in the keel. "Los Angeles" was accordingly decommissioned and the "Shenandoah" inflated with her helium; repairs to the German ship involved replacing the gas cells, but the chief reason she did not fly again until April 13, 1926, was the loss of two million cubic feet of helium in the "Shenandoah" disaster, and the slow rate of delivery from the Fort Worth helium plant. Thereafter the ship was almost continuously in operation until her decommissioning in 1932.

Dissatisfaction with the "high" mast at Lakehurst has already been mentioned, particularly with respect to problems of buoyancy changes with temperature fluctuations, and of access to the ship, which could be achieved only through the nose hatch. A dramatic misadventure on August 25, 1927, sealed the fate of the "high" mast. On that date "Los Angeles" had been brought out of the Lakehurst shed for the first time in two and a half months, and placed on the "high" mast. In the middle of the day the sea breeze, coming in from the opposite direction to the light prevailing wind, caught the big rigid under the tail, and despite a ground drag

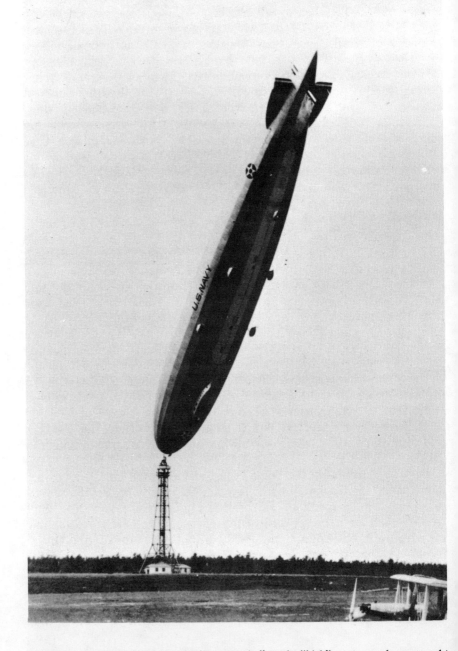

At midday on August 25 1927, with "Los Angeles" on the "high" mast, a sea breeze caught her under the tail and despite a ground drag aft weighing 2500 lb., lifted her until she was standing on her nose, then swung her around to lie in the opposite direction. The entire sequence of photographs are published here for the first time. (Dr. Smith DeFrance)

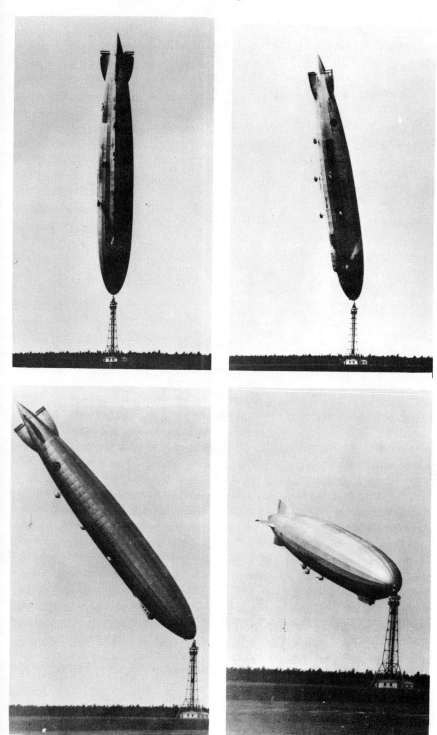

weighing 2500 lb made fast aft, lifted the tail until the 658-foot ship was standing vertically on her nose atop the mast! Then, gracefully pirouetting with the wind, she descended to lie headed in the opposite direction. None of the 25 men aboard were injured, and the only damage resulted from loose articles tumbling down the keel and going through the outer cover in the nose.

Within a few months, on October 5, 1927, first trials were made at the instigation of her commanding officer, Lieut. Comdr. Rosendahl, with an early version of the "stub" mast. This held the airship close to the ground while the rear gondola (or the lower fin in later ships) swiveled around the mast on a "mooring circle" with changes in the wind. In this situation the ship could be made heavy enough to assure that she could not lift her tail, and access could easily be had to the keel through most of her length for loading cargo, gas, fuel and ballast. The original stub mast was an old wooden pole 60 feet high with a fitting at its top and wire bracing, while a landing gear wheel from a heavy bomber was attached under the rear gondola.

Lakehurst in the Summer of 1931. "Los Angeles" approaching to make a flying moor to the mobile mast (right), mounted on crawler feet. The "big barn", as the 804-foot double hangar was called, appears in the left background. (Fred Tupper-Hepburn Walker collection)

Eight moorings were made to the stub mast during the next two months, and it was shipped to Panama in February to enable "Los Angeles" to land at France Field on February 27, 1928. Thereafter "Los Angeles" made only four more "high" mast moorings, one being at the end of a flight to Fort Worth in October, 1928. In July, 1928, a circular railway track was laid out around the mast, and the rear engine gondola, fitted with side braces to take lateral loads, was firmly attached to a flat car. In a later version appearing in mid-1929, the stub mast was made mobile, so the airship could be towed out of the hangar to the mooring circle; still later the lower fin was attached to a heavy "stern beam" for the tow out of the hangar. The Germans were not too proud to use the mobile mast when the "Graf Zeppelin" stopped at Lakehurst during a 1930 "triangle" flight to South America, and the "Hindenburg" routinely moored to it during all her 1936 flights to North America.

Moorings to the "Patoka" mast were so frequent as to be routine for the "Los Angeles," with a total of 44 being recorded during the life of the airship. Mooring to the seagoing mast was much facilitated by the automatic grapnel being used to couple the mast wire to the airship's mooring cable, the first use of this device being on June 6, 1925, off Annapolis. "Los Angeles" also made a single but well publicised landing on the deck of the aircraft carrier "Saratoga" at sea off Newport on January 27, 1928. The experiment was not repeated, as the different motions of the carrier as affected by the sea and of the airship as affected by the air currents kept the "Los Angeles" in constant movement on the deck.

Another career in which "Los Angeles" made a pioneering contribution was in developing the technique of picking up aeroplanes in flight and subsequently releasing them, in anticipation of aeroplanes being carried for self defence aboard the big Fleet scouting airships of the next generation. A number of haphazard experiments with primitive equipment had been made by the Germans, the British, and the U.S. Army in 1924 with a tiny Sperry Messenger biplane grossing only 862 lb; but the Navy intended to use standard service aircraft and the first "hook-on" plane was the two-seater Vought UO-1 with a gross weight of 2,305 lb. Early in 1926 the Bureau of Aeronautics approached the Goodyear-Zeppelin Company with a view to designing and installing a "trapeze" aboard the "Los Angeles" at Frame 100 amidships. The article produced by Goodyear was a stout structure of duralumin girders with a bar at the bottom which either could be winched up close to the airship, or

The flying moor nearly completed, with "Los Angeles", her yaw lines down to port and starboard, being winched down to the mobile mast by the main cable from the nose. (Fred Tupper-Hepburn Walker collection)

The first trapeze installed on Frame 95 of the "Los Angeles" in December 1928. Hangar tests are being made at Lakehurst with the Vought UO-1 aircraft. The early form of the aircraft hook shows in this view. (U.S. Navy)

lowered some 25 feet below. This was not delivered and installed aboard "Los Angeles" until December 1928. The first hook-on attempt was made on July 3, 1929, and others followed with increasing success. The aeroplane hook was attached to an overhead tubing structure above the center section of the upper wing and went through several modifications. Early in 1931 several pilots reported to Lakehurst for hook-on training with a view to their being assigned to the new "Akron's" heavier than air squadron, and beginning in July, the first assigned pilots began practicing with Consolidated N2Y aircraft fitted with hooks. On October 23, 1931, two pilots made the first hook-on landings with the little Curtiss XF9C-1 which was the prototype of the fighters intended to be carried aboard the "Akron." The last hook-on to the "Los Angeles" was made on October 26, 1931, with the XF9C-1. Thereafter the "Los Angeles" trapeze was cannibalized to provide parts for the "Akron's".[32]

[32] Richard K. Smith, "The Navy's First Sky Hook," *Journal of the American Aviation Historical Society*, vol. 6, No. 2, Summer, 1961, p. 91.

Finally, after seven years in service as a "civil airship," the United States Navy received permission from the former Allies who had imposed the original restriction to use "Los Angeles" in a Fleet problem in February, 1931. Technically her performance was a fine one, particularly for a 7-year-old craft, for she was away from Lakehurst for 27 days and traveled 14,500 miles in 272 flying hours. On February 4-5 she flew in 24 hours to Guantanamo Bay where she moored to the expeditionary mast. On February 6-7 she went on south to moor to the "Patoka's" mast in Dulce Bay, Costa Rica, on the Pacific side of Central America. From then until February 22 "Los Angeles" operated entirely from the seagoing base, sometimes from Dulce Bay and at other times from Panama Bay. Embarking the Honorable David S. Ingalls, Assistant Secretary of the Navy for Aeronautics, "Los Angeles" then made two flights of 38 and 36 hours each between February 16 and 20 in connection with the Fleet exercise, which represented the enemy approaching to attack the Pacific side of the Panama Canal. Most remarkable is the fact that between these two long flights, only 11½ hours were required to replenish and refuel the ship at the "Patoka" mast. "Los Angeles" was part of the "White" fleet defending the canal, and with her great range and endurance compared to the aeroplane, was misused in tactical close-in scouting for the approaching "Black" invasion fleet. She in fact was the first "White" unit to discover the enemy fleet, but in spite of skilful use of cloud cover, she was "shot down" by planes from the "Langley," the sole "Black" carrier.

The evaluation of the big rigid's performance in her first Fleet operation predictably reflected the prejudices of the commentators. Secretary Ingalls was "exceedingly gratified at the marked success attendant upon the use of the "Los Angeles" in connection with the Fleet manoeuvres." Admiral Moffett realistically observed that "to a comparatively small group who have had experience with airships. . . the performance of 'Los Angeles' was gratifying. To a much larger group. . . the 'Los Angeles' merely confirmed preconceived opinions that airships either are no good or are of so little practical use that their existence is not justified." Most influential of those in opposition was the Commander in Chief of the U.S. Fleet, Admiral Frank H. Schofield, who was opposed to "the proposed development of rigid dirigibles" on the grounds that their cost was "out of proportion" and their "appeal to the imagination. . . not sustained by their military usefulness."[33] The arguments were repeated in

---

[33] Turnbull & Lord, p. 281.

future years in relation to the participation of the "Akron" and "Macon" in Fleet exercises. The prejudices of senior admirals were never overcome, while the big rigids, never given a chance to show what they could do in the strategic role, were damned by the Fleet for their vulnerability in tactical problems. Panama demonstrated that World War I rigid airship scouting methods were out of date when the "enemy" brought his own aircraft to sea, not only on the catapults of cruisers, but also on the flight decks of the carriers "Langley," "Saratoga" and "Lexington." The logical next step was already forseen by some at the Bureau and at Lakehurst: the conversion of the rigid airship into a carrier for fast scouting aeroplanes.

Following the commissioning of the "Akron" on October 27, 1931, the "Los Angeles" was decommissioned on June 30, 1932, as an economy measure. Yet though she never made another flight, she continued in existence for another seven and a half years, occupying one side of the Lakehurst hangar and spending many hours out on the field in mooring experiments. After the loss of the "Macon" on February 12, 1935, operating personnel agitated for the old Zeppelin's return to flying duty, but the Bureau vetoed this due to her advanced age and airframe deterioration. In December, 1939, dismantling of the veteran "Los Angeles" began and the work was completed on January 3, 1940, with all scrap removed by the end of February.

One of the conditions under which the Council of Ambassadors had permitted the building of the "Los Angeles" was that on completion of the ship, the Zeppelin works and hangars were to be demolished. Accordingly, Zeppelin Company officials believed with reason that their enterprise could not survive in Germany and thoughts turned to carrying on in a foreign country. Ultimately this led to a partnership with the Goodyear Tire and Rubber Company of Akron, Ohio, in the United States, whose president, Paul W. Litchfield, saw a great commercial future for the rigid airship in the United States, and intended to found an industry which would design and build them. Litchfield and the Zeppelin Company were brought together by Harry Vissering, a Chicago railway supply manufacturer, who had become an ardent devotee of the rigid airship after visiting Friedrichshafen in 1919 and taking a flight in the small commercial airship "Bodensee." In October, 1923, Litchfield, William C. Young, and Vissering reached an agreement in Friedrichshafen with Eckener, Colsman and Lehmann which led to

"Los Angeles" in the Summer of 1931. Experimental water recovery condenser up on the hull over No.3 engine gondola, and retracted trapeze is visible amidships. (Fred Tupper-Hepburn Walker collection)

the establishment of the Goodyear-Zeppelin Corporation of Akron, Ohio. North American rights to the Zeppelin patents, and Zeppelin engineering and operating experience were to be conveyed to the American firm, together with key Zeppelin engineering personnel who expected to have no future in the Fatherland. The agreement went into effect with the delivery of the LZ 126 to the United States. Shortly after this event, in October, 1924, twelve Zeppelin Company engineers, with Dr. Karl Arnstein, the company's chief designer at their head, emigrated to America.

The genesis of the giant sister ships "Akron" and "Macon," which Arnstein was to design and Goodyear-Zeppelin to build, went back to March 1924 when Starr Truscott of the Bureau of Aeronautics' Lighter Than Air Design Section put some thoughts on paper concerning the Navy's next airship. Tentatively labeled Design No. 60, Truscott's proposal envisaged a craft of 6,000,000 cubic feet capacity, 780 feet long, 122 feet in diameter, with a maximum speed of 80 knots and a cruising speed of 60 knots. For defense and observation, the new design was to carry four fighter aircraft.

That the proposal led to the construction of the "Akron" and "Macon," despite public and congressional opposition to rigid airships in the wake of the "Shenandoah" disaster, is a tribute to Admiral Moffett's extraordinary political sense, tact, skill and ability in marshalling facts (ably assisted by Garland Fulton) to win over the admirals in the Navy Department and the legislators on Capital Hill. Moffett skilfully pleaded for the rigid airships "their great radius of action, their high speed relative to surface vessels, their ability to hover, their ability to receive and transmit information promptly, and their general long-range scouting ability... The rigid airship is primarily a scouting ship, the purpose of which is to travel long distances at high speed; carry observers who can see what is going on and report back by radio."[34] The Bureau of Aeronautics' Five Year Plan, as passed by Congress in 1926, authorized the construction of two large rigid airships, an airship base on the West Coast, and additionally a small experimental Metalclad airship by the Aircraft Development Corporation of Detroit, Michigan.

In my opinion, the Metalclad belongs in any history of the rigid airship, though some consider it merely a pressure airship with a

---

[34] HR 9690, "To Authorize the Construction and Procurement of Aircraft and Aircraft Equipment in the Navy and Marine Corps," etc., p. 1624.

sheet metal envelope rather than a fabric one.[35] The concept, owing little to the Schwarz metal-clad of 1897, originated with Ralph Hazlett Upson, a talented and imaginative engineer and free balloon racer with previous experience in pressure airship operations and building with Goodyear.[36] Acquaintance with advanced German metal aircraft design during a European trip in 1919 caused Upson to imagine an airship which would dispense with the redundant Zeppelin structure of girders, wires, outer cover, and gas cells, utilizing a simple metal shell as a gas container and strength member. Contact in 1920 with Carl B. Fritsche, who interested Edsel Ford and William Mayo of the Ford Motor Company, and Charles F. Kettering of General Motors, in Upson's concept, led to the founding of the Aircraft Development Corporation in 1922, with Upson as president (and chief engineer), and Fritsche as general manager. Several years of research followed on properties of aluminium alloys in sheets, design principles were elaborated and a water-filled model was constructed to check stress data. An indispensable technical achievement was the development by Edward J. Hill, the engineer in charge of construction, of an automatic riveting machine which, using aluminium wire .035 inches in diameter, could join sheets of the metal with three rows of rivets at the rate of 5000 per hour. In 1925 the design of a 200,000 cubic foot prototype was undertaken and proposals for construction of the ship (designated by the company the ZMC-2 for "airship, metal clad, 202,000 cubic feet"), were presented to the Navy. On March 1, 1928, the Aircraft Development Corporation received a contract for the ZMC-2 and construction started at once in a shed at Grosse Ile Airport near Detroit. The material used was duralumin sheet .008 inches thick coated with Alclad (pure aluminium) as a preservative. The 149 foot 5 inch hull, 52 feet 8 inches in diameter, was built in two

---

[35] There was still another American metal-clad airship which never flew—the Slate Aircraft Company's "City of Glendale." Built between 1927 and 1931 in a hangar at Glendale, California, the ship had a hull built up of corrugated, tapered longitudinal duralumin "planks" .011 in. thick and 18 inches wide, crimped together, with an overall length of 212 feet, a diameter of 58 feet, and a volume of 330,000 cubic feet, of which 30,000 cubic feet comprised a ballonet. Propulsion was by a "sirocco" fan at the nose throwing out air radially and supposedly creating a vacuum at the nose which would draw the airship forward. A steam turbine power plant with flash boiler was planned. Tethered and without a power plant, the "City of Glendale" made ascents for publicity photos, but two trial flights in 1929 and 1931 were failures, and the ship was dismantled. Wingfoot Lighter Than Air Society Bulletin, vol. 8, No. 11, pp. 4-6.

[36] Richard K. Smith, "Ralph H. Upson, A Career Sketch and Biography," *Journal of the American Aviation Historical Society*, vol. 13, No. 4, Winter, 1968, p. 282.

The "tin balloon", the Metalclad airship ZMC-2, landing at Lakehurst. Note the eight fins and rudders, positioned to raise the ship's nose. (Fred Tupper-Hepburn Walker collection)

halves — beginning with the bow and stern sections, two shells were erected, standing vertically on the hangar floor, with five transverse stiffening rings being inserted as construction advanced. Three and a half million rivets were driven with the automatic riveting machine. In February, 1929, the two halves of the hull were joined, and on August 10 the ship completed inflation with helium.[37] On August 19, 1929, the ZMC-2 made her first flight with five people aboard, the Army's Captain William E. Kepner being borrowed to command the flight crew. On September 12 the ship arrived at Lakehurst, and on September 25 was accepted by the Navy.

The "tin balloon" was unstable longitudinally, but this was due to her low fineness ratio (2.83 to 1) and not inherent in the Metalclad concept. Otherwise the ship as a prototype was very successful. She

[37] This was accomplished by first filling the metal shell from the bottom with carbon dioxide and displacing the air out the top; then helium was admitted from the top and the CO_2 drained out the bottom. Lastly any carbon dioxide mixed with the helium was removed by passing the gas mixture through a CO_2 scrubber. Carl B. Fritsche, "The Metal Clad Airship." *Transactions of the American Society of Mechanical Engineers*, vol. 1, no. 4, Oct.-Dec. 1929, p. 263.

had to be pressurized to resist forces on the nose at higher speeds (maximum 70 mph with two Wright Whirlwinds of 220 h.p. each), for a dent or wrinkle in the metal hull would have been much more serious than in a rubberized fabric one. The usual pressure seems to have been 4 inches of water, and was not to go below ½ inch of water in descents. Pressure was maintained by two ballonets, originally of the diaphragm type, displacing 22,600 cubic feet (forward) and 28,000 cubic feet (aft). These caused unacceptable distortion of the metal shell when full and were replaced by two cylindrical ballonets independent of the shell. The ship ordinarily flew with a crew of three, 200 gallons of fuel, 25 gallons of oil, and 420 lb of ballast. Gross lift with 100 per cent inflation with 92 per cent pure helium was 12,242 lb, and weight empty 9,115 lb. A feature of all the Metalclad designs was the use of eight fins and rudders, differential rigging of the controls permitting them to act as both elevators and rudders.

During a 12 year career the ZMC-2 made 752 flights totalling 2,256.5 hours, though only five hours were flown after 1938. In her old age the "tin balloon" suffered from gas leakage as the bituminous material coating her seams internally was dried out and cracking and it was not considered worth while trying to replace it. In the summer of 1941 she was cut up for scrap. It is unfortunate that she had no successors, for the design features were practical and the theoretical advantages, including life of the metal hull and gas tightness, were attractive. The Aircraft Development Company in fact proposed larger designs (MC-38 of 3,800,000 cubic feet, and MC-72 of 7,200,000 cubic feet), but the Bureau of Aeronautics, operating with restricted funds, felt a prior commitment to the conventional Zeppelin type airship. Charles P. Burgess of the Bureau of Aeronautics thought enough of the Metalclad concept to present it in his Design Memorandum No. 274 of August 1937 as the "Ultimate Airship," with a volume of 7,400,000 cubic feet, length of 618 feet, diameter of 154.5 feet, gross lift of 212.5 tons, and useful lift of 281,400 lb.[38]

Before calling for bids on the two large rigid airships, the Bureau of Aeronautics revised the specifications for Design No. 60 in the light of the structural weaknesses revealed by the "Shenandoah" crash. The diameter was increased from 122 to 135 feet, a measure which increased the beam strength of the hull by lowering the fineness ratio and which at the same time increased the gas volume to 6,500,000 cubic feet. In place of the flat "bicycle ring" main frame, the Bureau specified much stronger and inherently rigid deep rings of triangular section. These had at the same time independently been selected for the new British rigid, R 101, but whereas the British ship had no structure within the ring to prevent gas bag surging, the Bureau's design specified an "elastic bulkhead" to restrict gas cell movement. With much of the loss of life in "Shenandoah" occurring when the control car and engine cars, strut and wire braced to the hull, had carried away, the control car was to be firmly built onto the hull and the engines were to be carried inside the main framing.

Goodyear-Zeppelin was prepared to build such a craft and the Navy was willing to deal with them, but political considerations required that the Navy Department make the gesture of inviting competitive bids. Goodyear-Zeppelin's was the only serious entry in the 1927 design competition, the other entries being either amateurish or impractical, or where they showed some merit, their creators had no plant in which to build. But declaring Goodyear the winner (the Akron firm presented three alternative designs) did not clear the way for a contract. The subsequent intervention of the American Brown-Boveri Electric Corporation, which claimed to be able to design and build an airship more cheaply than Goodyear, persuaded Congress to order a second competition. The 1928 competition produced, besides another package of three Goodyear designs, a Brown-Boveri proposal evidently based on a hurried attempt to pirate the secrets of the Schütte-Lanz firm, and a series of drawings by Dr. Schütte himself. In essence, the Schütte design found no favor because the old master had no place in which to build. Brown-Boveri was prepared to construct a building hangar, but their design, presenting Schütte-type triangular duralumin tube girders, lacked supporting calculations and stressing data, while performance claims were rated overly optimistic. The Goodyear Project I won the Bureau's favor, and with some modification became the design of the "Akron" and "Macon." But the elaborate charade of "competition" put on for Congress' benefit had delayed by two years the start of construction.

On October 6, 1928, Goodyear and Navy representatives signed a contract whereby the Ohio company would build the two airships for the sum of $5,375,000 for the first one and $2,450,000 for the second. This was a lot of money in 1928, and enemies of the rigid airship did not fail to emphasize their high cost. While the final

design of the ZRS 4 and ZRS 5 was being elaborated, Goodyear
commenced work on the building shed at Akron. Dr. Arnstein played
a part in creating the unusual design for a streamlined structure with
hemispherical "orange peel" doors moving back nearly flush with the
walls as they opened; but the German pre-1914 sheds at Liegnitz and
Dresden had a similar layout. The Akron shed, however, was much
larger, measuring 1175 feet long, 325 feet wide, and 197 feet 6
inches high. The first arch was erected on May 21, 1929, and it was
virtually completed on November 7 of that year when construction
of the ZRS 4 officially began.

Meanwhile the Bureau of Aeronautics came up with an economical
solution to the question of what kind of aircraft the new airship
would carry. The prime requirement was that it must be able to pass
through an opening 30 feet wide and 24 feet long in the bottom of
the aircraft hangar. Three prototypes of small biplane carrier fighters
were then in the hands of the Bureau, and of the three, the Curtiss
XF9C-1 (though judged a failure for carrier operations) was selected
as the most suitable for the airships. Ultimately six production
F9C-2s, with a wing span of 25 feet 6 inches and a length over all of
20 feet 2 inches, were procured, while the six Consolidated N2Ys
purchased earlier were used as utility craft, or "running boats," by
the airship heavier than air units.

The design of ZRS 4 and 5, as evolved by Dr. Arnstein and
Goodyear-Zeppelin engineers in cooperation with the Navy
Department, closely followed the winning Project I of the 1928
design competition. The streamlined hull was 785 feet long and
132.9 feet in diameter, with a gas volume 100 per cent inflated of
6,850,000 cubic feet, making them the largest airships ever built
until the appearance of the "Hindenburg" in 1936. The hull
structure was immensely strong, based on 36 longitudinals, and of
the twelve main frames, ten were the stiff triangular "deep" rings
spaced 22.5 metres (74 feet) apart. No less than three intermediate
rings intervened between the main ones. The hull embodied not one
single keel at the bottom, but three, one being at the top of the hull
and the others to port and starboard in the lower hull. These
strengthened the framework particularly in the way of Cell VII
forward where there was a large opening in the bottom to give access
to the aeroplane hangar. Also, the lateral keels housed the eight
German Maybach VL-2 engines of 560 h.p. at Rings 57.5, 80, 102.5
and 125. With the engines fully enclosed in the hull (only possible
with helium inflation) streamlining was improved, though

A "Macon" F9C-2 hook-on fighter, one of six built by the Curtiss Aeroplane and Motor Co. of Buffalo, N.Y., especially for use from the "Akron" and "Macon". Wing span was 25 ft. 5 in., length 20 ft. 7 in., the engine a 438 h.p. Wright R-957-E3, and armament was two .30 cal. machine guns. One example, S/N 9056, exists today in storage at the National Air Museum, Washington, D.C. (U.S. Navy)

unexpected problems occurred due to the four outrigger-mounted swiveling propellers working all at the same level. There was considerable vibration, and air flow to the rear propellers was interfered with. Extending up the hull above each engine room were five water recovery condensers one above the other, flush with the hull. These were to prove a maintenance headache, and cleaning carbon out of their tubes with soap and water was an unpopular duty. There were twelve gas cells (the aftermost in the tail cone was not numbered) of cotton fabric gas-proofed with a synthetic gelatin-latex compound which was lighter than the formerly-used gold beaters' skin, as well as being cheaper. There were emplacements for eight .30 caliber machine guns – three along the ship's back in the upper keel; one at the extreme tail; two in the windows of the auxiliary control position in the lower fin; and two in the control car.

In two respects the final ZRS 4 and 5 design differed significantly from the successful Goodyear Project I of the 1928 design competition. The fins of Project I were long and slender, extending over 110 feet of the ship's length and being firmly attached to main frames 0, 17.5 and 35. Certain airship operators, however, objected that the lower fin was not visible from the control car — considered desirable as the lower fin made contact with the ground aft — and in a revision designed to meet this objection, the fins were shortened and deepened. They were now attached only to main frames 0 and 17.5, and extended forward only to intermediate Frame 28.75. At the same time the control car was moved aft about 8 feet. In later years, particularly after the loss of the ZRS 5 "Macon" originating in structural failure of the upper fin, much was made of these changes, particularly the fact that the leading edges of the fins were no longer attached to any main frame. Certain German "experts" claimed that the "Macon's" loss was occasioned by failure to strengthen the cantilever fins with cruciform bracing as in the Zeppelins. This argument may be dismissed as Nazi chauvinism. In the Zeppelins, cruciform girders were necessary in view of the flimsiness of the flat "bicycle wheel" main ring; the triangular deep ring had the inherent stiffness to take much higher loads.

Another derivative of the Five Year Plan and the contract for the large scouting airships was a project for developing a West Coast airship base to serve the Pacific Fleet. In the spring of 1929 a board of officers headed by Admiral Moffett and including Commander Garland Fulton and Lieut. Comdr. Charles E. Rosendahl met to consider 97 possible West Coast sites for an airship station. Eventually the competition narrowed down to Camp Kearney, just north of the Fleet base at San Diego, and Sunnyvale, about 30 miles south of San Francisco. Operational considerations caused the Board to recommend Sunnyvale, though the Fleet tended to feel offended that the airship designed to cooperate with it was located more than 350 miles north of the Fleet's exercise area.

Naval Air Station, Sunnyvale, Mountain View, California, centered around a huge airship shed with "orange-peel" doors and streamlined design resembling that of Akron, measuring 1,133 feet long, 308 feet wide, and 198 feet high. Construction of the hangar began in October, 1931, and was completed in March, 1933. The station was commissioned on April 12, 1933. Shortly afterwards on May 18, 1933, the station was renamed Moffett Field after the three-time Chief of the Bureau of Aeronautics lost in the "Akron" in that year.

The station still exists under this name, though the last lighter-than-air craft operating from there was deflated in August 1947.

Construction of the ZRS 4 commenced officially on November 7, 1929, when Admiral Moffett drove a golden rivet into the first main ring to be erected in the hangar. Further rings were built on the hangar floor, set upright and connected by longitudinal girders, the internal engine rooms completed, power plants and outriggers installed, the control car and fins built on, and the cotton outer cover applied and coated with aluminium powder dope to reflect the heat of the sun's rays.[39] On August 8, 1931, the ZRS 4 was far enough completed to be christened "Akron" by the wife of President Hoover. Even before this event, the papers had made much of the fact that the airship would be 22,282 pounds overweight compared to the 1928 design specifications.[40] This was a small figure compared to her gross lift 95 per cent inflated with helium of 403,000 lb, useful lift of 160,170 lb, and fixed weights of 242,830 lb. Furthermore, 3,532 lb of the excess weight represented Navy-authorized alterations.

The first flight of "Akron" was deferred until September 23, 1931. Lieut. Comdr. Rosendahl was in command, with 113 people aboard including as passengers the Secretary of the Navy, Charles Francis Adams; the Assistant Secretary for Air David S. Ingalls; Admiral Moffett; the ten-member Navy Board of Inspection and Survey; President Litchfield and other Goodyear-Zeppelin officials; and Garland Fulton, Dr. Arnstein, Charles P. Burgess, and Ralph Weyerbacher. Nine more trial flights followed, including the delivery flight to Lakehurst on October 21-22. "Akron" on these trials fell three knots short of her contract full speed of 72 knots, and the Press again made much of her "failure." On October 27, 1931, "Akron" was placed in commission at Lakehurst.

As the first of the Navy's really big rigids, "Akron" benefited from the sophisticated ground handling equipment now available, which in its final form had been perfected by Lieut. Calvin W. Bolster of the Construction Corps.[41] It would have been impossible to handle a

---

[39] Clear dope was used on the strakes over the lateral keels to permit light to diffuse through the cover for internal illumination, giving a curious effect as though the hull at this point was angled outward.

[40] Always in the limelight, "Akron" did in fact receive a consistently bad press, as noted by Richard K. Smith in his *The Airships Akron and Macon* (Annapolis, Maryland: U.S. Naval Institute, 1965), p. 53.

[41] United States Patent Office, 1,972,863, "Handling Apparatus for Airships," Calvin M. Bolster, United States Navy.

"Macon" at Sunnyvale, illustrating the last word in mechanical ground-handling equipment. The mobile railroad mast draws her out of the shed. The transverely-located stern beam is under the lower fin and barely seen exiting from the hangar. (U.S. Navy)

craft the size of the "Akron" in any kind of a wind with the German method of large numbers of ground personnel. With the mechanical procedure as refined by Bolster a few men could get the ship out of the shed and onto the field. In the hangar the big rigid's nose was connected to the travelling stub mooring mast, a massive quadrupod structure riding on double rails 64.5 feet apart. The lower fin was attached by clamps and cables to a transverse beam weighing 133 tons and spanning a width of 186.5 feet, which likewise rode on the 64.5 feet gauge rails (there was an adjustable connection between the mast and the stern beam). The whole affair, and the "Akron" with it, was drawn out of the hangar by a small diesel locomotive to the "hauling up circle," where the stern beam was transferred to circular railroad tracks by lowering two pairs of standard gauge railroad trucks to ride on the tracks surrounding the circle, lifting the beam off the hangar tracks in the process. Another locomotive then towed the stern beam around the circle until "Akron" was pointing into the wind, and she was ready for takeoff. The process was reversed on landing, with the bow and lower fin being attached to mooring mast

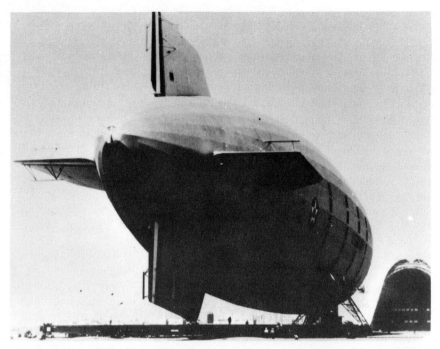

Another view of "Macon" on the south hauling-up circle at Moffett Field, the stern beam prominent in the foreground and the mast supporting the nose. (U.S. Navy)

and stern beam respectively, and then lined up with the hangar rails and pushed into the hangar. Sunnyvale had a north and south hauling-up circle 1300 feet in diameter at each end of the hangar; Lakehurst had only one, and an additional "mooring out circle" where the ship rode with a pneumatic wheel under the lower fin.

In the "Akron" the Navy at last had a large rigid airship specifically designed for fleet operations; and with little appreciation that she was merely the prototype for a fleet of ten such large rigids contemplated under U.S. Navy war plans, an ambitious schedule of exercises had been planned to test her capacities in operations with the Fleet. "Akron's" first year was plagued with operating difficulties and material deficiencies; training in fleet operations barely commenced; and an expedition to the West Coast between May 8 and June 16, 1932, in advance of the completion of the Sunnyvale facility, made it appear that the big rigid could not operate for an extended period without a hangar, and unfavorably impressed the Fleet commanders.

Nor was "Akron" materially ready for the first scouting exercise in January, 1932. The Naval Aircraft Factory had not completed the airship's trapeze in spite of cannibalizing the one from the "Los Angeles." In fact it was not delivered until February 7, and for various reasons, no hook-on flights to the "Akron" were made until May 3, 1932. The airship's participation January 9-12 in a Scouting Force exercise between Cape Lookout, North Carolina, and the Bahamas involved a fine technical performance, with 3000 miles travelled in three days, some of it through snow and icing conditions which no aeroplane could have survived, while the giant rigid easily carried over 8 tons of ice dynamically. Yet the airship, even though she discovered a force of one cruiser and 12 destroyers on the 11th, missed sighting some destroyers on the 10th which themselves sighted the airship. This was remarked on adversely by Vice Admiral Willard, Commander of Scouting Forces.

A serious setback on February 22 prevented "Akron's" participation in the Annual Fleet Problem on the West Coast in March. While being brought out of the Lakehurst hangar that morning in a 6 to 14 knot wind, the tail tore loose from the stern beam and as the runaway airship weather-vaned into the wind, the lower fin smashed repeatedly on the ground. Had it not been for the unusually sturdy hull design, more than the fin could have been shattered. Not until the end of April was the rebuilding of the lower fin completed, while the trapeze was at last installed. On May 8 "Akron" was hustled off to the West Coast, with the intention of flying a few exercises from Camp Kearney with the Scouting Force. Rough weather in West Texas, New Mexico and Arizona duplicated the problems of the "Shenandoah" on the West Coast flight eight years earlier. In attempting to land at Camp Kearney on May 11, three ground crew men were carried up on the lines, two falling to their deaths, to the gratification of news reel cameramen. Rosendahl valved much helium trying to save their lives and now had to go on to the incomplete Sunnyvale base to replenish. In subsequent exercises with cruisers of the Scouting Force, "Akron" was "attacked" by catapult float planes from the surface ships. To the Fleet, she seemed vulnerable to attack by aircraft, and the confidence of the aviators that the big rigid could be destroyed by dive bombing did not minimize this impression. Though the Chief of Naval Operations wanted "Akron" to remain on the Coast into the summer, her commanding officer insisted that she needed to be hangared for maintenance. The flight eastward began June 11, and again emphasized the problems of flying an aerostat designed for low altitude missions at sea over mountainous country: six tons of fuel, and finally the Curtiss XF9C-1 and Consolidated N2Y on board were released to compensate for the ship's heaviness. Fuel shortages forced a stop at the expeditionary mast at Parris Island, North Carolina, and not until June 16 was the airship back at Lakehurst.

Under the next skipper, Commander Alger Dresel, who relieved Rosendahl on June 22, the heavier-than-air unit "shaped up" with four pilots joining the two who had made the West Coast flight, while the six production Curtiss F9C-2 "Sparrowhawk" fighters were delivered through September 21, 1932. However, because of obstructing girders in the hangar (permission was given by the Bureau to hinge them, but this was not done before the ship's loss) only three of the diminutive fighters could be carried at one time. An accident with the stern beam on August 22 again laid "Akron" up for three weeks. Under Dresel, plans were made for sending two planes out beyond the limit of vision to each side of the scouting airship, enabling the formation to sweep a path 100 miles wide. Already it was apparent that the planes housed in the belly hangar of the dirigible were of more use for scouting than defence; unfortunately, the big airship aircraft carriers never received suitable long range scouting aircraft. A doctrine for their use, devised by Lieut. D. Ward Harrigan, the senior aviator of the unit, had considerable influence on later airship aeroplane operations.

"Akron's" last commanding officer was Commander Frank C. McCord, who relieved Dresel on January 3, 1933. With sea time in aircraft carriers, and over 2000 hours of flying time in airships, McCord was well aware of the need to sell the rigid airship to the Fleet. His three months in command included one flight to Guantanamo Bay in Cuba via the expeditionary mast at Opa-Locka near Miami; and a cruise to Panama without a landing. McCord's reports led to the erection of a mast at Guantanamo and plans to do the same in Panama. McCord also impressed everybody with his competence in handling the "Akron" when an East Coast storm with 30-knot gusts prevented her from landing at Lakehurst after a 43-hour flight. Taking a northerly course up the Hudson Valley, McCord then went west over Lake Ontario and Lake Erie to get behind the storm. From Cleveland he then proceeded east, following behind as the storm moved out to sea. In clearing weather, "Akron" landed at Lakehurst at sunset after a flight of nearly 72 hours.

Yet it was in a storm that "Akron" met her end three months

later. During the day of April 3, 1933, in lowering weather, the big ship was prepared for a two or three day flight to calibrate radio direction finding stations along the New England coast. Admiral Moffett came up from Washington to fly with the "Akron" as he had so often done, and there were 76 persons on board when the airship took off in fog at 7.28 pm. Though the fog extended from 300 to 1500 feet, there was no intimation or warning of really bad weather. Actually a cold front accompanied by severe disturbances was approaching rapidly from the west, with a thunderstorm developing over Washington and moving north-east.

Flying westward at first over Philadelphia, "Akron" followed the Delaware River south towards Wilmington. Here sharp flashes of lightning were seen to the south. Lieut. Comdr. Herbert V. Wiley, the executive officer, recommended flying west to get on the "safe semicircle" of the storm, but McCord had seen lightning to the west. The ship was headed east, then north-east, as lightning filled the southern sky. "Akron" increased her altitude to 1600 feet to stay above the top of the fog over the coast. At 10 pm she went out to sea on a heading of 83 degrees true. It was assumed that she made her departure from the vicinity of Asbury Park; actually a head wind had held her back, and she probably went out to sea near Bay Head, 11 miles south. To add to McCord's troubles, static prevented reception of one-third of the 2200 weather map, though Wiley saw a low pressure area centered on Washington.

McCord told Wiley at this point that he intended to ride out the storm at sea, passing ahead of it as it tracked north-east; but instead the lightning became even more vivid on all sides of the ship. At 2300 McCord reversed course to 268 degrees, nearly due west, and an hour later lights seen below were taken to be at Asbury Park. In fact, "Akron" was over Barnegat Inlet, some 45 miles to the south, being seen at this time by personnel of the Coast Guard station there as she once more headed out to sea on a course of 120 degrees. Wiley suggested that McCord, believing himself to be more to the north than he was, might have feared a collision with New York sky scrapers in the low visibility. More likely he believed that on the south-east course he could get behind the storm center which he believed to be moving off to the north-east.

Lightning flashes continued to fill the sky, and rain fell heavily. At 0015 the elevator man reported the ship falling rapidly; ballast was released, "Akron" leveled off at 700 feet, and began to rise rapidly. A few minutes later the air became very turbulent and again the ship was reported falling. Engine telegraphs were set for full power and the elevators put up to raise the nose and cause the ship to climb. "Akron" assumed an up angle of 20 to 25 degrees, and with 800 feet on the altimeter, there was suddenly a severe shock, like a violent gust, and the lower rudder controls carried away. Only later did Wiley realize that the shock was not a gust, but must have been caused by the lower fin and rudder striking the sea. "I was waiting for the shock of the stern hitting the water, but it never came." At 300 feet by the altimeter personnel in the control car sighted the surface of the water, and a few moments later the U.S.S. "Akron" was down in the sea, with water pouring through her control car windows. Partly due to a lack of lifesaving equipment, partly due to the coldness of the water, the loss of life was heavy – 73 dying including Admiral Moffett and Commander McCord, while only three were saved – Wiley, the executive officer; Moody Erwin, Aviation Metalsmith 2nd Class, and Richard E. Deal, Boatswain's Mate 2nd Class.

Due to the small number of survivors, it was difficult to determine what had caused the disaster. McCord was censured by the Court of Inquiry for "having committed an error in judgment in not setting such courses as would have kept him in the safe semicircle (to the west) of the storm, thereby probably avoiding the severe conditions finally encountered." Yet the low pressure disturbance moving north-east from Washington which the "Akron" was fighting when she met her end was merely one of many along a massive cold front rapidly advancing from the west and extending up and down the entire Atlantic seaboard.[42] McCord would have felt its unpredicted violence no matter which way he turned, though if he had gone inland the loss of life would have been small. But the storm did not directly cause "Akron's" destruction, and though Erwin and Deal, inside the hull, saw numerous girders breaking, these structural failures occurred *after* her tail slammed into the ocean. The plain fact is that at the bottom of the last descent, the ship did not have enough "sea room" to recover, and raising the elevators to make the ship climb instead forced the lower fin into the sea. This was confirmed when divers found the lower fin on the ocean floor at a distance from the wreckage, though apparently it was still tenuously attached to the hull when the wreck sank in 105 feet of water about

---

[42] I have vivid personal recollections of violent thunder and brilliant lightning repeatedly awakening me on the night the "Akron" was lost, and I was visiting my grandfather in Newton Center outside of Boston.

30 miles due east of Little Egg Inlet. The lower rudder was never found, and obviously tore off at the moment of impact with the water. The storm further played an indirect role through causing a false reading on the altimeter. I agree with the suggestion of Admiral Rosendahl that in the center of the low pressure area into which the airship was flying the barometer could have stood 0.32 inches lower than at Lakehurst, causing the altimeter to read at least 320 feet too high, and possibly even 600 feet too high. "Never was a 'non-barometric' altimeter more desperately needed than during the 'Akron's' last journey." [43] The final fall remains unexplained; possibly it was caused by a powerful down draft.

Though the sister ship "Macon" was nearing completion at the time of "Akron's" loss, the destruction of the latter can be seen, as Richard K. Smith observes, as the beginning of the end of the rigid airship in the United States. Not least of the repercussions of the disaster was the death of Admiral Moffett, the architect of naval air power and the staunch advocate of the rigid airship; though his support was never blindly uncritical. The heavy loss of life left Congressmen and citizens aghast, and once again there arose the cry, "no more airships!" The "Akron" had attempted to demonstrate the utility of the large rigid airship for strategic scouting at sea, but time had run out on her. For the "Macon" there was an eleventh-hour opportunity to succeed where her sister had failed.

ZRS 5, named for the city of Macon, Georgia, by Admiral Moffett's wife on March 11, 1933, was supposedly a sister ship of the ZRS 4 "Akron." Naturally, there were improvements reflecting experience with the prototype: in particular, better streamlining of radiators and outriggers, and efficient three bladed metal adjustable pitch propellers enabled "Macon" to attain 75.6 knots maximum speed compared to 69 knots in the "Akron." Through refinement in structure and fittings her weight empty was 8000 lb. less than that of the "Akron," with a corresponding increase in useful load. [44] At the same time, she might *not* have been a sister to the "Akron," but even bigger: Admiral Moffett favored inserting an additional 22.5 metre bay at Frame 57.5, the aftermost housing the ship's engines. This would have made her the largest airship ever built, with a gas volume of 7,430,000 cubic feet, and a length overall of 859 feet, too long for

[43] Charles E. Rosendahl, *What About the Airship?* (New York: Charles Scribner's Sons, 1938), p. 123.
[44] *The Airship*, vol. I, No. 3, Autumn, 1934, p. 63. The same article gives gross lift of "Macon" as 410,000 lb., useful lift as 173,000 lb., and fixed weights as 237,000 lb.

the Lakehurst shed, but not for Sunnyvale. Performance would have increased, the range at 50 knots, for instance, being increased by 25 per cent to 11,500 miles. The Chief of Naval Operations however did not want to ask Congress for the additional funds.

With Alger Dresel in command, and 105 persons aboard, "Macon" made her first flight on April 21, 1933. Three more test flights followed, then on June 23 she was placed in commission at Akron by Rear Admiral Ernest J. King, the new Chief of the Bureau of Aeronautics. A few hours later, with King on board, "Macon" was on her way to Lakehurst. Further trials at Lakehurst included training four heavier than air unit pilots in landing the F9C-2 aboard the airship (none of the little fighters had been aboard the "Akron" at the time of her loss). On October 12, 1933, "Macon" departed Lakehurst for the West Coast, having the usual troubles in West Texas, New Mexico and Arizona. Going through Dos Cabezos Pass between Willcox and Vail, Arizona, the ship was forced up by the terrain to 6000 feet and due to loss of helium through the automatic valves was 15,000 pounds heavy – a load carried by flying dynamically at a nose-up angle of 2 degrees.[45] On October 15, after a flight time of 3 days, 1 hour and 17 minutes, "Macon" moored to the mast at Sunnyvale and was moved into the hangar.

"Macon" was on the West Coast for only one reason – as stated by the Chief of Naval Operations, Admiral William H. Standley, to Admiral David F. Sellers, Commander in Chief U.S. Fleet, in July, 1933, she was "to be employed to the fullest extent possible in fleet exercises, so that her military value could be determined."[46] Sellers was to report in September, 1934, on her performance and to give his recommendations on the Navy's future airship policy. Unfortunately, the exercises in which "Macon" was ordered to participate, designed without regard for her strategic scouting capabilities, were held in a small area and involved "Macon" in tactical operations against large numbers of "enemy" ships. That she was repeatedly "shot down" by anti-aircraft fire or by carrier aircraft was not surprising, but gave ammunition to the airship's enemies on the score of her "vulnerability."

In the first exercises in which she participated, on November 15-16, "Macon" had two F9C-2 fighters aboard and they were used to a limited extent. In one case one of her planes discovered the

---

[45] *Log of the United States Ship "Macon"*, Saturday, October 14, 1933, p. 256. Xerox copy provided by Dr. Richard K. Smith.
[46] Smith, p. 103.

"enemy" advance force before the airship made contact. On the other hand, "Macon" was shot down three times, twice by anti-aircraft fire and once by enemy fighters. Each time she was transformed into the "ZRS 6" or "ZRS 7" and continued to operate. The exercises showed the need to use the aeroplanes for scouting while the more vulnerable airship remained in the background. This however required improvement in navigation of the airship, better radio communication between airship and aeroplanes, and a system for navigating the F9C-2s from the airship herself. Due to economic stringencies, the necessary equipment was slow in coming.

In the next series of exercises on January 3-5, 1934, "Macon" made a number of useful reports on the "enemy" fleet in a congested tactical situation, once reporting a convoy which was "wiped out" by an air strike from friendly carriers. On the other hand she was criticised for "sheltering" over a friendly cruiser division to enjoy the protection of its anti-aircraft batteries against attack by enemy aeroplanes. On the last day of the exercise, however, "Macon's" two hook-on planes were employed on a search pattern ahead of the airship in a "60-60" scheme devised by one of her officers, Lieutenant Donald Mackey. With the airship flying straight ahead at 50 knots, and the planes making 100 knots, the latter flew out on either side of the airship's path at a 60 degree angle to her course, and could count on meeting her again whenever they turned back inward at a 60 degree angle to her track. Twice the "Macon" was "shot down," once by anti-aircraft fire and once by enemy fighters.

The airship participated only briefly in exercises on February 20-21, due to bad weather, and was criticised by Admiral Sellers even though he admitted that "the weather was particularly unsuitable for all aircraft operations."[47] She also made a bad impression by letting herself be "shot down" by the battleships "New York" and "Texas" when she approached them at close range in murky weather. Dresel, however, was concerned about a threatening line squall, and for the safety of his ship he was heading for Sunnyvale even though he knew Sellers would hold it against the "Macon" that she was leaving the exercise.

History repeated itself on April 10, with "Macon" in a crowded tactical situation near the California coast being "shot down" once by enemy cruisers, and again destroyed by a squadron of dive bombers. It was then time for her to proceed to the Caribbean, where the Fleet was bound for manoeuvres designed to test its ability

[47] Smith, p. 113.

to transit the Panama Canal and cover it against an attack from the eastward. "Macon" was to be based during the exercises at the expeditionary mast at Opa-Locka. As usual, there was the high altitude problem of crossing the Continental Divide; Dresel would have preferred a longer but lower level route via the Isthmus of Tehuantepec, and the Mexican Government had given permission; but Admiral Sellers decreed that the ship would proceed east via the usual route.

The result was near-disaster, and "Macon" in the process sustained injuries which eventually proved fatal. She departed Sunnyvale on April 20, carrying 82,800 lb of fuel and 17,100 lb of ballast. By early morning of the next day, over Willcox, Arizona, she was at 6100 feet and had dropped 9000 lb of ballast and 7000 lb of fuel, yet due to loss of helium over pressure height was 20,200 lb heavy. Worse was yet to come: in West Texas the heated air was unusually turbulent, with vertical gusts so violent that men working in the catwalks had to hold on, while once Lieutenant Mackey saw his binoculars, parallel rulers and dividers "floating" above the chart table. Yet with the ship still 15,000 lb heavy, Dresel had to drive her with standard speed on all engines to hold her in the air dynamically.[48] The combination of vertical gust loads and aerodynamic loads, increasing as the square of the speed, was too much: just after noon two diagonal girders broke and one buckled in Frame 17.5 port side, due to excessive loads on the port fin bolted to the ring at this point. Quick action by Chief Boatswain's Mate Robert J. Davis led to the broken girders being promptly reinforced before the damage spread farther. The ship proceeded into smoother air with six engines on standard speed, and by the evening of the 22nd was at the Opa Locka mast. Here for 9 days she remained while a repair party from Goodyear-Zeppelin made more permanent repairs. It was realized that the ring structure at 17.5 was weak relative to the severe loads that might be imposed on it by the fins, and at a later date, after stress evaluations by the Bureau of Aeronautics and the Goodyear-Zeppelin Corporation, it was decided to reinforce the ring structure in the vicinity of the fins, and the fins themselves. Unfortunately this work was not considered urgent and was to be

[48] German practice was to minimize aerodynamic loads in rough air by dropping ballast and slowing the engines. In "Macon's" case, however, Admiral Rosendahl has pointed out to me that Dresel, flying through twisting canyons, needed high speed to control his ship, while he could not drop more fuel as he might not be able to reach Opa Locka. Lastly, "we thought those ships were so strong that they could take anything." Interview, Toms River, New Jersey, May 8, 1971.

"accomplished from time to time, as opportunity offers, at the discretion of the Commanding Officer"[49] in order not to interfere with operating schedules.

In scouting with the Fleet in the Caribbean, "Macon" was hampered by thunder squalls and poor visibility, and as usual found herself in a tactical situation with large numbers of ships within a relatively small area. It was demonstrated that the big airship could not approach within visual range of a force containing a carrier without being "shot down" by the latter's massed fighter squadrons, and the two F9C-2s on board could not possibly defend her successfully, partly because they could only be launched one by one from the hangar via the single trapeze.[50] As a result, "Macon" began experimenting with scouting methods which would keep the airship in the background. These included having two F9C-2s on station ahead, perhaps having them fly a 60-60 pattern back and forth across the airship's track; and an initial experiment where the "Macon," using radio and other intelligence, actually controlled the courses and distances flown by the fighters through the use of voice radio. Obviously the latter method was the best, but could not be depended on until better radio equipment was available, and a reliable homing radio beacon developed which could surely bring the fighters back to the airship in an emergency.

The cautious Dresel, to the annoyance of Admiral King and the disgust of Admiral Sellers, insisted on returning to Sunnyvale before the conclusion of the manoeuvres. He did not care to face the passes of West Texas, New Mexico and Arizona in the thunderstorm season in July and August, and felt that the weakness at Frame 17.5 should have prompt attention. "Macon" departed Opa Locka on May 16, and after a relatively uneventful flight of 51 hours returned to Sunnyvale.

As if in revenge, Admiral Sellers sent his evaluation of the "Macon" to the Chief of Naval Operations in June rather than in September. Carelessly assembled by members of his staff,[51] it complained that she was "overweight," a fault which was true of the

---

[49] Smith, p. 145.

[50] In August, 1933, a fixed trapeze, or "perch," had been installed at Frame 102.5 to enable an additional F9C-2 to be carried externally. The "Macon" heavier than air unit would have preferred to have all their aircraft out on "perches," ready for instant simultaneous release, on entering the combat zone; but this was not done.

[51] Airship men felt they had been victimized by Commander Holloway H. Frost of Sellers' staff. In an otherwise excellent book on the Battle of Jutland, Frost had gone out of his way to ridicule the performance of the German Zeppelins.

Curtiss F9C-2 fighter of the "Macon" HTA unit on the trapeze. Note shadow of the airship on the water to the right of photo. (U.S. Navy)

"Akron," and unrealistically expected her to perform at high altitudes. While admitting that "Macon's" performance had shown constant improvement, and that using her for tactical scouting put her at a disadvantage, Sellers had no suggestions about her employment. "Vulnerability" was pointed up with the observation that she could not operate with the Fleet for more than 12 hours without being "shot down". Sellers concluded that "The U.S.S. 'Macon' has failed to demonstrate its usefulness as a unit of the Fleet," and was "decidedly of the opinion that the further expenditure of public funds for this type of vessel for the Navy was not justified."[52] The Sellers report was obviously intended not so much to criticise "Macon" as to scuttle the airship in the U.S. Navy.

Admiral King's rejoinders received scant attention at higher levels in the Navy Department. Sellers' damning conclusions about the rigid airship's military uselessness did not of course destroy it, but they provided powerful arguments for highly placed opponents and

[52] Smith, p. 125.

confirmed their prejudices. Even if "Macon" had arrived fully trained and indoctrinated, and had put on a brilliant performance, it would seem that the result would have been the same.

Lieutenant Commander Herbert V. Wiley, the only officer survivor of the "Akron" disaster, brought a new drive and purpose to the "Macon's" activities when he took over as commanding officer on July 11, 1934. Under his direction the hook-on squadron came to play the chief role in scouting, while the airship served as carrier, radio relay station, and command center. A much talked of modification was at last made in the little F9C-2s, as the landing gear, unnecessary for operations from the airship at sea, was routinely removed at the start of a cruise and replaced by a 30 gallon fuel tank. Top speed rose from 176 to 200 mph, and flight time was increased to 5½ hours, increasing the radius from 175 to 255 miles from the airship. Long range operations of the aeroplanes became much safer with the development of a simple, foolproof low-frequency radio homing device by Dr. Gerhard Fisher, a civilian, and Lieut. Howard N. Coulter, the "Macon's" communications officer. Wiley finally tried out the pilot rescue gear – a life raft on the end of a long line – and briefly experimented with the "spy basket," or sub-cloud car, a much overrated device lowered 1000 to 1500 feet below the airship to direct her while the ship herself was hidden by cloud.

Wiley promptly devised some strategic scouting schemes of his own, the first one being intended also to give the "Macon" some favorable publicity. From newspaper reports and probable speeds he determined the probable course and position of the cruisers "Houston," with President Roosevelt aboard, and "New Orleans" en route from Panama to Hawaii, and in the course of a "protracted flight to sea" his planes discovered the two cruisers after being a little more than an hour in the air. The President and his entourage were astounded to find small fighter-type aircraft – *sans* landing gear! – "buzzing" the cruisers when the nearest land was 1600 miles away! They were thrilled when the "Macon" appeared and when the F9C-2s, after returning aboard "Macon," dropped newspapers, magazines and souvenir letters for the President. The Commander in Chief U.S. Fleet, now Admiral Joseph N. Reeves, was furious at the display of "misapplied initiative," but Admiral King, the Chief of the Bureau of Aeronautics, was highly pleased. Wiley later repeated the scouting procedure in contacting liners and freighters on the run between Hawaii and the West Coast.

In her first participation in Fleet exercises under Wiley's command, marking the return of the Fleet to the West Coast on October 8, "Macon" distinguished herself by tracking the carrier "Saratoga," and when attacked by six "Saratoga" dive bombers, Wiley foiled their diving approach by turning hard right and bringing all his guns to bear, while one of the F9C-2s joined in the fray. All officers and crew were on watch continuously from 0500 to 1800 on this day, and meals were served to lookouts and gunners at their stations. "Macon" was less successful in the next exercise on December 6-7, when her planes tracked and identified many units, but she was "shot down" twice in air attacks. The situation again was a tactical one in a crowded area, but at this time Admiral King was making headway with the suggestion that "Macon" undertake strategic search problems between the West Coast and Hawaii, utilizing the expeditionary mast at Ewa for layovers in the islands. Meanwhile, Wiley continued training his ship's company in frequent flights, and further drilled his hook-on pilots in new techniques. During an operation on January 15-16, 1935, the F9C-2s were able to take accurate radio bearings on "Macon" from 185 miles, and clear voice communications were possible out to 95 miles, with Morse code transmissions read with ease from 140 miles. Wiley was planning nothing less than an after-dark dive bombing attack with his F9C-2s on the carrier "Lexington" in the next manoeuvres: night operations with the hook-on planes were practically routine, while the surface carriers were then required to have their aircraft aboard before dark.

Structural failure on February 12, 1935, put paid to all these plans. In September, 1934, two boxes containing 598 pounds of reinforcement parts for Ring 17.5 and the fins attached to it were shipped from Akron to Sunnyvale, but these were put in a few at a time during seven overhaul periods between November 10, 1934, and February 10, 1935. By then the reinforcements were in place in the vicinity of the lower and horizontal fins, but work had not yet begun on the upper fin or the adjacent portion of Frame 17.5 One reason was that the gas cells I and II would have to be deflated, so this work was to be deferred until an overhaul period in March.

"Macon's" last flight, beginning at 0710 on February 11, involved scouting training while the Fleet moved from San Diego and Long Beach to San Francisco. Many flights were made by the F9C-2s which were constantly coming and going in every direction and sending in quantities of information. At 1310 on February 12

"Macon" was detached from the exercise, and some six hours later was off Point Sur en route to Sunnyvale when she was struck by an exceptionally severe gust and lurched violently to starboard. The heavy lateral force on the upper fin caused it to tear free of the ship, taking the top of Ring 17.5 with it. The entire upper fin then disintegrated, beginning at the forward end, and puncturing Cells II, I and 0 in the tail cone, which rapidly deflated. Even so the ship might conceivably have been saved, but on receiving news of the casualty aft, control car personnel dumped such large quantities of fuel and ballast that the stern-heavy ship, driven by her still-running engines, not only rose through pressure height, which was 2800 feet, but continued on up to 4,850 feet. So much helium was lost through the automatic valves that the ship was no longer buoyant, and her descent into the sea 24 minutes after the casualty was henceforth inevitable. In contrast to the "Akron" disaster, there was plenty of life-saving equipment, the water was warm, and cruisers from the Fleet were almost immediately on hand to rescue survivors. Only two persons were lost of the 83 on board.

The Court of Inquiry found that the primary cause of the loss of the ship was the failure of girders in the top of Ring 17.5 when overstressed by the gust load on the upper fin. Damage caused by broken girders caused three gas cells to deflate with a loss of lift of 30,000 to 40,000 lb. The keepers of the Point Sur Lighthouse, who were actually observing "Macon" through binoculars at the moment of the failure, gave valuable testimony concerning the break-up of the upper fin. The investigators also concluded that no less than 32,700 lb of fuel and water ballast had been dumped during the five minutes after the fin failure. Whether the dumping of weights made the big ship light or merely brought her into equilibrium, the engines should have been stopped. Possibly communications between the control car and the engine rooms suffered damage.[53]

"Macon" was the last rigid airship built and flown in the United States, and the last in the world excepting the later commercial Zeppelins "Hindenburg" and "Graf Zeppelin II." Convinced by an unremitting newspaper campaign that rigid airships were expensive killers and useless into the bargain, the public and Congress wanted nothing more to do with them. This prejudiced attitude was confirmed and hardened by the spectacular destruction of the "Hindenburg" at Lakehurst two years later. Commercial airships schemes, encouraged by Goodyear and its subsidiary, American

[53] Special Committee on Airships. Report No. 3. *Technical Aspects of the Loss of the Macon*. (Stanford: Stanford University Press, 1937).

Zeppelin Transport Co., had little chance after the loss of the "Macon," and none at all after the burning of the "Hindenburg." Nor did the rigid airship have many friends in the Navy. To senior admirals, and to personnel in the surface fleets, it had always been on trial, and it was easy to find fault with a peripheral weapon which was always in the experimental prototype stage. Nor did it number many friends in the Bureau of Aeronautics, dominated by heavier than air officers whose hearts belonged to the aircraft carrier. True, the Bureau still contained the Lighter-Than-Air Design Section, but this ceased to carry any weight after Captain Garland Fulton's retirement in 1940.

During the "years of confusion"[54] between 1935 and 1940, a number of interesting projects were put on paper. The Bureau conceived the idea of an airship carrying airplanes, not for scouting but for offensive purposes, and in 1936-7 Charles P. Burgess elaborated a design for a ZRCV airship of 9,550,000 cubic feet capacity, 897.3 feet long and 147.6 feet in maximum diameter, to carry nine dive bombers armed with 1000 lb bombs on retractible trapezes under the keel of the ship. It was claimed that three ZRCVs with 27 dive bombers would have the striking power of one aircraft carrier of the contemporary "Yorktown" class. Significantly, in the Bureau design, the eight Allison engines totalling 6,000 h.p. were carried in four external power cars, and the main hull frames were simple flat rings, reinforced at the bottom – deviations from the "Akron" design. Goodyear made drawings for an even larger ZRCV of 10,000,000 cubic feet, 963 feet long and 147.65 feet in diameter, to carry five dive bombers and three fighters. Neither design was ever presented to Congress.

A Five Year Program submitted by the Bureau for 1937-41 called for six blimps, a training airship to replace the "Los Angeles," two ZRS types with performance equivalent to that of the "Akron" and "Macon," and an experimental Metalclad airship of 1,500,000 cubic feet. The General Board refused to accept the programme in 1937 hearings, but acknowledged that the rigid airship had never had a fair chance to show its capabilities in strategic scouting, and gave encouragement to proponents of the airship carrier: "The conception of utilizing rigid airships as carriers of airplanes has not been thoroughly explored, but it is the field in which a naval airship's greatest possibilities seem to lie."[55] Nonetheless, the General Board would not recommend procurement of a large ZRCV "at this time"

[54] Captain Fulton's term.
[55] Smith, p. 165.

and recommended instead that the ZRN training airship be built – specifically of 3,000,000 cubic feet capacity and to carry at least two aeroplanes. Goodyear had no trouble in creating a design for such a craft, 650 feet long, 99.35 feet in diameter, and with retractible trapezes for three aeroplanes. Although authorized by Congress, this project came to nothing due to the adamant insistence of President Roosevelt that the training airship must be no longer than 325 feet – which would have resulted in a useless technical monstrosity. [56] Thus died the last rigid airship project in the United States – unmourned by the heavier than air men in the Bureau, or by the Navy generally.

Or not the *very* last, for in January, 1942, after becoming Commander in Chief of the U.S. Fleet, Admiral King, the former Chief of the Bureau of Aeronautics, attempted to revive the ZRCV concept. In the end he was persuaded that the time needed for development and construction, and the diversion of critical manpower and material in wartime, made it unrealistic to pursue a concept of "undemonstrated value."

American airship designers and operators had advanced the state of the art well beyond what they had learned from its German originators, as acknowledged by Zeppelin Company personnel themselves. Why was it then (leaving out the unreasoning prejudices of the public and economy-minded Congressmen) that the rigid airship never enjoyed with the U.S. Navy the popularity and acceptance that it was accorded in its heyday in the Imperial German Navy? One reason is that in Germany the Zeppelin was seen as a convincing, even overwhelming proof of German genius and technical superiority, while to pragmatic Americans it was "foreign" and therefore suspect. Another reason is that the German Navy, inferior to the British and on the defensive, needed the airship to safeguard its Fleet against surprise attacks. The offensive-minded U.S. Navy was disinterested in the scouting airship which had no attack capabilities (though the ZRCV was to cater to this point of view). A general reason was economic: airship men were fond of saying that the big rigids did not compete with aeroplanes, they supplemented them; but the competition was certainly intense when it came to dividing inadequate funds between airships and aeroplanes, not to mention the surface Navy. The cliché that forty flying boats could be

---

[56] Roosevelt seems to have been influenced in favor of the Metalclad design, and his otherwise irrational stand may be interpreted as intended to assure that Metalclad would receive a contract.

purchased for one rigid airship was constantly put forward and did not fail to make an impression. In the Bureau of Aeronautics there was prejudice in favour of the aircraft carrier and its attack group, and even Admiral Moffett, often misrepresented as adoring the airship as a child worships a toy, was too hard-headed to support the airship if it did not meet the needs of the Fleet. Too many losses occurred at critical times – in all probability *if* Lansdowne had lived and if the "Shenandoah" had survived, and *if* the "Akron" had not gone down off Barnegat with 72 men and the Chief of the Bureau of Aeronautics, their trained personnel would have gone on to prove the rigid airship as a scouting weapon. Lastly, too many of the operators failed to appreciate the need to change with the times. Carrier fighters and dive bombers made it suicidal to imitate the German scouting procedure, with the airship herself tracking the enemy forces. In the last six months of her life, "Macon" had developed into a sophisticated weapons system, capable of ranging thousands of miles from her base and throwing out her scouting aircraft, radio controlled and carrying homing equipment, for hundreds of miles to search ahead and to either side. But the Fleet had already rendered an adverse judgment; and when "Macon's" last voyage ended in the sea off Point Sur, the last chance passed for an eleventh-hour reprieve.

VII
The rigid airship in world commerce

During the First World War, the German Naval Airship Division, with 68 rigid airships, had made 325 raid flights, 1,205 scouting flights, and 2,984 other flights, for a total of 1,491,600 miles flown. Yet it could be argued that even the German Navy, with its extensive experience with the rigid airship, failed to exploit its capabilities as a long-range weight carrier. In another place,[1] I have argued that in the last two years of the war, when every effort was being made to bring England to her knees through the U-boat campaign against merchant shipping, the Zeppelins would better have been employed in scouting to the west of the British Isles. Loaded to capacity with more than 30 tons of petrol, the "height climbers," particularly the high speed ships of the L 70 class, would have had a range of 3000 miles – enough to enable them, flying via the north of Scotland, to cruise for several days in the Atlantic. What might they not have done to aid the unrestricted U-boat war by seeking out Allied convoys and directing the submarines onto them? Instead, carrying three tons of bombs and 27 tons of water ballast, they were sent in ineffective attacks against England; while the usual North Sea scouting flights lasted no longer than 20 hours. In fact, the "r" class of Zeppelin, appearing in the summer of 1916, had intercontinental capability, as was proven in July, 1919, when the British R 34, a copy of the German Navy's Zeppelin L 33, crossed the Atlantic from east to west in 108 hours, and returned in 75 hours.

This achievement had been foreshadowed by two flights made by German Zeppelins during the war. Oberleutnant zur See der Reserve Ernst Lehmann – the naval officer commanding Army airships, and destined to be Hugo Eckener's right hand collaborator in the period after the war – held original ideas on the employment of the big airships, and while commanding the Army's LZ 120 in the Baltic in 1917, argued that

> It was the concensus of opinion that it would be better, from a military view point, to maintain a ship on patrol for much longer periods of time – for example, 100 hours or more. We also concluded that the length of a flight

[1] Robinson, p.348.

250

might be limited solely by the petrol capacity of the ship. I say that was the concensus of opinion. It was universal among the members of our crew, but the other officers largely disagreed, for two reasons. They thought the motors would require overhauling before the completion of such a long trip and further, that the men could not stand the exertion and strain for such extended periods.[2]

The impending dissolution of the Army airship service on August 1 may have inspired Lehmann to test the proposition as a grand finale. Loading the Zeppelin with 2,650 lb of bombs, 7,700 lb of water ballast, 6,600 lb of machine guns, ammunition, equipment and provisions, and deducting 5,500 lb for the weight of the 29 men on board, Lehmann found enough useful lift remaining for 2,400 lb of oil and 37,300 lb of petrol. This would last for 56 hours at cruising speed on all engines, or more than 100 hours at reduced speed.

On the night of July 26, 1917, LZ 120 took off from Seerappen to begin her long flight. Once in the air the ship was put in order and the crew divided into watches, and those off duty climbed into the 20 hammocks along the gangway. Part of the experiment was to determine if the crew could tolerate the strain of prolonged flying by being divided into watches. Officers and men of the seaman branch stood alternate watches of 6 hours duration. By running most of the time on three engines, the machinists could be divided into three watches on duty 8 hours at a time.

Dodging thunderstorms kept the duty section busy on the first night, but the remainder of the flight was uneventful. Depending on the weather, the ship at first cruised in the western Baltic, and later in its eastern and northern portions. Twice the starboard after engine ran so roughly that connecting bolts at the upper end of the outrigger drive shaft were sheared through. Each time the Zeppelin free-ballooned while the outer cover was unlaced, and men climbed out on the propeller bracket to replace the bolts.

The weather map on the evening of July 30 indicated an approaching storm, and Lehmann set course for Seerappen, running on all six engines. LZ 120 landed at 3.40 am on July 31. She had been in the air for 101 hours, and fuel for three engines for 14 hours more still remained in the tanks.

Meanwhile, in one colony of the German Empire, German East Africa, troops under General von Lettow-Vorbeck were still holding

[2] Ernst A. Lehmann & Howard Mingos, *The Zeppelins* (New York: J. H. Sears & Co., 1927), p. 235.

out against superior British forces. In May, 1917, Dr. Zupitza, the former chief medical officer of the German West Africa garrison, suggested to the German Colonial Office that a Zeppelin be sent to von Lettow-Vorbeck with medical supplies. The project was approved in principle by the Navy Minister, Admiral von Capelle, and with the stimulus of LZ 120's endurance cruise, the Navy Ministry, the Colonial Office, the Leader of Airships, and the Zeppelin Company made a joint study of the requirements.

The southernmost airship base in territory controlled by the Central Powers was of course Jamboli in Bulgaria. The airline distance from here to Mahenge, in the heart of von Lettow-Vorbeck's territory, was 3,600 miles. A ship intended to cover this distance should have a still-air range of 4,350 miles, and travelling with four engines at a speed of 40 mph she would be in the air for 108 hours, or 4½ days. With a cargo of 16 tons – 11 tons of small arms ammunition and only three tons of medical supplies – a ship of 2,365,000 cubic feet capacity would be required.

L 59, the first Zeppelin to make an intercontinental flight, from Jamboli, Bulgaria, to Khartoum and return, 21-25 November 1917, with 15 tons of cargo and 22 persons aboard. The Zeppelin covered 4200 miles in 95 hours. (Luftschiffbau Zeppelin)

Even before reporting the plan to the Kaiser, the Navy Ministry ordered L 57, a series ship of the "v" class building at Friedrichshafen, to be lengthened by two 15 metre gas cells. This gave her a length of 743 feet, and a gas capacity of 2,418,700 cubic feet. On September 26, 1917, L 57 made her first flight, and on October 4 the Imperial consent was obtained. The project was set back a month when on October 7, 1917, L 57 burned accidentally at Jüterbog, together with 85 cases of precious medical supplies. Kapitänleutnant Bockholt, her commander, had made an error of judgment in bringing her out for a speed trial with a storm approaching, and she had been damaged and then caught fire during an attempt to return her to her shed in high winds.

Less than 48 hours later the Navy Ministry ordered the L 59, then building at Staaken, to be modified in the same manner as L 57. On October 25 L 59 made her first flight, again with Bockholt in command. Hastily she was loaded with the special cargo, amounting to more than 15 tons:

311,000 rounds of ammunition	16,950 lb
230 machine gun belts with 57,500 cartridges in the belts	3,855 lb
54 machine gun ammunition boxes with 13,500 cartridges	972 lb
30 machine guns	1,125 lb
4 infantry rifles (for the crew in case of forced landing)	530 lb
9 spare machine-gun barrels	377 lb
61 sacks of bandages and medicines	5,790 lb
3 sacks of sewing materials	265 lb
Mail	55 lb
Binoculars	62 lb
Spare rifle bolts	110 lb
Bush knives and sheaths	168 lb
Spare radio parts	73 lb
Total	30,332 lb [3]

On November 3, L 59 departed Staaken for Jamboli, where she arrived 28 hours later. Bockholt made two abortive attempts to fly to Africa, once getting as far as Symrna in Asia Minor. Finally, on the morning of November 21, the big Zeppelin got away loaded with 20,200 lb of ballast, 47,800 lb of petrol, the cargo amounting to 35,800 lb, and 22 persons on board. To avoid British aircraft based on the islands of the Aegean, Bockholt initially steered across Asia Minor to Symrna, leaving the mainland at the Gulf of Kos. By 10.15 pm on November 21 L 59 was off the eastern tip of Crete, and

[3] J. Goebel u. Walter Förster, *Afrika zu unseren Füssen* (Leipzig: Verlag von K. F. Koehler, 1925) p. 50.

went through a line of thunderstorms towards the North African coastline. At 5.15 am on the 22nd she reached the shoreline near Mersa Matruh. All through the day the Zeppelin cruised south above the desert, checking her navigation by crossing the Farafrah and Dakhla Oases. A hundred and fifty miles south of the latter, L 59 crossed the Tropic of Cancer and became the first airship to fly in the tropics. The heat of the sun blazing overhead expanded the hydrogen, and quantities blew off through the automatic valves. Very light from the superheat and consumption of fuel, Bockholt flew the ship nose down during the day to prevent further gas loss. Thermals rising from the baking sands, more violent than any that Bockholt's crew had ever experienced, tossed the ship about. Some of the men, veteran seamen with many years' service, were embarrassed to find themselves airsick.

At 4.20 pm the forward engine had to be shut down, and L 59 made the remainder of the journey on four engines. Just after dark she reached the Nile at Wadi Halfa. Now, with cooling taking place after sunset, the loss of gas during the heat of the day became painfully apparent; in fact the hydrogen was supercooled to 9 degrees below the temperature of the outside air. Anticipating a loss of lift after dark, Bockholt had released 4400 lb of water ballast and believed he could carry the rest of the load dynamically, flying 4 degrees nose up. At 3 am on the 23rd the ship stalled and fell, nearly striking a mountain peak in the Jebel Ain, and 6200 lb of ballast and ammunition had to be dropped in a hurry.

Meanwhile, at 12.45 am west of Khartoum, L 59's radio had received a message from Nauen, the big overseas station near Berlin, advising that von Lettow-Vorbeck had been defeated and the enemy had seized the greater portion of the Makonde Highlands, where the Zeppelin was to have landed. Bockholt was ordered to return. The East African garrison was in fact hard pressed, but von Lettow-Vorbeck succeeded in escaping into Portuguese Mozambique, where he captured supplies more than equal to those carried in L 59. He did not surrender until November 23, 1918.

There was some debate in the control car, with arguments that now more than ever von Lettow-Vorbeck needed the supplies and the ship should go on, but training and discipline prevailed and at 2.30 am on November 23, L 59 reversed course, being then some 125 miles west of Khartoum. "The realization of being on the verge of fulfilling the mission after overcoming all difficulties made it very difficult to turn back, and affected morale,"[4] wrote Bockholt later. There was a reaction to nervous tension, to say the least. Some of the men became feverish, very fatigued and suffered from insomnia, though they still stood their watches of 4 hours on and 4 hours off.

At 3.30 am on November 24, L 59 left the African continent at Sollum, and steered north-east at 10,000 feet on course for the Gulf of Adalia. That night there was a repetition of the near-catastrophe in the Sudan, and for the same reason — insufficient ballast released to compensate for evening cooling. Six thousand, six hundred pounds of ballast had to be discharged as the ship dropped while flying "heavy" above the mountains of Asia Minor. At 4.30 am on November 25 L 59 was over Jamboli, but did not land until 7.40 am. The flight had covered 4200 miles in 95 hours, and the 22,750 lb of fuel remaining on board would have driven the Zeppelin for 64 hours more.[5]

The success of L 59 in carrying 22 persons and 15 tons of cargo for a distance equal to that from Friedrichshafen to Chicago proved the intercontinental capability of the large Zeppelin airship, and was very much in the minds of all airship enthusiasts after the Armistice in 1918. There were some reservations: the excessive loss of gas and ballast, due to the extreme heat of the tropical sun, had been noted, Bockholt himself having written that "the ship should have 3000 kg (6600 lb) or 4 per cent of her lift to take care of cooling effect."[6] Thus, the amount of ballast which could be loaded (at the expense of payload and petrol), divided by 6,600 would seem to indicate the number of nights that the long distance airship could remain airborne in the tropics.

In the immediate post-war period there were two schemes to fly the Atlantic with the L 71 and L 72, both of which had the same gas capacity as the L 59. L 71's commanding officer, Martin Dietrich, indicated to me that the ideas of his crew on the subject did not deserve to be taken seriously, and represented them as simply reacting to the boredom of lying idle in Ahlhorn after the Armistice. Nevertheless, he forwarded to the authorities in Berlin their letter of

[4] Robinson, p. 292.
[5] After being reconstructed in Friedrichshafen to carry 14,100 lb. of bombs, L 59 returned to Jamboli on February 21, 1918, to conduct long distance raids in the Mediterranean. After an attack on Naples, and an abortive attempt to bomb Port Said, L 59 burned in the air over the Straits of Otranto on April 7, 1918, while en route to raid Malta.
[6] Robinson, p. 292.

November 30, 1918:

> The extreme danger of this hour, and the conviction that our beloved Fatherland stands at the brink of the abyss, forces on us airshipmen the question of whether the German people can be aided by dispatching to America by the quickest means suitable representatives of the new Government, who may bring to the attention of the free American people the frightful distress of our Fatherland, and who may request immediate help . . . It may sound dangerous to speak of crossing the ocean, yet we have no fear of it. We know that it is absolutely within the range of possibility and were it not for the war, German airships would already have crossed the ocean. We remind you of the Africa flight of the naval airship L 59, and of the 100-hour flight of the airship LZ 120, which were successfully carried out under the most difficult weather conditions. With reasonably favorable weather we could make the crossing in a flight of 100 hours and together with 30 passengers, we could transport a quantity of leaflets and other propaganda material . . . .
>
> Gentlemen! Please advise us of the Fatherland's needs. We are prepared to carry the German spirit across the seas and we hope that thereafter the pressure of events will contribute to opening the hearts of the enemy to the German people.[7]

No answer was ever received to this letter, and on December 8, 1918, L 71 was hung up in her hangar and deflated, and her crew dispersed.

The proposal to fly L 72 to America was much more serious, and assiduously pushed by Ernst Lehmann, who expected to be the commanding officer. As early as December, 1918, Lehmann was discussing the project with Baron von Gemmingen, who had succeeded Count von Zeppelin, his uncle, as head of the company on the latter's death on March 8, 1917. Gemmingen, who had served under Lehmann in wartime airships, threw the support of the firm behind the project. In the eyes of the *Luftschiffbau* (though not of the Entente powers) L 72, which was practically complete in Löwenthal at the time of the Armistice, was still the property of the Zeppelin Company as the German Navy had cancelled the contract. The ship was loaded almost exclusively with fuel, and Lehmann anticipated being able to make a two-way flight without refueling if the reception in America was unfavorable. For he was not totally blind to the political complications: he intended to depart secretly via the North German coast, slip by night down the English Channel or around the north of Scotland, and announce the flight only the day before reaching the North American continent with a message to the American authorities requesting permission to land. With

---

[7] Copy in possession of Oberst Martin Dietrich, Hamburg.

preparations well along, the Zeppelin Company in March, 1919, felt obliged to request the permission of the central government in Berlin. This was refused; undoubtedly the politicians foresaw more clearly than the chauvinistic Lehmann the storm of outraged protests that would come from the Allied powers, which might even lead to a French occupation of Friedrichshafen and the destruction of the Zeppelin works.

The Zeppelin Company in any case had plans of their own for commercial airship operations in the last months of 1918.[8] Unable to forsee the political and economic chaos that would prevail in Germay for at least five years, or the harsh terms of the Versailles *Diktat*, its directors naively expected to do business as usual. Their first thought was to revise the proposed design for the Navy's L 100 of 3,800,000 cubic feet, to be designated the "America airship." Perceiving that this was too ambitious a project at a time of uncertainty, the Zeppelin Board of Directors, on January 27, 1919, took up the question of a "small passenger airship." The craft was intended to advertise on a small scale the speed, safety and convenience of airship travel, and as Baron von Gemmingen remarked, "if it succeeds, won't it be good publicity for everything we plan to undertake further?"

In March, 1919, Dr. Paul Jaray, the project director, completed the final design and the ship, numbered LZ 120, made her first flight on August 20, 1919. She was christened "Bodensee" after the lake on which Friedrichshafen is situated, and the DELAG was revived to operate her on a regularly scheduled passenger service. "Bodensee" was in fact the first fully streamlined rigid airship,[9] 396.3 feet long, and 61.4 feet in diameter. The gas volume was 706,200 cubic feet, approximately that of the "Sachsen" of 1913, but whereas the latter had a useful lift of only 16,300 lb, the efficient "Bodensee" could carry 22,000 lb. With her clean design, the new rigid had the highest

[8] It is fascinating to speculate briefly on the future of the rigid airship had Germany won the war. All the technological know-how, vast building plant and numerous airship bases, and hundreds of trained personnel, would have been dedicated to creating a network of airship lines around the world. Probably transatlantic service to South America via Spain (always a friendly neutral) would have commenced within two years of the end of the war, followed by a North American service, then a route via the Mediterranean and India to the Dutch East Indies, with the Pacific being the last ocean to be conquered. Once more the Zeppelin would have reigned supreme in the hearts of its countrymen as the symbol of German prestige and leadership, and with the might of a powerful *Reich* subsidizing it as a weapon of Imperial exploitation, to the disadvantage of the aeroplane, the long range passenger airship might even be with us today!

[9] The fully streamlined British R 80, the inspired creation of Dr. Barnes Wallis, had been designed during the war but did not make her first flight until July 19, 1920.

trial speed yet recorded for an airship — 82.4 mph — even though her four 245 hp engines, wartime "altitude motors," could not be run at full throttle below 6000 feet. The most striking innovation was the placement of the passenger cabin. After some debate as to whether it should not be amidships, it was decided to locate it forward, with the control car built integrally into its fore part. The overall length of this external structure was about 80 feet. The long gondola was divided into five compartments, each seating four people. (Up to six additional passengers could be carried in wicker chairs in the aisle if the lift sufficed). Forward was a private compartment for a single V.I.P. passenger, who paid double fare, and aft were washrooms and a buffet. Though the meals served by the steward were not advertised as prominently as in pre-war days, he was undoubtedly well patronized on the 370 mile run between Friedrichshafen and Berlin-Staaken, which "Bodensee" was scheduled to make in 7 hours. The ship of course carried up-to-date radio equipment. The crew numbered 16.

The first scheduled flight north was on August 24, 1919. Thereafter flights took place daily, Sundays included, northbound on odd days of the month, laying overnight in one of the big building hangars at Staaken, and proceeding south the next morning. Sometimes afternoon excursions were made over Berlin after the north-bound flight to Staaken, and until October 4, 1919, there was usually an intermediate landing at Munich. The published schedule called for a 9 am departure from Friedrichshafen or Staaken, and a 4 pm arrival, but this was usually bettered, the fastest run being slightly under four hours, which compared very favorably with the pre-war running time by rail of 16 hours. As the DELAG's travel brochure put it in a lyrical burst of eloquence:

> The housing of the sleek airship in the airship shed at Staaken proceeds quickly, and it is still bright summer daylight. The magic journey which began at 10 am on Lake Constance is already completed before the fifth hour in the afternoon. No dust, such as weights down the body after a long train ride, no frayed nerves, but the spirit is surfeited with new, never-suspected impressions. Proud and happy one returns to earth, proud to have seen that which for thousands of years has only been longed for and longingly written of in fiction. A grateful departing glance rests on the gray, plump body of the airship, then one goes by swift auto into the tumult of the metropolis, there to submerge oneself, happy and unrecognized like the Prince of Fairyland, whom the earth-born never suspected of having been borne through the air by magic powers from a distance land.[10]

[10] DELAG-HAPAG brochure for "Bodensee" passengers (no title), p. 5.

The DELAG closed down flight operations on December 5, 1919. A second ship, LZ 121 "Nordstern," had been completed – built from the same plans as "Bodensee," she had an extra 10 meter gas cell amidships, and accomodation for 30 passengers. "Bodensee" was cut in two and similarly modified. Gas volume of both ships was now 795,000 cubic feet and the useful lift 25,350 lb. At this point the Interallied Commission of Control forced a suspension of operations, and both ships were ordered surrendered in partial compensation for the naval Zeppelins destroyed by their crews in the North Sea bases. "Nordstern" was delivered to France on June 13, 1921, and "Bodensee' to Italy on July 3.

There followed a time of acute crisis for the Zeppelin Company. The Versailles Treaty forbade the construction of any kind of military aircraft in Germany; and the London Protocol of May 5, 1921, limited the volume of commercial airships to 1,000,000 cubic feet – too small to fly the Atlantic. Struggling to keep its head above water, the Zeppelin Company turned to the manufacture of aluminium cooking utensils bearing the trademark "Ellzett".

Meanwhile, with the chairman of the company, Baron von Gemmingen, suffering from a fatal illness (he died in 1924), a bitter struggle for power was going on behind the scenes. Colsman, who had continued as business director throughout the war, was in the strongest position, but by 1922 had been discredited and supplanted by Dr. Eckener, the operational manager of the company, who in time succeeded Gemmingen as chairman. Firstly, the blame for the cancellation of the Hensley contract, for which he had been responsible, was laid at Colsman's door. Secondly, a journey which he made to the United States in 1920 to seek American financial assistance not only failed to obtain the support and interest of either Henry Ford or President Litchfield of the Goodyear Tire and Rubber Company,[11] but also with his stiff-necked Prussian manner and narrow provincial outlook, Colsman managed to offend the more informal American industrialists. By contract Eckener, a true cosmopolitan and one of the great men of his day, realized the urgent importance of American support if the Zeppelin was to survive, and needed only to be himself to be congenial to the Americans. His chief protagonist, Ernst Lehmann, not only spoke English, but after a trip to America with Harry Vissering on April, 1921, returned with a broader outlook and a respect for American

---

[11] Colsman blamed his failure on a fall in the price of rubber (Colsman, p. 232). In fact, his terms were exorbitant. The Goodyear firm was also being reorganized at the time.

methods. He is said to have initiated the struggle which deposed
Colsman from power. Eckener of course secured his claim to the
leadership of the company when he won the contract for the
LZ 126, and further, dared to pledge the assets of the company to
ensure its delivery when Colsman hesitated to do so.

A mystery of this period of the early twenties is the missing
numbers LZ 122 through LZ 125, for which no ships were ever built.
It is not even clear what designs might have been created for these
numbers. The only clue is in Vissering's book,[12] where a series of
drawings show: a 6-engined enlarged "Bodensee" of 1,765,000 cubic
feet "for medium distances and training purposes"; a 10-engined
"fast passenger Zeppelin for medium distances. Accomodation for 80
passengers" with a gas volume of 2,118,600 cubic feet; and an
18-engined "fast passenger Zeppelin" of 4,766,850 cubic feet. There
also appears in two versions a 12-engined "fast commercial Zeppelin"
of 3,531,000 cubic feet, one with a passenger cabin forward, the
other with a small control car resembling that in the Schütte-Lanz
airships. The last is almost certainly the LZ 125 which was offered
to Colonel Hensley, and otherwise advertised as "the America ship."

By securing a U.S. Navy contract for the construction of the
LZ 126, Hugo Eckener had literally saved the *Luftschiffbau
Zeppelin;* for otherwise its construction hangars would have been
demolished pursuant to the orders of the Interallied Commission of
Control; and without the building plant, the company could not
possibly have been resurrected in the impoverished Germany of the
1920s. Furthermore, LZ 126 herself had generated much favorable
interest in the rigid airship, not only in Germany where the trial
flights had been astutely arranged to cover much of the country, not
only in America where the big ship's safe arrival had rebounded to
the credit of her German operators and builders and had aroused
intense enthusiasm; but also throughout the world, which saw the
transatlantic flight as a symbol of Germany's resurgence as a major
power. It also brought Eckener to world prominence, and for the
next fifteen years his activities were front page news.

At the end of a triumphal tour, Eckener returned to Germany in
November, 1924. Lehmann stayed on longer to conduct negotiations
with the Goodyear Corporation. Friedrichshafen, after the emotional
excitement of the departure of the LZ 126, was like a deserted
ballroom on the morning after. Once again Eckener knew the

[12] Harry Vissering, *Zeppelin: The Story of a Great Achievement* (Chicago: privately printed, 1922), Plates 52, 53, 54, 55.

compnay would have to go forward or perish: the next step had to be a demonstration airship for international voyaging with passengers. But how to raise the funds to build one? The Weimar Republic, beset by mounting economic crisis, offered no encouragement for an aircraft palpably useless for military purposes. Further, the government's aeronautical advisors were to a man old *Frontflieger* in love with the aeroplane, dedicated to rebuilding in secret the German *Luftstreitkräfte* and hostile towards the "gas bag." Nor did they doubt that the aeroplane soon might cross the oceans commercially.

Remembering Echterdingen, Eckener thought the German people might help financially as they had when Count Zeppelin's fourth airship had crashed during the "great flight." The situation however was not now so dramatic, and "a whole people will not enthuse twice over one and the same cause."[13] But there was no other possibility, so the new Chairman of the Board of the Zeppelin Company organized the "Zeppelin-Eckener Fund" and went to work. Only through an exhausting series of lectures concerning the Zeppelins in general and the flight to America in particular, was it possible to raise the necessary cash, and in this strenuous effort Eckener was loyally supported by Flemming, von Schiller, Wittemann and Pruss, who had participated in the flight. In the midst of their labors came a bright ray of hope – on October 16, 1925, Germany signed with representatives of the former enemy powers the Treaty of Locarno which instituted a brief period of peaceful cooperation with Germany as an equal partner in the concert of Europe. One of Locarno's provisions rescinded the limitation on airship size. Now the transatlantic Zeppelin was possible.

After two years of effort, the "Zeppelin-Eckener Fund" contained only two and a half million of the four million marks needed for the transatlantic airship, but this sufficed to begin construction. Subsequently the German government was persuaded (Eckener does not say how) to give over a million marks to complete the work.

An immediate upper limit to the size of the new craft was set by the dimensions of the big construction shed in Friedrichshafen, which measured 787 feet long, 138 feet wide, and 115 feet high, "clear inner dimensions." The hull of the new craft, numbered LZ 127, measured 775 feet long and 100 feet in diameter, while the overall height of 110 feet from gondola bumpers to backbone girder brought her to within two feet of the underside of the hangar arches when

[13] Hugo Eckener, *Im Zeppelin über Länder und Meere*, p. 98.

being walked in or out. She was in effect a "stretched" version of the LZ 126 with parallel section amidships, with a gas volume of 3,955,000 cubic feet, hence less graceful than the earlier ship. The slender, inefficient lines of the relatively poorly streamlined hull were criticised abroad by "experts" who failed to realize that Dürr was not free to design the "ideal" airship. The hull was built on 28 longitudinal girders, with main rings spaced 15 metres apart. Each main ring was made up of twelve diamond-shaped trusses connected end to end in a circle (performing the same function as the kingpost bracing in the wartime ships), while at the bottom of the hull the keel, an inverted triangle, was heavily braced to the sides with compression girders. Between each main ring were two light unbraced intermediate rings 5 metres apart. The hull was divided by the main rings into 17 spaces, each containing a gas cell confected of gold beaters' skin glued onto light cotton fabric. As in LZ 126, the tail cone was large enough to accomodate a gas cell.

When fully inflated, however, LZ 127 contained only 3,037,000 cubic feet of hydrogen. The lower part of the space inside the hull through much of its length was filled by twelve "fuel gas cells" containing 918,000 cubic feet of "Blau gas," which resembled propane. This could power the airship's engines for over a hundred hours, whereas the 32 tons of petrol which might have been carried if the craft had been completely filled with hydrogen would have given her an endurance of only 67 hours. The real advantage of the "Blau gas" was that, weighing the same as air, its consumption did not lighten the ship, and hydrogen did not have to be wastefully valved off during the flight to bring the airship into static equilibrium, as would have been the case if petrol had been used.

Because the automatic valves of the hydrogen cells lay above the tops of the fuel gas cells, for the first time a central gangway ran through the ship (somewhat below the center line) so that the riggers could have access to the hydrogen cells and these valves.

The simple, thick fins were of full cantilever designs with no external bracing; internally they were supported by two sets of cruciform girders running right through the ship from one fin into the other. One cruciform was at the rudder post; the second 20 metres forward. Simple unbalanced rudders, and elevators balanced by external compensating surfaces ahead of the hinge line, were attached to the rear of the fins. A cramped auxiliary steering station was concealed in the thickness of the lower fin.

Forward was a mooring cone for attachment to mooring masts;

yet early in her career LZ 127, like the wartime ships, was landed on the field and walked into the shed. This was always true at the small landing ground at Friedrichshafen, and also at Lakehurst prior to 1930. Only later in her career, after the establishment of the service to South America in 1931, did LZ 127 regularly moor to a mast in Pernambuco.

A large gondola 98½ feet long and 20 feet wide under the hull well forward provided quarters more palatial than in any airship built up to this time, and arranged for long distance passenger carrying. In the nose of the gondola was the control room, with the rudder wheel right forward, elevator wheel to port with gas and ballast controls overhead, and engine telegraphs to starboard. Instruments included both a magnetic and a gyro compass for the rudder man, and altimeter, variometer, inclinometer, and air and gas thermometers for the elevator man. In addition, his station had indicators showing when the gas cells were 100 per cent full.

Immediately aft of the control room was a chart room running the width of the gondola, with a large chart table and drawers to hold aerial maps of every part of the world. Next to the rear was a radio room on the port side, and the galley to starboard. Both obtained their power from small wind-driven generators which could be extended on brackets from the gondola side. There was a 140 watt main transmitter and 70 watt emergency transmitter and receiver, together with a radio direction finder. The galley had a stove and two electric burners, a hot water heater, refrigerator, etc. The door for entering the gondola was immediately abaft the galley on the starboard side.

Next came a lounge running the width of the gondola and measuring 16½ by 16½ feet, lighted by four outward-slanting windows with four dining tables and 16 chairs. Curtains and carpets were a dark wine-red. To the rear, five pairs of sleeping cabins opened off a corridor, providing accomodation for 20 passengers.

Each cabin had its own window and was furnished with a sofa, a clothes closet, a small table, and a folding canvas stool. At night, the back of the sofa could be hinged upward and attached to the overhead to form an upper berth. Right aft in the gondola were wash rooms and toilet rooms. It should be noted that waste water, instead of being vented overboard, was retained and stored for use as ballast.

Five engines were carried in an equal number of streamlined gondolas, arranged in two pairs on the sides of the hull at Rings 95 and 125, and a single gondola under the hull aft at Ring 50. The

Lounge and dining salon aboard the "Graf Zeppelin". (Luftschiffbau Zeppelin)

engines were Maybach VL-IIs, uprated versions of the twelve cylinder VL-Is which had powered the LZ 126. With the compression ratio increased to 7 to 1, and revolutions to 1600 rpm, they produced 550 hp each, or 450 cruising hp at 1400 rpm. Dry weight increased slightly to 2315 lb. Each engine drove directly (without gearing) a 2-bladed wooden propeller.

The weight empty of LZ 127 was 122,000 lb, which included 66,000 lb of duralumin metal. The gross lift with full gas cells was 188,000 lb. The useful lift was 66,000 lb under standard conditions, of which 33,000 lb could be devoted to the 20 guests, their baggage and supplies, and mail and express. With full fuel cells, an endurance of 100 hours was possible at a cruising speed of 73 mph. With less pay load, and 17,600 lb of petrol carried in addition, a further 20 hours' endurance could be obtained. Speed at full power was 80 mph.

On July 8, 1928, which would have been Count von Zeppelin's 90th birthday, his only child, the Countess Hella von Brandenstein-Zeppelin, christened the LZ 127 "Graf Zeppelin". Thus began the eight-year career of the most famous of all airships.

Though the "Graf," as she came to be called familiarly, appeared to be complete at the christening ceremony, there was a lot of final detail work to do. Thus the ship did not leave her hangar for the first time until September 18, 1928. There were four short trial flights, the first three with petrol only; on the fourth, "Blau gas" was carried and used, the engines accepting it with no trouble. The fifth trial flight, on October 2-3, lasted 34½ hours, and took the ship north via Frankfurt and Düsseldorf to the Dutch border. Crossing Holland to the North Sea, the "Graf" that evening was seen over Lowestoft and Great Yarmouth, the first Zeppelin to appear over England since Peter Strasser in L 70 was shot down in flames in nearly the same spot ten years earlier. Then back across the North Sea to Kiel, Hamburg, and eventually to Berlin before returning to Friedrichshafen. Here Eckener found that the flight had been a sensation of the wrong kind — with the French accusing him of flying over the occupied Rhineland, and the Berlin government charging that he had crossed Holland to pay respects to the ex-Kaiser at Doorn! It was not the last time that the "Graf Zeppelin" would be involved in politics.

There was one more trial flight, and then, on October 11, 1928, at 7.54 am, the "Graf" was off on her first transoceanic voyage. Destination, the United States, specifically Lakehurst, where the American public eagerly awaited her arrival, and where American businessmen might be favorably impressed by the intercontinental passenger carrier. True, the Atlantic had been crossed before, by the R 34 both ways in 1919, by the LZ 126 in 1924, by the U.S. Navy's NC-4 and by Alcock and Brown in 1919, and by Lindbergh, Chamberlain and Byrd the year before. But here, for the first time, paying passengers were setting off for the New World by air (though only ten of the twenty were paying their way; four were representatives of the German Air Ministry, and six were journalists, including one woman, Lady Drummond Hay).

With storms over the central Atlantic, and lacking experience over the northern route via Scotland, Iceland and Labrador, Eckener chose to travel via the southern route. Initially following the Rhine to Basel, the big ship proceeded south across France to the Mediterranean. Passing down the French and Spanish coast, she was off Barcelona by evening, and traversed the Straits of Gibraltar just under 24 hours from her takeoff in Friedrichshafen. So far the weather had been fine, and over the Atlantic the "Graf Zeppelin" even picked up a tail wind. Eckener's sophisticated dead reckoning methods enabled him to hit Madeira squarely at 2 pm of October 12, and the Zeppelin went on westward. That evening, some 250 miles south of Terceira in the Azores, the airship took in a weather report from the islands warning of a squall front approaching from the north-west. For much of the night the watch in the "Graf Zeppelin's" control car observed almost continuous vivid lightning along the northern horizon, and it was no surprise when Dr. Eckener found athwart his course early next morning "a blue-black wall of cloud of very threatening aspect advancing towards us at great speed from the north-west." For some reason power was not reduced, and as the Zeppelin plunged into the squall line she surged upward in the violent up-drafts at an angle of 15 degrees. Passengers breakfasting in the lounge found their place-settings in their laps, and pots and pans fell to the deck in the galley; but Eckener congratulated himself that the ship had not broken up in the turbulence as had the "Shenandoah." His self-satisfaction was premature, however, for presently the master mechanic, August Grötzinger, climbed down the control car ladder to report that the bottom cover had been torn off the port horizontal stablizer by the violent aerodynamic forces as the ship entered the front.

This was a real emergency, for the flying tatters of cotton fabric could jam the elevators. While the engines were slowed, volunteers climbed out on the bare girders of the fin to cut away or lash in place the remains of the cover. Eckener took the weighty decision to send a radio message to the U.S. Navy Department to ask for assistance, and assembled the passengers in the lounge to report on the crisis. But as repairs were completed, and the engines could be opened up again, Eckener sent out a second message announcing that assistance was not necessary. The remainder of the flight was not uneventful, however: after crossing Bermuda on the evening of October 14, the ship faced another squall front. The chief engineer expressed doubt that the damaged fin could withstand the stress of a frontal passage. Eckener nonetheless decided to go through with the engines at half power. The ship pitched and bucked, while rain and hail beat on the outer cover, but after a few hours she was through the worst and continued towards Chesapeake Bay. A small tear was later found in the upper cover of the port fin.

The "Graf's" near escape from disaster over the Atlantic – or so it appeared in the black headlines all over America – had produced the most intense interest in the public, which Eckener now turned to advantage to show the Zeppelin to millions thronged below as he flew north over Washington and Baltimore to New York. After a turn around Manhattan he proceeded south to Lakehurst, where he received a tumultuous welcome from the thousands who had driven from every direction to witness the "Graf's" arrival. There was a ticker-tape parade up Broadway, a reception by President Coolidge in the White House, and a flood of invitations, particularly for the "Graf" to show herself over the Middle West.

These had to be declined, for it took twelve days to repair the damaged fin and the season, in Eckener's opinion, was then too far advanced. On the night of October 28, 1928, the "Graf Zeppelin" departed Lakehurst for Friedrichshafen via the northern route, Eckener having had enough of the frontal systems to the south. Lack of weather reports far out in the ocean caused the ship instead to be stressed once again by another frontal squall system off Newfoundland, but this time the engines were throttled down and there was no damage. Off the European coast the ship encountered another low pressure trough, which she followed to the south looking for improvement. Finally the Zeppelin turned east, flew through a few squalls and reached the French coast at the mouth of the Loire. Ten hours later she arrived over Friedrichshafen, to land some two hours after dawn.

The double crossing demonstrated that the ship had to be faster — the elapsed time westbound had been 111 hours 44 minutes, and eastbound 71 hours 51 minutes. It also demonstrated that Eckener already knew — that the "Graf" was really too small for regular transatlantic service. Lastly, it proved that October, with the precursors of winter storms over the North Atlantic, was really too late in the season for the ocean crossing. The "Graf" in her eight year career crossed the North Atlantic only seven times, and only once, on a later occasion, did she fly it so late in the year.

During the winter overhaul, the cotton covering on the fins was replaced with linen.

The transatlantic crossing by the "Graf Zeppelin" aroused enormous popular enthusiasm, and congratulations poured in from all sides; but there were no practical results, no capitalists offering to finance a Zeppelin air line, and no stirrings of government interest. At the time, as Eckener wrote, he had not realized how interested the great newspapers might be in providing operating funds for the airship, while the income to be realized from flying special covers for stamp collectors he had not dreamed of. So there remained only the possibility of interesting the government; and early in 1929 Eckener had the inspiration of embarking two shiploads of influential guests for two excursions to the sunny Mediterranean while winter still held central Europe in its frozen grip.

The first flight departed Friedrischshafen on March 23, and the guest list included the Minister of Commerce, the President of the *Reichstag,* the Minister of Posts, the President of Württemberg, several members of budget committees, and the editors of various influential newspapers. While they pulled on overcoats to warm themselves over Germany in the unheated passenger spaces, the scene changed when the airship arrived next morning over the sunny Mediterranean near Marseilles. Eckener now enjoyed himself, and enthralled his guests, as he moved at low altitude along the French Riviera, via Corsica, to Ostia by sea and then inland to circle over Rome. Southward the Zeppelin then went to Naples, thence eastward to Crete, which the passengers saw in the early morning. The day went on with the "Graf" reaching shore at Haifa in Palestine; there was a leisurely cruise over Jerusalem and the holy places, and in the evening, by bright moonlight, Eckener amused himself by descending to 1000 feet *below* sea level over the Dead Sea.

Unfortunately, Eckener had been refused permission by the British Government to fly over Egypt – because, he believed, the English themselves wished to impress the Egyptian *fellaheen* by being the first in the skies with their airships R 100 and R 101. So he contented himself with flying along the coast outside the three mile limit and sending a telegram to King Fuad regretting that "contrary winds prevent us from flying over the land of the wonders of a thousand years." This led to some questions in Parliament. Northbound once more, the "Graf" proceeded over the islands of the Aegean to Greece, looked in on the Athenians twice in one morning, and then journeyed home across the spurs of the Dinaric Alps. Once more it was winter, and snow plastered the control car windows as the President of the *Reichstag* broadcast midnight greetings to Vienna from the airship. The flight lasted 81 hours and 28 minutes. A second cruise of 56 hours and 53 minutes took place around the Iberian Peninsula on April 23-25, 1929.

Two years later, in April, 1931, the "Graf Zeppelin" *did* fly to Egypt, as a result of a special invitation from the British Air Minister. This followed on the fiery crash of the British airship, R 101, on the first leg of a planned flight to Egypt and India, in which almost all on board perished including the incumbent Air Minister, Lord Thomson of Cardington. Eckener, attending the funeral in London on October 12, 1930, knew the political climate had changed when the English Prime Minister, Ramsay MacDonald, came over to him as he stood outside Westminster Abbey and thnked him for attending. The flight, with paying passengers aboard, saw the Zeppelin soaring over the Pyramids (Eckener, a man of ready humour, could not resist parodying Napoleon by calling to the control car crew, "stand fast, boys! Forty-one centuries are looking up at you!"), landed briefly to take on distinguished Egyptian passengers, and carried them for a day's cruise over Palestine. The flight aroused great enthusiasm among the Mohammedan peoples of the Near East, and encouraged Zeppelin Company personnel in their secret hopes of establishing a commercial service to the Dutch East Indies.

A second transatlantic flight attempt a month later turned into a near-disaster. Departing Friedrichshafen in the early morning of May 16, 1929, the "Graf" made fast time down the valley of the Rhône with the help of a stiff northerly wind, the mistral. Above the Mediterranean she passed along the French and Spanish coast towards Gibraltar. One engine failed at noon with a broken crankshaft, but this caused little concern and the flight continued. Then in the evening, off Barcelona, a second engine failed. This was serious, and the ship was put on a reciprocal course to return to Friedrichshafen. The chief engineer of the *Zahnradfabrik,* the Zeppelin Company's gear-making subsidiary, was on board, and presently he came to tell Eckener that both failures had resulted from severe crankshaft vibration caused by modifications to the propeller couplings made by the ship's chief engineer without consulting the engine builders. With only three engines in operation, the air speed had dropped from 80 mph to 55, and progress across the Gulf of Lions and up the Rhône against the mistral was painfully slow. Then at 2.15 in the afternoon two more engines failed one after the other.[14] Hopeless now to think of reaching Friedrichshafen with one engine against the gale; and calmly, but with a heavy heart, Eckener began to look for a place to land. The ship would have to be sacrificed, but the passengers and crew could be saved.

Hating the *sale Boche* as they did with undisguised passion, Frenchmen watching anxiously the drama in the sky found it too much for them. The French Air Ministry at this point generously

---

[14] Sources differ as to why the fifth and last engine kept running for the entire 38½ hour flight: (a) its propeller coupling had not been modified, (b) with modified coupling the fifth engine likewise was damaged, but kept running because it was new while the others had about 350 hours on them.

relented, and radioed an offer of the French hangar at Cuers near Toulon. Gratefully Eckener accepted, and running with the wind the "Graf" made rapid time to Cuers. At last the ship was safe, berthed in the hangar which had once housed the ex-German Zeppelin L 72, renamed "Dixmude," and on the wall of which hung a main ring of the French "Méditerranée," the former German "Nordstern." New motors arrived from Friedrichshafen by rail, and on May 24 the "Graf Zeppelin" returned to the *Bodensee.*

The motor trouble was extensively investigated, while the "Graf" lay in her hangar without engines for two months. Meanwhile Eckener had been planning a bold undertaking – nothing less than a flight around the world, a feat accomplished only once before by the United States Army Air Service in 1924. The most difficult problem as usual was not aeronautical but financial: how to pay for the journey. William Randolph Hearst, the American newspaper millionaire and an unfailing friend of the Zeppelin, offered 150,000 dollars in exchange for exclusive press rights on the flight. When Eckener insisted that German newspapers would have to be represented, Hearst reduced his offer to 100,000 dollars. Three German publishing firms put up 12,500 dollars, and half the expenses were taken care of. The remainder came from stamp collectors, who took a great interest in the flight; while there were several paying passengers in addition to the official guests.

There was really little choice concerning the route; for the only suitable hangar in the Orient was the former Jüterbog double shed now re-erected at the Japanese Navy's air base at Kasumigaura near Tokyo. Lakehurst likewise was the only suitable shed in the Western Hemisphere.[15] Some thought was given to a flight east from Friedrichshafen via the Mediterranean, the Indian Ocean and the China Sea; but this route, of more than 8700 miles, approximated the still air range of the "Graf Zeppelin" at economical speed and was considered too long. A northern course north of the high mountains of central Asia via Lake Baikal and down the Amur Valley to Manchuria and Japan was only 6200 miles, but the danger of typhoons coming inland over Manchuria led to another route which was the one finally chosen. This crossed central Russia and Siberia to Yakutsk, and thence across the poorly charted Stanovoi Mountains to the Sea of Okhotsk. This path from Friedrichshafen to Tokyo led

[15] The U.S. Army's airship base at Scott Field, near Belleville, Illinois, had a shed measuring 800 ft. long, 123 ft. wide and 150 ft. high which could have accomodated the "Graf Zeppelin," but Lakehurst was much more suitable for Eckener's purposes.

far north, but approximated the Great Circle course. Thence the way led via the North Pacific to Los Angeles, adjacent to the Hearst palace at San Simeon; then across the United States to Lakehurst, and so home.

In actuality there were *two* world flights, for Hearst, as a condition of his support, required that the journey should begin and end with a circle around the Statue of Liberty in New York Harbour. So the American world flight was from Lakehurst to Lakehurst, while the German one was from Friedrichshafen to Friedrichshafen.

On August 1, with 40 crew members and 18 passengers on board, the "Graf Zeppelin" departed Friedrichshafen for Lakehurst, arriving on the 5th after an uneventful flight of 95 hours 22 minutes. While some of the passengers disembarked, Lady Drummond Hay, representing the Hearst Press, the explorer Hubert Wilkins, Commander Charles E. Rosendahl, commander of the U.S. Navy's "Los Angeles," and Lieutenant Richardson embarked for the return flight to Friedrichshafen. Flying around the south side of a large low

"Graf Zeppelin" during one of her four landings at Lakehurst, with a U.S. Navy ground crew. Note windmill generator extended below rear of the passenger gondola. (Fred Tupper-Hepburn Walker collection)

pressure area to obtain a strong tail wind, the Zeppelin made the
eastward crossing in the fast time of 55 hours between August 7 and
10. There was a 5-day layover in Friedrichshafen to check the ship
and engines. Here the German contingent boarded, mostly reporters
from the large newspapers; Dr. Megias of Madrid (the personal
physician to King Alfonso, he treated Dr. Eckener on the Pacific
crossing for gastroenteritis and an abcess), and Comrade Karklin
representing the Russian government; Commander Fuiyoshi of the
Japanese Navy, and two Japanese reporters. Altogether there were 20
passengers on board on the departure from Friedrichshafen on
August 15.

The eastward route was at first a familiar one, via Ulm,
Nuremberg, Leipzig and Berlin, where thousands waved as the
Zeppelin flew down the "Unter den Linden" at low altitude. Then it
was on to East Prussia with the ship crossing Danzig, Königsberg, and
at 6 pm the Russian border at Tilsit. Comrade Karklin now appeared
in the control car to insist that the Zeppelin must show itself over
Moscow, where thousands were waiting to greet it; Eckener refused
because a low pressure area over the Caspian Sea was causing east
winds over the capital, while he wanted to take advantage of a west
wind farther north. This was the first crisis of the flight, and a
political one at that; the complaints from Russia were so loud that in
September, 1930, the "Graf Zeppelin" made a special flight over
Moscow to assuage the hurt feelings of its citizens.

Helped on by the west wind, the airship was making nearly
70 mph over the ground with only four engines running. Gradually
the forests became more extensive, the habitations scarcer. Night in
these high latitudes was only two or three hours long. Shortly after
midnight the ship approached the Urals north of Perm, but had to
ascend only to 3300 feet to clear them. Much of the area below was
covered with smoke from forest fires. The land underneath, the
swampy *taiga,* was so empty, desolate and devoid of landmarks that
the Zeppelin's navigation now changed from local pilotage to dead
reckoning, as in ocean journeys. Finding the junction of the huge
rivers Irtish and Ob, the airship now headed across Siberia as from a
seacoast landmark for an ocean crossing. Ahead lay the monstrous
water course of the Yenesei, which came up ahead at dawn; a flight
to the north discovered the tiny hut-colony of Imbatsk, and this
served as a point of departure for a further compass course towards
the Tunguska River. Many remarked on the contrast between the
dismal swampland below and the comfort – even luxury – enjoyed

by the passengers looking down from the Zeppelin. Indeed, with the clock advanced an hour every seven hours as the airship rapidly transversed the meridians of longitude at 64 degrees north, the passengers complained of being fed too often, and threatened to go on strike!

Over the Tunguska the ship passed through an inky black and menacing-appearing squall line which however produced little turbulence. After the brief night, the Zeppelin came to Yakutsk on the River Lena, and dropped a wreath to commemorate the German prisoners of war of 1914-18 who were buried there. Ahead lay the most critical portion of the flight across Asia – the Stanovoi mountains. The ridges of these rose to 6500 feet, and the pass leading to Ayan on the Sea of Okhotsk was supposed to be 5000 feet high. Instead, the airship had to rise to 6000 feet and still was only 150 feet from the ground. Then the mountainside fell away abruptly, and ahead was the Sea of Okhotsk! There was a temptation to continue right on to Los Angeles – the fuel would have lasted with a predicted following wind – but political considerations triumphed, and Eckener followed the Japanese islands south to Tokyo and Kasumigaura. The journey from Friedrichshafen had taken 101 hours and 49 minutes at an average speed of 69 mph.

On August 23 the "Graf" was off for Los Angeles, having disembarked the importunate Russian and the first lot of Japanese, and replaced them with Lieutenant Commander Ryunosuke Kusaka, destined to be an aviation admiral in World War II; Major Shibata, and a reporter. Taking advantage of a south-west wind around the south side of a typhoon which had passed over Tokyo the day before, the Zeppelin made 98 mph over the surface. During the rest of the North Pacific crossing there were following winds, but the journey was very monotonous for the passengers as most of the time the Zeppelin was flying through thick fog or deep, solid cloud. At 0400 on August 25 San Francisco was in sight ahead, and the "Graf" continued down the coast towards Los Angeles.

The stop at the "City of the Angels" unpleasantly emphasized some of the disadvantages of the airship, whose lift may vary greatly depending both on the temperature of the hydrogen and on that of the surrounding air. Approaching to land at Mines Field at 0500 on August 26, the Zeppelin found at 1600 feet an inversion (an essential ingredient of the latter-day Los Angeles smog) with a temperature above the interface of 77 degrees, while below it was 66 degrees. The ship, 4000 lb "lighter" as it entered the top of the colder and denser layer, refused to descend, and some 35,000 cubic feet of hydrogen had to be valved before the "Graf" could go on down to the temporary Navy mast. The Pacific Ocean had been crossed in 79 hours 3 minutes.

For the take-off after midnight on August 26-27, the inversion would present the same difficulty, only in reverse, for the Zeppelin, rising to the top of the low layer of cool air, would refuse to ascend further into the warmer and less dense air above unless a lot of ballast was released. Yet it was found during the evening that the ship was too heavy and would not lift from the ground. The meagre amount of hydrogen available had all been piped into the ship during the afternoon, but even so did not suffice to replace the gas valved during the landing manoeuvre, while some may have been lost through the automatic valves through the hot sun warming and expanding the gas. The only thing to do was to lighten the ship; fuel and ballast were off-loaded, not to mention six crew members who were sent to Lakehurst by rail. Even then the "Graf" floated up only a few feet. Hoping to ascend dynamically, Eckener put the engine telegraphs to "full speed" and the Zeppelin began to move on four engines. Ahead loomed red warning lights atop the towers of a high tension line! The nose must go higher – and as the elevators depressed the tail, the lower fin and rudder furrowed the ground. The control car cleared the wires – and with cool precision, Eckener ordered the elevators put down in time to lift the stern over the wires likewise. Never had the "Graf Zeppelin" been so close to destruction; but in fact only a few girders had been bent in the lower fin.

In order to be able to maintain a low altitude, the Zeppelin flew south to San Diego, then east across Arizona and New Mexico to El Paso, avoiding the high Sierras and the Rockies. The route then led north-east across the central plains to Chicago, where the airship received a tumultuous welcome from thousands thronged along Lake Michigan. Then on to New York, the end of the "American" world flight, a bigger than ever ticker tape parade up Broadway, and a visit to President Hoover in the White House. But German pride and national feeling overflowed with the Zeppelin's return to Friedrichshafen on September 4. All kinds of records had been set: the "American" world flight had been made in 12 days 11 minutes flying time; the "German" flight in 12 days 12 hours, 20 minutes. The total distance covered on the "German" flight was 21,200 miles. Most important of all, 16 to 22 passengers had been carried on each leg, in such safety, comfort and luxury that the pioneering journey for them was a pleasure cruise as well as an adventure.

For the remainder of the year 1929, the "Graf Zeppelin" made flights in Europe, always with paying guests. Several were made over Switzerland, and were very popular with the Swiss themselves in spite of a price of 200 marks per person. The local flights over Germany were known to the crew as "circus flights," yet they were taken seriously by Dr. Eckener, who never tired of reminding his subordinates that the German people had put up the money for the "Graf Zeppelin" and therefore had the right to see her frequently.

Early 1930 brought the Zeppelin to Seville for the first time, and to the British airship base at Cardington, where R 100 was riding to the mast. Between May 18 and June 6 the "Graf Zeppelin" made her first flight to South America – a route which already appealed to Eckener as having commercial possibilities. This was of course in the nature of a trial run, but the Zeppelin at the same time was carrying as many as 38 passengers – many sleeping in the crew's quarters. Further, this was not to be a single crossing of the South Atlantic and return, but a "triangle flight" with a run north to Lakehurst before returning to Friedrichshafen. The price for the entire journey was 6500 dollars!

The first stage of the journey was from Friedrichshafen to Seville, where a number of Spaniards embarked, including the cousin of King Alfonso, the Infante Don Alfonso de Orleans. Next was a long leg from Seville to Recife de Pernambuco, on the north-east corner of Brazil, the flight proceeding via the Canary Islands, the Cape Verdes, St. Paul's Rock and Fernando de Noronha, all of which served as navigational check points. The flight time was 61 hours 52 minutes. In the "zone of calms" along the Equator the Zeppelin was heavily deluged with rain while passing through tropical squall lines; but was able to carry the 8 tons of rain which accumulated on the envelope with no difficulty. Nor, despite the formidable appearance of the towering cumuli of the weather fronts, was there much wind or turbulence. Eckener's experience contrasted favorably with Bockholt's over the Sudan 13 years before in two respects: the dynamic lift of the "Graf Zeppelin", amounting to 13 tons, was much greater than that of the lower-powered L 59, which was less than 3 tons. Further, the "Graf," flying over the ocean, did not lose so much gas from the sun's heat as did the L 59 transversing the hot sands of the Sahara.

For two days the "Graf" lay at the short mooring mast at Recife, then went on the further 1500 miles to the Brazilian capital, Rio de Janeiro. There were no facilities whatever at the Campo Affonso military air field; so the ship lay on the landing ground for less than an hour of speeches. She then returned to Recife, and after two more days departed on May 28 for Lakehurst.

The Spanish passengers had been looking forward longingly to a flight over Cuba – Spain's former colony – and a possible landing in the capital, Havana; but warnings of uncertain weather over Cuba, with strong north-east winds between there and Florida, obliged Eckener to keep further to the east, over Puerto Rico. The Spaniards were disappointed, but understood – Don Alfonso better than any – Dr. Eckener's responsibility for the safety of the ship. This did not prevent a German journalist on board from launching a bitter attack in the New York newspapers under the headline "Why Did The 'Graf Zeppelin' not go to Havana?" with lurid details of a "mutiny" among the passengers put down by the officers "with drawn revolvers."

As the Zeppelin proceeded northwards, a long north-south squall line was visible to port as a towering blue-black wall of cloud. East of Cape Hatteras Eckener turned and plunged into the front. There was a violent upthrusting of the entire airship, followed by a plunge like that of an elevator; then minutes later the ship was through, but the wind, which had been south at 38 mph, was now north at 45 mph. Eckener later described it as "the wickedest squall I have ever experienced, and I don't believe there could be a worse one."[16]

At Lakehurst the Zeppelin was led into the huge double shed by the travelling mooring mast, and remained for three days. The flight home across the North Atlantic via the Azores was uneventful; there was a brief landing at Seville to off-load the Spanish passengers. Going up the valley of the Saône, however, a small thunderstorm provided "a terribly dangerous situation, which I look back on with horror even after many years, and which came within a hair's breadth of being fatal for the ship and for all on board her."[17] Flying blind in cloud, the "Graf" began to pitch and bump, while lightning flashed close aboard. Suddenly an unprecedented cloud burst, far more intense than those of the tropics, poured down on the ship. Next, the large rain drops changed to hailstones the size of walnuts, and these, beating on the taut cover, began slowly but inexorably to force the airship to the ground although she was developing maximum dynamic lift with an up angle of 12 degrees. Feeling that a crash was inevitable, Flemming wanted to stop the engines. "No!" cried Eckener, "we need them more now than ever! Set them on

[16] Eckener, p. 329.
[17] *ibid.*, p. 335.

flank speed!" and just then the ship, though she was 22,000 lb heavy, began to climb slowly thanks to the added power from the engines.

Most of the ascents during the remainder of 1930 were "circus" flights over Germany. Between July 9 and 11 the Zeppelin proceeded up the Norwegian coast to Bear Island and Spitzbergen, and between July 16 and 18 to Iceland. In July, 1931, there was a second flight to Iceland. These were preliminaries for one more of the "Graf's" unforgettable pioneering adventures – a scientific expedition to the Arctic!

In the year 1926 the famous Polar explorer, Fridtjof Nansen, had founded the "International Association for Exploring the Arctic by Means of Airships," called "Aeroarctic" for short. Nansen interested Eckener in the possibility of using the "Graf" for an expedition to the Arctic, and when he died suddenly in 1930, Eckener found himself elected his successor as president of "Aeroarctic." Initially William Randolph Hearst offered to finance the flight on condition that the Zeppelin and Hubert Wilkins in a submarine should meet at the North Pole; but this never came to pass, and the flight was largely supported by stamp collectors. There was in fact an exchange of mail with the Russian icebreaker "Malygin" off Franz Joseph Land.

The scientific aims of the expedition, of which the Russian Professor Samoilowich was the leader, were threefold: firstly, to explore variations in the earth's magnetic field, both in direction and in intensity, in high latitudes. One of the rear sleeping cabins of the "Graf Zeppelin" was considered to be far enough removed from masses of iron and electrical currents to be suitable for housing the sensitive double compass provided through a grant from the Carnegie Foundation, together with other magnetometers. The observers in this area were the Swedish Dr. Ljungdahl and the Americans, Commander E.H. Smith of the U.S. Coast Guard and Lincoln Ellsworth. Secondly, to make meteorological observations, not so much of local variations during the flight as of high altitude readings by means of radiosondes carried by balloons. A special large hatch was made in the keel through which the balloons were dropped out; to prevent these from fouling the underside of the Zeppelin, they had a weight attached which was released after a minute to permit their climb to high altitude. The German Professor Weickmann and the Russian Professor Moltchankoff were in charge of this equipment. Thirdly, geographical exploration of unknown lands was an important part of the "Aeroarctic" program, which showed particular interest in the nearly unknown Severnaya Zemlya and the east coast of Novaya Zemlya. A panoramic camera invented by Professor Aschenbrenner of Munich, automatically taking nine photographs every few seconds, each showing the time and altitude, was mounted in one of the cabins in charge of its inventor. Altogether there were twelve scientists from four different countries on board as passengers, together with two reporters and a cameraman. The crew numbered 31, including a Russian radio man for working Soviet ground stations.[18]

Naturally the ship was much modified, with all passenger comforts removed, cabins appropriated for scientific instruments, and all hands sleeping in bunks along the keel. Survival gear to the amount of 11,200 lb. was loaded in the event of a forced landing on the ice, including emergency rations, hunting and fishing gear, sleeping bags, 23 sledges, cooking stoves and 12 tents.

The flight was officially considered to originate in Leningrad, where the "Graf" arrived on the evening of July 25, 1931, after a night's layover at the mooring mast in Berlin-Staaken.[19] At 9.05 am on the morning of July 26 the "Graf" departed with fuel for 105 hours on all five engines, including petrol for 21 hours. Crossing Lake Ladoga and then Lake Onega, the Zeppelin reached Arkhangelsk in the late afternoon, and proceeded out over the Barents Sea in pleasant weather. News of a low pressure area ahead decided Eckener to make first for Franz Joseph Land to the north, and then to follow behind the weather eastward to Severnaya Zemlya and the Taimyr Peninsula of Siberia. The Zeppelin in fact passed through a weather front shortly after leaving Arkhangelsk, and then had the low pressure area to starboard.

The following afternoon the edge of the ice field was in sight at 78 degrees north, with the snow-covered mountains of Franz Joseph Land ahead. At 1730 the "Graf" made a water landing near the icebreaker "Malygin" for the benefit of the philatelists. During the next six hours the Zeppelin manoeuvred over the islands of the Franz Joseph group, mapping them with the panoramic camera; the sunlight was continuous, but a sort of twilight with the sun low to the north at midnight hampered photography for several hours. The

[18] Dr. L. Kohl-Larsen, *Die Arktisfahrt des "Graf Zeppelin"* (Berlin: Union Deutsche Verlagsgesellschaft, 1931), chapter 10.
[19] Since Berlin was some 1200 feet lower than Friedrichshafen, the Zeppelin could carry 9000 lb. more fuel and equipment on departure from there.

airship then headed east for Severnaya Zemlya, looking for unknown islands along the route which of course were not found. Towards 0600 on the 29th the north cape of Severnaya Zemlya was in sight, and during the next six hours the airship flew down the west side of the island (the east side was shrouded in fog), mapping with the cameras and discovering for the first time that Severnaya Zemlya was really two islands instead of one. Then crossing the Siberian coast at Cape Chelyuskin, the Zeppelin steered inland to Lake Taimyr. A flight westward along the lake proved it to be much longer than drawn on the maps, while the mountains roundabout were much higher than previously reported. The "Graf" appeared over the isolated settlement of Dickson Haven at the mouth of the Yenesei River, then stood out north-west towards Novaya Zemlya. The airship flew down the east side of the two islands, taking many photographs while the scientists made copious notes. This ended the scientific side of the expedition. By 0354 hours of July 30 the ship was over Leningrad. The Zeppelin had been in the air for 90 hours, but still had fuel enough to reach Friedrichshafen. En route home Eckener was persuaded to land in Berlin for a civic welcome, ultimately reaching Friedrichshafen at 0440 on July 31. While Eckener felt he had been rather lucky in the good weather he had enjoyed over the Arctic Ocean following the frontal passage, he believed also that the flight had amply proven the value of the airship for Arctic exploration. Unfortunately, it was the last expedition of its kind, the "Italia" disaster of 1928 having previously discredited the airship as an Arctic vehicle, while later explorers preferred cheaper aeroplanes.

This was the last of the spectacular publicity journeys of the "Graf Zeppelin". In August, September and October, 1931, the "Graf" made three scheduled and advertised flights to South America. Because no proper airship base had been erected at Rio, the crossings terminated at the mast in Recife and the passengers went on via the German Condor air line. So successful were these voyages, both technically and financially, that the Zeppelin Company planned henceforth to minimize the "circus" and publicity activities, and to concentrate on the South American service. In 1932 there were nine passenger flights to South America, the last three terminating in Rio to stimulate the interest of the Brazilian Government in erecting an airship base. There was some variation in the route followed, either down the Rhône Valley to the Mediterranean or via the Bay of

Biscay, thence via the Canary and Cape Verde Islands and Fernando de Noronha to Pernambuco. Sometimes there were landings at Barcelona or Seville.

In 1933 there were nine passenger trips to South America; on the eighth one, the President of Brazil and some of his ministers were guests on the flight from Recife to Rio. This was the fruit of Dr. Eckener's determined efforts to persuade the Brazilian Government to establish an airship base near Rio; Eckener had stayed on in Brazil after the first crossing of the year, and eventually won a contract for the building of a shed, with traveling mooring mast, barracks for the crew, and a hotel for passengers, at Santa Cruz, some 25 miles south of Rio. The hangar was completed late in 1935.

The last ocean crossing of 1933 was a triangle cruise, the directors of the Chicago World's Fair having requested the appearance of the "Graf". The ship departed Recife on October 21 with 15 passengers, including an American couple bound for Chicago with a three month old baby. The journey proceeded via the mouths of the Amazon, the Guianas and Trinidad, and thence up the Leeward Islands. The Zeppelin then moored at the U.S. Navy's expeditionary mast at Opa-Locka, near Miami. Here, like the U.S. Navy's "Akron" before her, and "Macon" afterwards, the "Graf" had her troubles with sudden wind shifts and tropical cloud bursts. After a stay of only 13 hours the "Graf" cast off to avoid further unpleasantness and went on towards Akron. Now winter arrived on the heels of further cold fronts, and with the temperature at freezing, the passengers regretted that there was no heat in their quarters. Finally the ship landed and was walked into the huge Goodyear "air dock" in the early morning of October 25. Next day the Zeppelin made a brief appearance over Chicago and landed long enough for Eckener to disembark. A day later he rejoined the "Graf" at Akron, and from there she proceeded direct for Friedrichshafen via Seville. Despite the lateness of the season, there were no storms over the North Atlantic, merely a persistent north-east wind.

In 1934 the "Graf" was advertised to fly to South America every 14 days. Altogether 12 round trips were made that year. On the third one the Zeppelin went on to Buenos Aires in an attempt to interest the Argentinian Government in constructing an airship base; but nothing came of the effort and passengers were flown via the Condor air line from Rio to Buenos Aires. In 1935 the regular flights continued. An old time table in my possesion shows that ten round trips were advertised between June 15 and October 31, but the

The swastika in America: "Graf Zeppelin" on the field of the Goodyear Zeppelin Corporation at Akron, Ohio, during the 1933 "triangle flight". The display of the *Hakenkreuz*, forced on Dr. Eckener by the Nazi Propaganda Ministry, caused resentment and revulsion in other countries besides the United States. (Banks-Hepburn Walker collection).

"Graf" made 16 in all, completing the last one on December 10. In addition, three shuttle flights were made from Recife to Bathurst in British Gambia on the west coast of Africa, carrying mail ordinarily flown across the South Atlantic by the *Lufthansa* air line. Temporarily both *Lufthansa* catapult ships, "Westfalen" and "Schwabenland," had had to be withdrawn from service. The second of these flights, commencing on November 22 as the ship left Recife, inadvertently kept the "Graf" aloft for 118 hours 40 minutes. The crossing to Bathurst was uneventful, but during the return journey a revolution broke out in Pernambuco. Three days passed, while the Zeppelin cruised at minimal speed off the coast, before government troops were in control of the landing field. Advised by radio, Captain Lehmann brought in his ship to land at Recife on the evening of November 27.[20]

[20] Lehmann asserts that this flight surpassed the record set by the "Dixmude" in September, 1923, but this is not correct. E. A. Lehmann & Leonhard Adelt, *Auf Luftpatrouille und Weltfahrt* (Leipzig: Schmidt u. Günther, 1936), p. 34. For "Dixmude's" record, see p. 346.

It must not be thought that the South American flights took place in a political vacuum. Adolf Hitler's appointment as Chancellor of Germany on January 30, 1933, had important consequences for the Zeppelin airship – at first seeming to assure it of commercial predominance on the air routes of the world, it ended in bringing on the war which destroyed it forever. In the process, the Zeppelin did not escape becoming a propaganda appendage of the Brown Shirt regime. Initially it was taken up by the Propaganda Minister, Dr. Joseph Goebbels, who in the summer of 1934 contributed two million marks towards the completion of the new "Hindenburg." Stung to rivalry despite his hatred of the "gas bag," World War I fighter pilot and Air Minister Hermann Goering then intervened to set up in March, 1935, the *Deutsche Zeppelin Reederei,* in which the government air line, *Lufthansa,* was the dominant partner.

Gone was the independence of the Zeppelin enterprise, and nationalism was exalted in place of the international outlook which was the cornerstone of Eckener's philosophy. Outspokenly anti-Nazi, the great airship man might have been one of the victims when on June 30, 1934 – "the night of the long knives" – Hitler with the help of the SS murdered scores of political opponents. At the time Eckener was fortunately returning from Buenos Aires. Presumably his great international reputation and the affection in which he was held in America in particular, saved him from being executed or imprisoned.[21] With the founding of the *Reederei* in March, 1935, the direction of operations was taken out of Eckener's hands and entrusted to Ernst Lehmann. Eckener's loud public complaints about the misuse of the two airships "Graf Zeppelin" and "Hindenburg" in a propaganda flight in March, 1936, led an enraged Goebbels to declare "Dr. Eckener has placed himself outside the pale of society. Henceforth his name is not to be mentioned in the newspapers and his photograph is not to be published!" Thus Eckener became an "unperson," but was otherwise left alone even during the war years.

More and more the airships were used for propaganda purposes. In the triangle flight of October, 1933, the "Graf" had borne on her vertical tail surfaces the Nazi flag – a black swastika in a white circle on a scarlet background – on the port side, and on the starboard side the horizontal stripes of the German tricolor – black, white and

[21] I cannot put much stock on the story that Eckener was spared because President Hindenburg, on his death bed in July, 1934, made Hitler promise not to harm him. I do not doubt the testimony of his physician, Professor Sauerbruch, in relating Hindenburg's words, but cannot imagine that such a promise would deter the man who murdered millions from liquidating a single inconvenient opponent.

red.[22] Even then threats were made against "the Nazi ship" which caused her appearance in Chicago to be as brief as possible. As early as April, 1933, the "Graf" had overflown the massed celebration by a million Brown Shirts of "National Workers' Day" in Berlin. A month later the airship landed in Rome partly to salute the visiting Dr. Goebbels. In connection with the 1936 referendum ratifying the abrogation of the Locarno treaty and the occupation of the Rhineland, the "Graf" and the new "Hindenburg" were required to cruise over the *Reich* from March 26 to 29 to urge the populace by loud speaker and leaflet to vote for the *Führer* and his policies.

The "Hindenburg" represented Eckener's dream of the ideal transatlantic airship. The concept of a truly big craft of course antedated the design of the "Graf Zeppelin." One important preliminary goal was realized as early as 1929-30 when a new, large construction shed — erected with funds provided by the German government and the State of Württemberg — was built in Friedrichshafen with a length of 837 feet, height and width of 164 feet, "clear inner dimensions." With the construction number LZ 128, a design was produced for a ship with a capacity of 5,307,000 cubic feet of hydrogen, 761 feet long and 128 feet in diameter, driven by eight 500 hp Maybach engines in pairs in four gondolas, and with accomodations for 30 to 34 passengers. This proposal was shelved after the British R 101 crashed and burned at Beauvais on October 5, 1930, on the first leg of a projected flight to India. A new design, LZ 129, was undertaken to provide the same performance with safe helium. With nearly twice the volume of the "Graf Zeppelin," though only about 30 feet longer, LZ 129 had a gas capacity of 7,062,100 cubic feet in a hull 803.8 feet long and 135.1 feet in diameter. The "fat" hull was more efficient in that it contained more gas in proportion to structural weight, and was more resistant to bending forces. The large fins, of cantilever section and nearly 100 feet long and 50 feet in breadth were eleven feet thick at the root and so roomy that the lower one contained an auxiliary steering station in case of a breakdown of the main controls. The hull was of conventional Zeppelin design, with 15 transverse main rings — 36 sided girderwork polygons radially braced with hard-drawn steel wire — dividing the hull into 16 compartments to

[22] The Nazi flags do not appear in photographs of the airships in post-1945 German publications, invariably being air-brushed out. When I wrote a book on the "Hindenburg" in 1964, I began by telling the publisher that he faced a "political" decision — "swastikas or no swastikas?" His answer was to "show the ship just as she was."

contain the lifting gas cells. Thirty-six triangular girders ran from end
to end of the hull, tying the main rings together. Between each main
ring, themselves spaced 49.2 to 54.1 feet apart, were two unbraced
intermediate rings. The aluminium-doped cotton outer cover had a
total area of 367,000 square feet. Four streamlined engine gondolas
hung in pairs amidships and aft, and forward was a small control car.
On both sides of the keel running along the bottom of the ship from
bow to stern were arranged the crew's quarters, freight rooms, fuel
oil and ballast water tanks. For a transoceanic flight, 65 tons of fuel
were carried for the four Daimler-Benz 16 cylinder diesel engines
with a maximum output of 1320 hp each.

    In contrast to the "Graf Zeppelin", the passenger quarters in
LZ 129 were entirely inside the hull. Occupying only a minute
fraction of the ship's length, they nevertheless provided spaciousness
and luxury for her 50 passengers unmatched to this day in any kind
of aircraft. On the upper deck, which measured 49 by 92 feet, were
the public rooms – a dining salon to port and a comfortably
furnished lounge and writing room to starboard. In the center of the
deck were two-berth sleeping cabins, each with a washbasin with hot
and cold running water. On the lower deck were toilet rooms, the
galley and a smoking room with a pressure-lock door to exclude any
stray hydrogen.

    To minimize the risk of fire, the "Blau-gas" fuel in the "Graf
Zeppelin" had been eliminated, and non-flammable helium would be
sought in America. Yet hydrogen would not be entirely dispensed
with in the LZ 129. Every airship designer had to solve the problem
of the ship, weighted down to capacity with fuel at the start of a long
flight, becoming progressively lighter as the journey continued and
fuel was burned. In the early days the Germans simply valved
hydrogen to keep the ship in equilibrium. With helium seven times as
expensive as hydrogen, the American Navy recovered water from the
engine exhausts to maintain a constant weight. To the Germans, the
water-recovery condensers seemed unduly heavy and their air
resistance high. They would, instead carry small cells of hydrogen
safely enclosed within the large helium gas bags. The cheaper
hydrogen "antiballast" could then be valved to compensate for the
weight of diesel oil burned.

    An early drawing of LZ 129 shows a hydrogen cell rigged inside
the upper portion of a helium cell by a complicated system of
thwartships booms and bridles, and filling about one-third of the
space within the helium cell. Because of its position, the automatic

and hand-operated discharge valves of the hydrogen cell were deep within the hull — an innovation which may have had a bearing on the Lakehurst disaster — and were serviced from an axial gangway running straight through the center of the ship.

Work actually commenced on the LZ 129 in the autumn of 1931. This was the height of the Depression; a time of near-chaos in the political and economic life of the *Reich,* and with government backing dwindling, progress was initially very slow. Nine million marks from Hermann Goering's Air Ministry eventually assured her completion, and the new airship was essentially complete by Christmas, 1935.

The safety programme had received a setback when Dr. Eckener found it impossible to procure helium in the United States. The Helium Control Act of 1927 reserved to the Government all the gas produced in the United States, and forbade its export. Dr. Eckener had hoped that helium might be made available to a joint German-American airship operating company, but the world-wide economic depression rendered such plans impossible. It was too late now to change the ship's internal arrangements. The big cotton gas cells would now contain hydrogen instead of helium, and the small hydrogen cells were eliminated. But the automatic and hand-operated valves for release of hydrogen remained in their original location — deep inside the ship, just above the axial gangway, and exhausting into shafts reaching upward as much as 70 feet to the top of the hull.

Surprisingly, LZ 129 made her first flight on March 4, 1936, without a name — to seamen always a harbinger of misfortune. Ignorant rumors persisted that Eckener was fighting the *Führer's* demand that the new sky queen be christened "Hitler." Actually, the name "Hindenburg" had been chosen in advance, appearing, for instance, in the spring, 1935, issue of the British quarterly, *The Airship.* With her test programme curtailed by the propaganda flight, "Hindenburg" set off on her first long cruise, to Rio, on March 31 with 37 passengers. Eckener's forebodings were justified when on the outward journey one of the new Daimler diesels failed with a broken wrist pin, and a second failed in the same manner on the flight home. Nearly a month passed, while the motors were overhauled, before the Zeppelin made her next flight, a 7½ hour test ascent.

In February, 1936, Dr. Eckener, through the intervention of President Roosevelt, had obtained a revocable permit from the U.S. Navy Department to make ten round trips to Lakehurst during the

"Hindenburg" nearly complete in the building shed. Rudders at different angles as they have not yet been connected to the controls. (Luftschiffbau Zeppelin)

"Hindenburg" at Lakehurst: an unusual close-up from the top of the mobile mast. Main cable and port yaw line lead down to right. (Robinson)

year 1936. These were successfully carried out with no further difficulties, and keeping to a strict schedule, "Hindenburg" won the enthusiastic approval of the traveling public, and the growing interest of American financiers. On October 9, in a masterly propaganda gesture, Eckener played host to 72 American businessmen, industrialists, officials and newspaper men on the ten-hour "millionaires' flight" over New England. Meanwhile the "Graf" was continuing the South American service with thirteen flights to Rio via Recife, plus a postal flight from Recife to Bathurst and return. The "Hindenburg," having a longer range, went straight through to Rio in seven flights to South America during the year. Furthermore, in May the new intercontinental airship base at Frankfurt-am-Main was opened, with the "Graf" making the first landing there on May 11. The chief advantage of Frankfurt as a base was that being only 350 feet above sea level, the "Hindenburg" could lift 13,200 lb more than in a takeoff from Friedrichshafen, which lay 1000 feet higher. Because at first only one of the two Frankfurt hangars was

1936 aerial view of Lakehurst, with "Hindenburg" moored on the mooring out circle, and "Los Angeles" in the distance, decommissioned but still in use for mooring trials. (Robinson)

1936 aerial view of Lakehurst, with "Hindenburg" moored on the hauling up circle directly in front of the hangar. (Robinson)

completed, "Hindenburg" was in permanent possession while the "Graf" had to shuttle back and forth to Friedrichshafen as home base.

Thus, all participants were in high heart and optimistic about the future as preparations were made during the winter of 1937-8 for the next year's transatlantic season. With hydrogen as the lifting medium instead of helium, "Hindenburg" had considerable reserve lift, so during the winter layup in Frankfurt, nine more passenger cabins were built on "B" deck in places preempted from the crew's quarters, increasing the passenger capacity to 70. Further, a new ship, LZ 130, a sister to "Hindenburg," had been laid down on June 27, 1936, in the building shed in Friedrichshafen. Her first flight was planned for August, 1937, and in the timetable for that year she was advertised to make her first departure for Rio on October 27. Meanwhile the eight-year-old "Graf Zeppelin" was surveyed by government inspectors and pronounced fit for 3 more years of flying! Lehmann, as flight director of the *Reederei,* was busy shuffling personnel: no longer in command of any of the ships, he

"Hindenburg" at Lakehurst, 1936. Note the multiplicity of hatches and windows along the bottom of the ship. (Fred Tupper-Hepburn Walker collection)

assigned Max Pruss to command the "Hindenburg," Anton Wittenmann to command the old "Graf," while a third crew was formed for the LZ 130 and Hans von Schiller was provisonally designated as her commander. Further, during the winter a joint German-American consortium was formed to operate four airships in transatlantic service, two under the German flag and two under the American.

"Hindenburg" made the first ocean crossing of 1937 to Rio between March 16 and 27. "Graf Zeppelin" followed, with stops at Recife, between April 13 and 24. On April 27 the "Graf," temporarily commanded by von Schiller, departed for Rio, where she arrived on May 1. On May 3 the "Hindenburg" departed Frankfurt for the first of 18 scheduled flights to the United States. She was carrying 36 passengers and a crew of 61, many of them being trainees for the sister ship LZ 130. Her estimated time of arrival at Lakehurst was 0600 local time on May 6.

Head winds delayed the Zeppelin, and on the evening of May 5, Pruss radioed a new ETA of 1800 hours on the following day. About 1600 the big rigid was first seen near Lakehurst, but a cold front was moving east across the field accompanied by thunderstorms, and Pruss accepted the advice of Commander Rosendahl, the station commandant, that he delay his landing. Shortly after 1900, the "Hindenburg" came up over the field from the south-west, at an altitude of 600 feet, turned, and came back towards the mast, heading into the light south-east wind. Engines were reversed, and as she approached the mast for a "high" landing, the port and starboard yaw lines and the big mooring cable fell from the bow.

Though "Hindenburg" was no longer a sensation, her comings and goings were still news, and a number of photographers and reporters were on hand to record what all expected to be another routine arrival. It is thanks to them and their steadfast devotion to the traditions of their calling that the events of the next few moments constitute the outstanding recollection of today's older generation of the rigid airship era: not only in vivid photographs, but most of all through the agonized voice of a radio announcer who was making a recording of the Zeppelin's arrival.

Four minutes after the lines touched the ground, a big burst of flame suddenly blossomed atop the hull just ahead of the upper vertical fin. Almost immediately the entire stern section was aflame, showering fragments of hot metal on the ground below, while glowing particles of fabric whirled upward in a hot gale of flame coalescing overhead in a mushroom cloud of smoke. The stern dropped, the nose of the 803-foot hull pointed skyward; then, the glowing framework breaking in two amidships, the enormous metal structure collapsed on the ground as the flames ate their way forward. Amazingly, from the holocaust 62 of those embarked in the airship survived, some badly injured. But 13 passengers had perished together with 22 of the crew, including Ernst Lehmann, old DELAG captain and flight director of the Zeppelin *Reederei,* who died on May 7 of severe burns.

How the "Hindenburg" was destroyed is a subject still hotly debated to this day among surviving airship men and airship historians. One fact is beyond dispute: the Nazi sky giant would never have burned had she been inflated with helium, as her designers intended. What set her hydrogen on fire? The main arguments involve either accident or sabotage, with variations on both themes.

Remarkably, several crew members in the tail section at the time of the landing actually saw the start of the fire and survived. One testified at the investigation that he "heard above him a muffled detonation and saw from the starboard side, down inside the gas cell, a bright reflection through and inside the cell. The cell suddenly disappeared because of the heat."[23] Flames of course shot up the ventilation shaft between Cells 4 and 5, and it was these which blossomed atop the ship forward of the upper fin to signal the disaster to spectators on the ground.

The American and German investigating commissions, influenced large by testimony of Dr. Eckener and of Professor Dieckmann, a noted authority on electrostatics and atmospheric electricity, concluded that leaking hydrogen had been ignited by a static electrical discharge. Eckener persistently held to the belief that the final turn towards the mast had overstressed the hull, causing a bracing wire to break and slash open Cell 4 or 5. Considerable evidence was introduced to show that the ship had been stern-heavy for half an hour before the landing – suggesting leakage of hydrogen aft. Furthermore, gas had been valved from all cells ten minutes before the accident, and it was possible that the manoeuvring valve of Cell 4 had stuck open, permitting the continuing escape of gas. Captain Garland Fulton, airship expert of the U.S. Navy's Bureau of Aeronautics and an eye witness to the accident, considered that even

---

[23] Department of Commerce, Bureau of Air Commerce, Safety and Planning Division, Report No. 11. *The Hindenburg Accident. A Comparative Digest of the Investigations and Findings, with the American and Translated German Reports Included.* August, 1938. p. 36.

if the va ve had closed, an inflammable mixture of air and hydrogen could have remained in the shaft, inadequately ventilated with the Zeppelin flying at low speed.

As for the static discharge, Professor Dieckmann pointed out that several minutes after the "Hindenburg" dropped her landing ropes, there would be an equalization of the static charges in the ship and on the ground, and therefore the Zeppelin, having "become a piece of the ground elevated into the atmosphere," would discharge electricity into the atmosphere – the so-called brush discharge or St. Elmo's Fire. Though no brush discharges were seen by witnesses under the ship and around the mooring mast, the American report held that they could have been present unseen since it was still daylight, and that "such a discharge likely would have ignited any adequately rich stream of leaking hydrogen that reached it; and that from the point of ignition the flame would have shot back to the leak, there quickly would have burnt a larger opening and set going a conflagration of great violence and rapidity."[24] And here I was able to make a small but important contribution to the evaluation of the "Hindenburg" disaster: by chance I met in the year 1962 Professor Mark Heald of Princeton, N.J., who undoubtedly saw St. Elmo's Fire flickering along the airship's back a full minute before the fire broke out. Standing outside the main gate to the naval air station, he watched as the Zeppelin approached the mast and dropped her lines. A minute thereafter, by Mr. Heald's estimate, he first noticed a dim "blue flame" flickering along the backbone girder. There was time for him to remark to his wife. "oh, heavens, the thing is afire," for her to reply "Where?" and for him to answer, " Up along the top ridge" – before there was a big burst of flaming hydrogen from a point ahead of the upper fin.[25]

The investigators dealt very gingerly with the possibility of sabotage. A finding that this was likely would have been extremely embarrassing to both the German and American governments at a time when public opinion was inflamed by Nazi rearmament, the illegal occupation of the Rhineland, and the persecution of dissidents and Jews. Dr. Eckener, after having discussed possible sabotage with a reporter the morning after the accident, was forced by German government officials to make a broadcast to America denying the possibility. Yet a small non-metallic incendiary device, concealed adjacent to a gas cell, would have caused all the phenomena observed

[24] *ibid.*, p. 63.
[25] *Wingfoot Lighter Than Air Society Bulletin*, v. 10, No. 4, February, 1963, p. 2.

in the Lakehurst catastrophe, and would itself have been consumed. Lehmann concluded in a last conversation with Rosendahl "it must have been an infernal machine." Within a year, Rosendahl published an account suggesting that such a device might have been put in place in flight, and might have been pre-set when it was expected that the ship would be moored to the mast at 1800, and would have been empty of passengers and most of her crew.[26]

A book published in 1962[27] blamed the disaster on sabotage, and flatly accused an airshipman who died in the fire. Filled with much irrelevant material, the book was not well received by the friends of the rigid airship.

The views of Captain Pruss, too seriously burned to testify at the enquiry, never appeared in the printed record, but from the beginning he dissented from the offical finding that an electrostatic discharge had ignited escaping hydrogen. Through the years he became increasingly convinced that sabotage had caused the loss of his ship and of 36 lives. In 1957 he told me, "in the control car were remote reading instruments showing the percentage fullness of each cell on a panel, and I have no recollection of this instrument showing anything wrong in an after cell or in any other cell."[28] Furthermore, he pointed out, the fire originated at a point where a ladder from the keel gave access to the space between Cells 4 and 5. In the last year of his life Pruss became convinced that the saboteur had been a passenger whose behaviour he recalled as being suspicious.

At the time of the Lakehurst catastrophe the "Graf Zeppelin," under von Schiller's command, was homeward bound from Rio. Her shocked commander decided to keep the news from his passengers until the landing at Friedrichshafen on May 8. Von Schiller was prepared to take the ship out for South America on schedule on May 11, but Dr. Eckener cancelled the departure. In fact, this was the last passenger flight by a rigid airship. Hopefully there would be more operations with helium, but with the heavier non-inflammable gas, the historic "Graf" would not have the lift to cross the oceans. On July 19 the veteran of 1,060,000 miles and 13,000 hours' flying was ferried to Frankfurt, hung up in a shed and deflated, to serve as a museum.

With the new LZ 130 the Zeppelin Company hoped to carry on

[26]Charles E. Rosendahl, *What About The Airship?* (new York: Charles Scribner's Sons, 1938), p. 25.
[27]A. A. Hoehling, *Who Destroyed The Hindenburg?* (Boston: Little, Brown & Co., 1962).
[28]Interview, Neu-Isenburg, July 24, 1957.

with safe helium. For a time hopes were high, for American lawmakers, horrified by the funeral pyre on their doorstep, hastened to amend the Helium Control Act to permit the export of limited amounts of the gas under strict control. The new ship was modified accordingly: smaller passenger quarters were fabricated for only 40 guests (several cabins had outside windows), and the engine gondolas were enlarged, with tractor instead of pusher propellers, to accomodate sophisticated water recovery equipment.[29] Six members of the American cabinet were required, however, to agree unanimously on the issuance of every helium permit – and one of the six, Secretary of the Interior Harold Ickes, resolutely refused consent on the grounds that the helium filled Zeppelin might be useful in war. Dr. Eckener, making a special visit to Washington in the spring of 1938, left empty-handed, still hearing the "old curmudgeon's" accusation – "Your Hitler is going to make war!" – and knowing it was true.

There was nothing left to do but fly the new ship with hydrogen. On September 14, 1938, Dr. Eckener christened LZ 130 "Graf Zeppelin"[30] and commanded her on her first flight at Friedrichshafen. Though she never carried paying passengers, she made a total of 30 ascents, mostly "circus flights" to German cities.[31] Long after the defeat of the Thousand Year *Reich* it was revealed that Ickes was right in his suspicions that she might be used for military purposes. Taken over by the *Luftwaffe* Department of Signals and loaded with electronic gear, the new "Graf" made nine flights to spy on the defences of Russia and Great Britain. Probably a 44 hour 51 minute flight on July 12-14, 1939, was made along the east coast of England to spy on the future enemy's radar network. Certainly the LZ 130 made such a flight in 48 hours on August 2-4, as she was seen inland over Scotland and R.A.F. Spitfires were sent off to intercept her. No information was obtained – the Battle of Britain might have ended in a German victory if the flights had been successful – and ambitious plans to build four more Zeppelins for such "ferret" missions were shelved. At the outbreak of war the new "Graf" was laid up in a shed at Frankfurt. Here the enmity of

[29] Actually, Zeppelin Company personnel with whom I discussed helium problems in July, 1937, expected to keep the ship ballasted largely by recovering rain water from channels in the outer cover on top of the ship. This had proven reliable in the "Hindenburg," which collected up to 9 tons of water at a time by deliberately flying through rainstorms.

[30] Often written "Graf Zeppelin II" in publications to distinguish her from the older ship, she did not in fact have the number after her name on the bows.

[31] Information on flights of the LZ 130 from Hepburn Walker Jr. of Vero Beach, Florida.

Hermann Goering proved the undoing of both proud symbols of German aerial predominance: as early as February 29, 1940, he ordered their destruction, with the excuse that their metal was needed for aircraft production. The old and the new "Graf Zeppelin" were broken up in the spring of 1940 by a *Luftwaffe* construction battalion, their own crews having refused to do the deed. On May 6, 1940, on the flimsy pretext that they blocked the takeoff of bombers participating in the big battle in France, both the Frankfurt hangars, by Goering's direct order, were dynamited.

> "It was not the catastrophe of Lakehurst, dear Doctor, which destroyed the airship," wrote Pruss to me in 1960, "it was the war."

One other country besides Germany built and operated commercial type rigid airships. The story of the British R 100 and R 101 is an incredible tale of vision versus governmental muddling and indecision; of genius advancing the state of the art and of inexperience creating an airship that would have been grounded had she not been constructed by a government department; of proven success on the one hand, and well-nigh inevitable tragedy on the other which took the life of the responsible Cabinet minister and of 47 other persons.

In the summer of 1921, while the Imperial conference was meeting in London, A. H. Ashbolt, the agent for Tasmania, offered a proposal to set up an airship route via Cairo, India, Singapore and Australia to New Zealand, and another to South Africa, using six wartime rigid airships to be converted for commercial use. The distinguished delegates from the Antipodes, he pointed out, could then reach London in ten days, whereas the sea voyage took six weeks. The crash of R 38 on August 24, and the post-war depression, caused the Commonwealth governments to reply in the negative. In March, 1922, a commercial scheme for connecting England to India and Australia by airship was presented to the Air Council by Commander Dennistoun Burney, a well-to-do inventor connected with the Vickers armament firm. The original Burney scheme called for a biweekly service to India, and later a weekly service to Australia, with five rigids of 3,500,000 cubic feet. Government financial support was essential of course, and obtaining this, and then waiting on the inevitable meetings of committees and circulation of minutes, led to endless delays, so that ships expected to fly by 1924 were not airborne until five years later, by which time the competing aeroplane was already flying passengers to India. While the Conservative Party ruled through much of the period during which the airships were being designed and constructed, it was the first MacDonald government in power between January and October 1924 which set up the final program, and again Labour returned to office in May, 1929, when the ships were ready to fly. In particular, the Labour Secretary of State for Air, Christopher Birdwood Thomson, whose identification with the airships was shown by his taking the title of Lord Thomson of Cardington, was the driving force behind the whole airship program. A fanatic believer in the giant rigids, he at the same time had no technical background or aeronautical knowledge, and found it all too easy to override his experts whenever their doubts were opposed to his personal ambitions.

For the Burney scheme of commercial operation with government financial support, the Labourites in May 1924 substituted a state-operated experimental program. Surviving wartime airships were to be reconditioned for a comprehensive series of tests, and two large 5,000,000 cubic foot rigids were to be constructed. Commander Burney was not to be frozen out – his Airship Guarantee Company, a Vickers subsidiary, would be allowed to build one of the craft. The other, however, was to be a shining demonstration of governmental enterprise, to be constructed at the revived Royal Airship Works at Cardington. Inevitably the first craft, R 100, came to be called "the capitalist ship," while the R 101 was labeled "the socialist ship." The competition between the two, never friendly, became in time bitter and irreconcilable.

Further, in reaction to the loss of R 38, where faulty design and structural failure had cost 45 lives, the Government was determined that extensive study and research should be undertaken to the end that the new rigids would be safe and able to resist both aerodynamic and static loads. An Airship Stressing Panel established in 1922 had done useful work in calculating aerodynamic loads in high-speed manoeuvres; now an independent official agency was set up, the Airworthiness of Airships Panel, empowered to pass on the designs of both airships with respect to strength, with a view to licensing them for commercial service. Actually, in the opinion of a distinguished English designer, the Airworthiness of Airships Panel was too rigid in requiring a safety factor of 4 throughout, when 3 in girders and 2 in wires would have been adequate, hence the framework of R 101 was 25 per cent heavier than necessary.[32] Nor was aerodynamic research neglected: between 1924 and 1926, two streamlined hull forms with

[32] Professor E.H. Lewitt, quoted in Robin Higham, *The British Rigid Airship 1908-1931* (London: Foulis, 1961), p. 313.

seven different fin and rudder shapes were tested for the R 101 at the National Physical Laboratory, and it is known that the R 100 hull shape was tested in the wind tunnel also. Independently, both designers settled on the fat, fully streamlined hull, with a length/diameter ratio of 5.2/1 (R 100), and 5.5/1 (R 101), because of better aerodynamic efficiency and greater resistance to bending forces of the "fat" hull.

Other requirements of the R 100 contract signed on November 1, 1924 (R 101 was built to the same specifications) called for a gross lift of 150 tons with 5,000,000 cubic feet of hydrogen; full speed of not less than 70 mph and cruising speed of 63 mph; accomodation for sleeping and feeding 100 passengers; and structural (fixed) weights not to exceed 90 tons, giving a useful lift of 60 tons. Lastly, in view of the extensive flying done in the tropics in World War II with petrol engines, there was a curious superstition that petrol was dangerous with high temperatures, and the two airships were "to be operated on fuel which could safely be carried and used in sub-tropical or tropical climates."[33] This, in effect, meant diesel engines, though none such had ever been flown in an airship, and no experimental diesels were flown in aeroplanes until 1928.

In addition, five mooring towers of a new and massive design were erected at strategic locations in the Empire. Seventy feet across at the base and 200 feet high, each had winches at the base to reel in the airship's mooring cable and yaw lines, pumps and pipes to bring fuel and water to the mast head, and a 12 inch hydrogen main. A lift and stairway led up to the centre of the tower. Such masts were erected at Cardington (only one for two ships!), at Ismailia in Egypt, Karachi in India (with a large shed), St. Hubert near Montreal in Canada, and at Grautville, Natal, in South Africa.

For the experimental program, both R 33 and the damaged R 36 were to be reconditioned, but the latter, though repaired, never flew and was broken up in 1926. R 33, which had not flown since June, 1921, was refurbished at Cardington and on April 2, 1925, was walked out of the shed and flown to Pulham where she was moored to the high mast. Fourteen days later, in an accident resembling that to the U.S.S. "Shenandoah" a year earlier, she tore away from the mast in a gale, with the nose structure collapsed and No. 1 gas bag deflated. Fortunately her executive officer, Flight Lieut. R. S. Booth, and 18 men were aboard, and released ballast and started the

[33] Cmd. 3825, *Report of the R 101 Inquiry* (London: HMSO, 1931), p. 14.

engines. But because of severe damage to the bow, these could be run
for an air speed of only 30 knots. The 50 knot wind carried R 33
stern first over Holland, but next day, after a flight of 29½ hours, her
crew brought her safely back to Pulham and she was placed in the
shed. Repairs lasted until August. There was some further flying in
October which did not contribute to the development program, in
which a light aircraft, a DH 53, hooked onto the airship and was
released. In 1926 a pair of Gloster Grebe fighters were carried aloft
and released. No further flights were made; the metal structure
showed signs of increasing fatigue and the outer cover was slack. It
was now decided in view of the governmental economy program to
lay up R 33, and in May, 1928, she was broken up.

R 100 was built at Howden, where the Airship Guarantee
Company had purchased the largest of the wartime hangars. The
design team commenced work as early as 1924 in a London suburb,
and moved to Howden a year later. At their head was Dr. Barnes
Wallis, who had designed the streamlined R 80 during the war, and
his Chief Calculator was a rising young aeronautical engineer, N. S.
Norway.[34] It would appear that Wallis aimed to design the perfect
rigid airship by going back to first principles, an attitude that led to
trouble with such practical details as gas cells and outer cover. In
order to minimize the number of structural members in which the
stresses would have to be calculated, the huge framework, 709 feet
long and 133 feet in diameter, was kept as simple as possible, with
sixteen longitudinals and fifteen transverse frames, including the one
at the stern post. Intermediate transverse frames and reefing girders
were omitted, which led to problems in supporting the large panels
of the outer cover. An axial girder ran from end to end of the ship to
support the radial wire bracing of the main rings, but unlike that in
the "Graf Zeppelin" it did not give access to the gas cells. The
triangular girders were all alike, massive affairs 27 inches deep and
made of duralumin tubing, but much more efficiently and simply
manufactured than those developed by Schütte too late for his "g"
type ships. Each tube was made by machine by rolling a strip of
duralumin in a spiral and riveting the edge — 24 rivets to the foot of
tubing. There were fifteen gas cells, which for the sake of simplicity
and cheapness, were built by the Zeppelin subsidiary, B.G.

[34] Better known to the general public as Nevil Shute. Successful in two fields — aeronautical
engineering and writing — Shute completed two of his novels ("Marazan" and "So
Disdained") during the six years he was associated with the Airship Guarantee Company.

Textilwerke G.m.b.H. of Berlin.[35] Fabricated in 1927, they were two years old when R 100 made her first flight. The same appears to be true of the linen outer cover. Gas valves were of standard Zeppelin type, and bought from the Zeppelin Company. Fins were of cantilever construction, and the large rudders and elevators were unbalanced – Norway and his calculators having discovered mathematically that they could be turned by hand.

After considerable time and effort had been spent on an experimental engine burning hydrogen or kerosene, the project was abandoned as the power plant would not be ready in time. Wallis refused to employ the overweight diesels with which R 101 was burdened, and solved the power plant problem by obtaining six Rolls-Royce Condor aircraft engines, burning petrol, of 660 hp each and a dry weight of 1200 lb. Curiously these were second-hand, having been rebuilt after R.A.F. service since 1925. The engines, three of which had reversing gears, were housed back to back in three engine cars, two amidships to port and starboard, and one under the keel aft. The power plant installation weighed under 9 tons.

Forward, and inside the hull with windows in the cover, were the accommodations occupying three decks. The lowest deck comprised the crew quarters; the two upper decks housed the passenger accommodations, including two and three berth cabins, a dining salon, and a short promenade deck. There was an electric galley. Beneath the accommodation bay was the control car, about 50 feet long.

Inflation of R 100 commenced in July, 1929, and lift and trim trials gave the following results: with gas purity of 95 per cent and standard atmospheric conditions, the gross lift was 156 tons, six tons over the contract specification. The weight empty came to 105 tons, somewhat more than the 90 tons called for in the contract; but there was still a useful lift of 51 tons. Subsequent flight testing gave a maximum speed of 81 mph, over 10 mph above the contract speed, while R 100 easily made the stipulated cruising speed of 63 mph on six engines. At full speed, however, the outer cover fluttered badly particularly in the wake of the engine cars, and was so damaged that she only flew briefly at this speed on a few occasions. In fact, the only real faults of this successful airship were in the cover and gas

---

[35] Captain J. A. Sinclair asserts that these bags were cotton lined with a single layer of gold beaters' skin (*Wingfoot LTA Society Bulletin*, v. 7, No. 2, Dec. 1959, p. 7). If so, they must have been made thus at the request of the customer, as two layers of skins were standard for Zeppelin gas cells.

cells, many of the difficulties being attributable to the age of the fabric, while a faulty design of the gas exhaust hoods and trunks permitted cascades of rain water to fall between the gas cells, rotting them along with the twine gas cell netting. The second hand engines also gave more trouble than they should have. R 100 never experienced any major structural or power plant failures, was well liked by her crew and deserved a better fate than that which in the end overtook her.

Not until December 16, 1929, after R 101 had vacated the single mast at Cardington, did R 100 make her first flight from Howden to Cardington with Squadron Leader Ralph Booth in command and 57 persons on board. On the following day she made a flight intended to be a speed test, but this was aborted when a fabric sealing strip across a rudder hinge became unglued. The ship was then housed in the Cardington shed alongside R 101 for repairs and alterations, particularly intended to reinforce the outer cover. She was brought out of the shed on January 16, 1930, and ran speed trials the same day. On January 27-29 the ship made an endurance flight of 2 days, 6 hours, 52 minutes with 56 persons aboard. The flight was quite uneventful in spite of fog, low ceilings and rough air. Generally R 100 cruised on only three engines. She was then put in the shed and did not emerge until April 24. Some damage was done to one of the horizontal fins when a gust blew her against the shed entrance, and she was returned to the shed for repairs and did not reappear till May 21. A flight of 22 hours 50 minutes commencing that day resulted in an unusual minor accident: during a brief full speed run the slender pointed tail fairing collapsed due to high external air pressures not anticipated by the designers. The ship's crew knew nothing of this mishap until advised by radio from the Cardington tower. She was then put in the shed for repairs and did not re-emerge until July 26.

R 101, the "socialist" ship, was of course built at the government establishment, the Royal Airship Works at Cardington. Before any work could be done the wartime building shed there had to be lengthened to 812 feet and the roof raised from 110 to 156 feet, this being completed in May, 1927. Erection of the hull framework began in November.

The government design team was headed by Lt. Col. V. C. Richmond, a man with experience in fabricating non-rigid airships but with none in the design or construction of rigids. He had some able assistants, however, in Harold Roxbee Cox as Chief Calculator, and Squadron Leader F. M. Rope among others.* On the other hand, Richmond had to suffer a multiplicity of overseers. Not only was there his titular chief at the Air Ministry, the Air Member for Supply and Research (initially this was Air Vice Marshal Sir John Higgins, later it would be the future Battle of Britain leader, Air Vice Marshal Hugh Dowding, neither of whom had had experience with airships). At Cardington was the Director of Airship Development, Wing Commander R. B. B. Colmore, and the Assistant Director (Flying), Major G. H. Scott.

Two years were spent in testing various hull and fin shapes in the wind tunnel of the National Physical Laboratories, the shape chosen being fully streamlined with a length of 732 feet overall and a maximum diameter of 132 feet. Whatever her faults, R 101 was an esthetically beautiful creation, but her rakishly swept fins were of a type proven by Zeppelin Company wind tunnel tests to stall at low angles of attack, thereby losing their effectiveness. And within the sleek 30-sided hull were a myriad of innovations. Policy dictated an expensive and extensive program of research into all components of the huge craft, with the aim of making the government airship the safest as well as the most scientific ever. In the end, the outpourings of publicity from the Air Ministry press department fastened around the necks of the harassed Richmond and his staff a variety of impractical devices which had to go into the ship regardless of consequences, as the public had been told how wonderful they were.

Determined not to have a structural failure such as had doomed R 38, Richmond turned his back on light duralumin and fabricated his main girders of stainless steel. This was the material in the fifteen main longitudinals and in the fifteen main rings. Duralumin reefing girders (which could be screwed outwards to maintain tightness of the outer cover) alternated between the main steel longitudinals. The eleven largest main rings were of a novel design, not the flat wire-braced bicycle wheels of Zeppelin practice, but deep, stiff structures triangular in section with no transverse bulkhead wiring. The base members of the triangle were ten feet apart; the inner apex member rather farther. One disadvantage of the novel triangular ring was that it robbed the ship of some of her gas volume, roughly 500,000 cubic feet, equivalent to 15 tons of lift.[36] Another disadvantage of the deep ring was that lacking radial and chord

---

* Published claims that Dr Paul Jaray, the Zeppelin Company aerodynamicist acted as consultant in the design of R101 are denied by Roxbee-Cox (now Lord Kings Norton).

[36] Professor E.H. Lewitt, quoted in Higham, p. 298.

wiring, there was no bulkhead structure to prevent the gas bags from surging fore and aft. In the original design, however, the sixteen gas bags (manufactured at Cardington from fabric and gold beaters' skin) were firmly secured in all directions by an ingenious system of "parachute wiring" devised by Squadron Leader Rope. Each bag was encased in a network of longitudinal and circumferential wires, and attached to the lower hull framework by a system of bridles. Further, the gas bags were so restrained that they could not touch or chafe on the girders in the upper part of the hull.

Rope and Richmond were also responsible for an unusual gas valve which simultaneously served as an automatic and a manoeuvring valve. Located on the sides of the gas cells, the valve could be serviced only by climbing up inside the transverse ring. So sensitive was the valve that it would open automatically if tilted more than three degrees; later experience showed that R 101 often rolled further than this, causing a constant loss of gas which contributed to her chronic heaviness when flying. Thirty-eight tanks were provided for 29 tons of oil fuel; some could have the bottom cut out to release their contents as ballast. On the other hand, water ballast was carried which could not be released from the control car; incredibly, at the time of the final disaster, a rigger was being sent forward to drop a thousand pounds of ballast by hand! Another novelty was the pre-doped outer cover; this split and had to be renewed (like R 100's it was probably two years old when the ship first flew), and rotted to friability when reinforcing ties were stuck on inside with rubber cement. On the other hand the passenger quarters, on two decks inside the ship, were palatial and impressive: on the upper deck were inside sleeping cabins, a dining salon, and a lounge extending 32 x 60 feet between glassed-in promenade decks; on the lower deck, besides lavatories and a galley, there was a smoking room, fireproofed with asbestos sheathing and sheet duralumin. The control car was under the passenger accommodation. For the sake of streamlining, it was on two levels, with the chart room and the wireless room in the body of the ship on the lower passenger deck level.

There were five power cars, two forward ahead of the passenger accomodation, two abaft it amidships, and one on the center line aft. These embodied the most disastrous features of the ship — the Beardmore 8 cylinder in line diesel engines. Originally designed for railway locomotives, they weighed at least 4700 lb each, the entire machinery installation weighing 17 tons. Worse still, the Beardmores did not produce their expected power. It was hoped they could develop 700 bhp at 1000 rpm, but at 900 rpm the long crank shaft developed such severe torsional vibrations due to resonance that the engines could be operated at a maximum of not more than 585 bhp even after the crank shaft was stiffened (thus increasing the weight).

Richmond and his co-workers were early convinced that the diesels would raise the empty weight of the ship to the point where she could not carry fuel for intercontinental service; but their attempt to get authorization to use the lighter petrol-burning Condors was blocked by the responsible military bureaucrat, Dowding's predecessor as Air Minister for Supply and Research, on August 22, 1927. Thereafter Richmond could only reply to criticisms of R 101's heaviness by saying that "it was as absurd to blame her for her heavy engines as it would be to blame a man for wearing heavy boots if he were not allowed to change them."[37]Initially no reversing gear was fitted, as it was expected that variable pitch propellers could be developed; the prototypes however failed repeatedly under load, and R 101 was then equiped with conventional two-bladed wooden propellers. The port forward engine, however, was fitted with a reverse pitch propeller to provide reverse thrust as the airship approached or departed from the mast. Shut down at other times, it was a useless dead weight, while the other four power plants provided cruising power! Only just before the last flight were the two forward engines fitted with reversing gears.

There seems likewise to have been no control or running record of the weights going into R 101 during her construction, an elementary precaution in building a successful airship. The result was shockingly apparent when, after the beginning of inflation in July, 1929, lift and trim tests began on September 30. The gross lift was only 148.6 tons, instead of the anticipated 150, while the weight empty, instead of the specified 90 tons, was 113.6 tons. This left only 35 tons of useful lift instead of the expected 60. This meant that she could not carry enough fuel to fly from Karachi back to Egypt.

Another little-appreciated result of the ship being overweight was that the calculations of the members of the Airworthiness of Airships Panel had to be repeated. It could not be said, however, that the differences rendered R 101 structurally weak.

At this point, says Sinclair, "R 101 should have been scrapped."[38] This of course would not have been permitted after the

[37] J. A. Sinclair, *Airships in Peace and War* (London: Rich & Cowan, 1934), p. 248.
[38] *Wingfoot LTA Society Bulletin*, vol. 7, No. 2, Dec. 1959, p. 9.

government had staked its prestige by building her at a government factory, and after spending over £527,000 of the taxpayers' money. The rest of her short life was spent in a search by the designers for means of increasing her lift — a search which became ever more frantic as they found themselves being pressured by the responsible Secretary of State, Lord Thomson, who saw his political fortunes being glamorously enhanced by a successful flight to India in the craft which he had in effect created.

R 101 was brought out of the Cardington shed on October 12, 1929, and moored to the tower, making brief trial flights on the 14th and 18th. There were five more flights before the end of the year, one, on November 17–18, being an endurance flight of 30 hours 41 minutes. The ship was stable and performed satisfactorily considering her small useful lift. She was then put in the shed on November 30 and remained there for seven months. A number of already-anticipated changes were then made — the removal of fixed weights, including some of the sleeping cabins and a heavy servo

R 100 at the mooring mast at St. Hubert, south of Montreal, during the flight to Canada in August, 1930. Passenger quarters inside the hull are indicated by the windows below the number. (Hepburn Walker collection)

power steering system which had been found unnecessary, was calculated to lighten the ship by three tons. At the same time the gas bag wiring was let out to increase the volume of the cells, and hence the lift, by three tons more. A more drastic modification — cutting the ship in two and adding an extra bay and gas bag to increase the lift by a further 9 tons — was deferred until later.

The responsible engineers at Cardington do not seem to have anticipated the doubly disastrous consequences of letting out the gas bag wiring. A subtle effect was to render the craft statically unstable. No longer tightly restrained, the gas bags were free to surge forward and aft through the unbraced frames for a distance of as much as 14 feet.[39] This meant that the center of lift fluctuated through the same distance, and further, that when nose-up the nose-light moment would increase further, while when tail-up the tail would tend to rise further. Because of this static instability, R 101 in the future followed an undulating flight path, with hard-up and hard-down elevator being needed to overcome the static pitching moments produced by the surging gas bags. Further, the moving gas bags were now impinging on the girder structure in the upper part of the ship, wearing countless holes in the delicate fabric which, even if small, permitted a steady loss of hydrogen. This was brought to the attention of the Air Ministry by a conscientious inspector at Cardington. The matter was referred back to. Colmore, the Director of Airship Development, who suggested that the inspector was an alarmist and that padding the girders would take care of the problem. Ultimately over 4000 pads were installed on the framework.

That all was not well was amply demonstrated — at least in the opinion of Captain Booth and First Officer Meager of R 100, who flew in her at this time — when in June 1930 R 101 was brought out of the Cardington shed to appear at the R.A.F. display at Hendon. No sooner was the ship put on the mast than the outer cover split over 140 feet of its length. The next day a shorter split took place on top of the hull. These tears were repaired and strengthening bands applied with a rubber solution. On June 26 a short flight was made to test the repairs. On June 27 R 101 flew for over 12 hours to rehearse her role in the Hendon display, and on June 28 she made the display flight. The ship now showed an alarming tendency to put her nose down to as much as 25 degrees and dive — the cause being static instability with shifting gas bags — and full elevator was

[39] W. Newman Alcock, quoted in Higham, p. 312.

required to recover. During the rehearsal the ship was dived to within 500 feet of the ground, then pulled up sharply causing a gasbag wiring bridle to break. Evidence of serious loss of gas disturbed the R 100 officers, though the regular R 101 crew did not seem so concerned. At the end of each 12½ hour flight the ship was heavy when she should have been light from the consumption of fuel; on the 27th she had to release 9 tons of ballast to weigh off before making fast to the tower, on the 28th it was 10 tons. Gas bag damage was undoubtedly the chief culprit, though hydrogen probably spilled in addition from the valves while flying in rough air.

Lord Thomson was now pressuring the Cardington staff to have the ship ready to leave for India on the weekend of September 26-28, so he could return triumphant on October 16 at the height of the Imperial Conference (he is supposed to have had ambitions to be the next Viceroy of India). Clearly R 101 could not make the flight unless the new bay was inserted, so she entered the shed on June 30 and remained there for the rest of the summer. The new bay was 45 feet long and parallel sided, housing a bag of 510,300 cubic foot capacity. The gross lift was now 167.2 tons, the fixed weight 117.9 tons, the useful lift increasing to 49.3 tons. At the same time the rotten outer cover was to be renewed.

Now it was the turn of R 100 to occupy the limelight. A final condition for the acceptance of this ship was that she must demonstrate her airworthiness by an actual intercontinental flight, and since R 100 had petrol engines, she would go to Canada while R 101 with her diesels would make the journey to India. The personnel of the Airship Guarantee Company and the crew of R 100 had confidence in the ship, and while the Cardington work force had been frantically concentrating on R 101's problems, the "capitalist" ship's crew had been quietly preparing her for the transatlantic journey. On July 25, 1930, R 100 was brought out of the Cardington shed and put on the mast, and there was a trial flight on July 25-26, largely to test internal modifications designed to support the outer cover in the wake of the engine cars. At 0248 on July 29, R 100 departed the mast at Cardington, carrying 34.5 tons of petrol, 1.5 tons of oil, and 5.5 tons of water ballast. The crew numbered 37 and there were seven passengers and officials, including Burney and Norway, representing the Airship Guarantee Company; Colmore, the Director of Airship Development, and Squadron Leader Wann, the surviving captain of the R 38. Scott, the Assistant Director (Flying) was carried as a crew member, and in effect was in charge of the flight.[40]

The journey was uneventful, except for two emergencies at the end, and the airship normally cruised at 60 knots on three engines. On the other hand, she was able to use weather forecasts for "pressure pattern flying" in the Eckener tradition, achieving a higher ground speed by going around the north side of a low pressure area west of Ireland. Navigation was by sun sights, drift sights by day and night, and radio bearings and positions from steamers. At 2115 local time on July 30 the airship reached North America at Belle Isle, 46 hours and 27 minutes after leaving Cardington. From here to Montreal the wind was ahead, influenced by a deep depression over Hudson's Bay.

The first mishap of the journey occurred next day about 1500 over the Isle aux Coudres some fifty miles from Quebec. Booth had been persuaded to open up the engines to 70 knots, with a view to reaching Montreal before dark, when the ship was struck by violent turbulence spilling down from the mountains to the north. She rolled heavily (Norway thought at least 10 degrees) and pitched rapidly over the same range. Immediately the starboard and after engine gondolas rang for assistance. As in the "Graf Zeppelin's" encounter with the squall line on her first Atlantic crossing, the violent movement in turbulent air had been too much for the fin coverings, with tears in the lower and starboard fins, and in the lower cover of the port fin, "a hole large enough to drive a bus through."[41] The ship was held at low speed in the head wind over the Isle aux Oies for two hours, while riggers climbed about on the wires and girders of the horizontal stabilizers stitching tears together, and on the port fin, making fast a large patch derived from the corridor cover. The engines were then opened to half speed and the ship moved ahead past Quebec. At 1930 local time R 100 was near Trois Rivières and it was almost dark; a small but vicious-looking thunderstorm was approaching, and Scott chose to take the ship into the storm instead of going around it. Violent vertical gusts of 4000 feet per minute carried her to 4500 feet; at one time R 100 had a nose down angle of at least 25 degrees, and later the remains of supper were found to

[40] A curious arrangement contrary to all seafaring tradition, wherein the captain is the ultimate and absolute authority aboard ship. Booth, the C.O. of R 100, and Irwin, the captain of the R 101, seem to have had little independent authority, while Scott, who was always aboard, planned the flight in advance, chose the course, speed and altitude, and had the authority to give orders to flight personnel in the control car.

[41] Nevil Shute, *Slide Rule* (New York: William Morrow & Co., 1954), p. 113.

R 101 at Cardington. (Hepburn Walker collection)

have shot forward along the corridor to Frame 2 well forward. Luckily the airship suffered only minor damage in this entirely avoidable incident, two 12 foot tears in the lower fabric of the starboard fin being promptly repaired. After dodging some further thunderstorms the ship moored to the tower at St. Hubert at 0437 local time on August 1. The elapsed time on the flight was 78 hours 49 minutes, and 3364 nautical miles had been covered at an average speed of 42 knots. The engines had burned 29.5 tons of fuel, but the ship arrived with 4.5 tons more of water ballast than she had on board when departing Cardington, having collected rain water.

A 25 hour flight on August 10-11 carried 17 Canadian military and civic leaders and reporters on a tour over Ottawa, Niagara Falls, Toronto and Kingston. On approaching the mast the reduction gearing of the starboard forward engine failed, the gear casing breaking up and causing some damage. It was decided that R 100 could make the homeward flight safely on 5 engines, counting on the prevailing westerlies. This in fact proved to be the case, the return journey on August 14-16 being uneventful except for the failure of the electrical system in the passenger quarters, which meant there was no heating or hot food. The time homeward bound was 57 hours 36 minutes. The day following her return, R 100 was walked into the Cardington shed – never to emerge again in one piece.

All attention was now focused on R 101 and the planned flight to India. No drama in the history of the rigid airship is so poignant as the inevitable tragedy which followed. On the one side was the responsible Minister of State, Lord Thomson of Cardington, the enthusiastic amateur so blind as to have publicly declared "she is as safe as a house – except for the millionth chance." Determined to use the airship to promote his political future, he was demanding adherence to his personal schedule regardless of reality. On the other side were his subordinates – some of whom merely wished for more time, others who knew R 101 was a bad airship – who dared not confront Thomson with the truth. Dowding certainly would have had the courage to deal with the politician, but "was not sufficiently self-confident to set my individual opinion against that of the technical experts."[4][2] Those closest to the project were indeed still sanguine. Colmore would have objected to cancelling the India flight, and not merely from motives of self-interest; the displeasure of Lord Thomson would have put an end to the rigid airship program which had meant so much to the Cardington community over a period of six years. Richmond and Rope were satisfied, or else kept their opinions to themselves. Scott was a blind optimist in the Count Zeppelin and Peter Strasser tradition; certain critical decisions he took in connection with R 101's last flight made her destruction certain. Irwin, the captain, seems to have had premonitions of disaster, but had been robbed of the power and authority associated with his title, and was a very tired man. Brancker, the Director of Civil Aviation, who was expected to make the India flight, seems to have tried to reason with Thomson but swallowed his doubts along with his resentment when the minister accused him of "showing the white feather." Booth and Meager, after flying in R 101, thought of her as a thoroughly bad airship and were resolved not to fly in her further unless directly ordered to; but their advice was not sought.

Working desperately, the Cardington staff "gassed up" the rebuilt airship with the new bay on September 26, 1930, and had her ready to fly the following day; but not until October 1 was the weather calm enough to bring her out of the shed and to the tower. That

[4][2] Robert Wright, *The Man Who Won The Battle Of Britain* (New York: Charles Scribner's Sons, 1969), p. 52.

same day she made a trial flight. Intended to last 24 hours, it was cut to 16 hours 51 minutes so that in Colmore's words, "we may have a chance, if all goes well, of starting on Friday evening (October 3)."[43] The weather was very pleasant, and provided no test of the ship's ability to handle a storm. Nor was it possible to make a full speed test as the oil cooler broke down in the starboard forward engine. The ship in fact never did make a full speed test: it was even suggested that she should do this during the India flight!

Lord Thomson was now pressing for a start on the evening of October 3, or the morning of October 4, but was persuaded to delay the departure until the evening of the 4th to afford the crew a rest. In conversation with Colmore, Thomson is recorded as saying, "you must not allow my natural impatience or anxiety to start to influence you in any way. You must use your considered judgment."[44] This the harassed officials of the Royal Airship Works were not doing, and were not in a position to do. As Squadron Leader Booth, the commander of R 100, regretfully observed at the subsequent inquiry.

> I feel that their decision to leave, or their agreement to leave, at that time was biased by the fact of the Imperial Conference coming off, and the psychological moment in airships when they could carry the Secretary of State to India, and bring him back to time. It biased their judgment in agreeing to fly. If that Imperial Conference had not been coming off, I feel confident that they would have insisted on more trials.[45]

At 1503 on October 4, Irwin was handed a forecast which predicted for the period 1300 October 4 to 0100 October 5 "upper wind at 2000 feet. Direction 270° to 240°. Speed (mph) 20 to 30 mph in Northern France, lighter in southern France."[46] At 1836 the airship slipped from the Cardington tower, the wind freshening and gusty. On board was a crew of 5 officers and 37 men, six officials from the Royal Airship Works including Colmore, Scott, Richmond and Rope, and six passengers including Lord Thomson, his valet, and Sir W. Sefton Brancker, the Director of Civil Aviation. One official, Mr. Harry J. Leech; a wireless operator, Arthur Disley; and four engineers, Joseph Binks, A.V. Bell, A.J. Cook, and Victor Savory, were to be the only survivors of the tragedy which eight hours later left the enormous craft a blackened ruin in the fields near Beauvais.

[43] Cmd. 3825, *Report of the R 101 Inquiry* (London: HMSO, 1931), p. 62.
[44] *ibid.*, p. 67.
[45] *ibid.*, p. 66.
[46] *ibid.*, p. 105.

On departure R 101 was carrying 25 tons of fuel oil and 9¼ tons of water ballast, but 4 tons of this were dropped in departing the mast as the ship was already heavy. If more ballast had to be released forward, it would have to be hand-dropped by sending a man into the nose.

Rain was falling as R 101 circled Bedford, and climbed to 1500 feet, above her pressure height of 1000 feet, meaning that she lost about 3 tons of lift. At 2021 she was over London, and announced her intention of proceeding via Paris, Tours, Toulouse and Narbonne. At about this time an amended forecast was wirelessed to the airship indicating an unexpected deterioration in the weather: "Forecast next 12 hours flight S.E. England, Channel, Northern France Wind at 2000 feet from about 240 degrees, 40 to 50 mph."[47] In other words, on a dark, rainy night R 101 would have to battle a head wind which would reduce her ground speed to 10 to 20 mph, in worse weather than she had ever encountered. Norway, who was aboard R 100 when Major Scott ordered her steered through the thunder squall on the Canadian flight, severely criticises Scott for not abandoning the flight in the face of the forecast and returning to Cardington to wait for better weather.[48] The responsibility for going on was certainly Scott's, for Irwin had been left with no voice in decisions affecting the flight planning of the airship of which he was captain.

The crossing of the Channel took two hours, and it was not until 2336 that R 101 reported reaching the French coast at Pointe de St. Quentin. She was delayed by a loss in oil pressure in the rear engine which had to be shut down for two hours. Leech, Binks, and Bell were all involved in getting the engine going again. Meanwhile, as in earlier flights, R 101 was undoubtedly becoming heavy even while burning fuel, not only from the weight of rain water on the outer envelope, but undoubtedly from loss of hydrogen through the gas valves, and from damage to the gas bags as they surged back and forth while the airship pitched in the turbulent air. Leech, looking out of the rear gondola, estimated the ship's altitude over the Channel at only 700 to 800 feet, while Disley, in the control car at 10 pm saw the First Officer take the elevator wheel from the elevator man and himself climb the ship from 900 to 1000 feet, ordering the man thereafter "do not let her go below 1000 feet."[49] Witnesses on

[47] Cmd. 3825, p. 105.
[48] Shute, p. 137
[49] Cmd. 3825, p. 72.

the ground who watched her struggle against the wind agreed that she was very low; some thought she was trying to land. It took R 101 two and a half hours to cover the 62 miles from Pointe de St. Quentin to Beauvais, at a ground speed of 25 mph.

At 0200, as R 101 passed Beauvais, the watch changed. A few minutes later the airship got into a long and steep dive. She then leveled off, doubtless through the application of full up elevator, but failed to gain altitude, and then put her nose down again, striking the ground with the underside of her bows. Undoubtedly the control car personnel anticipated a crash, for before she reached the ground the engine telegraphs transmitted an order to slow the engines, while Disley, asleep in the crew's quarters, was awakened by Coxswain Hunt passing through and calling, "We're down, lads." Rigger Church, who lived for three days after the disaster, testifed that he was ordered forward to release half a ton of ballast in the nose, but before he could reach it the crash occurred. The impact was not severe, but was immediately followed by an explosion and a violent hydrogen fire.

The Court of Inquiry, presided over by Sir John Simon, had little to go on, and Lord Brabazon of Tara, one of Sir John's assessors, told Dr. Robin Higham years later that the Court never did find out what caused R 101 to crash.[50] Several hypotheses were eliminated at the outset: that there had been structural failure in flight was disproven by the intact state of the wreckage at the crash site; and that some long-drawn-out emergency had occurred, such as a progressive loss of gas or a fire in the crew's quarters, was disproven by the routine change of watch a few minutes before the crash. The official explanation as put forth in the "Report of the R 101 Inquiry" assumed a massive deflation of a forward gas bag, perhaps after failure of the outer cover on top of the ship. Extensive model tests were run at the National Physical Laboratory which demonstrated that the loss of lift from a sudden gas bag failure forward would inevitably bring the ship to the ground, though whether she would impact nose-down or tail down would depend on her attitude at the time of the gas bag deflation. One theoretical flight path, assuming 6 tons general heaviness, a 6 ton loss of gas from Cell 3, and a gust of 20 ft/sec with a 10 ft/sec downward component, very closely resembled the descent and crash as described by the survivors.[51]

[50] Higham, p. 308.
[51] Cmd. 3825, Figure 6, p. 126.

Much rarer than the "Report" is the "Minutes of the Proceedings at the Public Inquiry into the Loss of the Airship R 101,"[52] a 13-part document presenting in full the testimony on every one of the 13 days of the inquiry. I shall never forget my utter astonishment on reading in the "Minutes" testimony that R 101, *even with the new bay,* would not have had enough lift to return from Karachi to Ismailia in most months of the year, as high temperatures at Karachi would prevent her from loading sufficient fuel. In June the ship would require *24 tons of fuel over and above her normal lifting capacity* for the Karachi-Baghdad leg alone, and other summer and fall months were equally bad. These estimates had been prepared from meteorological data going back forty years, and were well known to Colmore, Scott and others, though apparently not to Thomson.

A final note of unintentional macabre humor is provided by the spiritualistic seances in which Major Villiers, a friend of Brancker, obtained "testimony" about the loss of R 101 from interrogating the ghosts of Brancker, Irwin, Scott and other officers of the ship. These offered the plausible suggestion that the entire party had set out knowing they could not even reach Egypt, but would at least vindicate their honor by starting out, and then landing in France, possibly at Le Bourget, and plead the bad weather as a reason for aborting the flight. Villiers attempted to persuade Sir John Simon to accept the spiritualistic evidence, with an effect on that distinguished jurist that can only be imagined.[53]

Today there stands at the side of the Beauvais-Paris road near the hamlet of Allonne an impressive monument bearing the arms of France and Great Britain and the inscription "À la Mémoire des Victimes de la Catastrophe du Dirigeable R.101 5. Octobre 1930." This does not of course mark the site, which is on a hill half a mile away. Here is where the ship crashed and burned, with her nose in the Bois des Coutumes and her tail in an open field. On the edge of the wood is a small obelisk, the *petit carrefour,* marking the site and bearing the simple inscription, "Dirigeable R 101, 5 Octobre 1930."[54]

[52] HMSO, London, 1931. Copy provided by Charles Keller.
[53] James Leasor, *The Millionth Chance, The Story of the R 101* (London: Hamish Hamilton, 1957), pp. 166-74.
[54] The ship breaking firm of Thomas Ward of Sheffield was hired to break up and cart away the wreckage, but when I visited the *petit carrefour* in the summer of 1937 the woods were full of the steel shear and gasbag wiring of the airship which the wreckers had not bothered to carry away.

It also marks the end of an Imperial dream. The loss of the giant airship from which so much had been expected, and whose thoroughly bad qualities had been concealed from the public, together with a Cabinet minister and so many brave men, produced a thrill of horror and revulsion, not only in the British public but also in the Labour government. Plans for a larger R 102 were abandoned, and the successful "capitalist" rival, the R 100, was broken up in the Cardington shed in 1931.

VIII
Does the rigid airship have a future?

Seemingly the rigid airship era came to an end with the dismantling of the LZ 127 "Graf Zeppelin" and LZ 130 "Graf Zeppelin II" at Frankfurt in the spring of 1940. Yet in the period since the end of World War II, literally countless proposals have been made to revive the rigid airship, and much design work has been done with a view to creating a craft as large as 33,000,000 cubic feet. Certainly the rigid airship has not lost its ability to fascinate and enthrall, and its supporters continue to see it competing successfully with both the surface ship and the aeroplane as a carrier of cargo. Unfortunately the last word has not rested with the engineers and technologists, but with the financiers: none of the dreamers has been able to obtain either from private capitalists or from the government the millions needed to bring back the large rigid airship.

It would be tedious to review all the proposals made, but the more serious ones by responsible organisations will be briefly recited, bearing in mind that this volume attempts to limit itself to rigid airships *built and flown*.

On the eve of World War II, with the "Graf Zeppelin II," the sister ship of the "Hindenburg," in limited operation, the Zeppelin Company of Friedrichshafen commenced work on the LZ 131. General arrangement drawings show that she would have closely resembled "Hindenburg" with an additional gas cell, giving a volume of 7,875,022 cubic feet, length of 869.46 feet, and diameter of 136.8 feet. The passenger accomodations would have extended over two bays for a total length of 108 feet, and there would have been fifty 2-berth cabins, 22 of which would have had windows on the outside of the ship. Only a few rings were completed before the war broke out; during the conflict the Zeppelin works, with its two building hangars, was bombed out of existence by the R.A.F.

Not until 1952, when Germany had recovered to some extent from the chaos of defeat, was an attempt made to revive the Zeppelin passenger airship. Dr. Eckener, 84 years old and convinced the airship could not compete with the transatlantic aeroplane, played no part in this attempted come-back, and died two years later

316

on August 14, 1954. It was left primarily to Max Pruss, the last captain of the "Hindenburg," to lead the effort. For the next eight years until his death on November 28, 1960, Pruss, with the slogan "if you want to travel quickly, take an aeroplane. If you want to travel comfortably, take an airship," fought continuously to interest financial circles in advanced Zeppelin designs. These began in 1957 with a reworking of the LZ 131 with four 1800 hp diesels to carry 100 passengers at a speed of 100 mph. A cargo airship of the same dimensions was to have carried 42 tons of freight at a somewhat lower speed. Still later in January, 1958, came a proposal for a 10,500,000 cubic foot Zeppelin, 920 feet long and 154 feet in diameter, which would have carried 200 passengers or 70 tons of cargo. All of these airships would have been inflated with American helium, with electrical heating units in the gas cells which in the hangar or at the mast could superheat the helium by $18°F$. Pruss did not succeed in finding any financial backing for these designs and the operations proposed with them. A major obstacle to realizing these German ambitions was the total destruction of the Zeppelin works.[1] Nor was the successor company, the *Zeppelin Metallwerke G.m.b.H.*, at all interested in rigid airships; it limited its production to radar antennae, tank trucks, and caterpillar tractors, for which it held the European manufacturing rights.[2]

The Goodyear Aircraft Corporation in the period immediately after World War II made a considerable effort to develop public and governmental support for a trans-oceanic airship line. It was intended that the ships be built in the Air Dock at Akron, operate from former naval airship stations on both coasts (the standard wooden arch blimp hangars built during the war at bases up and down both coasts measured 1026 feet long, 157 feet high and 235 feet wide), and no hangars were required at the overseas terminals, where the ships would have moored to stub masts. Initially Goodyear intended to build for this service 10,000,000 cubic foot ships of fairly conventional Zeppelin design, except for the introduction of bow elevators as well as the conventional ones at the tail. The hull would

---

[1] A new building shed measuring 936 x 181 x 181 feet was to be erected at Tettnang, 5½ miles east of Friedrichshafen. With all necessary facilities the cost was estimated at 15,967,000 marks. A new operating base at Frankfurt with one similar shed would cost 17,500,000 marks. On the other hand the cost of the reworked LZ 131 was estimated at 20,000,000 marks, and for the larger ship 24,000,000 marks.

[2] Luftschiffbau Zeppelin Friedrichshafen (Erich Hilligardt & Andreas Sperger): *Bericht über die Luftschiffstudie LZ 132. II. Nachtrag zum Bericht über die Luftschiffstudie LZ 132: 300,000 m³ Fahrgast u. Frachtluftschiff.*

measure 950 feet in length and 142 feet in diameter, and there would have been six engine gondolas in pairs. The operating range would have been 6000 miles with 35 per cent fuel reserve, and a crew of 40 with 20 stewards, cooks, etc. Unlike the Germans, who enclosed the passenger quarters within the hull, Goodyear's designers contemplated a long external gondola forward under the hull. Internally, this could be arranged to meet a number of requirements, from private staterooms with luxurious public rooms for 112 passengers to airline type reclining seats for 288 passengers on an overnight run to Hawaii, or an all-cargo version to handle 90 tons of freight on the same route.[3] At the invitation of President Litchfield of Goodyear, Dr. Eckener in 1947 spent seven months in the United States acting as consultant on this design.[4] No government subsidy was forthcoming, and the 10,000,000 cubic foot passenger ship was never built.

Great Britain, after the R 101 disaster, lost interest in the rigid airship, though plans were drawn at the time for an R 102, with a gas volume of 7,380,000 cubic feet, length of 814 feet, and diameter of 147 feet. Gross lift was to be 226.5 tons, and fixed weights estimated at 128 tons plus 19 or 15 tons further depending on different power installations, burning hydrogen and liquid fuel.[5] The ship was to carry 50 passengers, and a crew of 44, and to be suitable for either the North Atlantic service or the route to India. R 102 remained a paper scheme of course, and only the two hangars at Cardington survive today to recall Britian's onetime interest in the rigid airship. On the other hand, a British shipping firm, Manchester Liners, a pioneer in containerized cargo operations, has recently set up a subsidiary, Cargo Airships Ltd., under Mr. Max Rynish as managing director. Newspaper publicity indicates their intention to build cargo airships to handle containerized packages of up to 10 tons, which will be air-lifted to the top of the hull by helicopter and lowered into the hold by a lift. Thus the Rynish airship would not have to land at its destination. Detailed specifications have not been worked out, but the traditional Zeppelin construction methods will not be followed.

[3] P.W. Litchfield & Hugh Allen, *Why? Has America No Rigid Airships?* (Cleveland: Corday & Gross Co., 1945), pp. 119-24.
[4] This invitation reflected Litchfield's personal affection for Dr. Eckener rather than a need for his services. Following Eckener's death, Litchfield presented to the "Cathedral of the Air" at the Naval Air Station, Lakehurst, N.J., a beautiful stained glass window in his memory, depicting the progress of aerostatics. The burning hot air and hydrogen balloon of Pilatre de Rozier symbolizes "sacrifice," and the "Graf Zeppelin" represents "achievement."
[5] Information by courtesy of Mr. Donald Woodward.

The hull may be a stressed-skin shell of spun duralumin or plastic, with some internal girder reinforcement. If a prototype is built, it would be tailored to the dimensions of the Cardington hangars, but there is talk of ultimately building a 33,000,000 cubic foot craft (helium inflated, of course), 1300 feet long and with a useful lift of 500 tons.[6]

With the advent of atomic power, several engineers saw the peculiar advantages of mating the large rigid airship to the nuclear reactor. Many of the difficulties which caused the United States Government to abandon the program to power an aeroplane with a nuclear reactor would be eliminated by sending it aloft in a rigid airship: the considerable weight of the reactor and ancillary steam turbines and generators could easily be borne by the large rigid, indeed, the total weight of the nuclear installation might be less for the same horsepower than the conventional petrol or diesel power plant plus the tons of fuel needed for long distance ocean crossings. Further, the range of the nuclear airship would be essentially unlimited. Shielding of the airship crew against radiation would be easier than in the aeroplane, as the reactor could be installed at a considerable distance from the passenger and crew spaces. Lastly, nuclear power offers to the airship the peculiar advantage of a constant gross weight even on a long flight, eliminating the need either to valve helium or to recover water from the exhaust gases as in the airship with internal combustion engines. The atomic power concept was briefly introduced to the general public in 1957 by Edwin J. Kirschner in his *The Zeppelin In The Atomic Age:* The book was a general survey of the subject, but embodied sketches of a 10,000,000 cubic foot nuclear powered rigid with retractible floats for landing on water, radar inside the transparent nose and a large stern propeller.[7]

Kirschner offered no detailed plans, but such were elaborated about 1966 by Professor Francis Morse of Boston University, an engineer with some previous experience with the Goodyear Aircraft Corporation. His rigid craft, of 12,500,000 cubic foot volume, 980 feet long and 172 feet in diameter, was to carry 400 passengers at a top speed of 103 mph. The nuclear power plant would develop 6000 hp, of which 4000 hp would be absorbed by a pair of large contrarotating propellers in the tail cone, and 2000 hp by boundary

---

[6] *The Times,* May 15, 1971.
[7] Edward J. Kirschner, *The Zeppelin In The Atomic Age,* (Urbana: University of Illinois Press, 1957), p. 39.

layer control ducts installed aft. The palatial passenger quarters would be forward, and aft of them would be a hangar to accomodate an 18-passenger hook-on plane which could shuttle passengers between the ground and the airship. The nuclear plant would be still farther aft, 630 feet from the nose, in an expansion of the stem to stern axial corridor, the entire installation with shielding being enclosed in a pressurized steel sphere 13 feet in diameter. While the weight of the sphere would be 50 tons, this would still be less than the fuel required for long flights in such an airship with internal combustion engines.[8] Professor Morse's plans attracted considerable popular attention for a brief period, but no company was ever formed to build the airship, which certainly was technically feasible.

All these projects except the Rynish scheme involved conventional Zeppelin construction methods, with a hull framework built up of girderwork rings and longitudinals braced with wire, a doped fabric outer cover and separate gas cells of fabric lined with a gas-tight substance. The Zeppelin design, with a triplicated structure of a metal hull frame with separate fabric gas cells and outer cover, is often criticized as redundant. This complexity of structure is inefficient, particularly in terms of empty weight. However, it was conceived in an era when skilled labour was cheap. Such a hand-crafted vehicle, built today at prevailing wages, might be too expensive to compete in the transportation market.

Nonetheless, the only rigid airship built since the LZ 130 "Graf Zeppelin II" owed much to Zeppelin concepts. This craft, an experimental prototype named "Aereon III," was constructed at the Mercer County Airport within a few miles of my home in Pennington, N.J., U.S.A., and I was privileged to see it at every stage of its construction and to know the enthusiasts promoting the concept. The driving force behind the enterprise was the Reverend Monroe Drew Jr. of Trenton, N.J., a clergyman deeply concerned with the needs of undeveloped countries and their requirements for the transportation of goods in the absence of proper highways. Further, Rev. Drew had been impressed with the feats of Dr. Solomon Andrews, a physician of Perth Amboy, N.J., who between 1863 and 1865 built two airships — "Aereon I" and "Aereon II" — which he claimed could progress through the air without an engine. "Aereon I" consisted of three cigar-shaped balloons arranged to form a flat surface 80 feet long and 39 feet wide, and the resulting "lifting body" could be made to travel forward in ascension by releasing ballast, and in descent by valving

[8] *Wingfoot LTA Society Bulletin*, vol. 14, No. 1. November, 1966, p. 2.

gas. A speed of 25 mph was claimed and was probably achieved. "Aereon II" used the same inclined plane principle with a single balloon 85 feet long and 50 feet wide, which could be flattened by a strap running around it longitudinally in the vertical plane. Publicity concerning "Aereon III" suggested sometimes that it would progress without power in the same manner as its predecessors, but such was not the intention of its designer, the former Navy Lieut. Comdr. John Fitzpatrick, who had at one time been an engineering officer in a Navy airship squadron. He endeavored merely to create a gas-filled lifting airfoil as efficient as possible aerodynamically while not rendering the structure unduly complicated to build. He also intended to take advantage of all the technological and aerodynamic advances of the past twenty years insofar as they could be applied to airship design and construction.

The basic structure of "Aereon III" was thus three streamlined rigid hulls 83 feet long and 17½ feet in diameter, connected in parallel by a faired structure of airfoil section to form a low aspect ratio surface 55 feet in maximum width. The rigid hulls closely resembled Zeppelin practice, except that duralumin tubing substituted for triangular girders. There were seven 20-sided main rings with radial wire bracing attached to a central fitting, and three intermediate rings between each main one. There were 20 longitudinals of duralumin tubing, and shear wire bracing as in Zeppelin practice. The eighteen gas cells, fitted with manoeuvring and automatic valves, were fabricated of Tedlar plastic. The ship however was designed to be 400 lb. heavy when filled 85 per cent with helium, and in order to fly without releasing gas or ballast, the helium was to be warmed by propane burners under each cell. A double outer cover – Tedlar on the outside and doped nylon inside – was expected to minimize heat loss. The power plant was to be an 80 hp Solar Titan gas turbine right aft in the central hull, and turning a 21-foot 2-bladed helicopter rotor in the vertical plane. Two pilots occupied a glazed-in cockpit in the nose of the central hull and operated the large elevons between the hulls aft, and the two rudders attached to the fins located aft beneath the outboard hulls. There were steerable wheels at the bottom of the fins, and forward under the central hull, an ingenious "internal mooring mast," with a wheel at its lower end, which could be retracted into the hull to confer a negative angle of attack for tying down in a wind, or extended to create a positive angle of attack for a dynamic takeoff. [9]

[9] Douglas H. Robinson, "The 'Aereon III'." *Wingfoot LTA Society Bulletin*, vol. 9, No. 10, September 1962, p. 2.

Aereon 111 under construction at the Mercer County Airport, Trenton, New Jersey, U.S.A., probably in 1964. This view shows the triple-hull craft from the rear. The interior structure of the three Zeppelin-type rigid hulls is well shown, with longitudinals, diamond-truss main rings and intermediate rings made of duralumin tubing. The outer cover is of Tedlar plastic. One of the two fins under the outer hulls is shown, covered with duralumin sheet, also the elevons fitted horizontally between the ends of the hulls. The engine was to go in the open space at the rear of the centre hull. (Aereon Corporation, Princeton, N.J.)

The designers and builders were beset with a multitude of technical problems as well as financial difficulties, and the ship unfortunately never flew. I first became aware of "Aereon III's" existence late in 1960 on discovering a series of welded duralumin tubing rings of Zeppelin pattern on a hangar floor at the airport, and soon was let in on the secret, making my two small children promise not to tell what they had seen to anyone. A major stumbling block was the Solar Titan gas turbine; finally a McCulloch drone engine was substituted for it. Not until April 1966 was "Aereon III" taken out of its hangar for publicity photographs and taxiing tests, and in one of these came disaster − a gust of wind during a too-sharp turn flipped the bulky, lightweight craft upside down and then back on its wheels, badly smashed. Rebuilding not only involved enlarging the lifting body to a delta shape measuring 100 x 75 feet, completely filling in the space between the hulls, and skinning the craft with metal, but also using a gas turbine to turn the helicopter rotor. Financial difficulties at this point forced the company to cease operations and in the summer of 1967 the partially reconstructed "Aereon IIIB" was dismantled. The company's dream of building the "Aereon 340," a delta lifting body airship 340 feet long and designed to carry eight or more truck trailers at 150 mph, has not so far been realized.

Harking back to Chapter VI and the ZMC-2 Metalclad airship of Ralph Upson, there is considerable consensus among engineers and others familiar with the rigid airship and its capabilities that if any are built in the future, they will be of the Metalclad type. The ZMC-2 as a prototype convincingly demonstrated the multiple advantages of the simple Metaclad shell, not only as a load carrying structure but also as an impermeable gas container, while its durability was far superior to that of fabric outer cover or cotton and gelatin-latex gas cells. Further, the essential hull structure was rapidly fabricated by a more or less automatic machine riveting process (nowadays cementing the metal sheets with epoxy resins would be practical and even simpler). Certainly the production costs of a large Metalclad would be well below those of the conventional Zeppelin design today.

Summing up, it must be admitted that the rigid airship, superior in the early days in range and weight carrying capacity, was equalled in these respects by the still faster aeroplane after some forty years of development. Dr. Eckener, profoundly pessimistic after living through a second World War in which Germany was devastated as well as defeated, wrote in 1949,

> A tremendous war which, as always in life-and-death struggles between great
> peoples, had forced the rapid technical development of the weapons of
> victory without regard to cost and effort, had furthermore forced an
> enormous development and improvement in aeroplane performance, so that
> planes were now in a position to carry on a transoceanic service. The airship's
> monopoly was broken. And, since the aeroplane is much faster and can fly a
> given distance in half the time or less than is needed by an airship, the role of
> this aerial vehicle in commerce seems to have been ended after a brief period
> of glory, just as it had been developed to the point of acceptance, for speed
> and time-saving are trump cards in today's hurried age, which has almost
> completely discarded space and distance as obsolete concepts in its plans and
> undertakings. What does the airship have to offer now to the businessman or
> statesman in a hurry to cross the Atlantic Ocean?[10]

Dr. Eckener's admirer and supporter, F. Willy von Meister, the
American representative of the Zeppelin *Reederei* during the
"Hindenburg" era, believes that the transoceanic Zeppelin airship
might have survived economically until about 1950, if its operators
and supporters had not made four political mistakes: (1) using the
early Zeppelins for bombing civilians in World War I, leading to an
Allied resolve to destroy the German airship industry instead of
fostering its expansion for international commerce with American
participation. (2) the refusal of the United States Government to
permit the export of helium, seen in retrospect as being indispensable
to a safe passenger carrying operation. (3) Dr. Eckener's decision to
inflate the "Hindenburg" with hydrogen in the spring of 1936,
instead of waiting to see if the American Congress would not have
permitted the export of helium – this step leading directly to the
catastrophe at Lakehurst on May 6, 1937. (4) World War II being
provoked by the Nazi regime.[11]

Lastly, I believe myself that the gruesome photographs of the
"Hindenburg" burning at Lakehurst, faithfully reprinted by the
newspapers yearly on May 6, have served powerfully to convince the
American public that the rigid airship was an inflammable death trap,
and at this late date they are unlikely to believe otherwise.

Nonetheless, it is still a corollary of the immutable laws of physics
that a thousand cubic feet of helium will support 68 pounds in the
air, while the power to move the load carried *aerostatically* is far less
than that required both to move and to sustain in the air a similar

---

[10] Eckener, *Im Zeppelin über Länder und Meere*, p. 559.
[11] F. Willy von Meister, "My Decade with Dr. Eckener and his Zeppelins." *Wingfoot LTA
Society Bulletin*, vol. 18, No. 12, July-August, 1971, p. 2.

load *aerodynamically*. While initial costs may be high (they are high also today for the jet aircraft), the airship will always be the cheapest, though not the fastest, way to move cargo by air. Uncontestably it has in the past, and could still in the future, provide a degree of luxury and comfort for passengers that subsonic or supersonic jet airliners could never hope to match. All kinds of technological advances made in the last twenty years for the benefit of the aeroplane would benefit the airship also — the geared turboprop power plant comes to mind immediately as being ideal for the airship by reason of its simplicity and reliability; the large, low speed propellers would have variable pitch and be reversible; modern instruments, radios and electronic navigational aids would be equally adaptable to the airship. Ground handling problems were largely solved years ago by the U.S. Navy, and the atomic powered rigid airship could cruise indefinitely, entering a hangar only once a year to be inspected and overhauled. The obstacles are not technical, they are psychological and financial; and if attitudes change and the money is forthcoming, we may still some day see again the giants in the sky which thrilled and enthralled our parents with their awesome size and majesty.

Bibliography

CHAPTER I

Berg, Carl. *David Schwarz – Carl Berg – Graf Zeppelin. Ein Beitrag zur Geschichte der Luftschiffart.* München: Eigenverlag, 1926.

Eckener, Hugo. "Der Lenkbare Ballon" in *Die Eroberung der Luft.* Stuttgart: Union Deutsche Verlagsgesellschaft, 1909.

Report by Capt. Charles Renard, "The First Flight of 'La France'." *The Airship* (London), vol. 2, no. 8, Jan.-Mar. 1936.

Rolt, L.T.C. *The Aeronauts. A History of Ballooning, 1783-1903.* London: Longmans, Green & Co. Ltd. 1966.

Santos Dumont, Alberto. *My Airships.* London: Grant Richards, 1904.

Wykeham, Peter. *Santos Dumont. A Study in Obsession.* New York: Harcourt, Brace & World, Inc., 1962.

CHAPTER II

Anon. *Der Erste Aufstieg des Zeppelin-Ballon in Manzell bei Friedrichshafen am Bodensee 2. Juli 1900.* Zürich; Polygraphisches Institut A.G., n.d. (1900).

Colsman, Alfred. *Luftschiff Voraus!* Stuttgart u. Berlin: Deutsche Verlags Anstalt, 1933.

Dürr, Ludwig. *25 Jahre Zeppelin-Luftschiffbau.* Berlin: VDI-Verlag G.m.b.H., 1924.

Hacker, Georg. *Die Männer von Manzell.* Frankfurt am Main: Societäts-Druckerei G.m.b.H., 1936.

Hildebrandt, Hans (ed.) *Zeppelin-Denkmal für das deutsche Volk.* Stuttgart: Germania-Verlag G.m.b.H., n.d. (1925).

Eckener, Hugo. *Graf Zeppelin.* Stuttgart: J.G. Cott'sche Buchhandlung Nachfolger, 1938.

Eckener, Hugo. *Im Zeppelin über Länder und Meere.* Flensburg: Verlagshaus Christian Wolff, 1949.

Kollmann, Franz. *Das Zeppelinluftschiff.* Berlin: Verlag von M. Krayn, 1924.

Kriegswissenschaftliche Abteilung der Luftwaffe. *Die deutschen Luftstreitkräfte in ihrer Entstehung bis zum Ende des Weltkrieges 1918. Die Militärluftfahrt bis zum Beginn des Weltkrieges 1914.* Berlin: E.S. Mittler u. Sohn, 1941.

Lehmann, Ernst A., & Adelt, Leonhard. *Auf Luftpatrouille und Weltfahrt.* Leipzig: Schmidt u. Günther, 1936.

Luftschiffbau Zeppelin. *Das Werk Zeppelins, eine Festgabe zu seinem 75. Geburtstags.* Stuttgart: Kommissionsverlag Julius Hoffman, 1913.

Müller-Breslau, Prof. Dr. Ing. "Zur Geschichte des Zeppelin-Luftschiffes." *Verhandlung zur Beförderung des Gewerbfleisses.* Januar 1914, p. 35.

Rosenkranz, Hans. *Ferdinand Graf von Zeppelin.* Berlin: Ullstein Verlag 1931.

von Schiller, Hans. *Zeppelin: Wegbereiter des Weltluftverkehrs.* Bad Godesberg: Kirschbaum Verlag, n.d. (1967).

Wingfoot Lighter Than Air Society Bulletin, Akron, Ohio, vol. 12, no. 10; vol. 13, nos. 1,3,5,6.

Die Woche. Zeppelin: 15. Sonderheft der "Woche". Berlin: August Scherl Verlag, n.d. (1908).

Zeppelin, Dr. Ing. Graf, *Erfahrungen beim Bau von Luftschiffen.* Berlin: Verlag von Julius Springer, 1908.

CHAPTER III

Deutsche Luftschiffahrts-Aktien-Gesellschaft, *Passagier-Fahrten mit Zeppelin Luftschiffen.* Hamburg, 1911.

Eyb's DELAG-Fuhrer, *Im Luftschiff über Hamburg (Frankfurt am Main, Berlin, Leipzig,* etc.), Stuttgart: Verlag von Gustav Eyb, 1913.

Great Britain, Public Record Office, "Examination of 'M', an ex-employee of Messrs. Schütte-Lanz Airship Constructors at Mannheim-Rheinau, August, 1916."

Nauticus: Das Jahrbuch deutschen Seeinteressen. Berlin: E.S. Mittler u. Sohn, 1909.

Robinson, Douglas H. "Barnstorming With Champagne." *Journal of the American Aviation Historical Society,* vol. 7, no. 2, Summer 1962, p. 100.

Schütte, Johann (ed.) *Der Luftschiffbau Schütte-Lanz 1909-25.* München u. Berlin: Druck u. Verlag von R. Oldenbourg, 1926.

CHAPTER IV

Engberding, Dietrich. *Luftschiff und Luftschiffahrt in Vergangenheit, Gegenwart und Zukunft.* Berlin: VDI-Verlag G.m.b.H., 1926.

Gamble, C.F. Snowden. *The Story of a North Sea Air Station.* London: Oxford University Press, 1928.

Gladisch, Walter. *Der Krieg in der Nordsee.* vols. VI-VII. Berlin & Frankfurt: E.S. Mittler u. Sohn, 1937, 1965.

Great Britain. Admiralty War Staff, Intelligence Division. C.B. 1265, 1265A, *German Rigid Airships* (Confidential). London: Ordnance Survey, February 1917.

Groos, Otto. *Der Krieg in der Nordsee.* Vols. I-V. Berlin: E.S. Mittler u. Sohn, 1921-25.

Jones, H.A. *The War In The Air.* vols. III, V, with maps. London: Oxford University Press, 1934, 1935.

Lehmann, Ernst A., & Mingos, Howard. *The Zeppelins.* New York: J.H. Sears & Co., 1927.

Morison, Frank (Ross, Albert H.) *War On Great Cities.* London: Faber & Faber, 1937.

Morris, Joseph. *The German Air Raids On Great Britain 1914-18.* London: Sampson, Low, Marston & Co., n.d.

Neumann, Georg Paul. *Die deutsche Luftstreitkräfte im Weltkrieg.* Berlin: E.S. Mittler u. Sohn, 1920.

Robinson, Douglas H. *The Zeppelin In Combat.* London: G.T. Foulis & Co., Ltd., 1962.

Strahlmann, Dr. Fritz (ed.) *Zwei deutsche Luftschiffhäfen des Weltkrieges, Ahlhorn u. Wildeshausen.* Oldenburg: Oldenburger Verlagshaus Lindenallee, 1926.

CHAPTER V

Air Department, Admiralty. *Handbook on Rigid Airship No. 1.* Parts I and II and Appendix. 1913.

Airship Department, Admiralty. *Handbook on Rigid 23 Class Airships.* May 1918.

Byrd, Richard E. *Skyward.* New York: G.P. Putnam's Sons 1928.

Higham, Robin D.S. *The British Rigid Airship 1908-31.* London: G.T. Foulis & Co., Ltd., 1961.

Lewitt, E.H. *The Rigid Airship.* London: Sir Isaac Pitman & Sons Ltd., 1925.

Maitland, Edward M. *The Log of H.M.A. R 34.* London: Hodder & Stoughton, 1920.

Pratt, H.B. *Commercial Airships.* London: Thomas Nelson & Sons Ltd., 1920.

Sinclair, J.A. *Airships in Peace and War.* London: Rich & Cowan, Ltd., 1934.

Ventry, Lord, ed. *The Airship.* Quarterly: vols. I-VI, Spring 1934-Sept. 1939.

Whale, George. *British Airships Past, Present and Future.* London: John Lane, The Bodley Head, 1919.

CHAPTER VI

Burgess, Charles P. *Airship Design.* New York: The Ronald Press, 1927.

Department of the Navy, *Rigid Airship Manual.* Washington: U.S. Govt. Printing Office, 1927.

Eckener, Hugo. "Der Amcrikaflug des ZR III." In Hans Hildebrandt (ed.), *Zeppelin Denkmal für das deutsche Volk.* Stuttgart: Germania-Verlag G.m.b.H., 1925.

Fulton, Garland. *Helium Through WWs I and II.* Naval Engineers Journal, October, 1965, p. 733.

Gleason, Spencer. *Moffett Field. From Lighter-Than-Air to Faster-Than-Sound.* San Jose: Globe Printing Co., 1958.

Hunsaker, Jerome C. *The History of Naval Aviation.* vols. I-IX. Typescript, 1923, copied and mimeographed by Charles L. Keller, 1960.

Keller, Charles L. *U.S.S. "Shenandoah."* West Roxbury, Mass.: World War I Aero Historians, Inc., 1965.

Rosendahl, Charles E. *Up Ship!* New York: Dodd, Mead & Co., 1931.

Rosendahl, Charles E. *What About The Airship?* New York: Charles Scribner's Sons, 1938.

Seibel, Clifford W. *Helium, Child of the Sun.* Lawrence: The University Press of Kansas, 1969.

Smith, Richard K. *An Inventory of U.S. Navy Airships.* Typescript, xeroxed, 1964.

Smith, Richard K. "The Navy's First Sky Hook." *Journal of the American Aviation Historical Society, vol. 6, no. 2, Summer 1961, p. 91.*

Smith, Richard K. "Ralph H. Upson, A Career Sketch and Biography." *Journal of the American Aviation Historical Society,* vol. 13, no. 4, winter, 1968, p. 282.

Smith, Richard K. *The Airships Akron and Macon.* Annapolis, Maryland: U.S. Naval Institute, 1965.

Special Committee on Airships. Report No. 3. *Technical Aspects of the Loss of the Macon.* Stanford: Stanford University Press, 1937.

"Technical Aspects of the Loss of the U.S.S. 'Shenandoah'." *Journal of the American Society of Naval Engineers,* vol. XXXVIII, No. 3, August, 1926, p. 489.

Turnbull, Archibald J., & Lord, Clifford L. *History of United States Naval Aviation.* New Haven: Yale University Press, 1949.

Wittemann, Anton. *Die Amerikafahrt des ZR III.* Wiesbaden: Amsel-Verlag, 1925.

CHAPTER VII

(a) German

Brandt, Rolf. *Mit Luftschiff "Hindenburg" über den Atlantik.* Berlin: Verlag Scherl, n.d. (1936).

Breithaupt, Joachim. *Mit "Graf Zeppelin" nach Süd und Nordamerika.* Lahr (Baden): Verlag von Moritz Schauenburg, 1930

Eckener, Hugo. *Die Amerikafahrt des "Graf Zeppelin."* Berlin: Verlag August Scherl, 1928.

Geisenheyner, Max. *Mit "Graf Zeppelin" um die Welt.* Frankfurt am Main: Societäts-Druckerei, 1929.

Geisenheyner, Max. *E. A. Lehmann, Zeppelin-Kapitän.* Frankfurt-am-Main: Societäts-Verlag, 1937.

Goebel, J., und Förster, Walter. *Afrika zu Unseren Füssen.* Leipzig: Verlag von K.F. Koehler, 1925.

Hoehling, A. A. *Who Destroyed the Hindenburg?* Boston: Little, Brown & Co., 1962.

Knight, R.W. Department of Commerce. Bureau of Air Commerce. Safety & Planning Division. Report No. 11. *The Hindenburg Accident. A Comparative Digest of the Investigations and Findings, with the American and Translated German Reports Included.* August, 1938.

Kohl-Larsen, Dr. L. *Die Arktisfahrt des "Graf Zeppelin."* Berlin: Union Deutsche Verlagsgesellschaft, 1931.
von Langsdorff, Dr. Ing. W. *"LZ 127 Graf Zeppelin," das Luftschiff des deutschen Volkes.* Frankfurt am Main: H. Bechhold Verlagsbuchhandlung, 1928.
von Langsdorff, Dr. Ing. W. *"LZ 129 Hindenburg", das Luftschiff des deutschen Volkes.* Frankfurt am Main: H. Bechhold Verlagsbuchhandlung (Inhaber Breidenstein), 1936.
Robinson, Douglas H. *Famous Aircraft Series: LZ 129 "Hindenburg."* Dallas: Morgan Aviation Books, 1964.
von Schiller, Hans. *Kapitän von Schillers Zeppelinbuch.* Leipzig: Bibliographisches Institut A.G., 1938.
Vaeth, Gordon. *Graf Zeppelin: The Adventures of an Aerial Globetrotter.* New York: Harper & Bros., 1958.
Vissering, Harry. *Zeppelin: The Story of a Great Achievement.* Chicago: Privately printed, 1922.

(b) British

Burney, Sir Dennistoun. *The World, The Air and the Future.* London: Alfred A. Knopf, 1929.
Leasor, James. *The Millionth Chance. The Story of the R 101.* London: Hamish Hamilton, 1957.
Meager, George. *Leaves From My Logbook.* Akron: Wingfoot LTA Society, 1961.
Meager, George. *My Airship Flights, 1915-1930.* London: William Kimber, 1970.
Minutes of the Proceedings at the Public Inquiry into the Loss of the Airship R 101. London: HMSO, 1931.
Cmd. 3825, *Report of the R 101 Inquiry.* London: HMSO, 1931.
Shute, Nevil. *Slide Rule.* New York: William Morrow & Co., 1954.
Wright, Robert. *The Man Who Won The Battle of Britain.* New York: Charles Scribner's Sons, 1969.

CHAPTER VIII

Kirschner, Edward J. *The Zeppelin In The Atomic Age.* Urbana; University of Illinois Press, 1957.
Litchfield, Paul W., & Allen, Hugh. *Why? Has America No Rigid Airships?* Cleveland: Corday & Gross Co., 1945.
Luftschiffbau Zeppelin Friedrichshafen (Erich Hilligardt & Andreas Sperger). *Bericht über die Luftschiffstudie LZ 132. II. Nachtrag zum Bericht über die Luftschiffstudie LZ 132: 300,000 m³ Fahrgast- u. Frachtluftschiff.*

APPENDIX B

Du Plessis de Grenedan, Jean. *Les Grands Dirigeables dans la Paix et dans la Guerre.* Paris: Plon-Nourrit & Cie., 1926. vol. I, *Leur Passé, Leur Avenir, L'Experience du "Dixmude." Vol. II, Leur Technique.*
Comte J. du Plessis. *La Vie Héroïque de Jean du Plessis.* Paris: Plon-Nourrit & Cie., 1924.
Commandant de Brossard, *Lachez Tout!* Paris: Editions France Empire, 1956.
Hormel, W., & Rasch, F. *Taschenbuch der Luftflotten 1914.* München: J.F. Lehmann's Verlag, 1914.
Robinson, Douglas H. "The Mystery of the 'Dixmude'." *Journal of the American Aviation Historical Society,* vol. 9, no. 2, summer 1964, p. 96.
Service Technique et Industriel de l'Aeronautique. Bulletin Technique No. 57. Stapfer, Paul, Lieut. de Vaisseau. *Analyses des Experiences Aerodynamiques Faites en Vol à Bord du Dirigeable "Méditerranée".* Marzin, R., Ingenieur-adjoint principal de l'Aeronautique. *Experiences sur la Charpente du Dirigeable "Méditerranée."* Paris: Librairie Blondel-La Rougerie, 7, Rue Saint-Lazare, Mars 1929.

APPENDIX A

THE 161 RIGID AIRSHIPS BUILT AND FLOWN, 1897–1940

Builder's number	Builder's type	Owner	Name	Built at	1st flight	Volume 100% inflated (cu. ft.)	Length (ft. & in.)	Diameter (ft. & in.)	Gas cell no.	Useful lift (lb.)	Engines (no. & type)	Total h.p.	Trial speed (m.p.h.)	Remarks
SCHWARZ METALCLAD														
Schwarz		Schwarz		Berlin-Tempelhof	3/11/97	114,700	156'	44' 3"	1		1 Daimler	16	10.8	Metal clad hull. Crashed on 1st flight, dismantled
ZEPPELINS (LUFTSCHIFFBAU ZEPPELIN G.M.B.H.)														
LZ 1	a	Zeppelin Co.		Manzell	2/7/00	399,000	420'	38' 6"	17	1,430	2 Daimler	28.4	17	Dismantled after 3 flights, early 1901
LZ 2	b	Zeppelin Co.		Manzell	30/11/05	366,200	414'	38' 6"	16	6,180	2 Daimler	170	25	On second flight 17/1/06 force landed at Kisslegg, dismantled
LZ 3	b	Zeppelin Co.		Manzell	9/10/06	403,600	414'	38' 6"	16	6,180	2 Daimler	170	25	Lengthened Autumn 1908; dismantled at Metz, Autumn 1913
"	"	Ger. Army	Z I		21/10/08	430,800	440' 3"	38' 6"	17	6,400	"	210	27.8	
LZ 4	c	Zeppelin Co.		Manzell	20/6/08	530,000	446'	42' 6"	17	10,150	2 Daimler	210	30	Burned at Echterdingen, 5/8/08
LZ 5	c	Ger. Army	Z II	Manzell	26/5/09	530,000	446'	42' 6"	17	10,250	2 Daimler	210	30	Wrecked at Weilburg, 25/4/10
LZ 6	d	Zeppelin Co. / DELAG		Manzell	25/8/09	530,000 / 565,000	446' / 474'	42' 6" / 42' 6"	17 / 18	9,700 / 9,620	2 Daimler / 2 Daimler / 1 Maybach	230 / 375	30 / 35.2	Lengthened Spring 1910; burned 14/9/10 in shed at Oos
LZ 7	e	DELAG	Deutsch-	F'hafen	19/6/10	683,000	486'	46'	18	11,000	3 Daimler	360	37	28/6/10, crashed in the Teutoberg Forest

		Operator	Name	Builder	Date	Volume	Length	Diameter						Fate
f	LZ 10	DELAG	*Schwaben*	F'hafen	26/6/11	628,000	460'	46'	17	14,300	3M C-X	435	47.6	28/6/12, burned on field at Düsseldorf
g	LZ 11	DELAG	*Viktoria Luise*	F'hafen	14/2/12	660,000	486'	46'	18	14,300	3M C-X	510	50.5	Dismantled Autumn 1915
f	LZ 12	Ger. Army	*Z III*	F'hafen	25/4/12	628,000	460'	46'	17	14,300	3M C-X	435	47.6	Dismantled at Metz, Summer 1914
g	LZ 13	DELAG	*Hansa*	F'hafen	30/7/12	660,000	486'	46'	18	13,860	3M C-X	510	50	Dismantled at Johannisthal, Summer 1916
h	LZ 14	Ger. Navy	*L 1*	F'hafen	7/10/12	793,600	518' 2"	48' 6"	18	20,700	3M C-X	495	47.4	9/9/13, lost in storm off Heligoland, 14 dead
h	LZ 15	Ger. Army	*Ersatz Z I*	F'hafen	16/1/13	690,000	466'	48' 6"	16	18,080	3M C-X	510	51.6	19/3/13, wrecked by storm after forced landing at Karlsruhe
h	LZ 16	Ger. Army	*Z IV*	F'hafen	14/3/13	690,000	466'	48' 6"	16	16,700	3M C-X	510	48.9	Dismantled at Jüterbog, Autumn 1916
h	LZ 17	DELAG	*Sachsen*	F'hafen	3/5/13	690,000	466'	48' 6"	16	16,300	3M C-X	510	48.9	Dismantled at Düren, Autumn 1916
						736,000	486'	48' 6"	17	17,400	3M C-X	540	47.6	
i	LZ 18	Ger. Navy	*L 2*	F'hafen	9/6/13	953,000	518' 2"	54' 6"	18	24,500	4M C-X	660	47.0	10/17/13, burned in air at Johannisthal, 28 dead
h	LZ 19	Ger. Army	*Ersatz E Z I*	F'hafen	6/6/13	690,000	466'	48' 6"	16	15,850	3M X-C	495	45.5	13/6/14, forced landing at Diedenhofen, wrecked
h	LZ 20	Ger. Army	*Z V*	F'hafen	8/7/13	690,000	466'	48' 6"	16	15,850	3M C-X	495	46.6	27/8/14, shot down by A.A. fire, Mlawa, Poland
						736,000	486'	48' 6"	17	16,700	3M C-X	540	45.5	
k	LZ 21	Ger. Army	*Z VI*	F'hafen	10/11/13	736,000	486'	48' 6"	17	19,350	3M C-X	540	46.6	6/8/14, damaged by gunfire at Liege, crashed near Bonn
l	LZ 22	Ger. Army	*Z VII*	F'hafen	8/1/14	780,000	510'	48' 6"	18	19,500	3M C-X	540	45.5	23/8/14, shot down by A.A. fire, St. Quirin, Lorraine, France
l	LZ 23	Ger. Army	*Z VIII*	F'hafen	21/2/14	780,000	510'	48' 6"	18	19,500	3M C-X	540	45.5	23/8/14, shot down by A.A. fire, Badonviller, Vosges, France

Builder's number	Builder's type	Owner	Name	Built at	1st flight	Volume 100% inflated (cu. ft.)	Length (ft. & in.)	Diameter (ft. & in.)	Gas cell no.	Useful lift (lb.)	Engines (no. & type)	Total h.p.	Trial speed (m.p.h.)	Remarks
LZ 24	m	Ger. Navy	L 3	F'hafen	11/5/14	794,500	518' 2"	48' 6"	18	20,250	3M C-X	630	47.4	17/2/15, forced landing on Fanö I., Denmark, 16 interned
LZ 25	m	Ger. Army	Z IX	F'hafen	29/7/14	794,500	518' 2"	48' 6"	18	20,250	3M C-X	630	50.9	8/10/14, bombed by British aircraft in Düsseldorf shed
LZ 26	n	Ger. Army	Z XII	Frankfurt	14/12/14	880,000	528' 6"	52' 6"	15	26,950	3M C-X	630	51.1	8/8/17, dismantled at Jüterbog
LZ 27	m	Ger. Navy	L 4	F'hafen	28/8/14	794,500	518' 2"	48' 6"	18	20,100	3M C-X	630	51.4	17/2/15, forced landing at Blaavands Huk, Denmark, 11 interned, 4 missing
LZ 28	m	Ger. Navy	L 5	F'hafen	22/9/14	794,500	518' 2"	48' 6"	18	20,250	3M C-X	630	52.1	6/8/15, forced landing due A.A. fire over Dunamünde, Russia
LZ 29	m	Ger. Army	Z X	F'hafen	13/10/14	794,500	518' 2"	48' 6"	18	20,250	3M C-X	630	50.9	21/3/15, forced landing at St. Quentin, France, due A.A. fire
LZ 30	m	Ger. Army	Z XI	Potsdam	11/11/14	794,500	518' 2"	48' 6"	18	20,250	3M C-X	630	50.9	20/5/15, blew away from shed at Posen, burned
LZ 31	m	Ger. Navy	L 6	F'hafen	3/11/14	794,500	518' 2"	48' 6"	18	19,150	3M C-X	630	52.0	16/9/16, burned accidentally in Fuhlsbüttel shed
LZ 32	m	Ger. Navy	L 7	F'hafen	20/11/14	794,500	518' 2"	48' 6"	18	18,500	3M C-X	630	52.0	4/15/16, shot down off Horns Reef by British cruisers, 11 dead, 7 prisoners
									18	18,850	3M C-X	630	52.0	Crashed at Tirlemort

	Service	Name	Built at	Date	Volume	Length	Diameter		HP	Engines		Speed	Fate
LZ 35	m	Ger. Army	LZ 35	F'hafen	11/1/15	794,500	518' 2"	48' 6"	18	20,250	3M C-X	630	50.9	13/4/15, forced landing Poperinghe, Belgium, due A.A. fire
LZ 36	o	Ger. Navy	L 9	F'hafen	8/3/15	879,500	529' 3"	52' 6"	15	24,365	3M C-X	630	52.8	16/9/16, burned accidentally in Fuhlsbüttel shed
LZ 37	m	Ger. Army	LZ 37	Potsdam	28/2/15	794,500	518' 2"	48' 6"	18	20,250	3M C-X	630	50.9	7/6/15, brought down in flames by British aircraft, Ghent, Belgium, 9 dead, 1 survivor
LZ 38	p	Ger. Army	LZ 38	F'hafen	3/4/15	1,126,400	536' 5"	61' 4"	16	33,100	4M C-X	840	56.6	7/6/15, bombed by British aircraft in Evere shed
LZ 39	o	Ger. Army	LZ 39	F'hafen	24/4/15	879,500	529' 3"	52' 6"	15	22,100	3M C-X	630	51.0	18/12/15, forced landing near Kovno, Russia, due A.A. fire
LZ 40	p	Ger. Navy	L 10	F'hafen	13/5/15	1,126,400	536' 5"	61' 4"	16	35,000	4M C-X	840	57.7	3/9/15, burned in thunderstorm off Neuwerk I, 19 dead
LZ 41	p	Ger. Navy	L 11	Löwenthal	7/6/15	1,126,400	536' 5"	61' 4"	16	34,800	4M C-X	840	57.0	Apl. 1917, dismantled at Hage
LZ 42	p	Ger. Army	LZ 72	Potsdam	15/6/15	1,126,400	536' 5"	61' 4"	16	30,800	4M C-X	840	59.6	26/2/17, dismantled at Jüterbog
LZ 43	p	Ger. Navy	L 12	F'hafen	21/6/15	1,126,400	536' 5"	61' 4"	16	34,900	4M C-X	840	59.5	10/8/15, burned at Ostend after A.A. damage in raid on England
LZ 44	p	Ger. Army	LZ 74	Löwenthal	8/7/15	1,126,400	536' 5"	61' 4"	16	35,700	4M C-X	840	61.6	8/10/15, rammed a mountain in the Schnee Eifel
LZ 45	p	Ger. Navy	L 13	F'hafen	23/7/15	1,126,400	536' 5"	61' 4"	16	34,250	4M C-X	840	59.7	Apl. 1917, dismantled in Hage
LZ 46	p	Ger. Navy	L 14	Löwenthal	9/8/15	1,126,400	536' 5"	61' 4"	16	33,800	4M C-X	840	59.2	23/6/19, wrecked by airship crews at Nordholz

Builder's number	Builder's type	Owner	Name	Built at	1st flight	Volume 100% inflated (cu. ft.)	Length (ft. & in.)	Diameter (ft. & in.)	Gas cell no.	Useful lift (lb.)	Engines (no. & type)	Total h.p.	Trial speed (m.p.h.)	Remarks
LZ 47	p	Ger. Army	LZ 77	F'hafen	24/8/15	1,126,400	536' 5"	61' 4"	16	35,700	4M C-X	840	61.6	21/2/16, shot down in flames by A.A. guns at Revigny, 11 dead
LZ 48	p	Ger. Navy	L 15	Löwenthal	9/9/15	1,126,400	536' 5"	61' 4"	16	34,600	4M HSLu	960	59.7	1/4/16, brought down by A.A. fire in Thames Estuary, 1 dead, 17 prisoners
LZ 49	p	Ger. Army	LZ 79	Potsdam	2/8/15	1,126,400	536' 5"	61' 4"	16	35,700	4M C-X	840	61.6	30/1/16, crashed at Ath, Belgium, due A.A. fire in raid on Paris
LZ 50	p	Ger. Navy	L 16	F'hafen	23/9/15	1,126,400	536' 5"	61' 4"	16	34,200	4M HSLu	960	59.7	19/10/17, wrecked at Nordholz by a crew in training
LZ 51	p	Ger. Army Lengthened in Dresden, Sept. 1916	LZ 81	Löwenthal	7/10/15	1,126,400 1,264,100	536' 5" 585' 5"	61' 4" 61' 4"	16 18	35,700 39,500	4M HSLu 4M HSLu	960 960	61.6 60.1	27/9/16, forced landing at Tirnova, Bulgaria, due A.A. fire
LZ 52	p	Ger. Navy	L 18	Löwenthal	3/11/15	1,126,400	536' 5"	61' 4"	16	33,800	4M HSLu	960	59.7	17/11/15, burned accidentally in Tondern shed, 1 dead, 7 injured
LZ 53	p	Ger. Navy	L 17	F'hafen	20/10/15	1,126,400	536' 5"	61' 4"	16	33,100	4M HSLu	960	58.1	12/28/16, burned accidentally in Tondern shed
LZ 54	p	Ger. Navy	L 19	F'hafen	27/11/15	1,126,400	536' 5"	61' 4"	16	33,700	4M HSLu	960	60.4	1/2/16, lost in North Sea after raid on England, 16 dead
LZ 55	p	Ger. Army	LZ 85	Potsdam	12/9/15	1,126,400	536' 5"	61' 4"	16	35,700	4M C-X	840	61.6	5/5/16, brought down at Salonika by A.A. fire
LZ 56	p	Ger. Army Lengthened in Dresden, Summer 1916	LZ 86	Potsdam	10/10/15	1,126,400 1,264,100	536' 5" 585' 5"	61' 4" 61' 4"	16 18	35,700 39,500	4M C-X 4M C-X	840 840	61.6 60.1	4/9/6, wrecked in landing at Temesvar, 9 dead

LZ 5…	q	Ger. Navy	L 20	F'haten	21/12/15	1,264,100	585' 5"	61' 4"	18	39,250	4M HSLu	960	55.7	3/5/16, wrecked in Norway after raid on England
LZ 60	p	Ger. Army	LZ 90	Potsdam, Summer 1916 / Lengthened in Dresden, Summer 1916	1/1/16	1,126,400 / 1,264,100	536' 5" / 585' 5"	61' 4" / 61' 4"	16 / 18	35,700 / 39,500	4M HSLu / 4M HSLu	960 / 960	61.6 / 60.5	7/11/16, blew away unmanned from Wittmundhaven in storm
LZ 61	q	Ger. Navy	LZ 21	Löwenthal	10/1/16	1,264,100	585' 5"	61' 4"	18	38,800	4M HSLu	960	57.5	28/11/16, shot down in flames off Yarmouth by British aircraft, 17 dead
LZ 62	r	Ger. Navy	L 30	F'hafen	28/5/16	1,949,600	649' 7"	78' 5"	19	61,600	6M HSLu	1440	62.2	Summer 1920, dismantled at Seerappen
LZ 63	p	Ger. Army	LZ 93	Potsdam, June 1916 / Lengthened in Dresden, June 1916	23/2/16	1,126,400 / 1,264,100	536' 5" / 585' 5"	61' 4" / 61' 4"	16 / 18	35,700 / 39,500	4M C-X / 4M C-X	840 / 840	61.6 / 60.5	Summer 1917, dismantled at Trier
LZ 64	q	Ger. Navy	L 22	Löwenthal	2/3/16	1,264,100	585' 5"	61' 4"	18	38,600	4M HSLu	960	59.0	14/5/17, shot down in flames off Terschelling by British aircraft, 21 dead
LZ 65	q	Ger. Army	LZ 95	F'hafen	31/1/16	1,264,100	585' 5"	61' 4"	18	38,800	4M HSLu	960	60.0	22/2/16, crash-landed outside Namur base due A.A. gunfire damage
LZ 66	q	Ger. Navy	L 23	Potsdam	8/4/16	1,264,100	585' 5"	61' 4"	18	40,700	4M HSLu	960	57.3	21/8/17, shot down in flames off Lyngvig by British aircraft, 18 dead
LZ 67	q	Ger. Army	LZ 97	Löwenthal	4/4/16	1,264,100	585' 5"	61' 4"	18	40,100	4M HSLu	960	60.0	5/7/17, dismantled in Jüterbog
LZ 68	q	Ger. Army	LZ 98	Löwenthal	28/4/16	1,264,100	585' 5"	61' 4"	18	40,100	4M HSLu	960	60.0	Aug. 1917, dismantled in Schneidemühl
LZ 69	q	Ger. Navy	L 24	Potsdam	20/5/16	1,264,100	585' 5"	61' 4"	18	40,300	4M HSLu	960	57.3	28/12/16, burned accidentally entering Tondern shed
LZ 71	q	Ger. Army	LZ 101	Potsdam	29/6/16	1,264,100	585' 5"	61' 4"	18	40,100	4M HSLu	960	60.0	Sept. 1917, dismantled in Jüterbog
LZ 72	r	Ger. Navy	L 31	Löwenthal	12/7/16	1,949,600	649' 7"	78' 5"	19	62,500	6M HSLu	1440	63.8	2/10/16, shot down in flames at Potters Bar by British aircraft, 19 dead

Builder's number	Builder's type	Owner	Name	Built at	1st flight	Volume 100% inflated (cu. ft.)	Length (ft. & in.)	Diameter (ft. & in.)	Gas cell no.	Useful lift (lb.)	Engines (no. & type)	Total h.p.	Trial speed (m.p.h.)	Remarks
LZ 73	q	Ger. Army	LZ 103	Potsdam	8/8/16	1,264,100	585' 5"	61' 4"	18	40,100	4M HSLu	960	60.0	Aug. 1917, dismantled in Königsberg
LZ 74	r	Ger. Navy	L 32	F'hafen	4/8/16	1,949,600	649' 7"	78' 5"	19	64,900	6M HSLu	1440	62.6	Sept. 24, 1916, shot down in flames at Billericay by British aircraft, 22 dead
LZ 75	r	Ger. Navy	L 37	Staaken	9/11/16	1,949,600	644' 8"	78' 5"	19	62,400	6M HSLu	1440	63.0	Summer 1920, broken up at Seddin
LZ 76	r	Ger. Navy	L 33	F'hafen	30/8/16	1,949,600	644' 8"	78' 5"	19	66,100	6M HSLu	1440	64.2	24/9/16, forced down at Little Wigborough by A.A. fire, 22 prisoners
LZ 77	q	Ger. Army	LZ 107	Potsdam	16/10/16	1,264,100	585' 5"	61' 4"	18	40,100	4M HSLu	960	60.0	July 1917, dismantled in Darmstadt
LZ 78	r	Ger. Navy	L 34	Löwenthal	22/9/16	1,949,600	644' 8"	78' 5"	19	68,600	6M HSLu	1440	64.0	28/11/16, shot down in flames off West Hartlepool by British aircraft, 20 dead
LZ 79	r	Ger. Navy, Feb. 1, 1917, No. 1 engine removed	L 41	Staaken	15/1/17; May 5-June 17, 1917, streamlined rear gondola installed	1,949,600	644' 8"	78' 5"	19	62,900	6M HSLu, 5M HSLu	1440, 1200	63.5	23/6/19, wrecked by airship crews at Nordholz
LZ 80	r	Ger. Navy, Feb. 1, 1917, No. 1 engine installed	L 35	F'hafen	12/10/16; Mar. 17-June 13, 1917, streamlined rear gondola	1,949,600	644' 8"	78' 5"	19	67,900, 74,584	6M HSLu, 5M HSLu	1440, 1200	64.2	15/11/18, broken up at Jüterbog
LZ 81	q	Ger. Army	LZ 111	Potsdam	20/12/16	1,264,100	585' 5"	61' 4"	18	40,100	4M HSLu	960	60.0	10/8/17, dismantled at Dresden
LZ 82	r	Ger. Navy, Feb. 1, 1917, No. 1 engine removed	L 36	F'hafen	1/11/16	1,949,600	644' 8"	78' 5"	19	71,600, 75,139	6M HSLu, 5M HSLu	1440, 1200	64.0	7/2/17, lost in forced landing at Rehben-an-der-Aller

LZ 85	r	Ger. Navy	*L 45* Aug. 26-Sept. 20, 1917, streamlined rear gondola installed	Staaken	2/4/17	1,949,600	644' 8"	78' 5"	19	68,800	5M HSLu	1200	64.2	20/10/17, forced landing at Sisteron, France, 17 prisoners
LZ 86	r	Ger. Navy	*L 39* Feb. 1, 1917, No. 1 engine removed	F'hafen	11/12/16	1,949,600	644' 8"	78' 5"	19	71,600 76,734	6M HSLu 5M HSLu	1440 1200	63.5	17/3/17, shot down in flames by A.A. fire at Compiègne, 17 dead
LZ 87	r	Ger. Navy	*L 47* Sept. 26-Oct. 7, 1917, streamlined rear gondola fitted	Staaken	11/5/17	1,949,600	644' 8"	78' 5"	19	70,600	5M HSLu	1200	63.4	5/1/18, destroyed in Ahlhorn explosion
LZ 88	r	Ger. Navy	*L 40* Feb. 1, 1917, No. 1 engine removed	F'hafen	3/1/17	1,949,600	644' 8"	78' 5"	19	71,600 76,808	6M HSLu 5M HSLu	1440 1200	62.4	17/6/17, wrecked in forced landing at Neuenwald
LZ 89	r	Ger. Navy	*L 50*	Staaken	9/6/17	1,949,600	644' 8"	78' 5"	18?	70,800	5M HSLu	1200	62.6	20/10/17, lost fore gondola at Dammartin, France; ship lost in Mediterranean, 4 dead, 16 prisoners
LZ 90	r	Ger. Army	*LZ 120*	Löwenthal	31/1/17	1,949,600	644' 8"	78' 5"	19	71,600	6M HSLu	1440	65.0	25/12/20, surrendered to Italy; dismantled at Ciampino, June 1921
LZ 91	s	Ger. Navy	*L 42* June 29-July 24, 1917, streamlined rear gondola installed	F'hafen	21/2/17	1,959,700	644' 8"	78' 5"	18	78,900	5M HSLu	1200	62.0	23/6/19, wrecked by airship crews at Nordholz
LZ 92	s	Ger. Navy	*L 43*	F'hafen	6/3/17	1,959,700	644' 8"	78' 5"	18	80,300	5M HSLu	1200	62.0	14/6/17, shot down in flames off Vlieland by British aircraft, 24 dead
LZ 93	t	Ger. Navy	*L 44*	Löwenthal	1/4/17	1,970,300	644' 8"	78' 5"	18	83,400	5M HSLu	1200	64.5	20/10/17, shot down in flames by A.A. fire at St. Clement, 18 dead
LZ 94	t	Ger. Navy	*L 46*	F'hafen	24/4/17	1,970,300	644' 8"	78' 5"	18	83,400	5M HSLu	1200	64.2	5/1/18, destroyed in Ahlhorn explosion
LZ 95	u	Ger. Navy	*L 48*	F'hafen	22/5/17	1,970,300	644' 8"	78' 5"	18	85,800	5M HSLu	1200	66.9	17/6/17, shot down in flames at Theberton by British aircraft, 14 dead, 3 survivors

Builder's number	Builder's type	Owner	Name	Built at	1st flight	Volume (cu. ft.) 100% inflated	Length (ft. & in.)	Diameter (ft. & in.)	Gas cell no.	Useful lift (lb.)	Engines (no. & type)	Total h.p.	Trial speed (m.p.h.)	Remarks
LZ 96	u	Ger. Navy	L 49	Löwenthal	13/6/17	1,970,300	644' 8"	78' 5"	18	87,200	5M HSLu	1200	65.8	20/10/17, forced landing at Bourbonne-les-Bains, 19 prisoners
LZ 97	u	Ger. Navy	L 51	F'hafen	6/7/17	1,970,300	644' 8"	78' 5"	18	87,000	5M HSLu	1200	66.1	5/1/8, destroyed in Ahlhorn explosion
LZ 98	u	Ger. Navy L 52 Apl. 26-May 15, 1918, Mb IVa engines fitted	Staaken	14/7/17	1,970,300	644' 8"	78' 5"	18	86,600	5M HSLu / 5M Mb IVa	1200 / 1225	66.4	23/6/19, wrecked by airship crews at Wittmund
LZ 99	u	Ger. Navy L 54 Mar. 15-31, 1918, Mb IVa engines fitted	Staaken	13/8/17	1,970,300	644' 8"	78' 5"	18	87,100	5M HSLu / 5M Mb IVa	1200 / 1225	66.6	19/7/18, burned in Tondern shed in British air attack
LZ 100	v	Ger. Navy L 53 Apl. 16-23, 1918, Mb IVa engines fitted	F'hafen	8/8/17	1,977,360	644' 8"	78' 5"	14	89,200	5M HSLu / 5M Mb IVa	1200 / 1225	66.0	11/8/18, shot down in flames off Terschelling by British aircraft, 19 dead
LZ 101	v	Ger. Navy	L 55	Löwenthal	1/9/17	1,977,360	644' 8"	78' 5"	14	89,600	5M HSLu	1200	64.6	20/10/17, forced landing at Tiefenort-an-der-Werra, dismantled
LZ 102	w	Ger. Navy	L 57	F'hafen	26/9/17	2,418,700	743' 0"	78' 5"	16	114,700	5M HSLu	1200	64.0	8/10/17, wrecked and burned at Jüterbog
LZ 103	v	Ger. Navy L 56 July 8-22, 1918, Mb IVa engines fitted	Staaken	24/9/17	1,977,360	644' 8"	78' 5"	14	85,100	5M HSLu / 5M Mb IVa	1200 / 1225	66.0	23/6/19, wrecked by airship crews at Wittmund
LZ 104	w	Ger. Navy L 59 Dec. 20, 1917-Feb. 14, 1918, rebuilt, gondolas relocated	Staaken	10/10/17	2,418,700	743' 0"	78' 5"	16	114,400	5M HSLu	1200	64.0	7/4/18, burned in air over Straits of Otranto, 23 dead
LZ 105	v	Ger. Navy	L 58	F'hafen	29/10/17	1,977,360	644' 8"	78' 5"	14	87,200	5M Mb IVa	1225	66.5	5/1/8, destroyed in Ahlhorn explosion

	Operator	Name	Built	Volume	Length	Diameter	Engines		Engine arrangement	H.P.	Speed	Disposition
LZ 108 v	Ger. Navy	*L 60*	Staaken	1,977,360	644' 8"	78' 5"	14	85,200	5M Mb IVa	1225	66.1	19/7/18, burned in Tondern shed in British air attack
LZ 109 v	Ger. Navy	*L 64*	Staaken	1,977,360	644' 8"	78' 5"	14	86,100	5M Mb IVa	1225	66.0	21/7/20, surrendered to England, dismantled at Pulham 21/6/21
LZ 110 v	Ger. Navy	*L 63*	F'hafen	1,977,360	644' 8"	78' 5"	14	87,000	5Mb IVa	1225	71.6	23/6/19, wrecked by airship crews at Nordholz
LZ 111 v	Ger. Navy	*L 65*	Löwenthal	1,977,360	644' 8"	78' 5"	14	86,200	5Mb IVa	1225	71.6	23/6/19, wrecked by airship crews at Nordholz
LZ 112 x	Ger. Navy	*L 70*	F'Hafen	2,195,800	693' 11"	78' 5"	15	97,100	7M Mb IVa	1715	81	5/8/18, shot down in flames off Cromer by British aircraft, 22 dead
LZ 113 x	Ger. Navy Oct. 3-28, 1918, lengthened, single-engine gondola aft.	*L 71*	F'hafen	2,195,800 / 2,418,700	693' 11" / 743' 2"	78' 5" / 78' 5"	15 / 16	98,500 / 112,700	7M Mb IVa / 6M Mb IVa	1715 / 1470	72.7	1/7/20, surrendered to England; dismantled at Pulham 1923
LZ 114 x	Ger. Navy	*L 72*	Löwenthal	2,418,700	743' 2"	78' 5"	16	112,700	6M Mb IVa	1470		13/7/20, surrendered to France; 21/12/23, exploded off Sicily, 50 dead
LZ 120 y	DELAG Winter 1919, lengthened by one gas cell	*Bodensee*	F'hafen	706,200 / 795,000	393' 4" / 426' 1"	61' 4" / 61' 4"	11 / 12	22,000 / 25,350	4M Mb IVa	980	82.4 / 80.5	3/7/21, surrendered to Italy; dismantled July 1928
LZ 121 y	DELAG	*Nordstern*	F'hafen	795,000	426' 1"	61' 4"	12	25,350	4M Mb IVa	980	80.5	13/6/21, surrendered to France; dismantled Sept. 1926
LZ 126	U.S. Navy	*ZR 3*	F'hafen	2,762,100	658' 4"	90' 8"	14	101,430	5M VL-1	2000	79.5	30/6/32, decommissioned; dismantled at Lakehurst Dec. 1939
LZ 127	Zeppelin Co.	*Graf Zeppelin*	F'hafen	3,995,000	775' 0"	100' 0"	17	66,000	5M VL-II	2650	69.5	Spring 1940, dismantled at Frankfurt

Builder's number	Builder's type	Owner	Name	Built at	1st flight	Volume (cu. ft.) 100% inflated	Length (ft. & in.)	Diameter (ft. & in.)	Gas cell no.	Useful lift (lb.)	Engines (no. & type)	Total h.p.	Trial speed (m.p.h.)	Remarks
LZ 129		Zeppelin Reederei	*Hindenburg*	F'hafen	4/3/36	7,062,100	803' 10"	135' 1"	16	224,200	4 Daimler-Benz	4200	82.6	6/5/37, burned at Lakehurst, 35 dead, 61 survivors
LZ 130		Zeppelin Reederei	*Graf Zeppelin II*	F'hafen	14/9/38	7,062,100	803' 10"	135' 1"	16	224,200	4 Daimler-Benz	4200	82.6	Spring 1940, dismantled at Frankfurt

SCHÜTTE-LANZ (LUFTSCHIFFBAU SCHÜTTE-LANZ G.M.B.H.)

Builder's number	Builder's type	Owner	Name	Built at	1st flight	Volume (cu. ft.) 100% inflated	Length (ft. & in.)	Diameter (ft. & in.)	Gas cell no.	Useful lift (lb.)	Engines (no. & type)	Total h.p.	Trial speed (m.p.h.)	Remarks
SL 1	a	Ger. Army	*SL 1*	Rheinau	17/10/11	734,500	432' 0"	60' 5"	7	11,000	2 Daimler	480	44.5	16/7/13, wrecked in storm at Schneidemühl
SL 2	b	Ger. Army Lengthened May-Aug. 1915	*SL 2*	Rheinau	28/2/14	861,900 / 981,600	474' 0" / 513' 3"	59' 10" / 59' 10"	15 / 16	17,300 / 22,800	4M C-X / 4M C-X	780 / 840	55.0 / 55.5	10/1/16, wrecked in storm at Luckenwalde
SL 3	c	Ger. Navy	*SL 3*	Rheinau	4/2/15	1,143,500	502' 4"	64' 10"	17	31,300	4M C-X	840	52.6	1/5/16, crashed in Baltic off Gotland
SL 4	c	Ger. Navy	*SL 4*	Sandhofen	25/4/15	1,146,500	502' 4"	64' 10"	17	30,800	4M C-X	840	52.8	11/12/15, wrecked by storm in Seddin shed
SL 5	c	Ger. Army	*SL 5*	Darmstadt	21/5/15	1,146,500	502' 4"	64' 10"	17	30,800	4M C-X	840	52.5	5/7/15, wrecked by storm at Giessen
SL 6	d	Ger. Navy	*SL 6*	Leipzig	19/9/15	1,240,300	534' 5"	64' 10"	18	34,750	4M C-X	840	57.9	18/11/15, exploded in air near Seddin, 20 dead
SL 7	d	Ger. Army	*SL 7*	Rheinau	3/9/15	1,240,300	534' 5"	64' 10"	18	34,600	4M C-X	840	58.9	6/3/17, dismantled at Jüterbog
SL 8	e	Ger. Navy	*SL 8*	Leipzig	30/3/16	1,369,300	570' 10"	65' 11"	19	42,500	4M C-X	840	56.1	20/11/17, dismantled at Seddin
SL 9	e	Ger. Navy	*SL 9*	Leipzig	24/5/16	1,369,300	570' 10"	65' 11"	19	43,200	4M HSLu	960		30/3/17, burned in air off Pillau, 23 dead
SL 10	e	Ger. Army	*SL 10*	Rheinau	17/5/16	1,369,300	570' 10"	65' 11"	19	47,400	4M HSLu	960	58.8	28/7/16, disappeared in Black Sea, 16 dead

							570' 10"	65' 11"	19	47,400	4M HSLu	900	36.8	8/4/17, burned in collapse of Leipzig shed
SL 14	e	*SL 14*	Ger. Navy	Rheinau	23/8/16	1,369,300	570' 10"	65' 11"	19	47,800	4M HSLu	960	58.8	11/5/17, broke in two in landing at Wainoden, dismantled
SL 15	e	*SL 15*	Ger. Army	Rheinau	9/11/16	1,369,300	570' 10"	65' 11"	19	47,400	4M HSLu	960	58.8	8/17, dismantled at Sandhofen
SL 16	e	*e 9*	Ger. Army	Leipzig	18/1/17	1,369,300	570' 10"	65' 11"	19	47,400	4M HSLu	960	58.8	8/17, dismantled in Spich
SL 17	e	*e 10*	Ger. Army	Zeesen	22/3/17	1,369,300	570' 10"	65' 11"	19	47,000	4M HSLu	960	58.8	8/17, dismantled at Allenstein
SL 20	f	*SL 20*	Ger. Navy	Rheinau	10/9/17	1,989,700	651' 0"	75' 3"	19	78,200	5M HSLu	1200	62.8	5/1/18, destroyed in Ahlhorn explosion
SL 21	f	*f 2*	Ger. Army	Zeesen	26/11/17	1,989,700	651' 0"	75' 3"	19	77,500	5M HSLu	1200	64.7	2/18, dismantled at Zeesen
SL 22	f	*SL 22*	Ger. Navy	Rheinau	5/6/18	1,989,700	651' 0"	75' 3"	19	82,600	5M HSLu	1200	64.7	6/20, dismantled at Jüterbog

BRITISH RIGID AIRSHIPS

No. 9		*No. 9*	Br. Navy	Vickers, Barrow	27/11/16	890,000	526'	53'	17	8520	4 Wolseley Maybach	720	42.5	6/18, dismantled at Pulham
No. 23		*No. 23*	Br. Navy	Vickers, Barrow	19/9/17	940,000	535'	53'	18	13,400	4 Rolls-Royce	1000	54.5	9/19, dismantled at Pulham
No. 24		*No. 24*	Br. Navy	Beardmore, Inchinnan	27/10/17	940,000	535'	53'	18	13,800	4 Rolls-Royce	1000	54.5	12/19, dismantled at Pulham
No. 25		*No. 25*	Br. Navy	Armstrong, Selby	14/10/17	940,000	535'	53'	18	13,000	4 Rolls-Royce	1000	54.5	9/19, dismantled at Cranwell
R 26		*R 26*	Br. Navy	Vickers, Barrow	20/3/18	940,000	535'	53'	18	14,050	4 Rolls-Royce	1000	54.5	10/3/19, dismantled
R 27	23X	*R 27*	Br. Navy	Beardmore, Inchinnan	6/18	990,600	539'	53'	18	16,800	4 Rolls-Royce	1000	56.5	16/8/18, burned in shed at Howden

Builder's number	Builder's type	Owner	Name	Built at	1st flight	Volume 100% inflated (cu. ft.)	Length (ft. & in.)	Diameter (ft. & in.)	Gas cell no.	Useful lift (lb.)	Engines (no. & type)	Total h.p.	Trial speed (m.p.h.)	Remarks
R 29	23X	Br. Navy	R 29	Armstrong, Selby	6/18	990,600	539'	53'	18	19,400	4 Rolls-Royce	1000	56.5	24/10/19, dismantled at East Fortune
R 31		Br. Navy	R 31	Short Bros., Cardington	8/18	1,535,000	614' 8"	64' 10"	21	37,000	6 Rolls-Royce	1500	70.0	7/19, broken up at Howden
R 32		Br. Navy	R 32	Short Bros., Cardington	8/19	1,535,000	614' 8"	64' 10"	21	37,000	5 Rolls-Royce	1250	65.0	27/4/21, broken up at Howden
R 33		Br. Navy	R 33	Armstrong, Selby	6/3/19	1,950,000	643' 0"	78' 9"	19	58,100	5 Sunbeam Maori	1250	60.0	1928, dismantled
R 34		Br. Navy	R 34	Beardmore, Inchinnan	14/3/19	1,950,000	643' 0"	78' 9"	19	58,100	5 Sunbeam Maori	1250	60.0	27/1/21, wrecked at Howden
R 36		Br. Air Ministry	G-FAAF	Beardmore, Inchinnan	1/4/21	2,101,000	675'	78' 9"	20	35,900	3 Sunbeam Cossack 2M Mb IVa	1540	65.0	1926, dismantled at Pulham
R 38	Admiralty "A"	Br. Air Ministry : U.S. Navy	R 38 ZR 2	R.A.W., Cardington	23/6/21	2,724,000	699'	85' 6"	14	102,144	6 Sunbeam Cossack	2100	71.3	24/8/21, broke up over Hull and burned, 44 dead
R 80		Br. Air Ministry	R 80	Vickers, Barrow	19/7/20	1,200,000	535'	70'	15	39,900	4 Wolseley Maybach	920	60	1925, dismantled at Pulham
R 100		Br. Air Ministry	R 100	Airship Guarantee Co., Howden	16/12/29	5,156,000	709'	133'	15	114,000	6 Rolls-Royce	3960	81	1931, dismantled at Cardington
R 101		Br. Air Ministry	R 101	R.A.W., Cardington	14/10/29	4,998,000	732'	132'	16	78,500	5 Beardmore Diesel	2925	?	5/10/30, crashed and burned at Beauvais, France, 48 dead
		Lengthened Summer 1930				5,508,800	777'	132'	17	108,000				

UNITED STATES BUILT RIGID AIRSHIPS (lift with helium 95% full)

				Date	Volume	Length	Diameter			Engines		Speed	Notes
ZRS 5	*Macon*	U.S. Navy	Goodyear-Zeppelin, Akron	21/4/33	6,850,000	785'	132' 11"	12	173,000	8 Maybach VL-II	4480	87.2	12/2/35, crashed at sea off Point Sur, 2 dead, 81 survivors
ZMC-2		U.S. Navy	Aircraft Development Corp., Detroit	19/8/29	202,000	149' 5'	52' 8"	1	3,127	2 Wright	440	70.0	1941, scrapped

FRENCH BUILT RIGID AIRSHIP

				Date	Volume	Length	Diameter			Engines		Speed	Notes
Spiess	*Spiess*		Sociéte Zodiac, St. Cyr	3/4/13 Lengthened 1913	451,000 580,000	370' 469'	44' 5" 44' 5"	14 17	?	1 Chenu 2 Chenu	200 400	43.5	1914, dismantled

Appendix B: Rigid airships of other nations

FRANCE

One rigid airship was built in France, and three more were acquired as spoils of war from Germany in 1920 and 1921.

In 1873 an Alsatian, Joseph Spiess, patented a rigid airship design which supposedly antedated the Zeppelin, but the patent drawings show a flimsy basket-like structure enclosing a series of ordinary spherical balloons. The rigid airship which Spiess financed over 35 years later had nothing in common with the 1873 patent, and must be considered a Zeppelin copy, though the hull framework was built of wooden girders. There is evidence that the original 1910 design was for a ship only 278 feet long, 44.4 feet in diameter, and with 293,000 cubic feet of hydrogen in twelve gas cells. For the sake of increased lift the dimensions were enlarged, and the craft completed in 1912 by the Société Zodiac airship builders at St. Cyr was 370 feet long, 44.4 feet in diameter, and had a volume of 451,000 cubic feet with 14 gas cells. The hull, like that of the Zeppelins, had a long parallel section with short tapered bow and stern, and fins, rudders and elevators very much as in "Schwaben." A triangular external keel ran almost the full length of the ship, and two gondolas slung in openings in the keel were to contain two Chenu engines of 200 hp each driving four 2-bladed propellers on brackets on the hull. The craft was so lacking in lift that the engine had to be removed from the rear gondola. With only the engine in the forward gondola, "Spiess" made at least two flights on April 3 and May 2, 1913. She was then lengthened by three gas cells, the work being completed in November, 1913, and was now 469 feet long and 580,000 cubic feet in volume, with the second Chenu engine installed in the rear gondola. In this form the ship first flew on December 9, 1913, and on January 16, 1914 made a flight over Paris that caused much popular enthusiasm. As far as can be determined, "Spiess" made no further flights and was broken up after the outbreak of World War I. Figures are not available on useful lift and empty weight, but it is apparent that the airship was not efficient. The maximum speed however was 43½ mph. The design was not repeated.[1]

Under the Versailles Treaty the French received three former Zeppelins – L 72,the latest product of the Friedrichshafen firm, delivered to the Maubeuge shed by a German civilian crew on July 13, 1920; the old ex-Army LZ 113, delivered to Maubeuge on October 9, 1920; and the ex-DELAG passenger carrier "Nordstern," delivered to St. Cyr on June 13, 1921.

Of these, L 72 renamed "Dixumude" and assigned to the French Navy, turned in the most remarkable performance. This is largely to the credit of her commander throughout her operational life, Lieut. de Vaisseau Jean du Plessis de Grenedan. A passionate and dedicated believer in the rigid airship, and a martyr to the airship cause, he deserves to be remembered with Peter Strasser, Ernst Lehmann, Edward Maitland, George H. Scott, Zachary Lansdowne, and William A. Moffett.

Determined as he was to demonstrate with "Dixmude" the value to the French Navy of the long-ranged rigid, du Plessis first had to battle for her existence. Notified that L 72 would be scrapped unless he could fly her out of Maubeuge to clear the hanger for LZ 113, du Plessis, with a scratch crew which had never flown in a rigid airship, managed to ferry the big Zeppelin to Cuers-Pierrefeu near Toulon on August 11, 1920. There followed three frustrating years during which "Dixmude" and her captain were grounded, always with the threat that for reasons of economy, the ship would be dismantled and her crew returned to general service. In September, 1921, an attempt to inflate the ship with the old German gas cells proved they were hopelessly porous. Du Plessis dared to suggest to his superiors that "Dixmude" could be flying in three months if they would order through an intermediary a new set of gas cells from the original manufacturer, the Zeppelin subsidiary at Berlin-Tempelhof. Instead, the Ministry of Marine, for reasons of national pride, chose to create a whole new industry to fabricate gas cells lined with gold beaters' skin. The contract went to the Astra-Nieuport firm, and the cells were delivered in the last week of June, 1923. These too were defective – fatally so – du Plessis writing "during flight the gas cells developed numerous small tears not corresponding to any defect in installation. It seems probable that they are due to the use of cotton

---

[1] *Wingfoot LTA Society Bulletin*, vol. 18, No. 1,2,3,4. Also Hormel & Rasch, *Taschenbuch der Luftflotten* (Munich: W. F. Lehmann's Verlag, 1914), pp. 20-21; 70-71.

of inferior quality."[2] But du Plessis was impatient, and they would have to do.

He had an ambitious plan – nothing less than to prove the extraordinary range and endurance of the big rigid airship by a series of voyages from Cuers across French North Africa. The plan, as approved by the Aviation Department of the Ministry of Marine, envisaged firstly a three-day flight around the western Mediterranean, then there might follow a long-distance cruise to the West African naval base at Dakar, 2500 miles from Cuers. Ambitious and daring indeed – particularly with an untried and untrained crew handling a lightly built "height climber" designed for the veterans of the German Naval Airship Division. Du Plessis certainly knew he was attempting too much with too little experience. Yet he had to take risks – after three years of agitation and expenditure, he had to justify promptly the sacrifices made to get "Dixmude" into the air, and to rally public opinion behind the airship cause. To hesitate meant that the entire French rigid airship program, which depended on "Dixmude" alone, would come to naught.

The flights that followed were indeed spectacular, and caught the fancy of the public. After two relatively brief ascents in the neighbourhood of Cuers on August 2 and 9, 1923, there followed a 50 hour flight to North Africa, touching at Algiers and Bizerta and returning via Sardinia and Corsica. The next cruise, commencing on September 25, went across the Mediterranean to Touggourt on the northern edge of the Sahara Desert. On his return to Cuers, du Plessis found the weather so favorable that he went on north to appear in triumph over Paris. It was a flamboyant gesture that aroused public enthusiasm, and brought to France the world's endurance record of 118 hours and 41 minutes.[3]

Between October 17 and 19 the big dirigible showed herself for publicity purposes over large cities in the south and west of France – Toulouse, Bordeaux, Rochefort, Nantes, Tours, and Lyons. On her next flight between November 21 and 24, "Dixmude," scouting with the Fleet off Bizerta, was blocked from reaching Cuers by a widespread storm in the western Mediterranean. For lack of a suitable base in North Africa, du Plessis was forced to fight his way through the turbulence of a thunderstorm front. He reached Cuers

---

[2] Jean du Plessis de Grenedan, *Les Grands Dirigeables dans la Paix et dans la Guerre* (Paris: Plon-Nourrit et Cie., 1925), Vol. I p. 250.
[3] The previous endurance record of 108 hours 12 minutes had been set by R 34 in her westward crossing of the Atlantic in July, 1919.

with only three tons of ballast, nine tons of rain water soaking the ship, and the crew exhausted. After the "flight through the tempest" du Plessis expressed unlimited confidence in the strength of his ship; yet the hull framework may have been more strained than he realized.

On December 18, 1923, "Dixmude" left Cuers for what was to be the last flight before the grand journey to Dakar. The goal was In Salah, a small oasis deep in the Southern Territories of Algeria. Fueled and provisioned for a 72-hour cruise, the big rigid was carrying 35,300 lb of petrol, 2200 lb of oil, 26,400 lb of water ballast, 4410 lb of provisions and stores, 3310 lb of drinking water, and 6620 lb of spare parts and tools. The 40 men of the crew and 10 passengers were figured at 7720 lb.

Routine messages came in as "Dixmude" passed west of Sardinia, reached the African coastline west of Bizerta, and went on south to Ouargla. At 1600 on December 19 the airship was over In Salah, dropping a bag full of mail from the crew. Returning north, du Plessis was to make an intermediate landing at Baraki air field outside Algiers. A gathering storm over the western Mediterranean was bringing freshening northwest winds over the coast of Algeria, and after battling the head wind for four hours, du Plessis reversed course and steered east. In deteriorating weather, the airship was seen in the evening darkness of December 20 proceeding at low altitude across Tunisia amid showers of sleet. At this time du Plessis apparently made up his mind to return home ahead of the storm, up the Tyrrhenian Sea, using the counterclockwise circulation around the storm to speed him on his way. The subsequent Court of Inquiry estimated that "Dixmude" was making between 50 and 87 mph over the ground as she departed the coast of Tunisia on a north-north-east course. Her radio signals were being read loud and clear, not only at Bizerta, but even by the battleship "Paris" over 500 miles away on the coast of Provence. At 0208 on December 21, "Dixmude" radioed "reeling in antenna due to thunderstorm." Twenty minutes later, as the 743-foot monster, *en plein vol* with her six Maybachs thundering through the night, approached the coast of Sicily, she and her crew were suddenly blasted into fragments by a violent explosion which lit the heavens and the earth for miles around.

Railway men assembled at the Sciacca station to take out the 2.30 am train were astonished to see a great fire, "like an aurora borealis," lighting the sky to the west, and sinking out of sight behind the high hill of Cape San Marco. A hunter on the seashore

south of Menfi, watching a thunderstorm offshore, saw a big flash of
lightning strike a cloud before him; immediately the interior of the
cloud was lit up by an enormous red glare, followed a few seconds
later by four blazing objects falling from the bottom of the cloud; on
reaching the water they gave off flame and smoke and were
extinguished at once. Morning revealed two aluminium fuel tanks on
the shoreline at Sciacca numbered "75 L-72" and "S-2-48 LZ 113".
Many pieces of scorched or charred gas cell and outer cover fabric
had blown in from the west across Cape San Marco. Even small
pieces of duralumin girder structure, electrical wires, and tatters of
electrically heated flight clothing had been carried to shore by the
strong westerly wind. Yet these unusual phenomena attracted no
attention from the outside world. Seemingly the big air cruiser had
simply disappeared with 50 souls aboard. In Paris, the Ministry of
Marine, reluctant for political reasons to admit the possibility of
disaster, fed the press and public for days with fantastic reports and
rumours suggesting that "Dixmude" was still in the air over Africa.
The "mystery of the 'Dixmude'," if there was a mystery, started
right there, in a responsible bureau of the French government.

All hopes and all uncertainties were ended when on December 26,
some fishermen of Sciacca, hauling their nets 4 miles south of Cape
San Marco, found the mutilated corpse of du Plessis. Papers in the
pockets of his fur-lined flight jacket provided positive identification,
and his watch had stopped at 2.27.

While the body of "Dixmude's" commander went home to Toulon
aboard the cruiser "Strasbourg," French warships began dragging
south of Cape San Marco. Many small objects were recovered
including a portion of one of the airship's girders; electrical cables; a
complete gas valve; the ship's two tricolored ensigns; and fragments
of the fur lined, electrically-heated flight jackets worn by the crew.
Adhering to one end of an electrical heating cable was a piece of
human skin the size of the palm of the hand. Two mutilated human
heads and numerous fragments of bodies were also recovered, but
aside from du Plessis' corpse, only one identifiable body was ever
found.

Without doubt, from the testimony of the eyewitnesses and the
widespread distribution of the wreckage, "Dixmude" had exploded
with incredible violence, instantaneously shattering framework, outer
cover, and gas cells, and leaving as the only large fragments the six
gondolas, hung below the hull, to fall to the sea a mile below amid a
last flare-up of flaming petrol. Du Plessis' injuries demonstrated that

he had been slammed with great force against a control car window frame and, already dead, precipitated out into the night. Though gas purity figures are conspicuous by their absence, it is clear that the defective Astra-Nieuport gas cells had permitted the inward diffusion of air, and it was the contaminated lifting gas which blasted "Dixmude" out of the sky. My conclusion is that in the turbulence inside the thunderstorm the ship had risen uncontrollably over pressure height and hydrogen was blowing off from her cells into the electrically-charged atmosphere. Possibly the light "height climber's" structure broke up in turbulence, in which case her doom was certain.

Thus perished one of the most fascinating figures in the history of the rigid airship, and with Jean du Plessis de Grenedan there ended the dream of aerial giants flying the French tricolor, crossing the Atlantic, ranging far over Africa, and binding the motherland to the French colonies in the Orient. True, there were two other rigid airships in French service, but neither was handled with the same boldness as the "Dixmude."

The ex-German Army LZ 113, assigned to the French Army, never left the shed at Maubeuge. The real reason, sneered their rivals in the French Navy, was that none of the soldiers knew how to fly her! She was shortly dismantled after a series of "experiments." The "Nordstern," renamed "Méditerranée," was originally assigned to the Army also and for a year remained at St. Cyr; she made several flights to train crewmen of the "Dixmude." Subsequently she was turned over to the French Navy and under the command of Lieutenant de Vaisseau Stapfer arrived at Cuers on July 28, 1922. Here, for obvious reasons, she was patronizingly referred to as "the little one" by du Plessis' crew. Her small size fitted her only for training flights and cruises along the coast. It is known that on August 28, October 8 and November 3, 1925, she was making experimental flights involving speed tests and pressure readings on the hull. In August 1926 "Méditerranée" was decommissioned in Hangar 2 at Cuers, and stripped of gas cells, engine cars and passenger gondola, and all accessories in the keel. In September 1926 her framework was progressively tested to destruction under loads.

ITALY

Italy received three former Zeppelins – L 61, delivered at Ciampino near Rome on August 30, 1920; LZ 120, delivered at Ciampino on

December 25, 1920; and the ex-DELAG passenger craft "Bodensee," delivered on July 3, 1921.

L 61 was five days en route from Wittmundhaven to Ciampino. On August 25, 1920, she merely made it to Friedrichshafen-Löwenthal, where she lay for three days. Not until Captain Heinen had been replaced by Captain Hans Kurt Flemming, a former Navy wartime airship commander, did L 61 depart for Ciampino on the afternoon of August 29. She landed at the base near Rome in the early morning of the 30th.[4]

Renamed "Italia," the ex-German height climber made a few flights, including one in which she rose to 7,500 feet with 85 passengers on board. In January, 1921, she was badly damaged in a landing accident and dismantled as no spare parts could be obtained to repair her.

LZ 120, the last military airship left in Germany, made the journey to Ciampino in two stages – Seerappen to Staaken on November 29, 1920, and Staaken to Ciampino on December 24-25. Though renamed "Ausonia," she appears not to have been flown by the Italians. While deflated and hung up in her shed, she was wrecked in June, 1921, when the hangar roof was severely damaged by a gale.

The ex-"Bodensee," renamed "Esperia," had a longer career. She made a number of flights, including one to Barcelona in company with the semirigid N 1, the later polar airship "Norge," and from Rome to Tripoli and back in less than 24 hours' flying time. On July 18, 1928, "Esperia" was put out of service and dismantling commenced three days later.

JAPAN

Japan received the old L 37, but had no place to house her and no interest in the type. She was dismantled in the shed at Seddin and the parts shipped to the Far East. The Japanese built and flew several semi-rigids designed by Nobile from the base at Kasumigaura, where the former Jüterbog hangar was erected, but they made no attempt to build or procure rigids.

---

[4] R. Strazzeri, *Report on the Delivery of the Airship L 61*. Strazzeri represented the Italian Army on the flight.

BELGIUM

Belgium was awarded the old L 30, but had her broken up at Seerappen.

RUSSIA

I have not been able to convince myself that the Russians ever built and flew a rigid airship, though they constructed a number of semirigids to the design of Nobile.

Glossary of airship terms

A

Airspeed Meter: Pitot-tube actuated, it presented the speed through the air in metres per second or miles per hour. Corrections had to be made for decreased air density with increased altitude, and it did not of course give speed over the ground.

Altimeter: An aneroid instrument, actually a barometer measuring air pressure, graduated to give the altitude in feet or metres. Changes in barometric pressure after takeoff could produce false readings, though corrections might be obtained by radio.

Antifreeze: Alcohol was invariably used in airship engine cooling systems. Glycerine was used in water ballast sacks by the Germans until shortages required the use of a substitute, calcium chloride, whose damaging corrosive effects on duralumin were not at first realized. American airships used alcohol exclusively in water ballast sacks.

Automatic Valves: Spring-loaded valves in the bottom of each gas cell opened automatically whenever the internal pressure exceeded the external by 8 to 10 mm. of water, as when an airship with full gas cells ascended to a higher altitude, expanding the gas. The larger valves in the large cells had a diameter of 31½ inches. In "Hindenburg" and "Graf Zeppelin II" the automatic valves were in the center of the gas cells at the level of the axial gangway. The British R 101 had combination automatic and manoeuvring valves halfway up the side of the bags which were very sensitive, opening with a pressure of only 2 mm of water.

Axial Cable: A stranded wire cable running through the gas cells from bow to stern of the ship, and connecting the wire bracing of all the main rings at their centers, reducing the loads on the framework if there was an inequality in pressure between adjacent cells. A Schütte-Lanz patent, the axial cable *(Zentralverspannung)* was introduced in the Zeppelin L 30.

Axial Gangway: In some of the later and larger rigid airships, the axial cable was replaced by an axial gangway. A girderwork structure running from end to end of the ship, the axial gangway served the same structural purpose as the axial cable, while permitting riggers access to gas valves and gas cells. "Graf Zeppelin" was the first with a gangway through the gas cells, though this was below the center line of the ship. R 100 had an axial girder but this was too small to serve as a gangway. "Hindenburg" and "Graf Zeppelin II" had axial gangways.

B

Ballast: To enable the airship to ascend to higher altitudes, or to compensate for gas loss or increased loads on the ship, droppable ballast was carried. Though the German naval airships briefly carried sand in 110 lb sacks early in 1917, water was the usual form of ballast.

352

Ballast Sacks: Most of the ballast was carried along the keel in rubberized cloth sacks holding 2,200 lb of water. Fourteen of such were fitted in L 30. Toggles in the control car were pulled by the elevator man to empty them as necessary, and the big sacks drained completely in 60 seconds. In some of the later ships, water ballast was carried in tanks rather than bags. In "Hindenburg" each ballast tank contained 5500 lb of water.

Ballonet: In pressure airships (qv), an air-filled compartment inside the main envelope which, being kept under pressure by a blower or other means, maintained a constant pressure in the large bag, regardless of changes in the volume of the gas.

"Breeches": To quickly lighten the ship at bow or stern, as in take-off or landing emergencies, water ballast was carried in small sacks near the nose and tail. L 30 and later ships had four sacks holding 550 lb each at each end of the ship. These, because their shape suggested half a pair of pants, were called "breeches", and unlike the large 2,200 lb sacks in the keel, the "breeches" emptied their entire contents instantly (often on the heads of the ground crew!) when the elevator man pulled their toggles in the control car. In "Hindenburg" these sacks at nose and tail each contained 2200 lb of water.

C

Ceiling: The maximum altitude attainable by an aircraft under certain conditions. The ceiling varied with the amount of useful load retained on board and prevailing temperature conditions and barometric pressure. Late in the 1914-18 war the German Navy Zeppelins were built very lightly to attain 20,000 feet with 6600 lb of bombs, but commercial Zeppelins, and the U.S. Navy's helium-filled airships, generally operated below 3000 feet to minimize loss of lifting gas through the automatic vlaves.

Compass: Though ships carried gyro compasses after 1911, these were much too heavy for airships, which through World War I and afterwards were steered by magnetic compasses. LZ 126 was the first rigid to have a gyrocompass, manufactured by Anschütz, with several repeater compasses. With these the course could be held within 3/10 of a degree instead of 5 degrees with the magnetic compass.

Control Car: In early Zeppelins, the open forward engine gondola had a control position partly shielded by a transparent wind screen, with rudder and elevator wheels, ballast and gas valve controls, and rudimentary instruments. Later an enclosed control car was provided for the commander, the navigator, and watch officers, with rudder and elevator men. Initially slung under the ship on struts and wires, the control car was built securely onto the hull, and glass and celluloid windows provided good all-round visibility except right aft. The rudder man handled the rudder wheel in the bow of the car. On the port side of the car (on the starboard side in British rigids) was the elevator wheel, with ballast releases and manoeuvring valve controls also in charge of the elevator man. A small chart table was on the starboard side of the car, with engine telegraphs overhead to transmit orders to the engine gondolas aft. Usually the sound-proofed radio cabin with transmitters and receivers was to the rear, but in later ships such as R 101, "Akron" and "Hindenburg," the radio room was in the keel above the control car.

Cover: Made of light cotton fabric. Large panels were laced to the girders, and the lacing covered with glued-on fabric strips. Clear dope was applied in the earlier Zeppelins; black dope to the underside of the hulls of German Navy airships late in the war; and aluminium dope was first used in the U.S.S. "Shenandoah" to reflect solar radiation. In the German Navy Zeppelin L 49 the top outer cover weighed 100 grammes per square metre undoped, and 140-158 grammes per square metre doped; the bottom cover weighed 80-90 grammes per square metre undoped, and 125 grammes per square metre doped. The entire outer cover weighed 4,704 pounds.

Crew: An airship crew was constituted as in a seagoing vessel, with comparable ranks, ratings and duties. During the commercial airship period three watches were carried, the seaman branch in "Hindenburg" standing 4 hour watches with 8 hours off, the engineering personnel 3 hour watches with 6 hours off. "Hindenburg's" crew consisted of 39 persons, as follows:

1 captain
3 watch standing officers
3 navigating officers
3 rudder men
3 elevator men
1 chief rigger
3 riggers
1 chief radio man
3 assistant radio men
1 chief engineer
3 charge hand engineers
12 engineers
1 chief electrician
2 assistant electricians.

D

Docking Rails: The only mechanical ground handling aid used with German rigid airships until the "Hindenburg". Running through the sheds and for 200 yards out into the field on each side, the rails carried so-called trolleys (q.v.) to which the ship was made fast fore and aft by tackles, so that she was prevented from moving sideways in a wind while entering or leaving her shed.

"Dope": A solution of cellulose acetate in acetone, brushed on to the outer cover after it was in place, to tauten and waterproof it.

Drift: The lateral motion of an aircraft over the ground, due to wind blowing at an angle to its course. To steer a true course over the ground, the wind strength and direction must be known.

Duralumin: Name applied to a family of alloys of aluminium, with small and varying amounts of copper and traces of magnesium, manganese, iron and silicon. Its properties were first discovered by Wilm in 1909 and it was first manufactured in Düren, Germany. Being much stronger than the parent metal, duralumin was used for the first British rigid airship, "Mayfly," in 1910, and for all Zeppelin girder-work beginning with LZ 26 of 1914.

Dynamic Lift: The positive (or negative) force on an airship hull, derived from driving it at an angle with the power of its engines. With a large amount of engine power, flying a ship "dynamically" could readily compensate for considerable degrees of lightness or heaviness. At full power and with an angle of 8 degrees, "Los Angeles" developed a dynamic lift of over eight tons.

E

Echo Altimeter: The *Echolot* measured in German commercial airships the true altitude above the surface by timing the interval between a blast of compressed air and its return to the ship.

Elevators: Movable horizontal surfaces at the tail of the airship (though in very early Zeppelins they were fitted forward also); motion upward or downward inclined the ship's nose up or down, and caused her to ascend or descend.

Engine Cars: Small streamlined enclosures attached by struts and wires to the hull of the airship, designed to accomodate an engine or engines, and personnel attending them, and to provide enough space to work on the engines in case of a breakdown.

F

Fins: Vertical or horizontal stabilizing surfaces at the tail of the airship, at the after ends of which were attached the movable control surfaces. Fins were flat, with extensive wire bracing, until 1918 when the Zeppelin firm introduced thick cantilever-section fins with a minimum of external bracing.

Fixed weight: Total weight of structure and other permanent installations of an airship — in a Zeppelin, includes framework, bracing wire, gas cells, outer cover, passenger accomodation, gondolas, engines, fuel tanks and piping, ballast sacks, instruments, etc. In wartime Zeppelins, these might be as low as 37½ per cent of the gross lift; safety requires a heavier structure in commercial airships, and the figure should then be nearer 45-50 per cent.

"Free Lift": At take-off, it was German practice to drop about 500 lb. of water ballast, to give an equivalent ascending force, or "free lift."

Fuel Gas: In the "Graf Zeppelin" alone among rigid airships, "Blau gas", a hydrocarbon resembling propane with a specific gravity the same as that of air, was used for fuel and carried in gas cells in the lower part of the hull.

G

Gangway: See keel.

Gas capacity: The gas content of all cells filled 100 per cent full. Usually derived from calculation.

Gas cells: Filling the entire interior of the airship when 100 per cent full of gas, the cells were held in place by wire and cord netting, and made to be both light in weight and as gas-tight as possible. Initially, rubberized cotton fabric was used, with a weight of 240 grammes per square metre. Gas loss was excessive, and there was a great improvement about 1911 when bags were first made of 6 layers of gold beaters' skin (qv). This material weighed about 150 grammes per square metre. These cells were fragile and expensive. With L 3 in 1914 was first used "skinned fabric" cells — two or three layers of gold beaters' skin glued to light cotton fabric. The weight of this was 145 grammes per square metre. "Skinned fabric" cells were used throughout the war, and with silk substituted for cotton in 1918, the weight was reduced to 135 grammes per square metre. The blockade caused a shortage of gold beaters' skin (principally imported from Argentina) and in the last two years of the war, inferior types of ordinary gut produced in Germany had to be substituted. Fabric cells with gold beaters' skin were used by British and American rigid airships, as well as by the Germans post-war. A synthetic gelatin-latex film was developed in place of gold beaters' skin for the "Akron" and "Macon," and a similar synthetic was used in "Hindenburg."

Gas shafts: A Schütte-Lanz patent, these, made of wooden hoops and netting, extended upwards between the gas cells to conduct hydrogen from the automatic valves in the bottom of the gas cells to exhaust hoods along the back bone of the ship. Early Zeppelins had no gas shafts, and the free hydrogen diffused upward in the "mantle space" between the gas cells and the outer cover, and through the cover at the top of the ship which was left undoped. Only in 1916, in the L 34, did the Zeppelin Company introduce gas shafts in their ships.

Girder: Transverse rings, and longitudinal members, being required to resist compression and bending loads, were built up of light girders of triangular section. The Zeppelin Company employed rolled duralumin channels connected by stamped lattice pieces. A section of main longitudinal girder, 16.4 feet long, 14.7 inches high, and 10.63 inches wide, weighed only 10.2 lb but could support a compression load of 4,928 lb. The Schütte-Lanz girders were built up of aspen plywood bonded with one of the earliest applications of casein glue, and waterproofed with paraffin and lacquered. A section of their wooden girder 8.6 feet long, 3.4 inches wide and 9.45 inches high, weighed 6.45 lb but could support a compression load of 9,930 lb.

Gold Beaters' Skin: Superb gas-tightness, together with light weight, was attained by lining the inside of the gas-bags with gold beaters' skin. This was the delicate outer membrane covering the *caecum* of cattle, each animal yielding only one skin measuring not more than 39 x 6 inches. For a single large gas cell, some 50,000 skins would be needed. The careful handling required in the slaughter houses, the quantity of skins required, and the skilled hand-work needed in assembling the skins at the gas-cell factory, caused the bags so made to be enormously expensive − in 1917 a single large gas-bag cost £2,000.

Gondola: Generic name for any car suspended below an airship, possibly derived from the fact that the early Zeppelin gondolas were not only shaped like open boats, but were intended to float on the water.

Gondola bumpers: One or two located under each centre-line gondola, to cushion the shock of landing. These were rubberized air bags enclosed in a framework of canes and covered with strong canvas. Only in the last two Zeppelins, "Hindenburg" and "Graf Zeppelin II," were the bumpers replaced by low pressure air wheels under the control car and the lower fin.

Gravity Tanks: Fuel tanks permanently installed over each engine car and feeding the engines by gravity. Machinists' mates of the different cars were responsible for keeping them filled by hand-pumping petrol up from the slip tanks (qv) along the keel. In L 30 there were eight gravity tanks, each holding 148 gallons.

Gross Lift: The total lift, under standard conditions, of the gas contained in an airship; equal to the total weight of the air displaced minus the weight of the gas.

Ground crew: German airships were walked in and out of their sheds, and manhandled on the ground by trained teams of men. Three or four hundred men were required to handle the larger airships. Only with the "Hindenburg" and "Graf Zeppelin II" did the Germans use mechanical handling equipment – a travelling mooring mast. The U.S. Navy needed 157 men to ground handle the "Los Angeles," but with the complete mechanical equipment devised for the "Akron" a dozen men could do the job.

H

Hangar: Large buildings at the airship bases, designed to contain one or two airships each, and with huge rolling doors at either end. The leeward door was always used for entry and exit except in very light winds. German practice required that the airships be housed in hangars when not in the air, and no mooring-out equipment was used.

Helium: The second lightest gas known, developed for airship use by the United States, which has a monopoly of its production from natural gas. Helium has the great advantage for airship use of being non-flammable, but it has only 93 per cent of the lifting force of hydrogen. In rigid airships, the expense of helium required the installation of heavy condensers to recover water from the engine exhausts to compensate for the weight of fuel burned and to eliminate the need to valve the lifting gas as the fuel was consumed.

Hydrogen: The lightest gas known, cheaply manufactured by a variety of methods. Produced for German airships at the airship bases in large plants utilizing the Messerschmitt process of passing steam over hot iron. Hydrogen is not only flammable, but is also explosive when contaminated by as little as 6 per cent of air. The Germans were able to use hydrogen in their airships with relative safety by very strict attention to gas purity. Between flights the gas cells were kept inflated 100 per cent full and under slight positive pressure to minimize inward diffusion of air, and purity was checked almost daily; if the purity fell too low the cell was emptied and filled with fresh hydrogen.

I

Inclinometer: An instrument which informed the elevator man of the up or down angle of the airship.

Intermediate rings: One or two intermediate rings were spaced between the main rings (qv) at 5 metre intervals to reduce bending loads on the longitudinal girders. A ring of girders circled the ship, but there was of course no transverse wire bracing.

K

Keel: A triangular-section corridor running from end to end of a rigid airship, composed of the two bottom longitudinals of the hull and an apex girder. At the bottom of the keel was the catwalk, about a foot wide. (Though there were no hand-rails, nobody was ever lost by stepping off it and through the outer cover!) Heavy loads such as bombs, fuel tanks and water ballast sacks, were hung from sturdy box girders along the keel, and here were slung hammocks for the crew.

"Akron" and "Macon" were unique in having three keels, one in the top of the ship, and two in the lower hull to port and starboard, containing the engine rooms in their after portions.

L

Landing Ropes: In the wartime German ships, a long landing-rope 410 feet in length, and two shorter ones 249 feet in length, were stowed in the nose on hatches which could be opened by wires from the control car. When low over the field, these would be released and the bows of the airship hauled down by the ground crew. Other shorter ropes were attached along the keel.

Longitudinals: The main longitudinal girders were the main lengthwise strength members of the airship. In L 30 there were thirteen, twelve of them triangular, 14.17 inches deep and 10.63 inches wide, and the top longitudinal was a doubled girder of W-section. The intermediate longitudinals, of which there were twelve in L 30, were lighter, did not extend all the way to the tail, and were designed primarily to support the outer cover.

M

Main Rings: Main rings or frames were the chief transverse structural members of the rigid airship, and were polygons built of girders (13-sided in L 30). The ability of the main ring to withstand the forces exerted by the lifting gas and by the weight of the ship's structure and lading was a basic consideration in airship design. Main rings were heavily braced with both radial and chord wires. In L 30, where the main rings were 10 metres apart, an intermediate ring – unbraced – occurred between each pair of main rings; in L 53 and later ships, with main rings spaced 15 metres apart, there were two intermediate rings. Beginning with L 30, main and intermediate rings were numbered with the distance in metres from the stern-post, which was Ring 0.

In contrast to the flat "bicycle wheel" main rings of Zeppelin practice, R 101, "Akron" and "Macon" had inherently stiff main rings of triangular section, without transverse wire bracing.

Manoeuvring Valves: Fitted in the tops of certain gas cells, these enabled the commander to trim his ship by releasing gas from one end, or on occasion, to make the entire ship heavy. The valve pulls were handled by the elevator man. Because the manoeuvring valves in the top of the ship were practically inaccessible and might stick open, standing orders in the German Naval Airship Division were to make the ship heavy by driving her over pressure height (q.v.), and discharging gas from the automatic valves. When the manoeuvring valves were used to make the ship heavy, they were opened all together for a measured time interval by attaching their toggles to the rim of a wheel. In L 70, with cells 75 per cent full, "valving on the wheel" for one minute would make her 1,100 lb heavier.

Maybach: In 1909, Count Zeppelin had backed the construction in Friedrichshafen of an engine designed by Carl Maybach especially for airships. The engine was further developed and manufactured by the Maybach Motor Company, a Zeppelin subsidiary. Because of their superior reliability and fuel economy, Maybach engines were used in all Zeppelins beginning with LZ 10 "Schwaben," all Schütte-Lanz ships except the first, and in the American "Akron" and "Macon." The Maybach VL-I was designed for the LZ 126 "Los Angeles," the VL-II for the LZ 127 "Graf Zeppelin."

The following table gives specifications of all the Maybach engine types:

Year	Type	hp	rpm	Wt (lb)	lb hp	Fuel consumption gm/hp/hr	Cyl inder no.	Compression ratio
1910	C-X	145	1100	993	6.85	240	6	
1913	C-X	180	1200	1020	5.75	225	6	
1914	C-X	210	1250	913	4.34	225	6	4.8/1
1915	HSLu	240	1400	805	3.35	200	6	5.45/1
1917	MbIVa	245	1400	882	3.59	200	6	6.08/1
1918	MbIVa	245	1400	860*	3.51	200	6	6.7/1
1924	VL-I	400	1400	2100	5.2	190	12	5.3/1
1928	VL-II	550	1600	2315	4.2	210	12	7/1

All engines were built in right-hand and left-hand versions, the C-X being coded "Edulare(chtsdrehend)", and "Edulali(nksdrehend)", the HSLu "Mulare" and "Mulali". The VL-I and VL-II could be reversed by stopping the engine, shifting cam shafts and restarting in the opposite direction.

Metalclad: Trade name for the product of the Airship Development Corporation of Detroit, Michigan. Their only craft to fly, the experimental ZMC-2, was built of riveted duralumin sheet .008 inches thick coated with Alclad (pure aluminium), the resulting shell serving simultaneously as gas container, outer cover and strength member.

Mooring Mast: Realizing that the Germans' inability to walk their Zeppelins in and out of their sheds in stiff cross winds imposed a severe operational handicap, Major G.H. Scott in the early post-war period devised the mooring mast, to which a rigid airship could be moored in the open, ready to take the air regardless of the wind direction. At the "high" mast developed by the British, the ship required constant attention because of changes in buoyancy, and for this and other reasons, the U.S. Navy later developed the "low" or "stub" mast, to which the airship was secured on the ground. The nose was held by the mast while the tail, resting on the ground, swung with the wind on a weighted car.

Mooring Point: A reinforced fitting in the keel forward of the control car, to which the landing ropes (qv) were made fast.

N

Non-Rigid Airship: A small pressure airship (qv) consisting of a rubberized fabric gas-bag whose streamlined shape is maintained by gas pressure, and from which a single gondola is suspended.

*Aluminium pistons replacing cast iron.

O

Oxyhydrogen: A gaseous mixture of oxygen and hydrogen, or loosely, of air and hydrogen; always potentially explosive.

P

Payload: That portion of the useful load (qv) which earns revenue; devoted to the carriage of paying passengers, or of cargo and mail.

Pressure airship: Generic term including both the non-rigid and semi-rigid airship (qv), in both of which the shape is maintained by gas pressure. Contrasts with the rigid airship, which (though very rarely) may be described as a "pressure-less airship."

Pressure height: The height at which decreasing atmospheric pressure permits the lifting gas to expand and build up a relative pressure inside the cells such that the automatic valves open and gas is "blown off." Following ascent to a preselected pressure height, the commander may ascent or descend at any altitude below this height without fear that gas will be released – an important consideration in flying a hydrogen ship through thunderstorms.

Propellers: Early Zeppelins had inefficient two or four-bladed metal propellers made of sheet aluminium riveted to steel tube frames. Beginning with LZ 26 the propellers were exclusively 2-bladed, built up of laminations of West African and Honduras mahogany and American walnut, and often covered with walnut veneer. Usually they were geared down to about 540 rpm from an engine speed of 1400 rpm, and were of large diameter averaging about 17 feet. "Graf Zeppelin" and "Hindenburg" had four-bladed wooden propellers. Wooden propellers were standard in rigid airships of other nations, but "Macon" was unique in having 3-bladed all metal Hamilton Standard ground-adjustable propellers.

R

Rate of Climb Indicator (statascope): An instrument which indicates to the elevator man the rate of ascent or descent in feet per minute or metres per second.

Rigid airship: An airship with a rigid frame which maintains its shape regardless of whether it is inflated with gas.

Rudder: Movable vertical surfaces at the tail of the airship, whose motion steer the ship to port or starboard.

S

Semi-Rigid Airship: A pressure airship with a rigid keel running the length of the bag, either suspended beneath it or faired into its underside, for the attachment of engines and gondolas and the distribution of fuel, ballast and other loads. Permits construction of airships larger than the non-rigid type.

Shear wires: Hard-drawn steel wires providing diagonal bracing in all rectangular panels formed by longitudinal girders and transverse rings, and taking the shear loads on the rigid hull.

Shed: See hangar.

Slip-Tanks: Aluminium fuel tanks distributed along the keel. In L 30 there were thirty-two of 64 gallon capacity, and any one of these could be dropped through the cover in an emergency if no other ballast was available.

Stall: In aircraft, a condition where an extreme angle of attack causes a loss of lift, and the aircraft falls out of control. It should be noted that while a "heavy" airship flying nose-up can stall downward like heavier-than-air craft, it can also "stall upward." When flying "light" and nose down, it may be inclined downward so far that the dynamic force on the top of the hull diminishes and the excess static lift of the "light" condition will cause it to rise out of control.

Static Lift: The lift of an airship without forward motion, and due solely to the buoyancy of the gas. Contrasts with dynamic lift (qv).

Streamlining: The shaping of a body so as to cause the least possible disturbance in passing through the air, and hence causing a minimum of resistance, or "drag." Early in World War I, much research on streamlining was done by Dr. Paul Jaray in the Zeppelin Company's wind tunnel at Friedrichshafen. Among Jaray's discoveries was that even at relatively low speeds, careful streamlining of all structural protuberances – fins, gondolas, struts and wires – was important for aerodynamic efficiency of the airship.

Sub-Cloud Car (Spähkorb): An observation device used solely by the German Army airships in 1914-17, much overrated as a result of its being featured in post-war movies. A small streamlined nacelle hanging in clear air half a mile below the Zeppelin and connected by telephone with the control car, it enabled an observer to direct the airship hidden in the clouds above. With its steel cable and winch driven off one of the airship's engines, it weighed over half a ton.

Supercooling: A condition (usually obtaining at night) where the gas is cooler than the surrounding air; since the density of the gas is increased, its lifting power is less. As much as -9 degrees F. of supercooling has been recorded.

Superheating: A condition (usually due to sun's heat being trapped within the hull) where the gas is warmer than the surrounding air. Since the density of the gas is decreased, its lifting power is greater. During her flight to America, on July 4, 1919, R 34 experienced superheating of +66 degrees F.

T

Thermometer: In the control car was an air thermometer, and a remote-reading electrical thermometer giving (somewhat inaccurately) the temperature in one of the gas cells. The data provided by these instruments was essential to determine the lift of the airship, particularly with superheating or supercooling.

Trim: The attitude of an airship in the air in response to static forces. When weights and lifting forces are properly balanced so that the centre of gravity is located directly under the centre of lift, the airship is on an even keel and said to be "in trim." If this is not the case, she is "Out of trim"; if the nose is inclined downward, "trimmed by the bow," if the tail is inclined downward, "trimmed by the stern."

Trolley (Laufkatze): A wheeled truck, pulled by hand and rolling on docking rails (qv). Trolleys served as points for attachment of tackles made fast to the airship fore and aft.

U

Useful lift: The amount of lift remaining after substracting the fixed weights of the airship from the gross lift.

Useful Load: The load that the airship can carry, equal in weight to the useful lift. Includes fuel, oil, water ballast, crew, spare parts, passengers, cargo, or armament and bombs.

W

Water Recovery: In American airships, to avoid valving scarce and expensive helium as the airship became lighter through consumption of fuel, the exhaust gases from the engines were passed through condensers hung above the gondolas in order to recover the water of combustion. In theory, 145 lb of water could be recovered for every 100 lb of petrol burned; in practice the figure was 110 to 122 lb depending on the outside air temperature. The condensed water was piped to ballast bags in the keel.

"Weighed Off": The state of an airship whose lift and load have been adjusted so as to be equal, or whose excess of lift or load has become known by test. (Colloquially, if said to be "weighed off," an airship is in equilibrium, while she will otherwise be said to be "weighed off — pounds 'heavy'," or "weighed off — pounds 'light'.") Before leaving the hangar an airship, through release of ballast, was weighed off so precisely that one man at each end could lift her off the trestles under the gondolas. In flight, an experienced elevator man could tell a good deal about her static condition from the "feel" of the ship, but good practice demanded that before landing, the ship should be "weighed off" in the air. The engines were stopped and ballast released if it were found that she sank, while gas was valved if she rose.

Weight Empty: Equals fixed weights (qv).

Index